The Myth of the Twelve Tribes of Israel

The Myth of the Twelve Tribes of Israel is the first book to explore the traditions of peoples all around the world who have claimed an Israelite identity as part of a continuous history of Israelite identity construction from biblical times to the present. By treating the Hebrew Bible's accounts of Israel as one of many efforts to create an Israelite history, rather than the source material for later legends, Andrew Tobolowsky brings a long-term comparative approach to biblical and nonbiblical "Israels". In the process, he sheds new light on how the structure of the twelve tribes tradition enables the creation of so many different visions of Israel, and generates new questions: How can we explain the enduring power of the myth of the twelve tribes of Israel? How does "becoming Israel" work, why has it proven so popular, and how did it change over time? Finally, what can the changing shape of Israel itself reveal about those who claimed it?

ANDREW TOBOLOWSKY is an Assistant Professor of Religious Studies at the College of William and Mary. An acknowledged expert on the twelve tribes tradition and on Israelite history, he is the author of *The Sons of Jacob and the Sons of Herakles* (2017), and numerous articles on both topics, as well as on the value of thinking through cross-cultural comparisons.

The Myth of the Twelve Tribes of Israel

New Identities Across Time and Space

ANDREW TOBOLOWSKY

College of William and Mary, Virginia

CAMBRIDGE
UNIVERSITY PRESS

CAMBRIDGE
UNIVERSITY PRESS

Shaftesbury Road, Cambridge CB2 8EA, United Kingdom

One Liberty Plaza, 20th Floor, New York, NY 10006, USA

477 Williamstown Road, Port Melbourne, VIC 3207, Australia

314–321, 3rd Floor, Plot 3, Splendor Forum, Jasola District Centre, New Delhi – 110025, India

103 Penang Road, #05–06/07, Visioncrest Commercial, Singapore 238467

Cambridge University Press is part of Cambridge University Press & Assessment, a department of the University of Cambridge.

We share the University's mission to contribute to society through the pursuit of education, learning and research at the highest international levels of excellence.

www.cambridge.org
Information on this title: www.cambridge.org/9781009094092

DOI: 10.1017/9781009091435

First published 2022
First paperback edition 2023

A catalogue record for this publication is available from the British Library

Library of Congress Cataloging-in-Publication data
NAMES: Tobolowsky, Andrew, 1985– author.
TITLE: The myth of the twelve tribes of Israel : new identities across time and space / Andrew Tobolowsky, College of William and Mary, Virginia.
DESCRIPTION: Cambridge, United Kingdom : Cambridge University Press, [2022] | Includes bibliographical references and index.
IDENTIFIERS: LCCN 2021053918 (print) | LCCN 2021053919 (ebook) | ISBN 9781316514948 (hardback) | ISBN 9781009094092 (paperback) | ISBN 9781009091435 (epub)
SUBJECTS: LCSH: Twelve tribes of Israel. | Lost tribes of Israel. | Bible–Influence.
CLASSIFICATION: LCC BS574 .T63 2022 (print) | LCC BS574 (ebook) | DDC 933/.02–dc23/eng/20211206
LC record available at https://lccn.loc.gov/2021053918
LC ebook record available at https://lccn.loc.gov/2021053919

ISBN 978-1-316-51494-8 Hardback
ISBN 978-1-009-09409-2 Paperback

Contents

Acknowledgments

It may be that writing a globe-trotting book is always an act of hubris, but it is surely more so if you go it alone. There is scarcely a section in this book that does not make me think with fondness of the people who made it possible, and often enough, became good friends along the way. Matthew Chalmers' expertise on the Samaritans was indispensable to Chapter 2, Christopher Cannon Jones' on the Mormons to Chapter 4 – which also benefited from the advice of Evan Criddle, and the archival work of the ever-generous Ardis E. Parshall, who pointed me in many interesting directions. Chapter 3 would be very different, and a good deal worse, without Josh Mugler's help in learning about the Crusades, and Daniel Picus' ever-patient explanations of the complexities of rabbinic literature. I was also blessed throughout, as I have long been blessed, to have brilliant conversation partners, of whom Jacqueline Vayntrub, Catherine Bonesho, Eva Mroczek, and Thomas Bolin merit special mention, and most especially Ian Douglas Wilson and Daniel Pioske who have taught me so much about memory and the past. And ever since we fetched up in the same graduate program in the early 2010s, Kerry Sonia and Zackary Wainer have been extraordinary sources of support, encouragement, and good ideas. To all of you: your insights, intellectual courage, and creativity were my inspiration, every step along the way. Anna Cwikla was instrumental in turning this book into what it was meant to be, and Matt Neil went to extraordinary lengths to finish the job. Both are incredibly gifted editors and writing coaches – and Matt, I want you to know that you battled. I would also like to thank Beatrice Rehl, editor extraordinaire, for taking a chance on this book, and the whole crew at Cambridge for their ever-courteous assistance. But most of all,

I absolutely could not have done any of this without my wife Robyn Schroeder, my partner for more than ten years, nor would I want to try. Like everything I write, this book is a map, for me, of where we were when I was working on it – this page a balcony in Providence in spring, that one a Chapel Hill café in summer. This argument came to me on 85, lit up by tail-lights, that one with our small grey dog jingling beside. I have built this book out of our lives together, which the process of writing it saw transformed, from years of living apart, to finding a home together, to starting a family, and what is best about it comes from that fact. And so, most of all, I dedicate this book to our son Judah, new to this planet, born between contract and copy-edits. You came into this world so loved, and you will always be so loved, by people who will try so very, very hard. I hope you like myths; they mean a lot to your mom and me.

Introduction

The Twelve Tribes Tradition and the Hidden History of "Becoming Israel"

His father's stolen blessing in hand, the young Jacob, not yet a patriarch, lights out for the territories. His flight rewinds history, retracing the thread of family destiny back to Harran, where once his grandfather Abraham heard the voice of a new god speaking: *lech lecha*, take yourself and go. This time, it is the voice of his mother Rebekah that Jacob heard, telling him "look, Esau your brother is consoling himself by plotting to kill you" (Gen. 27:42).[1] He chooses the better part of valor and his life not only begins, but, happily for him, continues. In Harran, in the home of his uncle Laban, Jacob will marry, not once but twice, and become the father of thirteen children – one daughter, and twelve sons (Gen. 29–30).[2] After fourteen years, Jacob and his family return to Canaan, and near the end of his life, travel from Canaan to Egypt (Gen. 46). In Egypt, in the fullness of time, the descendants of Jacob's twelve sons become the twelve tribes of Israel, a populous and powerful nation.[3]

From the book of Exodus on, the myth of the twelve tribes of Israel is the beating heart of the story the Bible tells. It is the tribes that Moses leads out of Egypt, into the wilderness, and the tribes who conquer Canaan with Joshua. It is the tribes who divide it between them, into

---

[1] Biblical translations in this study are my own, save where otherwise indicated.

[2] Reuben, Simeon, Levi, Judah, Issachar, and Zebulun are Leah's sons; Dan and Naphtali are Bilhah's; Gad and Asher are Zilpah's; and Joseph and Benjamin are Rachel's. In many tribal lists, Joseph and Levi are not included, but Joseph's sons Manasseh and Ephraim are. Dinah is Leah's daughter, born between Zebulun and Joseph.

[3] In fact, the first use of this phrase is in Genesis 49:28, at the end of what is usually called the "Blessing of Jacob," Jacob's deathbed blessing to his sons: "all these are the twelve tribes of Israel." The second usage appears in Exodus 24:4.

twelve parts, over the course of seven, detail-heavy chapters that strain the attention span of even the most zealous consumer of biblical lists and ephemera (Josh. 13–19). Four hundred years later, it would be "all the tribes of Israel" that come to David at Hebron, pledging to him "we are your bone and flesh" (2 Sam. 5:1). Ahead, near and far, lay the division of David's kingdom, conquests and destructions, exiles and at best partial returns. But even in the last days of the Hebrew Bible's history, when the people of Judah gather to celebrate the completion of the great "Second Temple" in Jerusalem, the centerpiece of the ceremony is a tremendous sacrifice: "one hundred bulls, two hundred rams, four hundred lambs ... and twelve male goats, according to the number of the tribes of Israel" (Ezra 6:17). From one perspective, here the curtain closes on the twelve tribes of Israel and their world.

The Hebrew Bible, however, is very far from the only body in which that heart beats. Instead, from the perspective of peoples all around the world, the story of the twelve tribes of Israel has *never ended at all.* The book closes, but, like something out of a modernist novel, the tribes climb out, escaping through the hole that is the Bible's silence on their ultimate destiny. They spread across the globe. Today, as for much of the last two thousand years, we live in a world full not only of legends about where the tribes went, what happened to them next, and what they became, but *Israels* – people who claim to be the people Israel, or have that identity claimed for them. And in each and every case, these Israels of the world understand themselves, or are understood by others, not as part of a sequel to the Bible's account, and certainly not as a fundamentally different kind of narrative, but simply the next chapter in a tribal history that is still unfolding. The myth of the twelve tribes of Israel is at the center of these stories, too – the permanent, impermeable vision of who Israel is, and always will be.[4]

My purpose in this book is to tell the story of a world full of Israels, if not as they themselves see it, then as they understand it: as a continuous one, from biblical times to today. In fact, it is to identify, for the first time – and so investigate – an ongoing phenomenon that I call "becoming Israel." This is the art, and the long-term historical practice – from the right perspective, one of the oldest, continuous, and most productive literary preoccupations in the world – of telling stories about Israel's tribes, and in fact, of acquiring and adapting Israelite identities. This

---

[4] Not all accounts of, or identifications with Israel involve traditions about the tribes explicitly or implicitly, especially in Christian communities. But a great many do.

phenomenon, ancient and modern, popular and poorly known, has been hidden in plain sight. Through the medium of five case studies, starting with the Israel of the Hebrew Bible itself, and continuing with discussions of the Samaritans, of Lost Tribe legends in the medieval age, of the Mormons, and the Beta Israel of Ethiopia, I plan to uncover it, exploring what inspires people to "become Israel," how it works, and how, at last, it made its way around the world.

In what remains of this introduction, however, I will explain why no scholarly attempt to study biblical and nonbiblical accounts of Israel on approximately equal terms – and as expressions of the same phenomenon – has yet been written, and why the time is finally right. And in that direction, the first point to make is that the absence of a comparative history of constructions of Israel does not mean that the traditions involved have never interested scholars. Far from it. Biblical scholars have studied the Hebrew Bible's tribal traditions as assiduously as any in that book and likely more than most. And there are now, finally – amidst a still buzzing cottage industry of publications by conspiracy theorists and treasure hunters – a growing number of serious, scholarly inquiries into the body of narratives generally referred to as "Lost Tribe" traditions.[5] The name is a little misleading; it comes from the fact that many, though far from all of these stories, take, as their starting point, 2 Kings 17's account of the exile of ten of Israel's tribes to Assyria never to return.[6] Still, the point is that these stories are known, and they have been explored.

At the same time, the study of biblical and nonbiblical tribal traditions have been quite siloed off from each other, made the province of different scholars, with different interests, and different expertise. Those who study Lost Tribe narratives often do refer to biblical traditions, but more as source material for later traditions than as a subject of inquiry of equal interest and value.[7] Scholars of the Hebrew Bible rarely refer to nonbiblical tribal traditions at all.[8] Certainly, no previous study has suggested a

---

[5] These include Zvi Ben-Dor Benite's *The Ten Lost Tribes* and Tudor Parfitt's *The Lost Tribes of Israel*. They also include a number of collected volumes and articles which I will discuss throughout.

[6] Actually, 2 Kings 17 does not say how many tribes there are, but since 1 Kings 11–12 says that Israel had ten of twelve tribes, and no subsequent text claims otherwise, it is the legend of the "Ten Lost Tribes" that has gone down in history.

[7] See, for example, Benite, *The Ten Lost Tribes*, 31–56; Parfitt, *The Lost Tribes of Israel*, 1–27.

[8] An exception of sorts may be found in Barmash, "At the Nexus of History and Memory."

fundamental equality between biblical and extrabiblical efforts to recount tribal history.[9] No one has asked why literally identifying as Israel has proven so popular, or even so possible. No one has explored whether there is anything about the myth itself that makes it such a useful tool for the constant production of new stories, new histories, and new visions of Israel, or investigated the mechanisms of presenting, acquiring, and adapting Israelite identities in order to see what light they may shed on how they are used in any particular case.

There are reasons these silos exist, some of which we can safely ignore. The scholarly hesitance to directly compare biblical traditions to nonbiblical traditions as fundamentally similar kinds of efforts extends far beyond tribal histories and is a reflection of the sui generis status the Bible enjoys in parts of contemporary culture.[10] It has nothing to do with anything particular to how biblical traditions were composed, or what role they played in ancient Israelite and Judahite society. Other reasons that withstand little scrutiny include a long-term tendency to privilege biblical traditions specifically over early Jewish and Christian traditions about ancient Israel and Judah because of the canonical status the Hebrew Bible *came* to enjoy – and even an internalization, quite unspoken, of a general sense of "scripture" as somehow different from "tradition," for all that "scripture," too, is a determination applied to biblical traditions only externally, and only after they were composed.[11]

---

[9] Although I first introduced the idea that the biblical vision of Israel is more similar to Lost Tribe traditions than many realize, if without substantial discussion, in Tobolowsky, *The Sons of Jacob*, 244. My point was simply that if the Judahites indeed used the twelve tribes tradition to lay claim to an Israelite identity from a place outside of Israel, after the heyday of the tribes as described, they would be performing a similar action to other "Israels" of the world.

[10] I have elsewhere made a general case for comparing biblical and extrabiblical uses of the same basic traditions on equal terms from the perspective of a comparative mythology (Tobolowsky, "The Hebrew Bible as Mythic 'Vocabulary,'" 459). I call these "two-way" comparisons – in which we use two examples of the use of a tradition, in anything from literature, to art, to film, not so that one can illuminate the other but so that each can tell us about both. This is by no means an unheard of form of comparison, but it is quite rare when biblical traditions are involved.

[11] For a discussion of how the cultural "hegemony of the biblical" is often inaccurately applied, in scholarship, to biblical texts before the period when they gained cultural ascendancy over other traditions, see Mroczek, "The Hegemony of the Biblical"; Mroczek, *The Literary Imagination in Jewish Antiquity*. As for scripture, as Dexter E. Callender Jr. and William Scott Green observe, in a similarly-minded discussion not of scripture and tradition but scripture and "myth," it "is a generic native category that biblical based religions use to depict themselves, though some scholars apply it to other

Other concerns, however, have more to them. Biblical accounts of tribal history are significantly older than any others I will discuss, except, perhaps, some of the Samaritan traditions in Chapter 2, and they are closer to the actual world of the tribes. In many cases, they likely do have more of history about them than the majority of Lost Tribe traditions which may be – in Tudor Parfitt's recent, blunt summary – "nothing but a myth."[12] At the very least, no Lost Tribe claim to descent from ancient Israel has yet passed a scholarly standard for empirically demonstrable truth. This difference between "history" and "myth," dull instruments as these terms may be, can be important, especially to the historian.[13]

Strange as it may seem, however, we no longer think that there is so much difference between ethnic traditions that have something of history about them and those which, under the historian's gaze, seem to have less.[14] Fundamentally, stories about the past that are believed to be true operate in the same way whether or not they actually are. And of course, there is no evidence that any of the "Israelites" discussed in this book hold or feel their Israelite identity any less deeply or sincerely than the ancient Israelites themselves. So, questions of ethnic truth or fiction seem to be of far greater interest as pure academic concerns than as aspects of our lived reality. Meanwhile, even when we know a given story about the past is true, or partially based on real events, we can still ask why it is being told rather than another one, perhaps equally true but neglected, and we can still ask how its telling is shaped by the context and occasion that gave it birth.[15]

---

religions as well" (Callender Jr. and Green, "Introduction: Scholarship Between Myth and Scripture," 1).

[12] Parfitt, *The Lost Tribes of Israel*, 1. "The fact is that over the last two thousand years, plenty of evidence of different sorts has been presented as proof of the continuing existence of the Lost Tribes. As far as I am concerned none of it is satisfactory as evidence. That is the standard view of scholars throughout the academic world."

[13] Here, I refer to conventional understandings of these categories – though not necessarily scholarly understandings – where history is something with a truth aspect and myth is something largely without it. An extended discussion of either term is far beyond the scope of this introduction, and certainly of a footnote, but my own sense is that the two terms increasingly refer to similar concepts. See Tobolowsky, "History, Myth, and the Shrinking of Genre Borders." See also the discussion in Tobolowsky, *The Sons of Jacob*, 203–6.

[14] Jonathan M. Hall refers to the now "sterile debate between ethnic truth and ethnic fiction" in his study of the construction of ancient Greek ethnicity over time (Hall, *Ethnic Identity in Greek Antiquity*, 19).

[15] Often, especially where ancient Israel is concerned, scholarship on descriptions of the tribes of Israel understands the ability to *represent* and to *express* in opposition to each other. That is, the idea is that if an account is true, it simply represents the past, rather

Developments like these certainly crack the door open to re-evaluating the long-operating distinction between biblical and nonbiblical tribal traditions in scholarship on the subject. The hammer that breaks the silos, however, was forged somewhere else. The haft is made out of an entirely underappreciated feature of the myth of the twelve tribes of Israel, which, for the rest of this book, I will more often refer to as the "twelve tribes tradition." The head is shaped by a new way of thinking about biblical traditions themselves, which makes these appear far more similar to "other" Israelite histories than anyone previously suspected – although this particular ramification has not yet been recognized.

First, then, the twelve tribes tradition is of a particular type known as a "segmented" genealogical tradition. The term is usually defined in contrast to "linear" genealogies which are those that follow a single line of descent, father to son or mother to daughter, typically to legitimate the current claimant to a throne, priesthood, or similar.[16] "Segmented" genealogies are those that follow multiple lines of descent at once instead, like a family tree.[17] The familiar biblical sequence, Abraham, Isaac, and Jacob is a linear genealogy, while – of course – the genealogy of the twelve sons of Jacob is segmented.

Segmented genealogical traditions have been a focal point of my scholarship nearly as much as the twelve tribes tradition has, and they are fascinating structures. I have often argued that a lack of attention to how segmented frameworks operate as ethnic charter myths has seriously inhibited scholarly analysis of biblical tribal traditions, and I will explore this topic again in the first chapter.[18] In the larger arc of this study, however, the functionality of segmented systems has another significance. It is the hidden filament that connects each act of "becoming Israel" to all the rest – because it is the hidden engine that makes "becoming Israel" go.

---

than expressing an ideology, "representation" being a key term in the study of history. However, as Megan Bishop Moore observes, even though objectivity can be a "regulative ideal" in modern historiographies, "history writing still requires historians to make decisions and value-judgements that are necessarily subjective to some degree" (Moore, *Philosophy and Practice*, 9–10). And this refers to modern historians – how much more so for those ancient historians who may have been "bound loosely to a historical past by their source material but untroubled by modern epistemological concerns birthed only in the past three centuries" (Pioske, *Memory in a Time of Prose*, 15).

[16] See, for example, Wilson, *Genealogy and History in the Biblical World*, 114–24, 132.
[17] Tobolowsky, *The Sons of Jacob*, 4.
[18] Especially in Tobolowsky, *The Sons of Jacob*; Tobolowsky, "The Problem of Reubenite Primacy."

There are many things to say about segmented systems, and I will hopefully say them throughout the book, but we need to understand that they are not stable *statements* of identity, they are negotiable claims about them, or maybe, an ongoing medium through which negotiable claims can be made. We can see this already in the book of Genesis. There is no good reason that the sons of Isaac, Jacob and Esau are the ancestors of two different peoples – Jacob of Israel, Esau of the Edomites (Gen. 25:30, 36:1–9) – while all twelve of Jacob's sons are one people. This is simply what the text says. And comparative examples tell us that the roads not taken in one articulation of identity can be taken in the next. One day, the Edomites and the Israelites might decide that they are one people after all, having descended from brothers just as surely as Reuben and Simeon did.[19] Or, the Reubenites might decide that they are *simply* Reubenites, not Reubenites and Israelites.[20] Or, the members of a given segmented framework might do a little reorganizing. In Gen. 29–30, the twelve sons of Jacob are born to four different women, Rachel, Leah, and their enslaved women Bilhah and Zilpah. Under the right circumstances, the Bilhahites might decide that they have had just about enough of the Leahites – and so on. The flexible structure segmentation provides makes all these reorientations, emancipations, and reorganizations possible.

Where "Lost Tribe" traditions are concerned, the essential feature of the segmented framework of Israelite identity is also its most obvious one: that segmented systems give permanent expression to the idea that many different groups are also, simultaneously, one group without losing their distinctiveness. The fact that Israel was born divided – so to speak – is what allows it to *be* divided, even across the world. The fact that Israel

---

[19] As Bruce Lincoln observes, "basic to the segmentary pattern is the principle of fission and fusion whereby the members of a total social field can recombine at different levels of integration to form aggregates of varying size ... To take an arbitrary example, when a man of lineage 1 struggles with a man of lineage 2, they invoke Ancestors 1 and 2 respectively ... When the time arrives to make peace, however, they invoke Ancestor A together: the figure through whose recollection may be formed that social group in which they are reunited" (Lincoln, *Discourse and the Construction of Society*, 19–20). When we think of "Ancestor A" as Jacob and "1 and 2" as, say, Ephraim and Judah, we see what we are dealing with here. There were instances in which "1 and 2" were opposed to each other in biblical history, but the prevailing vision of "all Israel" suggests that no recombinations occurred as a result.

[20] Some biblical texts suggest that these kinds of disaggregations happened, and notably the famous "shibboleth" episode in Judges 12, where Manassites are able to identify, and kill, Ephraimites on the basis of a difference in pronunciation. By and large, however, it is Israel and not the individual tribes that matter, and this is universally true in nonbiblical traditions.

was always understood as a conglomeration of different groups allows these various Israels to go on being different from each other, sometimes very different indeed. And the fact that Israel always had many different heirs at once is what allows so many different stories to co-exist, in so many different places. In short, the ability to explain that Reuben and Simeon are different, but both Israel, is also the ability to explain how the Mormons who are the subject of Chapter 4 and the Beta Israel who are the subject of Chapter 5 are different, but both Israel.[21]

Here is where recent scholarship on the Hebrew Bible's own accounts of Israelite history comes in. Today, we increasingly recognize that similar explanations are needed to make biblical history *itself* seem like an Israelite history – though, again, it has never been put quite this way before. First, even the Hebrew Bible itself admits that, upon the death of the mighty Solomon, the twelve tribes of Israel were permanently split between two different historical kingdoms, Israel and Judah (1 Kgs. 11–12), never to be reunited. Second, scholars have broadly acknowledged that the major developments that produced not only the Hebrew Bible as a whole, but its two lengthy narrative histories – the so-called "Primary History" spanning Genesis through Kings, and the "Secondary History" of Chronicles – occurred in Judah, not Israel, and only some time between the sixth and fourth centuries BCE, which is to say, between roughly 350 and 550 years since Solomon is supposed to have ruled.[22]

In a sense, then, the fact that what survives is really "Judah's Bible," as Daniel Fleming recently put it, is not exactly news.[23] What is new, however, is a raft of changes in how we think about identity, tradition, and memory that force us to reckon with what the relatively late, Judahite origins of the biblical accounts of Israelite history and identity really means.[24] Basically, we can no longer deny that if a narrative account

---

[21] As Malkin notes, segmented genealogies are "open to free manipulation and conflicting claims" and "capable ... of differentiating and relating nations at the same time" (Malkin, *The Returns of Odysseus*, 61).

[22] Whether Solomon is a historical figure is a difficult question that I will address to some extent in the first chapter, but if he was king of Israel, it would have been in the tenth century BCE.

[23] Fleming, *The Legacy of Israel in Judah's Bible*.

[24] The bibliography on this topic is vast and will be touched on at various points throughout this book. Some of the studies that I rely on throughout include Hall, *Ethnic Identity in Greek Antiquity*; Malkin, *The Returns of Odysseus*; Brubaker, *Ethnicity Without Groups*; Brubaker, *Nationalist Politics and Everyday Ethnicity*; Malešević, *The Sociology of Ethnicity*; Gil-White, "How Thick Is Blood?"; Crouch, *The Making of Israel*; Miller, "Ethnicity and the Hebrew Bible."

emerged in sixth through fourth century BCE Judah it *is* a sixth through fourth century BCE Judahite narrative.[25] Which means it reflects what Judahites living in this period thought Israel was, and to some extent, wanted it to be, and that theirs is a fundamentally Judahite vision.[26]

This is not to say that none of the traditions preserved in the Hebrew Bible are based on even much earlier ones, or for that matter, are Israelite rather than Judahite. In fact, my suspicion is that early Israelite traditions – and early Judahite traditions – are preserved better in the Hebrew Bible than in most other narratives based on older materials. There is a certain oddity in how much of the Primary History especially is composed, more through a kind of collage than a free composition.[27] The result is a multivocalic account that often contradicts, but also presumably preserves the literal wording of source materials, and a diversity of opinion, in a way and to an extent that is quite unusual.

In my own work, however, I have compared the problem of the biblical accounts of history, especially the Primary History, to the problem of the museum exhibit.[28] No one has to deny that these contain real artifacts, even from very ancient periods, and even in a good state of preservation, in order to recognize the primary role the curators who design the exhibit play in how we understand it. It is *their* exhibit, not the artifacts' own. The curators choose what to include, they organize it, they arrange it, they interpret it. Different curators can make very different exhibits even with the same artifacts, and of course, have. And if we somehow could not recognize that here, we will learn it, over and over again, throughout

[25] As Fleming put it, "the inheritance of Israelite material takes place after the realm was definitely called Judah and may be considered literally Judahite" (Fleming, *The Legacy of Israel in Judah's Bible*, 4).

[26] As Ian Douglas Wilson observes, "there is no doubt that many of these works have their roots in much earlier periods, and that they underwent long, complex processes of scribal reception, editing, and expansion that took place over centuries." Nevertheless, the biblical books in question are "representative of a particular discursive horizon, located across the fifth to early third centuries BCE" (Wilson, *Kingship and Memory in Ancient Judah*, 6, 10).

[27] This mode of composition may be totally unique. Although scholars such as Jeffrey Tigay have drawn attention to the existence of editorial seams in Gilgamesh, for example, as Seth Sanders points out, these seams in Near Eastern literature tend towards adding context and explaining further, while in the biblical narrative they often make things more confusing (Tigay, *Empirical Models for Biblical Criticism*; Sanders, "What If There Aren't Any Empirical Models for Pentateuchal Criticism?"). It also means the Hebrew Bible likely preserves a number of different perspectives better than other similar texts.

[28] Tobolowsky, "The Primary History as Museum Exhibit."

this book. There are worse ways to think about all these Israels of the world than as different exhibits of the same basic artifacts.

Additionally, by the time the mid-sixth century rolled around – again, just about the earliest date most contemporary scholars can imagine something like the biblical vision of history existing – a series of dramatic changes had occurred in the region. To be clear, even in the era when the two kingdoms co-existed, the books of Kings describe frequent wars between them, bitter conflicts that sometimes seem more the rule than the exception.[29] But the kingdom of Israel was conquered by Assyria in 722 BCE, and Judah itself, by Babylon in 586. Both conquests were accompanied by significant deportations away to Mesopotamia which, if not so complete as the Bible itself suggests, were significant nonetheless.[30]

Then, in 539 BCE, Persia would conquer Babylon, inaugurating at once the "Persian period" itself and the era of various "Returns" from Babylonian Exile. All of these, and many other events besides are of the sort that scholars of identity broadly agree dramatically reshape how peoples understand themselves.[31] Some key events in Judahite history did not even meaningfully include the Israelites, the Babylonian Exile among them, which many regard as a formative experience.[32] But even more prepossessing is the math. I count myself among the scholars who think the Persian period was the true crucible in which the biblical visions

---

[29] There was war, we are told, "all the days" of Rehoboam and Jeroboam (1 Kgs. 14:30). There was war all the days of Rehoboam's son Abijam (1 Kgs. 15:6), and after Abijam, "there was war between Asa and King Baasha of Israel all their days" (1 Kgs. 15:16). Jehoash, a later king of Israel, defeated Amaziah of Judah so badly that he broke down the wall of Jerusalem, which is typically the act of a conqueror attempting to prevent a new vassal from staging a rebellion (2 Kgs. 14:13). And in the end, the Assyrians may well have come down against Israel at the invitation of the Judahites, facing a devastating alliance between Israel and the neighboring kingdom of Aram-Damascus. We are told of an alliance between Rezin of Aram and Pekah, king of Israel, against the Judahites, and that in time they came to besiege Jerusalem itself (2 Kgs. 16:5). In response, Ahaz of Judah sent a request for aid to Tiglath-Pileser III of Assyria, along with a large amount of gold and silver, in response to which Tiglath-Pileser conquered Damascus (2 Kgs. 16:7–9). If a real event, this would have occurred less than two decades before the Assyrian conquest of Israel, and it is difficult not to connect the two.

[30] As we will see in Chapter 2, the 2 Kings 17 account of the Assyrian conquest, which is the real origin point for the "Lost Tribes of Israel" tradition, dramatically overstates how many Israelites were exiled to Assyria.

[31] As Carly L. Crouch notes, "there are perhaps as many specific kinds of social change which might impel the explicit articulation of identity discourse as there are ethnic groups" (Crouch, *The Making of Israel*, 97).

[32] Knoppers, *Jews and Samaritans*, 121.

of the past were forged. And at the moment it began, it would already have been five hundred years since any imaginable tribal age, nearly as many since the tribes could have been unified within a single political institution, and likely two hundred or more since all twelve tribes had even existed – if indeed they ever had.

Taken all together, what new recognitions about the context in which the biblical visions of history emerged, and were marked by, mean, is simply this: that the Hebrew Bible's traditions represent an act of "becoming Israel" too. In fact, an increasingly large number of scholars wonder whether this might be literally true – that the Judahites may not have originally thought of themselves as Israelite, but only acquired an Israelite identity for themselves after the Assyrian conquest of Israel.[33] I think this is likely enough, and I will discuss this debate in the first chapter, especially with respect to the possibility that the twelve tribes tradition itself might be a Judahite invention, based on an older, shorter Israelite form. But standing at the tail end of this long, tempestuous, *independent* history from Israel, Judahite authors still did not have to identify with Israel any longer, even if they previously had. They did not have to construct their visions of Israelite history and identity in a particular, time honored way, rather than one that suited them in their particular context. If they did not make Judah into an Israel for the first time, which again they well might have, they were nevertheless responsible for making Judah into a *particular* vision of Israel that was all their own.

We can, therefore, say it with confidence: the myth of the twelve tribes of Israel was already doing in the Hebrew Bible what it would go on to do everywhere else. It was already explaining how a people who lived outside of Israel, after the heyday of Israel, was Israel nonetheless – despite what would otherwise seem to be the eloquent testimony of history, geography, and politics. By repeatedly centering the twelve tribes tradition, which they did not have to do, by placing that familiarly beating heart in a new,

---

[33] This idea has its origins in the work of Philip Davies, especially *In Search of "Ancient Israel"* (1992); *In Search of "Ancient Israel,"* 2nd ed. (2004); "The Origins of Biblical Israel." Since then, the idea has grown increasingly popular, especially in recent years. See, among others, Kratz, *Historical and Biblical Israel*; Na'aman, "Saul, Benjamin and the Emergence of 'Biblical Israel' Part I"; Na'aman, "Saul, Benjamin and the Emergence of 'Biblical Israel' Part II"; Na'aman, "The Israelite-Judahite Struggle for the Patrimony of Ancient Israel"; Na'aman, "The Jacob Story and the Formation of Biblical Israel"; Fleming, *The Legacy of Israel in Judah's Bible*; Monroe and Fleming, "Earliest Israel in Highland Company"; Hong, "Once Again"; Finkelstein, *The Forgotten Kingdom*; Leonard-Fleckman, *The House of David*.

Judahite body, the authors of these biblical narratives built a bridge across a gap between ancient Israel and another place and time, and they built that bridge to spec – as so many others would in days to come.

Additionally, it was already the segmented structure of the twelve tribes tradition that made the biblical act of "becoming Israel" possible in the first place, which is where its role as "hidden filament" comes in. The segmentation of Israelite identity – the basic fact of the twelve tribes tradition's *e pluribus unum* structure – is what provides the means of explaining how both Judahites and Israelites are Israelites at once, despite different histories, political structures, and destinies. It is what explains how the Judahites could still be Israelites across a border, despite their own political structures, contextual realities, and particular experiences. Indeed, before the end of the biblical period, it was even already at work explaining how a conceptual "all Israel" survived not just its division between kingdoms, but between Israel and Assyria, Judah and Babylon, and soon, the wider Near Eastern and Mediterranean worlds. In later days, the exact same features of the exact same tradition would explain how very different peoples, all around the world, could still be part of the one and only Israel, across oceans, continents, and great gulfs of time.

Finally, because even "biblical Israel" is really Judah's Israel, every claim to an Israelite identity that survives is similarly animated by a set of unspoken assumptions that are by no means obvious or intuitive. The first is that the twelve tribes model of Israelite identity is *eternally relevant*, no matter what happens. In a vacuum, we might logically expect that the split of the kingdoms, the wars between them, or their conquests, exiles, and returns would have altered how the Judahites understood themselves with respect to an embracing all Israel identity. But already in ancient Judah, the idea was that nothing could alter the fundamental salience of "all Israel" and the twelve tribes of Israel – not the division of the kingdoms, nor the destruction of one, nor the loss of many of the tribes into exile and into the silence of history. And afterwards, every act of "becoming Israel" is based around the insistence that "all Israel" never lost this salience, and that it never could.

Second, in every context including the biblical, individual tribal identities primarily function as a synecdoche, a part forever channeling the presence of the whole. Even in the Hebrew Bible, the important thing is typically not that the tribe of Naphtali is *Naphtali*, but that "Naphtali" is an admission ticket to the larger structure of an Israelite identity. And after the biblical period, the individuality of the tribes is even less important. The main relevance of the Mormon story of Manasseh in America, or the tradition of the tribe of Dan in Ethiopia, is that *Israel* is in these places – Israel first and foremost. Manassite and Danite identities still function as a way of explaining how Israel came to a new place and changed in various ways. But it is *being* Israel that matters most.

And so, the long, continuous history of "becoming Israel" stands revealed. Not two roads that diverged, after all, but only one, the long path, winding through the wood, yellow as the fading sun. And as we will see throughout this book, telling the story of "becoming Israel" from biblical times to the present, with the twelve tribes tradition at the center, offers many advantages towards better understanding both the phenomenon as a whole and each individual case study. First, and simplest, the crucial role the tradition plays in the construction and reconstruction of Israelite identities has never itself properly been understood, precisely because virtually no study of "Israels" anywhere has considered the formal features of segmented systems, and their utility, at any length. My hope is that a large-scale comparative investigation will do here what comparison does everywhere: help us see now just how an apple differs from an orange, but *also* how orange an orange can be.

In other words, I want to explore what one act of "becoming Israel" can teach us about another, but also how a comparative perspective on so-familiar traditions, such as the Bible's, can make us see what was hiding in plain sight. And such an investigation is all the more useful because the *same* aspects of the twelve tribes tradition that allow Israelite identity to be adapted to so many different contexts across the world are also the ones that allow for the constant redescription of Israelite identity in any given time and place, over and over again. Every Israel "becomes" Israel more than once – and the transhistorical unity of "becoming Israel" as a practice is not just a matter of continuities across time and space, but also of inside and out. Thus, the study of how *an* Israelite identity changes over time feeds directly into our investigation of how new visions of Israel were created.

Additionally, a chronological account of the development of "becoming Israel" as a practice from biblical times to the present will help reveal how way led on to way. As we will see, different threads in the tapestry of "becoming Israel" gained and lost prominence at various times or combined with other traditions to allow for sometimes startling transformations. New encounters and new audiences sometimes gave Israel new significance, and often in ways that built on previous developments in general understandings of what Israel meant or portended. Tracing the genealogy of these developments is, as ever, the best way to understand them – and so to understand how what was once a local, Levantine concern became a global phenomenon. But we also understand what "becoming Israel" means in any given context best, to those in the business of "becoming," by understanding what Israel had *come* to mean by the period in question.

In the end, when we break the silos – when we allow ourselves to think about the Hebrew Bible's constructions of Israelite identity, and of the history of Israel's tribes, not through the lens of the Bible's own claims to incomparability, not overawed by the authority it enjoys in religious circles in comparison to other traditions, but as representative of a *common species* of literary and ideological activity for more than two millennia – we begin to see this extraordinary phenomenon as it truly is. And the through-line is the twelve tribes tradition, whose flexible, segmented structure is grist for the mill of "becoming Israel," the fertile soil in which new visions of Israel grow.

The case studies in this book are arranged chronologically. The first chapter, naturally, will be about the Hebrew Bible. Rather than focusing on the history of tribal Israel itself, I will discuss instead the existing scholarly methods for interrogating the Bible's accounts of tribal Israel. Today, I argue, most scholars approach biblical tribal lists and traditions in one of two ways. First, there is the older but still more popular method that I call the "preservative" method, because those who employ it mainly interrogate the details of tribal lists for what they preserve about early Israelite realities. In recent years, a second method has developed, which I call the "cultural invention" method.[34] Essentially, these scholars are interested in the twelve tribes of Israel tradition in the Hebrew Bible as a Judahite *invention* of an Israel that never was. For the most part, this approach begins with the argument mentioned above, that the Judahites only came to think of themselves as Israelites in later periods. Its proponents mainly study tribal lists to determine when a twelve tribe vision embracing both Israel and Judah first developed, why, and from what earlier Israelite traditions, trying to trace the process through its reflection in the development of tribal concepts.

The problem with both methods is that neither fully explains the actual data of biblical tribal depictions, of which there are many, but most from relatively late, Judahite authors. Since identity is indeed fluid over time, the date of most lists, composed after so many changes, means that it is

---

[34] I am grateful to Matthew Neil for this terminological suggestion.

not very likely that they reflect such early constructions of Israelite identity. Meanwhile, their sheer number suggests that they cannot be well explained by any *general* argument about where the twelve tribe concept comes from originally. In other words, the basic twelve tribes framework might be a Judahite invention or not, but that in and of itself would not explain why so many *different* Judahite authors produced so many different visions of it.[35]

I will, therefore, propose a third method of interrogating biblical tribal lists, which I will call the "redescriptive method," and which I intend to be the universal method employed throughout this book. Basically, I will argue that the majority of biblical tribal lists are simply what they appear to be: the fruit of many late, Judahite efforts to redescribe Israelite identity in various ways. By exploring the capabilities of the twelve tribes tradition as a tool for redescription, we will be able to identify something of the different agendas that inspired these various depictions of tribal Israel. Such a conclusion not only has the potential to add greatly to our knowledge of *what* Judahite agendas shaped the production of biblical visions of the past but opens the door to the productive comparisons around which this book is built. Each chapter will reveal something new about how the twelve tribes tradition can be used to adapt Israelite identities, and these can add to our understanding of what biblical authors were doing in their adaptations while also revealing the fundamental similarity between Judahite and extrabiblical acts of "becoming Israel."

In the second chapter, I will discuss the still-extant people known as the Samaritans who descend, for the most part, from the Israelites of the northern kingdom of Israel who were not exiled by the Assyrians – which is what they have always claimed. Until recently, however, their history tended to be interpreted by scholars and outsiders through the lens of a biblical text, 2 Kings 17, in which more or less the entire population of Israel was removed to Assyria and replaced by a motley crew of foreigners drawn from diverse parts of the Assyrian empire. The growing recognition that this biblical story is propaganda has presented contemporary researchers with a number of complicated questions, especially since it still seems most likely that Samaritanism itself, like Judaism, is not

---

[35] Indeed, as James C. Miller observes, "the fact that ethnic identity is a changing social phenomenon rather than a 'thing' possessed by a group means that no single configuration of Israel's 'ethnic identity' existed" (Miller, "Ethnicity and the Hebrew Bible," 173).

precisely a phenomenon of the biblical period, but an early post-biblical one. That is, recognizably Samaritan beliefs and practices probably developed, like Jewish ones did, in continuity with those that came before, but only over the course of the last centuries BCE and the first centuries CE.

The second chapter, then, addresses an open scholarly question: if many of the people living in Israel after the Assyrian conquest were still Israelites, *and* they were not yet Samaritans, what was the real state of the relationship between Israelites and Judahites between those two developments? If 2 Kings 17 is false, might it also be an outlier? Might most of the people of the two regions have understood the other more or less as Israelites like themselves for far longer than we used to think? As this question has started to be asked, scholars have begun to turn their attention to evidence that suggests precisely this. This includes, as a key example, 2 Chronicles 30, another biblical account of Israel in the aftermath of the Assyrian conquest which shows the people of Israel and Judah coming together to celebrate a Passover in Jerusalem, despite what 2 Kings 17 claims.

While these new approaches raise many important questions and make many fine points, I will argue that – in the same vein as the first chapter – recent scholarship on the subject of Israelite and Judahite conceptions of Israelite identity often fails to consider the redescriptive qualities of depictions of all Israel. In other words, because 2 Kings 17 explicitly rejects the Israelite identity of the northerners post-conquest, there is a tendency to treat any evidence that Judahites and Israelites could acknowledge the Israelite identity of the other as the rhetorical opposite. However, within segmented structures especially, an acknowledgment of a shared identity is very often only the first step towards claiming cultural superiority and distinction. In fact, all of the Israels of the world simultaneously claim to be part of the *same* Israel as all the others *and* unique, and privileged. Looked at from this perspective, much of the evidence that is supposed to reveal the absence of competition between Israelite and Judahite claimants to an Israelite identity actually confirms its existence – only couched in another register than 2 Kings 17's full-throated denial.

Chapter 2's discussion of north–south competition over Israelite identity, between Israel and Judah, will serve many purposes in the arc of the larger study. It will, first of all, offer a considerable opportunity to explore the specific role that segmented identity systems play in ethnic competitions and in advancing claims to distinction amidst commonalities. Additionally, this chapter will continue to reveal how the formal features of the twelve tribes tradition allowed for the constant and dynamic redescription of Israelite identity even in the biblical world, *and* how claimants to an Israelite identity could use the twelve tribes tradition to explain even substantial differences from each other.

In Chapter 3, I will turn my attention to "becoming Israel" in the medieval world. Throughout the medieval period, legends about the Lost Tribes of Israel were part of a much larger interpretive framework for many European Christians and Jews. The Crusades especially brought Europeans into contact with new realms and rumors in what was, from their perspective, the east. To explain these new encounters and experiences, medieval commenters turned to traditions about the tribes and blended them with others, especially those concerning Prester John, the great Christian king of the east, and Alexander the Great, in addition to biblical and extrabiblical traditions of other sorts.

Here, I will make concrete one of the main claims of the previous chapters: that, indeed, the features that would carry the twelve tribes of Israel around the world were those the tradition already had in ancient Israel and Judah. The ability of the segmented framework to allow Israel to exist in multiple places at once, and to feature in multiple different stories, would, in the medieval period, allow for the nearly constant production of new visions of Israel that could accommodate new developments of all sorts – in this case, from the perspective of Jewish and Christian Europe. And as in the first chapters, the capacity of descriptions of Israel to express perspectives and agendas turned accounts of where Israel had gotten to, and what its destiny would be, into a mirror to the complex geography of the hopes and fears the potential return and restoration of Israel engendered among both Jewish and Christian communities.

At the same time, the dynamic cross-pollination of traditions that is the main feature of tribal speculation in the medieval period also played a crucial role in spreading the phenomenon of "becoming Israel" still farther. It created a host of new associations for Israel, and new significances, while elevating some that already existed into a new prominence. By the end of the medieval age, the search for Israel had expanded to India and Ethiopia, and promise of the discovery and return of Israel had become firmly associated with the end of the world. The development of a kind of European habit of identifying newly encountered peoples with Israel, combined with these apocalyptic expectations, would indeed prepare the way for "becoming Israel" to emerge as a global phenomenon, even among Christian communities.

In the fourth chapter, we will study the development of Mormon views of Israelite identity. Because the role of the twelve tribes tradition in Mormon beliefs is still so poorly understood, it is all the more important to situate the Mormon adaptation of the tradition within the larger context of "becoming Israel." The Book of Mormon describes the arrival of a family out of the tribe of Manasseh to America and the war between two branches of that family that ultimately consumes one branch entirely. The other became the Native Americans – some or all, depending on who you ask – which gave the Mormons their earliest sacred task: to convert the Natives by reminding them of their own Israelite ancestry. By very early periods, however, the Mormons began to think of themselves, too, as literal Israelites. Thus, today, Mormon missionizing is often conceptualized, in explicitly tribal terms, as a hunt for others of Israel, who will be recognized by their openness to the Mormon message. Many of the main institutions of Mormon religious practice are based on this identification with Israel, especially the Mormon patriarchal blessing. In fact, as a central part of this blessing – an important coming-of-age ritual – the recipient's ancestral tribe is revealed.

Ultimately, the study of the twelve tribes tradition in Mormonism offers clear examples of two major themes of our discussion. First, the historical development of Mormon understandings of Israelite identity reveals extremely clearly how the accumulation of new features to the basic tradition laid the groundwork for surprising new developments. The arrival of Israel in America was accomplished in part by the aforementioned European habit of identifying the unknown with the tribes. Similarly, the perceived connection between the restoration of Israel and the Second Coming dovetailed with more widespread early American views on the need to convert the natives.

Second, the Mormon adaptation of the twelve tribes tradition is an object lesson in the capacity of the basic twelve tribes tradition to be "particularized" to fit the needs and characteristics of new circumstances. In each of our case studies, the tradition offers those who claim it the sanction and prestige of a broadly shared, broadly recognizable Israelite identity. At the same time, the inherent flexibility of the system allows the basic concept to be adapted in multiple places at once, in ways particularly suited to each context. In the case of Mormonism, the end result of these processes of development and adaptation is the enduring settlement of an "Israel" in America, which can teach us quite a lot about how Israels appear anywhere, and how they survive and attract members. Since the origins of Mormonism lie in so relatively recent a period and are so well documented, in comparison to the subjects of previous chapters, a discussion of the development of Mormon concepts of Israel over time will show the processes of "becoming Israel" at a level of granular detail previously unavailable to us – especially after the Mormon trek to Utah and settlement there.

Finally, in Chapter 5, we will investigate the story of the twelve tribes tradition among the Beta Israel of Ethiopia. This, our last case study, is also a story of tangled roots and surprising results. In Ethiopia, an old and very general identification with ancient Israel – and a surprisingly "Jewish" seeming and equally old Ethiopian Christianity – provided the foundation for the appearance of a specific Beta Israel identity sometime between the fourteenth and fifteenth centuries CE. At that time, the Beta Israel's sense of themselves as Israel was shaped by Ethiopian realities, and even proceeded from an ancient Ethiopian tradition, the *Kebra Nagast*, or "glory of kings." Israel was also a point of contention between the "Israels" of Ethiopia, since the *Kebra*, from the thirteenth century until the twentieth, also served as the charter myth for Ethiopia's Christian emperors.

In the nineteenth and early twentieth centuries, however, interactions with Christian and Jewish missionaries combined with developments within Ethiopia to produce not only a transformation of Beta Israel identity, but a remarkable substitution of one tradition of Israelite origin for another. Instead of the *Kebra Nagast*, the Jewish world interpreted the history of the Beta Israel through the lens of an ancient Jewish legend concerning the Danite Jews of Ethiopia – or Kush – and soon enough, many Beta Israel adopted this history for themselves. This latter story would clear the way for the Beta Israel to be brought to Israel in the 1980s and 1990s, per Israel's mandate to "ingather the exiles."[36] At the same time, the particulars of this new version of Israelite identity have caused a number of issues for the Beta Israel, as far as their comfortable settlement *in* Israel is concerned.

Basically, as we will see, the return of this Lost Tribe set up a collision among different ways of thinking about "being Israel." Again, it is true that in every case where the exact same twelve tribes tradition is being used, each vision of Israel purports to be the same *Israel*, and specifically biblical Israel. However, since each vision of Israelite identity is a distinct discursive formation from the rest, *including* biblical Israel, every Israel is

---

[36] Soroff, *The Maintenance and Transmission of Ethnic Identity*, 29.

constructed differently. What happened for the Beta Israel is that the twelve tribes tradition provided a means for this people, and for Jewish authorities in Israel, to explain their relationship to each other, but not to fully rationalize or reconcile the fundamental differences between them. In rationalizing these differences as the consequence of the survival of a "pre-Talmudic" form of Judaism in Ethiopia, these Israeli authorities described native Beta Israel practices as less than their own, and in need of reforming. Indeed, the earliest Beta Israel immigrants were even required to undergo a modified conversion ceremony, which caused a great deal of controversy and contributed to an ongoing sense of alienation. And today, the struggle for Beta Israel equality goes on.

This case study is a fitting conclusion to the book for two reasons. First, the tensions that persist between the Beta Israel and the authorities of the State of Israel are the same tensions at work in every chapter. Every construction of Israel presents itself as part of *the* Israel, every construction is unique – and when Israels meet, these unique features raise existential questions. Second, in every case, it is these unique features of a given vision of Israel that reveal the character of every construction of Israel, and something of its history. Naturally, in internal, ethnic contexts, these differences inevitably raise questions about which account of Israel is the correct one, with resulting tensions, and scholars have often followed suit, evaluating the character of self-identifying Israels on the basis of the validity of their historical claims. But from an external perspective, the unique features of each Israel are the key to understanding the unique history and character of them all.

Ultimately, by breaking down the barriers between the use of the twelve tribes tradition to construct visions of Israelite identity in the ancient world and the modern, we will emerge with our continuous story. We will see the twelve tribes of Israel in their native land, first united, then riven by political faction. We will see some taken into the great fastness of the Neo-Assyrian empire, the juggernaut of its day. We will see some remain behind, in the vicinity of the ancient city of Jerusalem, David's capital, where the Jewish faith would develop out of its ancient roots in the last centuries of the first millennium BCE. We will see another Israelite history unfold in what had once been "Israel" itself: the northern region, where the Samaritans still live today, calling themselves by the name of Israel and worshipping in the same place their ancestors had for at least 2,500 years.

After these stories, we will see many more. We will see the tribes of Israel go on, sometimes together, sometimes quite alone. We will see them move deeper into Asia, where they were often found in the medieval period, and into North Africa, where a people called the Beta Israel of Ethiopia would be brought to the modern State of Israel in fulfillment of the promise made at that nation's founding to become a home for all the children of Israel. We will watch Israel make its way even across the mighty Atlantic Ocean, to America. In some cases, we will see what happens when two Israels from different worlds meet and make accommodation with each other – or do not but change in the process nonetheless. We will see what happens when self- or other-identified tribes of Israel are found, and how their discovery changes both them and their discoverers, as stories meet, match, and mix in the fluid middle grounds of encounter, colonization, and empire.

Most of all, of course, we will discover "becoming Israel" itself. The myth of the twelve tribes of Israel is not one story, it is not the possession of a singular people, it is the raw material of stories, the place where the stories start. And once we understand that – once we can investigate what was done with it, context to context, without the prejudices of familiar categories – we reveal a hidden structure, spanning with its bulk more than two millennia, a kind of labyrinth, full of hidden ways. An awareness of "becoming Israel" as an *ongoing* phenomenon is our guide through it, the silver thread unspooling through its depths, shining to show us its shape. The greatest treasure of this labyrinth is the mirror at its heart, in which we will see reflected something of all those who have stood before it, clad in Israel's raiment, similar but different, and beyond them, the shadows of all those who *will* come in future days, along paths still unknown. Our task is to look into that mirror and see what Israel has meant, and where, and why – to them, to us, to the world.

I

Judah's Israels

The Twelve Tribes of Israel in the Hebrew Bible

In the morning, when the Rabbi asked her what she'd thought of the book, she hesitated, searching for the right words. "Were these real people?" He raised an eyebrow. "Would my answer change your understanding of them?"
—Helene Wecker, *The Golem and the Jinni*, 87.*

Even in antiquity, stories often began *in medias res*. The *Iliad* opens on the last year of a ten-year conflict, plunging us head-first into the animosities of two men, Achilles and Agamemnon, whose anger towards each other we are ill-equipped to understand. The *Odyssey* begins on Ithaca, in Odysseus' absence, where Telemachus, the son who never knew his father, stands on the brittle brink of adulthood. When we first meet Odysseus, in book V, he is not about to embark on his famous journey, but already on Calypso's island, two stops from home. He will tell his story once he makes it to Phaeacia, but the Cyclops and the Sirens are already long behind him. Today, of course, a story might begin anywhere at all – in the middle, at the end, or both at once. James Joyce's *Finnegans Wake* begins with the end of a sentence that the end of the book begins, while the great Flann O'Brien starts his *At Swim-Two-Birds*: "One beginning and one ending for a book was a thing I did not agree with."[1]

---

* From *The Golem and the Jinni*, published by HarperCollins Publishers. Copyright © 2013 by Helene Wecker. Reprinted by permission of The Frances Goldin Literary Agency as agents for the author.

[1] In Joyce's case: "Riverrun, past Eve and Adam's, from swerve of shore to bend of bay, brings us by a commodious vicus of recirculation back to Howth Castle and Environs" (Joyce, *Finnegans Wake*, 3; O'Brien, *At Swim-Two-Birds*, 1).

Still, where clarity is concerned, nothing beats a story told straight from the beginning, which, for the twelve tribes of Israel tradition, is the Hebrew Bible. And since my purpose is to show that the act of "becoming Israel" – of constructing new visions of Israelite history and identity out of the tradition – *is* a continuous story, what I intend to demonstrate in this chapter is that the things people far away from and after ancient Israel did with Israelite identity were already being done in the Hebrew Bible. I will reveal, here as well as in the next chapter, that the features which would eventually carry "becoming Israel" around the world were features the tradition always had. And I will explore how thinking in terms of this continuous story can shed light on the use of the twelve tribes tradition, even in the Bible itself.

The real beginning of our story, then – the beginning of the beginning – is the fundamental tension at the heart of the Hebrew Bible's vision of the twelve tribes of Israel. On the one hand, we have the absolute centrality of the twelve tribes of Israel to both of the Hebrew Bible's narrative histories – the "Primary History" of Genesis through Kings and the "Secondary History" of the books of Chronicles.[2] We have the sheer, and rarely considered, mass of tribal lists, which is to say, complete or nearly complete descriptions of tribal Israel, in the Hebrew Bible. There are roughly twenty-six lists in all, including nineteen in the Primary History and six in the Secondary – which also happens to start with a massive, nine-chapter-long recapitulation of the entire history of Israel in the form of a tribal genealogy.[3] We have the last tribal list, in Ezekiel 48, in which an apocalyptic vision of a restored Israel and a restored Jerusalem is repeatedly presented as the restoration of the twelve tribes of Israel as well. All these details have been taken as an intimation of the

---

[2] These, of course, are scholarly terms, and not necessarily appropriate ones. They reflect an outdated perspective on the relationship between the two narratives and their respective value. However, for our purposes, the main point remains simply that these narratives exist.

[3] Counting lists is not an exact science because multiple lists can occur in the same chapter, and some lists are not complete. These are the lists that appear to be comprehensive or nearly comprehensive, while also remaining distinct efforts. For a discussion of my methodology see Tobolowsky, *The Sons of Jacob*, 43. There are four lists in the book of Genesis (Gen. 29:32–30:24; 35:22–26; 46:8–27; 49:1–27), one in Exodus (Exod.1:1–6), eight in Numbers (Num. 1:5–15; 1:20–43; 2:3–33; 7:12–83; 10:14–27; 13:4–15; 26:5–62; 34:14–28), two in Deuteronomy (Deut. 27:12–13; 33:1–29), two in Joshua (Josh. 13:15–19:48; 21:4–40), and two in Judges (Judg. 1:1–36; 5:14–23). The Chronicles lists are 1 Chron. 2:1–2; 2:3–9:1a; 6:40–48; 6:49–66; 12:25–38; 27:16–22.

overwhelming importance of tribal Israel, not just in biblical literature, but in Israelite and Judahite history, and it is not hard to see why.

At the same time, biblical tribal discourse, considered as a whole, overwhelmingly profiles as late and Judahite in origin, which is to say that a substantial majority of the Hebrew Bible's tribal texts were produced by authors who lived in the kingdom, then region, called Judah, centuries after Judah and Israel could have been united politically – in the great "United Monarchy" of David and Solomon or otherwise. This includes at least eleven of the fifteen tribal lists in the Pentateuch, which are routinely attributed to the so-called "Priestly" author, or authors, likely at work between the sixth and fourth centuries BCE, and who are also held to be responsible for the majority of the Pentateuch's tribal narratives.[4] It includes the six lists in the books of Chronicles, as well as the books themselves. These were probably composed as a whole only in the "Persian period," which began with Cyrus of Persia's conquest of Babylon in 539 BCE, nearly half a millennium after Judah could have been part of Israel, and after many dramatic changes. It includes Ezekiel 48, an apocalyptic vision of the future restoration of Israel and Jerusalem in tribal terms, probably also from this rather later period.[5]

Already that accounts for eighteen of twenty-six lists, and there is no compelling reason to suspect that all the rest are early or Israelite. Judges 5 is likely a very early tribal text – perhaps the oldest text in the entire Bible – and Genesis 49 and Deuteronomy 33 are often supposed to have early cores as well.[6] But I suspect the real number of late Judahite tribal lists, which is to say late, Judahite visions of tribal Israel, is something like

---

[4] Older reconstructions of P did sometimes suggest an earlier date but P is seldom believed to have been at work prior to the sixth century BCE today, especially because of the similarities between P's vocabulary and concerns and the (largely sixth-century) book of Ezekiel (Olyan, *Rites and Rank*, 15–50; Carr, *The Formation of the Hebrew Bible*, 297; Klawans, *Impurity and Sin in Ancient Judaism*). See also Blenkinsopp, "An Assessment of the Alleged Pre-Exilic Date," and the various studies in Shectman and Baden, *The Strata of the Priestly Writings*. P is often held to be responsible for Gen. 35:22–26, 46:8–27; Num. 1:5–15, 1:20–43, 2:3–33, 7:12–83, 10:14–27, 13:4–15, 26:5–62, 34:14–28. Exod. 1:1–6 is usually assigned to P, or an even later redactor, R. I have argued that the two Genesis lists attributed to P were actually written by an even later author, too, but the main point is that they *are* late, and Judahite (Tobolowsky, *The Sons of Jacob*, 116–25, 135–38).

[5] Zimmerli, *Ezekiel*, 197; Sparks, *Ethnicity and Identity in Ancient Israel*, 297–99; Tuell, *The Law of the Temple in Ezekiel*; Carr, *The Formation of the Hebrew Bible*, 297.

[6] On Judges 5, see especially Smith, "Why Was 'Old Poetry' Used in Hebrew Narrative?," 197–203; Smith, *Poetic Heroes*, 211–20.

twenty-three or twenty-four, and that is just the start.[7] Obviously, all of these lists now appear in narratives that themselves could only have been crafted by Judahite authors of the sixth through fourth centuries BCE – which is to say, in a time and place when not only would any imaginable tribal age have been half a millennium in the past, but a number of tribes likely no longer existed.[8]

The tension, then, is between what these tribal traditions purport to be – depictions of the historical experience, and historical reality, of an institution that was foundational to Israelite identity – and what they actually are: largely, late Judahite compositions within late Judahite accounts of Israel's history. And whatever the history of tribal concepts, or even of a tribal institution, we certainly cannot deny that it was the *interests* of late Judahite authors and their extraordinary enthusiasm for describing and redescribing tribal Israel that gave biblical tribal discourse its characteristic shape. Neither can a simple desire to preserve an ancient tradition intact account for this enthusiasm; the sheer quantity of late Judahite visions of tribal Israel; or the sometimes substantial differences between them.[9]

Today, the scholarly study of the Hebrew Bible's tribal traditions is largely divided between two approaches. The first of these is what I call the "preservative method" of interrogating tribal traditions – an older method, but still the most popular. Its proponents are mainly interested in reconstructing early tribal Israel, so they interrogate the details of tribal depictions for what they may preserve about early tribal realities. Crucially, these scholars understand the differences between biblical accounts of the twelve tribes of Israel – differences in order, or

---

[7] Another two lists, in Joshua, might be Priestly, if there are Priestly lists there, and likely late regardless. Meanwhile, there is no good reason to think Deut. 27:12–13 or Judg. 1:1–36 are particularly early, although this case has sometimes been made, especially in earlier scholarship. See Tobolowsky, *The Sons of Jacob*, 72–73. I have also argued in various places – and certainly not I alone – that Genesis 49 may have an early core, but represents a late Judahite reconstruction nonetheless. See especially Fleming, *The Legacy of Israel in Judah's Bible*, 85–90; Schorn, *Ruben und das System der zwölf Stämme Israels*; Macchi, *Israël et ses tribus selon Genèse 49*; Tobolowsky, *The Sons of Jacob*, 55–56.

[8] That is to say, any age in which the tribes lived and worked together as the primary political structure of Israel.

[9] As I've observed elsewhere, if the order of the tribes in a given list is taken into consideration, "*none* of the tribal lists in biblical literature are exactly like any other" (Tobolowsky, *The Sons of Jacob*, 45). In other cases, scholars are quite familiar with the fact that some tribal lists include Joseph and Levi and some Ephraim and Manasseh, and there are various instances in which some tribes are not mentioned in lists or described in unusual ways.

arrangement, and sometimes even number – to reflect developments in the organization of the institution itself, though not always directly. Thus, the preservative method is a method of extracting historical data about early Israel from the details of twelve tribe narratives and lists.

In more recent years, a second major approach has developed, which I call the "cultural invention" method. The scholars in this camp are responding not only to the relatively late Judahite origins of so many biblical tribal traditions, but other evidence that suggests biblical tribal traditions were composed to forward Judahite interests. The proponents of this method argue that the twelve tribes concept itself was a Judahite invention, if based on earlier Israelite tribal traditions, and they are mainly interested in exploring when it developed, out of what, and why. The cultural invention method involves interrogating the details of tribal traditions for what they reveal about the process through which Judah "invented" itself as Israel.

Of these two approaches, I think the second is a better explanation for a number of different aspects of biblical tribal traditions, and I will explain why below. At the same time, any true solution to the problem of predominantly late Judahite tribal traditions in the Hebrew Bible's histories of Israel must explain not only their prominence, or the context in which most emerged, but their *frequency* and *variety*. In other words, a method that treats the majority of tribal traditions as various accounts of an actual early institution explains their centrality to biblical traditions, and their variety. Treating the twelve tribes concept as a Judahite invention explains their date. Neither, however, can explain why so many late Judahite authors were interested in describing the twelve tribes of Israel so often and differently from each other.

When we consider what *can*, we can reflect that here we stand at the beginning of a book about an ongoing fascination with redescribing and adapting Israelite identity, through the twelve tribes of Israel tradition, that spans not only the history of ancient Israel and Judah but *the next two thousand years and more*. We stand on the brink of a discussion of how often, and in how many places, Israelite identity was redescribed by manipulating the details of tribal traditions, and for how many reasons. To suggest that precisely this impulse to repeatedly redescribe Israel was alive and well already in ancient Judah cuts against a knee-jerk impulse to understand biblical traditions as fundamentally Israelite, and fundamentally different than the traditions of Israel that came after. But such an impulse does explain what we actually have in the Hebrew Bible's many tribal traditions much better than the approaches just described.

A "redescriptive" method – a third method that explores how the segmented structure of the twelve tribes tradition works to allow the constant, dynamic redescription of Israelite identity, and what the study of redescriptions can reveal – will, therefore, offer considerable insight here, and in chapters to come.

In what follows, I will first describe the history of the preservative method, and why, despite its continued popularity, it should be definitively abandoned. I will then explore the origins of the cultural invention method and explain what I think it gets right, but also its significant limitations. Next, I will lay out this "redescriptive method," which I intend to be useful not only here, but as a universal method throughout this book – a kind of "grand unified theory" of the twelve tribes tradition.[10] Treating the majority of biblical tribal traditions, first and foremost, as what they appear to be – a number of different, late Judahite efforts to redescribe Israelite identity – is what allows us to understand what these authors were doing with Israelite identity. But it is also what reveals the fundamental continuity between the redescription of Israelite identity in the Bible and its redescription everywhere else, where so many things were "done" with Israelite identity. And as we will see, universally, those who *describe* Israel also *inscribe* it with what they want, need, believe, and hope for – and these are inscriptions we can translate, if we know how.

1.1 THE ORIGINS OF THE PRESERVATIVE METHOD

We can start with what the preservative method is not – it is not the vague, general belief that *some* aspects of the Hebrew Bible's account of tribal Israel may preserve early tribal realities to *some* extent. Nobody really doubts that, though there is a range of opinions on just how much might be preserved, and how much preservation factors into the traditions we now have, as we have them. Still, there are early tribal texts, especially Judges 5, and in all probability, even later tribal traditions were often built around earlier ones. This is the way of inherited traditions, even when they are really dynamically reinvented – new visions piggyback off the authority of the old, and preserve much in the process.[11]

---

[10] I recently pioneered some aspects of this method in Tobolowsky, "The Problem of Reubenite Primacy."

[11] In the case of Greek mythological genealogies, as Margalit Finkelberg observes, "rather than changing the system, the experts who were responsible for the creation of new

The preservative method is, however – well – a method. Certainly, it is animated by a more robust faith in the capacity of biblical traditions to preserve early realities than we find elsewhere, but it is, nevertheless, a quite particular set of techniques, animated by an equally particular set of assumptions, aimed at extracting information about early tribal Israel from the details of tribal traditions. More specifically, it is a method for extracting this kind of information from perceived hints in biblical accounts of tribal history and from the differences between depictions of the order and organization of the tribes. It is, basically, a particular way of hunting for what are sometimes called "kernels of truth," the traces of early realities supposedly preserved in early traditions, sometimes quite without the knowledge of those doing the preserving.

Interestingly enough, the preservative method emerged out of what was actually a rejection of much of the biblical history of Israel's tribes.[12] By the turn of the century, scholars had begun to realize, generally grudgingly, that it was unlikely that anything like an Israelite conquest of Canaan had occurred. Violent conquests tend to be the kind of thing that show up in the archaeological record, and the archaeological record did not suggest anything of the sort at any time when a plausibly histor- ical Israel might have arrived from outside. In response, Albrecht Alt developed the so-called "peaceful infiltration" model of the Israelite entry into the region, in which small groups gradually made their way over a long period of time.[13] Through this model, the basic sense of the biblical narrative was preserved, since the Israelites would still be outsiders, but the absence of evidence for conquest could be explained away.

Yet the development of the method itself is mainly the work of Martin Noth, another German scholar of the early- to mid-twentieth century. Noth's initial contribution in this direction was his argument that, before they had entered Canaan, the groups involved had not really been *Israelite* at all.[14] Instead, in Noth's rendition, Israel, as Israel, had

---

genealogies would modify their client's lineage so that it fitted into the pre-existing schema" (Finkelberg, *Greeks and Pre-Greeks*, 29). In fact, this is not always the case, and modifications can be more creative than that, but often.

[12] Notably, in Noth, *Das System der zwölf Stämme Israels*; Noth, *Überlieferungsgeschichte Des Pentateuch*; Noth, *Geschichte Israels*.

[13] Alt, "Judas Gaue unter Josia"; Alt, *Die Landnahme der Israeliten in Palästina*; Alt, "Das System der Stammesgrenzen im Buche Josua"; Alt, *Die Staatenbildung der Israeliten in Palästina*.

[14] C. H. J. De Geus observes that "the amphictyony hypothesis of Martin Noth was not a matter of spontaneous generation ... it was already to be found in the works of Ed. Meyer and G. Beer; while E. Sellin, R. Kittel, and E. Auerbach came close to it ... It might

emerged for the first time in Canaan itself, only in the few centuries before the rise of the Israelite monarchies, and only after the majority of the events the Bible describes as tribal experiences would already have happened.[15] This first and oldest Israel, naturally, had taken the form of a twelve tribe league – or an "amphictyony," Noth's preferred term, borrowed from Greek mythology – which explained to his satisfaction the centrality of the twelve tribes tradition to the biblical accounts of history.[16] In his words,

Israel was constituted in the form of an amphictyonic twelve-tribe association; this fact was of basic significance for the whole subsequent course of history. Israel, at any rate, always thought of itself as a community of twelve tribes, and upheld the conception in spite of all later attacks on its external form.[17]

The center of the league, Noth argued, had been a sanctuary near the Israelite city of Shechem, and it had formed there starting in the mid-fourteenth century BCE.[18] Furthermore, the processes through which Israel had formed were quite complete "at least a hundred years before the accession of Saul" – something like 1150 BCE.[19]

Where the preservative method is concerned, the crucial aspect of Noth's new history of Israel is that it was also a history of Israel's traditions, and specifically, of the traditions of the Pentateuch.[20] Basically, Noth argued that the narrative sequence that appears in the Pentateuch was actually formed with Israel itself, and in more or less the same

---

be objected that, in contrast to Noth's hypothesis, all these earlier covenants of the tribes, leagues and amphictyonies had always been imagined as prior to the entry into Canaan, usually as having their centre in Kades, or sometimes in Transjordan. Yet also H. Winckler and R. Kittel already placed their tribal leagues after the Entry, and in Palestine. The peculiarity of Noth's hypothesis, however, is that he no longer regards the amphictyony or tribal league as a phase to be postulated in the vague past of Israel, but depicts it most concretely as a living institution, whose influences may be pointed out even far into the time of the kings. Indeed, he goes further still, and ascribes the very origin and formation of Israel to this amphictyony!" (De Geus, *The Tribes of Israel*, 69). See especially Noth, *A History of the Pentateuchal Traditions*, 257–59.

[15] Noth, *The History of Israel*, 96. "That the Old Testament tradition took too simple a view of the events which led to the development of Israel as a totality is obvious from the fact, already mentioned, that the tribes of Israel did not all settle on the soil of Palestine at the same time but, judging from various statements in the tradition that has come down to us, their occupation of the land was divided into at least two distinct phases" (Noth, *The History of Israel*, 72).

[16] Ibid., 90–92.   [17] Ibid., 96.

[18] That is, at "the undoubtedly very ancient tree shrine east of the city" (ibid., 91–92).

[19] Ibid., 81.   [20] Van Seters, *Abraham in History and Tradition*, 144.

way.[21] The pre-Israelite groups that feature in Noth's reconstruction had entered Canaan with their own independent traditions, and these had been brought together as those groups were. In neither case was simple combination involved, but a more complete reinvention in "all Israel" form that nevertheless left the outlines of previous realities and narratives somewhat intact.[22] He called the resulting – and quite hypothetical – narrative the *Grundlage*, or "common basis," meaning that it was the basis of all major later pentateuchal traditions, already rendered in familiar order and form.[23] Thus, "the decisive steps on the way to the formation of the Pentateuch were taken during the preliterary stage, and the literary fixations only gave final form to material which in its essentials was already given" – and they were given, for the first time, as the charter myth of the league in its earlier days.[24]

On the one hand, the combination of these arguments meant that even late pentateuchal *texts* were really Israel's earliest *traditions*, written down much later on, which explained to Noth's satisfaction why so many late Judahite compositions might nevertheless reveal, primarily, early Israelite realities. On the other hand, the same arguments also meant that the vast majority of the biblical account of tribal history was not literally true. The Pentateuch, after all, describes the experience of the tribes, as the twelve tribes of Israel, from the birth of the tribal ancestors to the death of Moses, prior even to the conquest itself – and Noth had started with the

---

[21] "This traditio-historical collocation of themes, which occurred under the given assumption that the 'twelve tribes of Israel' first became a permanent unity upon Palestinian soil in the form of a sacral league, was a product of the formation of tradition in the sphere of the tribes that had already become settled" (Noth, *A History of the Pentateuchal Traditions*, 256).

[22] "Of course, originally, most of the tradition-materials in the Pentateuch were quite limited in their reference, indeed limited more to locality than to tribal history, and often this reference shows through clearly in the transmitted form. But in the Pentateuch these materials manifestly have *only* an all-Israelite significance. Thus it is clear that the Pentateuch did not come into being by the summation of individual narratives, which, having been gradually accumulated from the sphere of all Israelite tribes and connected with one another in manifold ways, finally yielded by virtue of their combination an overall picture of a history or of a prehistory of *all* Israel" (Noth, *The History of Israel*, 43).

[23] Ibid., 39. In the "*pre*literary history" of the pentateuchal narrative, the tradition achieved "a pattern that came to be firmly fixed in all its essentials." Later authors may have added certain things and reworked what they inherited to some extent but "apart from the primeval history ... added no really new theme, either in great or small matters" (ibid., 44).

[24] Ibid., 1–2.

position that there had been no twelve tribes until after the era of the conquest was over.

Predictably, Noth, like Alt before him, hedged on just how unreliable this made the Pentateuch as a source for history. Since he believed that the *Grundlage* had been built from pre-Israelite traditions, he thought they might well preserve something of the pre-Israelite experiences that produced them, perhaps including events much like Abraham's journey from Mesopotamia, or the exodus from Egypt. In this telling, these would only have happened to *some* of the ancestors of *some* of the members of the early Israelite community, and would only have become part of an "all Israel" narrative after all Israel had formed – but they would have happened, for some given value of "happened." Certainly, Noth argued explicitly that both "the 'patriarchs' and Moses are to be reckoned as historical figures in the prehistory of the Israelite tribes."[25]

The same logic could not be applied, however, to the Pentateuch's many descriptions of the twelve tribes themselves. Neither could it be applied to pentateuchal accounts of the organization and arrangement of the tribes, nor of its key institutions. After all, the twelve tribes of Israel itself was, specifically, what had not yet existed prior to the era recounted in the book of Judges. How, then, could these traditions represent the actualities of Israel's tribal history in any meaningful way? The question gains urgency from the fact that the Pentateuch is the epicenter of the Bible's accounts of the tribes, containing its major traditions of origins, the reception of the law at Sinai, and no fewer than fifteen of the Hebrew Bible's twenty-six lists.

In an odd way, Noth's solution to the problem of what I earlier called the tension between the biblical description of the heyday of the tribes of Israel and his own sense of when those traditions had emerged, mirrors my own quite well. Basically, he concluded that biblical tribal traditions did not *represent* the historical realities of tribal experience, but *reflected*, somewhat obliquely, those of the era of their composition.[26]

---

[25] Noth, *A History of the Pentateuchal Traditions*, 257.

[26] "It goes without saying that the tribes had a history of their own before they entered Palestine and in the Old Testament certain tribal traditions from that early period have been preserved which are undoubtedly genuine ... On the other hand, these traditions were first given definitive form within an Israel that was already united in Palestine and they were conditioned by its point of view ... in their existing form they are based on presuppositions which did not exist until the tribes had already settled on Palestinian soil" (Noth, *The History of Israel*, 53).

Because, however, Noth believed this was the era of the tribal league itself, in an oral form that long preceded their emergence as texts, it was the realties of the league that he believed they preserved.

As to how they reflected a period which, in fact, neither they nor any other biblical text even describe, Noth suspected that the original authors of pentateuchal tribal traditions had inscribed the realities of their own age backwards onto its charter myths in order to justify them. More than that, because there are so many different, sometimes contradictory tribal traditions in the Pentateuch, he suspected that many different aspects of the tribal age and its history had been preserved, likely including snapshots of the league in different arrangements. This meant that a careful scholar who knew how to read the way in which these shifts were reflected in these texts, and could put them in something like chronological order, would be able to reverse engineer the history of the league through them, including its prehistory to whatever extent the processes through which the tribes entered Canaan and came together had been preserved.

This, in a nutshell, is the preservative method: a supposed way of divining the realities of the early history of Israel, the origins of the tribal league, and something of its development over time out of the details of surviving tribal traditions. The details in question did not represent those realities in a literal way, but reflected them in a manner that could be discovered through interpretation. In a sense, the method makes of tribal traditions what Abraham Malamat, an enthusiastic practitioner, would later call a "code," and made the art of the scholar a kind of code-breaking.[27] With the proper cipher, the whole history of early Israel might be revealed.

For Noth, then, a detail like the order of the birth of the tribal ancestors in Genesis 29–30, as well as the fact that they had been born to four different women – Jacob's wives, Rachel and Leah, and their enslaved women, Bilhah and Zilpah – could reveal, through interpretation, the order in which the tribes entered Canaan and something of the pre-league arrangements between them. Since, for example, Leah was Jacob's first wife, and since she had six children, Noth extrapolated the existence of a six tribe league that preceded the twelve tribe league in Canaan, consisting of the tribes represented by Leah's sons.[28]

---

[27] Malamat, *History of Biblical Israel*, 47–48.

[28] At one point in his *History of Israel*, he argues that "the older form begins with a group of six tribes which, following Gen. XXIX, 41 ff, are usually called 'Leah Tribes.'"

Or, the fact that Reuben is described as Jacob's eldest son despite the fact that the Reubenites never seem to be an important tribe might reveal an era of Reubenite pre-eminence so long ago it had otherwise been totally forgotten.[29] The fact that some versions of the twelve tribes tradition include Joseph and Levi, and some Ephraim and Manasseh, might reflect a moment when Levi had left the secular tribal institution to serve as the priestly tribe, and Joseph had been split in two to preserve the traditional number of twelve.[30] The tradition in Genesis 48, which describes the adoption of Joseph's sons Ephraim and Manasseh by Jacob, would have developed retroactively to justify this new reality. In such hints and whispers did Noth believe the history of early Israel was written.

In fact, for Noth, the preservative method would not serve as *a* way of reconstructing the history of early tribal Israel, but *the* way. It is hard to overstate how little evidence there is for so much of what Noth suggested other than the fruits of the method. Obviously, no biblical text directly suggests the order in which the tribes entered Canaan, or the processes through which they formed a league, since in the Bible no such thing ever happened. No biblical text even describes a league centered on Shechem, nor does any extrabiblical evidence suggest such a thing.[31] Yet through this form of textual divination alone, Noth would render a fantastically detailed account of the early history of Israel, and so would many who came after.[32] So, indeed, do many today.

At another, "one must assume that the 'Leah tribes,' Reuben, Simeon, Levi, Judah, Zebulun, and Issachar, had once formed a six-tribe association at a time when the first named of these tribes were still in full possession of their original position and Joseph and Benjamin had not yet completed their occupation, and that this six-tribe association was the forerunner and basis of the later twelve-tribe association" (Noth, *The History of Israel*, 86, 89).

[29] Ibid., 88–89; Cross, *From Epic to Canon*, 56, 70; Curtis, "Some Suggestions," 247–49.

[30] Noth, *The History of Israel*, 12.

[31] Joshua 24 describes an assembly of the tribes at Shechem, but stops far short of explaining the historical relationship between the two. And Shechem is important elsewhere, but not obviously as the tribal capital.

[32] See, especially Noth, *The History of Israel*, 55–97 and to a lesser extent, Noth, *A History of the Pentateuchal Traditions*, 71–101. De Geus observes that aspects of Noth's approach "found very many adherents, so many even that for about thirty years ... [it] practically ruled all possible conceptions of early Israel" (De Geus, *The Tribes of Israel*, 42).

I.2 THE PRESERVATIVE METHOD TODAY

In most respects, the 1970s began an era of rapid change in biblical studies that would only accelerate over the following decades. The fact that the preservative method not only survived, but thrived, owes not only to the ongoing influence of Noth, but to the work of a number of scholars in that period, especially Robert Wilson and Abraham Malamat, to set it on supposedly firmer foundations.[33] It was Wilson and Malamat who drew scholarly attention to the potential utility of two different sets of comparisons. The first was with then-recently translated Assyrian and Babylonian "Kinglists" from the early second millennium BCE.[34] These Kinglists, they argued, proved that recording political realities in genealogical form was an ancient Semitic practice. In Wilson's phrase, they demonstrated an "Amorite custom of using genealogies for political and social purposes," which their study could therefore reveal.[35] Since the Hebrew Bible often describes the ancestors of the Israelites as Mesopotamian Amorites, and of course as Semites, this seemed very important.

The second comparison was with the oral genealogical traditions of various African cultures, and especially the Nuer.[36] These had been studied earlier in the century, but had only recently come to the attention of biblical scholars. What they suggested, as comparative evidence, is that Noth's instincts had been basically right – genealogical representations of society *do* shift as society shifts. As a result, the progress of these shifts over time might indeed be reverse engineered out of them. Thus, for

---

[33] Malamat, "King Lists of the Old Babylonian Period"; Malamat, "Tribal Societies"; Johnson, *The Purpose of the Biblical Genealogies*; Wilson, "The Old Testament Genealogies in Recent Research"; Wilson, *Genealogy and History in the Biblical World*; Wilson, "Between 'Azel' and 'Azel.'"

[34] See Gelb, "Two Assyrian King Lists"; Finkelstein, "The Genealogy of the Hammurapi Dynasty".

[35] Wilson, "The Old Testament Genealogies in Recent Research," 175.

[36] Especially Evans-Pritchard, *The Nuer*. Thus, Malamat: "... allow me to quote a statement by Evans-Pritchard on the Nuer: 'When the brothers [*of certain Nuer lineages*] are spoken about as quarreling, migrating and so forth, it must be understood that the lineages and the local communities of which they form part are being personified and dramatized.' Such personifications are equally characteristic of the Biblical genealogies" (Malamat, *History of Biblical Israel*, 48; Evans-Pritchard, *The Nuer*, 242). A quick glance through Wilson's discussion of oral genealogical traditions in his *Genealogy and History* will reveal citations to studies of African cultures on almost every page, including Evans-Pritchard but many others as well, notably John Middleton's *Lugbara Religion* and various references to the work of Laura and Paul Bohannan (Wilson, *Genealogy and History in the Biblical World*, 13–55).

Malamat too, the details of tribal traditions were rich with historical information relevant to early Israel, preserving "the complex processes involved in the rise and decline of the specific sub-units within the tribal framework – the continual fluctuation of dissolution and eventual unification, the transmigration of one branch to another tribal territory," and so on.[37] For Wilson, the genealogies did not preserve a "historical record," but "may nevertheless be considered historically accurate in the sense that they frequently express actual domestic, political, and religious relationships" – which could be reconstructed if the scholar knew how to interpret these expressions.[38] Ultimately, Wilson's 1977 monograph, *Genealogy and History in the Biblical World*, would prove to be a watershed study, cited frequently even today.[39]

It is largely on the strength of these two comparisons that the preservative method continues to dominate the study of tribal traditions even today. In fact, this is true even in many contemporary histories of Israel that are quite skeptical in most other respects. In one study from 2016, for example, the authors describe the twelve tribes tradition as a "theological construct" that likely did not appear before the fifth century BCE. At the same time, they also argue that it preserves a "social memory" reaching back to the tenth century BCE, courtesy of the (hypothetical) "palace schools of Samaria and Jerusalem."[40] The idea that the tribal traditions would be at once carefully preserved in palace schools to the point of preserving the literal realities of an era half a millennium earlier, *and* fundamentally reinvented into a totally new form, shows something of the tension at the heart of the contemporary use of the method more generally.

Similarly, the author of a study published in 2005 acknowledges that the "reliability" of biblical accounts of the era of Israel's formation is "highly dubious" and singles out "the lists or descriptions of the 'Twelve Tribes of Israel' in particular."[41] He acknowledges that, when social realities are encoded in genealogical form, it is generally true that "a whole tribe may be added or subtracted, a fake affiliation inserted," and even that the "systematization of the tribes and the idea of a large

---

[37] Malamat, *History of Biblical Israel*, 47–48. Both men were not only theorists of the method, but frequently employed it as well.

[38] Wilson, "The Old Testament Genealogies in Recent Research," 189.

[39] Wilson, *Genealogy and History in the Biblical World*. See, for example, Blum, "The Israelite Tribal System," 203–6.

[40] Knauf and Guillaume, *A History of Biblical Israel*, 46, 45.

[41] Liverani, *Israel's History and the History of Israel*, 59.

tribal federation" likely developed into its present form only in the sixth century BCE, fairly late in time.[42] Nevertheless, because "the representation of social relations in a genealogical form is typical of the Iron Age," in this case meaning the era of Israel's origins centuries earlier, he argues that it remains possible to "salvage some elements of a more ancient historical context" and frequently attempts exactly that.[43] In his view, for example, the "pairing" of tribes like Benjamin and Ephraim must be "attributed" to ancient historical realities, while the "dislocation of the typically pastoral tribe of Gad/Gilead, Reuben, and half of Manasseh to east of the Jordan (Josh. 13) is connected to historical events . . . beginning in the time of Saul" and so on.[44] Here, the statement that "the representation of social relations . . . is typical of the Iron Age" overcomes the author's awareness of the mutability of genealogical traditions over time to allow genealogical details to become the basis of key elements of his history, despite being an axiom rather than a demonstrated reality.

Still other recent studies embrace the preservative method more or less straightforwardly, without even these caveats.[45] The author of one recent study argues, for example, that Israel's "proto-history," including the accounts of the "twelve eponymous tribal fathers, and the Exodus narratives," is "conceived in general principle and . . . constructed backwards from the tangible historical experience through the earlier, more vaguely known stages."[46] As a result, the author concludes, just as Noth would have, that the account of "the twelve sons of Jacob/Israel . . . represents the corporate entity of the people, and due to the birth sequence and the matrilineal relationships it actually reflects the settled people in the land."[47] Another treatment, also from 2009, suggests that the "concept of 'bastard tribes' of Dan, Naftali, Asher and Gad" – born, in Genesis 29–30, to the enslaved Bilhah and Zilpah, rather than Jacob's legal wives – reveals, or we might say encodes, the "heterogeneous origins"

---

[42] Ibid., 59–60.   [43] Ibid., 42, 59–60.   [44] Ibid., 62.

[45] And not about the tribal genealogies alone. In one recent study of the "toledot" genealogies of Genesis – supposedly beginning different sections of Genesis with the assertion "these are the generations of" various characters throughout the book – the author argues "these genealogies truly act as preservatives, allowing the story to continue forward with its ever-narrowing focus, while preserving and honoring the memory and identify of these secondary characters of Israel's world, covered by the blessing of God" (Thomas, *These Are the Generations*, 95).

[46] Kallai, "The Beginnings of Israel," 194.

[47] "Thus, it may be contended that the upper border of the tangible elements of the proto-history of Israel is the established people and its tribal structure" (ibid., 195). This is more or less Martin Noth's position as well.

of Israel itself.[48] Indeed, the effort to render early tribal history from the tribal birth narratives remains common.[49] These are just a handful of examples, but they represent the general state of affairs fairly well.[50]

Again, the problem with the continued popularity of the preservative method is not that the Hebrew Bible's various tribal traditions cannot preserve early realities, or at least earlier traditions. Neither is it that the details of tribal traditions, genealogical traditions, and origin traditions generally cannot reveal information about realities and developments that goes beyond what they literally say. The studies of the Nuer and others have held up in certain key respects, and especially in this: we still think there is something of a code embedded in segmented genealogical traditions, and that what is encoded reflects the world of the authors of the tradition. There is still decoding to be done, and this is what the "redescriptive method" is.

The problem does, however, begin to emerge from where I began this discussion. The method is not the vague belief that tribal traditions preserve useful historical information; it is a specific approach to what *kind* of information, from *what* period, and how it might be extracted. And while Noth, Wilson, Malamat, et al. did have – equally specific – reasons for believing that the details of tribal traditions mainly "encoded"

---

[48] Dijkstra, "Origins of Israel Between History and Ideology," 73.

[49] Kristin Weingart argues that the story in Genesis 29–30 and the "Joseph-story" "do much more than merely dress actual tribal developments in the garb of a family story … They inform their addressees about their social environment and that is their primary intention as is easily seen in their underlying etiological tendency. As a result, the question of the historical and political context of these texts is first and foremost that of the situation that they inform about." In the same study, she asks – noting that certain more recent studies suggest that a tribal concept developed after the fall of Israel "to consolidate and strengthen Northern Israelite identity" – "why are there so many loose ends? Why the prominence of Reuben as a first born and Simeon as second? Why is there a close connection between Benjamin and Joseph? Why is Judah included?" She answers "that an early origins of the tribal concept is still the more plausible assumption" (Weingart, "Concepts of Israel in the Monarchic Period," 26–27). Or, see Weingart's efforts to make sense of biblical details about Benjamin and Reuben with respect to earlier Israel, if not earliest Israel, in Weingart, "All These Are the Twelve Tribes of Israel," 28–29.

[50] See, for example, Zevit, *The Religions of Ancient Israel*, 648–49; Kallai, "The Twelve-Tribe Systems of Israel"; Kallai, "A Note on the Twelve-Tribe Systems of Israel"; Provan, Long, and Longman, *A Biblical History of Israel*, 168; Rendsburg, "The Internal Consistency"; Williams, "Israel Outside the Land"; Kessler, *The Social History of Ancient Israel*, 55–62; Matthews, *A Brief History of Ancient Israel*, 49. This approach also appears in earlier, influential treatments, including Westermann, *Genesis 1–11*; Westermann, *Genesis 12–36*; Westermann, *Genesis 37–50*; Miller and Hayes, *A History of Ancient Israel and Judah*, 89–93.

the developing realities of early tribal Israel, these reasons were themselves a product of the eras in which they worked. And they have all since
been repudiated, knocking the foundations of the method out from
under it.

Consider, for example, how Noth negotiated the tension I described at
the beginning of this chapter between what he believed tribal traditions
represent and when (and where) most of them were actually written
down. Again, Noth knew perfectly well that most pentateuchal tribal
traditions are late Judahite compositions. A basically modern reconstruction of the compositional history of the Pentateuch had emerged even by
the end of the nineteenth century. More than that, Julius Wellhausen,
who was largely responsible for popularizing this new chronology,
already acknowledged that the role of late Judahites in producing the
whole made it very unlikely that any effort to reconstruct early Israelite
history could succeed, just as many do today.[51] Noth did not deny the
accuracy of a basically Wellhausian chronology or propose an alternative;
he simply argued that it was irrelevant. His theory of the *Grundlage*, the
"common basis," meant that whenever any pentateuchal tribal tradition
had been written down, it should, in some general sense, be a product of
the early tribal age.[52]

Yet Noth could only be so blasé about the extraordinary distance
between any imaginable tribal age and the main eras of tribal composition, and all the changes along the way, because of another specific set of
assumptions that are no longer applicable, in this case about the nature of
the relationship between a people and their historical traditions. He was,
for example, a firm believer in the so-called "Great Divide" model of
literary production – essentially a nineteenth-century idea that a people, in
the flush of their national youth, compose their great traditions naturally,
and orally, which are only set down in writing much later.[53] He believed,
like many of his day, that a certain kind of tradition, of which the

---

[51] Wellhausen, *Prolegomena to the History of Ancient Israel*, 332–425.
[52] Because, again, "the literary fixations only gave final form to material which in its
essentials was already given." Noth, *A History of the Pentateuchal Traditions*, 1–2.
[53] As Jacqueline Vayntrub observes, "the past few decades have seen attempts to move past
a Great Divide view of how the biblical authors might have produced their texts. Scholars
such as Susan Niditch, Raymond Person, Karel van der Toorn, and David Carr, each with
their own proposed models, emphasized the simultaneity of oral and written text
production, how written and oral modes of communication blend in complex ways,
and the role of memory in these processes" (Vayntrub, *Beyond Orality*, 2–3). See also
Niditch, *Folklore and the Hebrew Bible*, 7; Kawashima, *Biblical Narrative and the Death
of the Rhapsode*.

pentateuchal account was a type, could only have been composed in early periods, to be replaced later on with less creative and more formulaic genres such as historiography.[54] Noth embraced what would now be called a "primordialist" approach to ethnic identity, in which a people's identity is formed once, long ago, and survives in much the same form ever after.[55] Together, these beliefs made it easy to imagine that an authoritative early, oral tradition would be handed down through the generations largely intact, and to a group of Judahites who would find the same meaning in them their distant ancestors had – because, after all, they understood their Israelite identity the same way their ancestors did.

Today, however, scholars in every field concerned with the study of tradition universally acknowledge the ongoing fluidity of traditions, and historical memory, over time.[56] We acknowledge that "the image of the solitary biblical author composing finalized, lengthy works in a single lifetime, safeguarded after publication from further alterations" is

---

[54] Thus, Gunkel, who believed "the writing of history is not an innate endowment of the human mind; it arose in the course of human history and at a definite stage of development. Uncivilised races do not write history; they are incapable of reproducing their experiences objectively, and have no interest in leaving to posterity an authentic account of the events of their time ... Only at a certain stage of civilization has objectivity so grown and the interest in transmitting national experiences to posterity so increased that the writing of history becomes possible" (Gunkel, *The Legends of Genesis*, 7). For Noth "the vigorous growth of a saga-tradition ... is usually found in a situation where the history of a people is borne by the community of its tribes ... During the time of statehood, the saga-tradition is replaced, as a rule, by written history" (Noth, *A History of the Pentateuchal Traditions*, 44). See also Kirkpatrick, *The Old Testament and Folklore Study*, 43.

[55] Here, ethnic identities are understood as the reflection of "a primitive social substructure that had managed to live on in historical times." In this case, Jan Paul Crielaard is referring to groups such as the Ionians and Dorians, but it applies to the "Israelites" of Israel and Judah perfectly well (Crielaard, "The Ionians in the Archaic Period," 37–38). As he further notes, "this way of looking at ethnicity meant that myths about common origins and ethnic identity found in ancient literary sources were believed to contain a kernel of historical truth."

[56] As Mait Koiv observes: "It has been increasingly realized that the very reason for the existence of the tradition is to explain and justify the present and that any account about the past will be preserved only insofar as it is important for the social group transmitting it. Stories about the events losing their significance are constantly replaced by new ones, and those preserved are in turn perpetually remodeled to meet the requirements of changing conditions" (Koiv, *Ancient Tradition and Early Greek History*, 14). In point of fact, the work of F. C. Barlett, R. H. Lowie, and others had begun to show that "the older ideal of a folk community preserving its traditions faithfully over the centuries could no longer be substantiated" even in the 1910s and 1920s (Kirkpatrick, *The Old Testament and Folklore Study*, 45; Lowie, "Oral Tradition and History"; Bartlett, "Some Experiments on the Reproduction of Folk Stories").

fundamentally wrong.[57] We suspect that the idea of the kind of "social memory" that would need to exist to even imagine such an unbroken chain of transmission requires tremendous re-thinking to be workable.[58] And unlike Noth, we know that identity changes constantly "through ongoing interaction with others and self-reflection prompted by such interaction ... [and] as groups encounter new environments and fresh experiences."[59] And without Noth's means of navigating around the tensions just described – without being able to treat late, Judahite texts *simply* as literary renditions of early oral traditions – the problem of the late Judahite origins of most biblical tribal traditions and descriptions re-emerges.

As for the supposedly bolstering comparisons employed by Wilson, Malamat, and others, these should have fared no better, popular as they still remain. Here, too, the supposed relevance of Mesopotamian Kinglists composed nearly a millennia before the oldest biblical compositions was not a product of any general similarity to biblical tribal genealogies – in fact, they are not very similar.[60] Instead, scholars in the mid-to-late twentieth century thought Israel's ancestors *were* early second millennium Mesopotamians, à la the Abraham story – so anything the latter group did would necessarily be relevant to Israelite tradition production.[61]

---

[57] Pioske, *Memory in a Time of Prose*, 3.

[58] As Ian Douglas Wilson has recently observed, while there is no doubt that humans are social beings and that society has a role to play in what the past seems to be, "it should be noted, however, that there is no such 'thing' as social or collective memory" (Olick and Robbins 1998, 112; Wertsch 2009a, 118–24). There is no 'mystical group mind,' as Jeffrey Olick and Joyce Robbins (1998, 112) put it; there are, instead, 'sets of mnemonic practices in various social sites' ... In theorizing about social memory, one may transfer what we know about the process of individual cognition to the level of society, but only metaphorically and heuristically. Astrid Erll (2010, 5) writes, 'Societies do not remember literally; but much of what is done to reconstruct a shared past bears some resemblance to the processes of individual memory, such as the selectivity and perspectivity inherent in the creation of versions of the past according to present knowledge and needs'" (Wilson, *Kingship and Memory in Ancient Judah*, 24). The references are to Olick and Robbins, "Social Memory Studies"; Wertsch, "Collective Memory"; Erll, "Cultural Memory Studies."

[59] Miller, "Ethnicity and the Hebrew Bible," 172–73.

[60] For one thing, early Mesopotamian Kinglists are *linear*, where the twelve tribes genealogy is segmented – as Wilson himself observed (Wilson, "Between 'Azel' and 'Azel,'" 13).

[61] "... genealogies ... were used by Old Babylonian tribal groups having Amorite connections. The biblical patriarchs are also traditionally connected with the Amorites, and the OT places a number of genealogies in the patriarchal period" (Wilson, "The Old Testament Genealogies in Recent Research," 175). As John Bright put it, in a history first written in the 1950s but still popular today, "as the Bible presents it, the history of Israel began with the migration of the Hebrew patriarchs from Mesopotamia to their new

Today, not only do we no longer possess this confidence in the historicity of the Abraham story, we do not think of ethnic descent in such a way that compositions from so much longer ago and farther away would seem to be terribly relevant even if we did.[62]

Similarly, we can ask why precisely we should think that African oral traditions are a good comparison for what are, after all, fundamentally literary ones. Again, the answer will be period specific, emerging from the Nothian belief that these literary traditions were, somehow, *really* oral. If we simply take them as the literary texts they are, not only will this comparison seem less useful, a more appropriate one – with similar literary traditions – will suggest the opposite of what the preservative method does.[63] Basically, instead of preserving the realities of much earlier ages, inherited *literary* genealogical traditions serve as a constant medium for the redescribing of identities, for making claims, and for advancing agendas of various sorts. The idea that the twelve tribes tradition might have been used in this way, not just by those who first formed it, but by all those who inherited it, would not only be fatal to the preservative method, it would explain the actual chronological and geographical profile of biblical tribal traditions much better.

Then again, there is a sense in which the comparison with African oral traditions suggests as much already. After all, if the point is that these shift constantly in response to societal changes, why should that suggest anything like the idea that fairly late, Judahite compositions *preserve* much earlier realities faithfully over such long periods of time, rather than the opposite? And here again, we encounter ideas that have outlived their

---

homeland in Palestine. This was indeed the beginning, if not of Israel's history properly speaking, at least then of her prehistory" (Bright, *A History of Israel*, 23).

[62] In fact, the general rejection of the historical validity of the Abraham narrative began just *before* Wilson published *Genealogy and History*, especially in Thompson, *The Historicity of the Patriarchal Narratives*; Van Seters, *Abraham in History and Tradition*.

[63] This, too, was recognized to some extent decades ago, though few have followed it up since. In the early 1990s, John Van Seters already observed that Wilson's "Near Eastern linear genealogies, which derive from highly structured literate societies, bear very little resemblance to the segmented genealogies found in the book of Genesis. On the other hand, his discussion of the segmented genealogies and their comparison with Genesis is based upon anthropological studies of oral traditions in illiterate societies and this has created an artificial social and form-critical dichotomy" (Van Seters, *Prologue to History*, 197–98). For my own discussion of this topic, see especially Tobolowsky, "The Problem of Reubenite Primacy," 30–31; Tobolowsky, *The Sons of Jacob*, 4–5.

welcome. The answer to this question is that we would not – not without Noth's, Wilson's, and Malamat's confidence that fluidity is *only* a feature of oral traditions, and only in the context in which they were first composed, which is to say that an older, outdated model of the historical development of Israel's traditions is much more of a prerequisite of the preservative method than many seem to realize.

More than that, the argument that those who inherited tribal traditions would not alter them, even if they *were* originally early, oral traditions is misguided. Wilson, for one, explicitly argued that the basic tribal concepts were "frozen" in "pre-Davidic form" because they "could not have functioned politically" during the monarchy.[64] But this presumes that the only function adapting genealogical traditions can have is to reflect straightforward shifts in the political arrangement of the entities involved, at the time when they compose the primary political structure of a people – and not other kinds of shifts in ideology, memory, or even ambition. Not only is this untrue, the history of "becoming Israel" – of adapting the twelve tribes tradition to new realities from biblical times to the present – would be impossible if it were, another benefit of thinking in terms of this longer history.

Meanwhile, more recent studies of precisely the kinds of traditions that so interested Wilson, Malamat, and others – the oral traditions of diverse African cultures – make explicit arguments in favor of the need for a "critical reassessment of many of our most cherished anthropological notions of the nature of kinship," precisely meaning the assumptions the scholars discussed above were, and are, working with. In J. Teresa Holmes' recent study of the Luo people, for example, she explicitly observes that – where we once saw codified kinship relations preserving memories of a much earlier age – now we can see that the Luo use "more flexible and encompassing notions of relatedness to construct socially significant identities" over and over again.[65]

Similarly, just as I am speaking of "becoming Israel," rather than "being Israel," as if the question was only whether the Judahites were or were not Israelites *once upon a time*, Holmes notes the existence of "a process of *becoming wuon lowo*, rather than merely *being wuon lowo* – 'owner of the land' – through the creation of links between various

[64] Wilson, *Genealogy and History in the Biblical World*, 193–94.
[65] Holmes, "When Blood Matters," 51.

landed populations based on ties through women" – which is to say, through adapting genealogical descriptions, especially through expanding the scope of a genealogical tradition.[66] Similarly, "becoming Israel" was a process that kept on happening after the tribal age, and the twelve tribes tradition kept being a tool of it. The capacity of even those who have "been" Israel, in a sense, to "become Israel" in a new way is a crucial part of the picture – and so is the ongoing availability of an Israelite identity via genealogical expansion.

Ultimately, then, we need to realize that the continued popularity of the preservative method is a residual popularity. It is a machine that keeps working long after its engine has fallen apart, a consensus that persists mainly because it has persisted.[67] And at least as much as we need to reject the confidence that the details of biblical tribal traditions preserve the realities of early Israel to any significant degree that is still so common, we need to reject the belief that they would do this *more than they do anything else* – more, for example, than they reflect the subjectivities, desires, and situatedness of their actual authors, in the actual period when they were composed.

As we saw above, even many contemporary arguments that acknowledge that the twelve tribes tradition could have been dynamically adapted over time suggest that adaption is both limited and easy to identify. In fact, what the evidence suggests – including the evidence of who is really responsible for so many biblical tribal traditions – is that the adaptation of inherited tribal traditions to further the agendas of those responsible for them was not only constant, it takes the exact same form as the kinds of modifications that were once regarded as reflections of early developments. Not only, then, were these traditions adapted more

---

[66] Ibid., 57, 68. Women, in patriarchal societies, play a crucial role in genealogical traditions because their marriages outside of their immediate kinship group create links between genealogical stemmata.

[67] As Lester Grabbe notes: "Once a consensus has been established, it develops a momentum that is hard to stop. It is not so much that we examine carefully and then reject a new idea. It is that if the new idea cannot be proved beyond a reasonable doubt, the old consensus is assumed to be confirmed. Unfortunately, that ignores how a consensus becomes established. Sometimes a consensus is established because someone comes up with a brilliant argument ... But often a consensus develops for very nebulous reasons – because a noted authority once expressed an opinion or even because nothing better has been advanced. Unfortunately, the consensus starts to assert a powerful influence simply because it has been around awhile" (Grabbe, "The Case of the Corrupting Consensus," 91).

constantly, and in ways that are harder to distinguish from earlier efforts than many suspect, but focusing so narrowly on the ability of tribal traditions to preserve early realities robs us of the opportunity to explore what else they can reveal.

Finally, within the larger arc of this study, the rejection of the preservative method is significant for a number of reasons. After all, the idea that tribal traditions are fundamentally Israelite – and fundamentally early – despite when they were written down, plays a key role in constructing them, mentally, as different from extrabiblical tribal traditions. The idea that they preserve and represent, rather than reinvent, is what makes them notionally different from post-biblical tribal traditions, which are more clearly reinventions. However, as soon as we imagine Judahite authors using an inherited tribal tradition to redescribe Israelite identity in ways that made sense to them, the essential similarity between Judahite and other redescriptions of Israel emerges.

Meanwhile, in the other direction, the simple fact that so many authors did freely adapt the twelve tribes tradition to the realities of their context – in so many different ways, *long after the biblical period* – is itself a powerful argument in favor of the conclusion that ancient Judahites did the same. In a vacuum, we might think that sixth through fourth century BCE Judahites were too overawed by the reverence in which they held early Israelite traditions to alter them in any significant way, which seems to be the general view of many of the scholars whose work is described above. An early benefit of our looming, never before attempted comparison, however, is that they make us realize the fallacy of this view. Whatever forbidding authority Israelite tribal traditions had in Judah, it would surely have paled in comparison to the *full* canonical authority of the Hebrew Bible in later contexts. And yet, the dynamic adaptation of tribal traditions, the reinvention of tribal histories, and the redescription of their basic significance goes on and on.

Ultimately, a method that explores what the redescription of Israelite identity through tribal traditions can reveal about those doing the redescribing can and will serve equally well in all contexts in which the twelve tribes tradition is given new life, including the Hebrew Bible. Before exploring how such a method would work, however, we turn our attention to a newer approach to analyzing tribal traditions – one that responds to the late Judahite profile of so much biblical tribal discourse in a way the preservative method cannot.

1.3 THE "CULTURAL INVENTION" METHOD

The term "cultural invention" originally emerged in the early 1980s out of the work of Eric Hobsbawm, Terence Ranger, and others in response to an increasing scholarly awareness that some "ancient traditions" were not, in fact, so ancient after all.[68] At the time, these scholars were attempting to distinguish these "inventions" from what they called "genuine" traditions, which is to say, traditions that emerged in "historic continuity" with older forms.[69] Today, the whole topic of cultural invention seems considerably more complicated, in ways that I will discuss below, and for reasons that have ramifications for the study of biblical tribal traditions in precisely the direction I want to take them. It is, however, generally the original form of cultural invention that animates the cultural invention method of analyzing biblical tribal discourse.

Basically, the proponents of this method understand the twelve tribes tradition as a Judahite invention, and one that is party to another even more dramatic development – the invention of an Israelite identity in Judah, period. Since the 1990s, at least some scholars have been arguing that the Judahites did not understand themselves as Israelites until after the Assyrian conquest of Israel.[70] And as radical as this proposal may seem, its increased popularity in recent years is a natural result of other broadly accepted developments in how scholars think about the history of Israel and the accuracy of biblical narratives. For one thing, even in fairly conservative scholarly histories, the eras in which an "all Israel" entity could even have existed have now shrunk to the few centuries before the split of the kingdom. We no longer think there is much to say, with any confidence, about the "pre-monarchical" period in this direction – or, for the most part, about "Israelite identity" itself in that era.[71]

---

[68] Hobsbawm and Ranger, *The Invention of Tradition*. See especially Hobsbawm, "Introduction: Inventing Traditions," 1.

[69] Hobsbawm, "Introduction: Inventing Traditions," 7–8.

[70] See footnote 27 in the introduction.

[71] As Miller observes: "Any attempt to speak of 'pre-monarchic Israel' involves one in a host of controversial issues ... Most scholars working specifically on Israelite ethnicity in the pre-monarchic period regard the biblical narratives portraying this era as late and historically unreliable ... Although most of these same scholars believe these ... may contain memories of genuine historical events ... the historical realities that may lie behind these narratives are believed to be simply too difficult to reconstruct with any confidence" (Miller, "Ethnicity and the Hebrew Bible," 176). Fleming adds that "the entire discussion of ethnicity for the southern Levant before the ninth century is fraught with assumptions about identity that the evidence cannot sustain ... in the early Iron Age, the region was indeed inhabited by a 'motley crew,' but this was not simply the raw

Thus, even in these conservative histories, the United Monarchy of David and Solomon is the last remaining plausibly historical period in which a recognizable Israel and Judah could have been politically unified. Today, many scholars doubt that it even existed, and there is certainly no clear evidence that it did.[72] And even its champions now acknowledge that it must have been a good deal smaller and less powerful than the Bible suggests, raising questions about what else these narratives get wrong.[73] Today, we can even wonder about the relevance of such an institution for later Judahite constructions of Israelite identity. Certainly, the United Monarchy was terribly important to Judahite self-conceptions in later periods, but, through the lens of contemporary understandings of the fluidity of identity over time, we can still ask how much it *had* to matter in, say, sixth century BCE Judah that their ancestors had been politically unified with the ancestors of the Israelites long ago and for a fairly brief time.

Meanwhile, it is surprisingly difficult to prove that historical Judahites and Israelites thought of each other as one people in any early period. Certainly, there is little evidence that their neighbors were aware of any specific relationship between them. The Assyrians, who were significantly involved in the region for a period of several centuries, never mention it.[74] And some scholars have claimed to detect, especially in prophetic texts, a shift from treating Judah as Judah to Judah as part of a larger Israelite identity sometime in the seventh or sixth century BCE.[75] And if the

---

material for eventual Israelite ethnicity" (Fleming, *The Legacy of Israel in Judah's Bible*, 254).

[72] For the debate, see especially Mazar, "Jerusalem and Its Vicinity in Iron Age I"; Mazar, "The Search for David and Solomon"; Leonard-Fleckman, *The House of David*; Finkelstein, "A Great United Monarchy?"; Finkelstein, "King Solomon's Golden Age?"

[73] Mazar, one of the best known champions of the historicity of this monarchy, suggests that David's Jerusalem may have been "a medieval Burg ... the centre of a meaningful polity," and the United Monarchy itself "a state in an early stage of evolution, far from the rich and widely expanding state portrayed in the biblical narrative" (Mazar, "Archaeology and the Biblical Narrative," 57).

[74] "A review of the Assyrian sources," as Tammi Schneider notes, "reveals that they saw no special connection ... The main question is why the Assyrians would not reveal a special connection between the two when the Bible does? It is difficult to believe that the Assyrians did not know about the relationship, since they were engaged in the area for more than 130 years before the destruction of Israel" (Schneider, "Through Assyria's Eyes," 14).

[75] See, for a review of this debate, Tobolowsky, *The Sons of Jacob*, 35–37. See also Kratz, "Israel in the Book of Isaiah," 115; Na'aman, "Saul, Benjamin and the Emergence of 'Biblical Israel' Part I," 212–13; Høgenhaven, *Gott und Volk bei Jesaja*, 14–22; Fleming, *The Legacy of Israel in Judah's Bible*, 5–14; Davies, "The Origins of Biblical Israel," 146;

Judahites did "become Israel," in a sudden act of cultural invention after the Assyrian conquest of Israel, a number of different reasons have been suggested for why this might have happened. Some argue that "becoming Israel" would have allowed the Judahites to claim vacated Israelite territory, or even the greater cultural prestige of its more powerful, northern neighbor.[76] Others suggest the arrivals of Israelite refugees in Judah are to blame, bringing with them Israelite traditions that, in an eerie echo of Noth, would also form the basis for a new "all Israel" vision of history.[77]

Obviously, if an all-embracing "all Israel" identity did not exist in early Israel or Judah, neither did the twelve tribes tradition to reflect it. And as we have already seen, the basic shape of tribal discourse in biblical literature may suggest precisely this; we have a preponderance of late Judahite twelve tribe compositions and very few early ones. Even more interestingly, Judges 5, almost universally considered the oldest surviving tribal composition, simply does not include the tribes most often associated with Judah in biblical literature, which are Judah, Levi, and Simeon. Deuteronomy 33, another potentially early list, is also missing Simeon, and some scholars were arguing that Judah and Levi were only added to it – and Judah, Levi, and Simeon to Genesis 49 – long before anyone suspected that Israelite identity might not be as ancient in Judah as in Israel.[78] Remarkably, then, the differences between early and late tribal

Miller, "Ethnicity and the Hebrew Bible," 194. Again, the basic idea that Judah invented itself as an "Israel" first emerged in the work of Philip Davies, especially in Davies, *In Search of "Ancient Israel."*

[76] For the possibility that "being Israel" allowed Judahites to claim Israelite territory, see Tobolowsky, *The Sons of Jacob*, 31–32; Na'aman, "Saul, Benjamin and the Emergence of 'Biblical Israel' Part I," 211–24; Na'aman, "Saul, Benjamin and the Emergence of 'Biblical Israel' Part II"; Fleming, *The Legacy of Israel in Judah's Bible*, 45; Knauf, "Bethel: The Israelite Impact on Judean Language and Literature," 316–19. Na'aman has also argued that Judahites wished to co-opt Israelite prestige by analogy to Assyria's occasional efforts to co-opt Babylon's (Na'aman, "The Israelite-Judahite Struggle for the Patrimony of Ancient Israel").

[77] For the argument that this new concept allowed for the incorporation of refugees, see especially Finkelstein and Silberman, *The Bible Unearthed*, 243–45; Finkelstein and Silberman, *David and Solomon*, 129–38. For an argument against the existence of these refugees, see Na'aman, "Dismissing the Myth."

[78] More precisely, scholars have wondered whether Judah and Levi were added to Deuteronomy 33, and suspected that the portion of Genesis 49 that includes the Judahite tribes might have been substantially edited in later periods, for a long time. For general treatments of Deuteronomy 33 that make this point, see Cross and Freedman, "The Blessing of Moses," 202–3; Labuschagne, "The Tribes in the Blessing of Moses," 101; Mayes, *Deuteronomy*, 402; Sparks, *Ethnicity and Identity in Ancient Israel*, 269–70; Sparks, "Genesis 49 and the Tribal List Tradition in Ancient Israel," 329.

compositions may reflect the shift from a more limited, Israelite tradition to one embracing "all Israel" quite straightforwardly.

Ultimately, the cultural invention method attempts to trace the development of an "all Israel" identity in Judah through its reflection in the expansion of the tribal tradition into the familiar twelve tribe form. The proponents of this method are particularly concerned with two questions. First: what did the original northern Israelite tribal tradition actually look like? Second: how, when, and why did the twelve tribe concept emerge? So, for example, Daniel Fleming has argued that an eight tribe vision embracing the north alone was expanded by the addition of Judah, Simeon, Levi, and Benjamin.[79] Ulrike Schorn makes a similar argument, but with Reuben, Simeon, Levi, and Judah, and so does Jean-Daniel Macchi, especially on the basis of Genesis 49.[80] Nadav Na'aman has made a convincing case that the narrative account of the life of Jacob in the book of Genesis was rewritten by southern authors aiming to create a Pan-Israelite vision of Israel that did not previously exist, something I have also argued.[81] This would include the addition of Judahite sons, Judahite places, and much else besides.

As it happens, I agree with the conclusions the cultural invention method is based on and have even had occasion to forward them myself.[82] Most recently, I pointed out that in many of the instances where particularly early Israelite and Judahite traditions are likely to have been brought together, the Israelites tend to be referred to as members of tribes while the Judahites are not – exactly what we would expect, if tribal

---

For the blessing of Judah, in Deut. 33 specifically, see Beyerle, *Der Mosesegen im Deuteronomium*, 108–35, 285; Sparks, *Ethnicity and Identity in Ancient Israel*, 330–31; Sparks, "Genesis 49 and the Tribal List Tradition in Ancient Israel," 269–71; Fleming, *The Legacy of Israel in Judah's Bible*, 79. For Genesis 49, see Westermann, *Genesis 37–50*, 223, 228; Tobolowsky, *The Sons of Jacob*, 55–56; Sparks, *Ethnicity and Identity in Ancient Israel*, 109–24, 267–72; Macchi, *Israël et ses tribus selon Genèse 49*; Fleming, *The Legacy of Israel in Judah's Bible*, 85–90; Schorn, *Ruben und das System der zwölf Stämme Israels*.

[79] Fleming, *The Legacy of Israel in Judah's Bible*, 79–80.

[80] Schorn, *Ruben und das System der zwölf Stämme Israels*, 63–79; Macchi, *Israël et ses tribus selon Genèse 49*. Overall, Schorn argues that Reuben never existed.

[81] Na'aman, "The Jacob Story and the Formation of Biblical Israel." Casey Strine has also argued that the Genesis version of the Jacob story developed only after the fall of Israel, but as a northern Israelite response to trauma (Strine, "Your Name Shall No Longer Be Jacob"). See also Hong, "The Deceptive Pen of Scribes"; Hong, "Once Again"; Quine, "Reading 'House of Jacob'"; Finkelstein, *The Forgotten Kingdom*, 153.

[82] See especially Tobolowsky, *The Sons of Jacob*, 43–77; Tobolowsky, "The Problem of Reubenite Primacy," 33–36.

paradigms were older than Israel in Judah.[83] Obviously, then, I find the arguments just mentioned interesting and valuable, especially if new studies continue to bear out their foundational theses.

At the same time, the cultural invention method is much better at explaining where the twelve tribes tradition came from, and why, than how it is actually used in biblical literature. Given the uncertainties surrounding the historical relationship between Israel and Judah, the late Judahite context in which most, or all, twelve tribe compositions clearly emerged, and the place of honor the Judahite tribes often have within them, it does make sense to think that the basic concept was developed in Judah to redescribe Judah as Israel. But neither the basic concept nor any account of its origins can explain why so many *different* biblical authors describe the twelve tribes of Israel differently from *each other* – or so very frequently. In other words, a simple desire to claim an Israelite identity does not explain why there are eight different descriptions of the twelve tribes of Israel in the book of Numbers alone, or four in Genesis, or six in 1 Chronicles. Nor does it explain the substantial differences between visions of twelve tribe Israel, such as why Levi and Joseph sometimes are, and sometimes aren't counted among the twelve tribes, or why the order of tribes is so often rendered differently – any more than a simple desire to preserve an important ancient tradition does.

For that matter, neither the cultural invention method nor any approach which does not consider how the twelve tribes tradition was used after it developed can explain other oddities in the pattern of that use. Why, for example, are references to the tribes, omnipresent in the histories, so nearly absent from wide swathes of the rest of the Hebrew Bible? It is, as I observed elsewhere,

one thing to say that Ezekiel 48 is the only full list in the books of prophets and another to point out how completely it accounts for all the evidence that prophets were aware of or interested in the tribes. Reuben, Simeon, Asher, and Issachar never appear in another prophetic text. Naphtali, Zebulun, and Manasseh are only mentioned additionally in Isaiah 9.[84]

Nor can a method unconcerned with use explain why, between presence and absence, it is absence that is generally supported in extrabiblical traditions where references to tribal identities are extraordinarily rare.[85]

---

[83] Tobolowsky, "Othniel, David, Solomon."   [84] Tobolowsky, *The Sons of Jacob*, 44.

[85] Tribal identities are "not a standard characterization in ancient documents or inscriptions. Most people are identified by name, father's and grandfather's names and maybe town, such as found in most material of the first millennium BCE, including legal

It seems clear that some form of tribal identity existed and was important in Judah, in the sixth through fourth centuries BCE, especially where the tribes of Judah and Benjamin are concerned, and in Israel even earlier. Whether the tribes were as important to individual Judahites as they were to the authors of the histories is another question, and a more difficult one.

We might say, then, that the cultural invention method amounts to the conclusion, simply, that cultural invention *has taken place*, and that the twelve tribes tradition reflects it. This is an important conclusion, and since it swims against existing currents, hyperfocus on the fact of invention makes sense. But once we have identified when the original twelve tribes tradition developed, why, and what it looked like – if this is indeed what happened – we still have to figure out what was *done* with it, later on. In the face of so many different biblical visions of tribal Israel, and at the beginning of a book about so many more, we need a method that explains both origins and use – or, as I put it in the beginning of this chapter, not only the prominence of the twelve tribes tradition and the late Judahite context that birthed the discourse, but the frequency and variety of biblical twelve tribe descriptions as well. We need a method that acknowledges that the biblical rendition of the twelve tribes of Israel is, fundamentally, a Judahite one, *and* that this isn't the end of the story. We need one that acknowledges that the descriptions of the twelve tribes throughout the Bible represent not one but many visions of Israel. And we need one that acknowledges that, whenever the concept emerged, the differences between these many renditions of the twelve tribes of Israel are meaningful – as they would be ever since, long after and far away.

1.4 TOWARDS A REDESCRIPTIVE METHOD

Before I describe and demonstrate the redescriptive method, one more prefatory point will prove useful. As I observed above, the cultural invention method is based on the concept of cultural invention as it was

documents among Elephantine and Wadi Daliyeh papyri and votive and funerary inscriptions. Of the four hundred votive inscriptions dating to the third century BCE found on Mount Gerizim, for example, none carries a tribal name. I cannot recall any Palestinian inscription with a tribal name" (Hjelm, "Tribes, Genealogies and the Composition of the Hebrew Bible," 27). There is an apparent reference to the "men of Gad," perhaps the tribe of Gad, on the ninth century BCE Mesha stele.

originally understood – sometimes quite explicitly.[86] In recent years, however, an increasing awareness of the general fluidity of both traditions and identities has caused a dramatic expansion in the scholarly understanding of what cultural invention is.[87] Today, and for some time now, scholars of invention have argued that "all traditions – Western and indigenous – are invented" because all traditions are "constructed in the present and reflect contemporary concerns and inherited legacy."[88] In other words, even those traditions that are based on much earlier versions of *themselves* are still dynamically reinvented over time – we might say, "redescribed" – in a way that is hard to distinguish from what used to be called "invention."[89] The times, the places, and the purposes that bring someone to tell a particular story, especially a story about the past, always leave their mark, and it is a dynamic one.[90]

One result of this new way of thinking about invention, and perhaps a surprising one, is that where the redescriptive method is concerned, it really doesn't matter that much whether an Israelite identity was in conventional terms or not. The twelve tribes construction of Israelite identity would have been reinvented many times over regardless. And here we might say is the major flaw of both older methods – that they are each based, to some extent, on the assumption that Israelite identity was

---

[86] Fleming, for example, employs Hobsbawm's original formulation of cultural invention as a model in the conclusion of his study, which is in fact called "Genuine (versus Invented) Tradition in the Bible," but without engaging with new scholarship on the subject (Fleming, *The Legacy of Israel in Judah's Bible*, 304–22). He argues "all Israelite narratives, the material that serves Israelite identity in the social and political matrix of corporate 'Israelite,'" – meaning as opposed to Judahite narratives – "may be considered 'genuine traditions'" (ibid., 308).

[87] Theodossopoulos, "Laying Claim to Authenticity"; Handler, "Reinventing the Invention of Culture"; Handler and Linnekin, "Tradition, Genuine or Spurious"; Linnekin, "Cultural Invention and the Dilemma of Authority"; Bayart, *The Illusion of Cultural Identity*.

[88] Linnekin, "Cultural Invention and the Dilemma of Authority," 447.

[89] "Another problem with the notion of cultural invention is its indirect presupposition of inauthenticity ... To evade some of these problems, we can easily replace 'invention' with alternative terms ... 'revitalization,' 'revival,' and 'revaluation' ... or even more broadly, terms that that allude to social change, such as 'transformation' ... or 'restructuring'" (Theodossopoulos, "Laying Claim to Authenticity," 350).

[90] "Everyone is given to tinkering with his or her identity, depending on the alchemy of the circumstances. To that extent, the idea of continuity is debatable. It suggests too strongly that we belong to one, aggregate identity, which is supposed to dictate our interests and passions ... [but] historical experience shows that an individual's act of identification is always contextual, multiple, and relative" (Bayart, *The Illusion of Cultural Identity*, 85, 92).

invented only once, either very long ago or somewhat more recently. Correspondingly, practitioners of both methods have a strong tendency to make the question of whether biblical accounts of the twelve tribes tradition reflect early Israelite realities or late Judahite inventions *dependent on whether the basic tribal concept is an early Israelite or late Judahite one* – and beyond that, whether Judah and Israel were ever actually one.

In other words, scholars broadly assume that biblical tribal traditions would reflect historic realities if there really had been an early, twelve tribe institution, and would not if there was not. But this assumption is wrong. Even very late versions of a tradition may reflect much earlier ones to some degree, and therefore reflect something of the realities that gave it birth. But even if the first tribal tradition, whether preserved in the Bible or not, was an eyewitness account of the tribes in their first homes, later ones would be Judahite inventions, because again, invention is a constant. And in other contexts, as we will see again and again, the segmented structure of the twelve tribes tradition is most useful, and most often used, to dynamically adapt Israelite identity to new realities and new requirements – why not in the Hebrew Bible itself?

After all, what we most clearly have in the Hebrew Bible is precisely – precisely – many different accounts of Israelite history and identity, constructed in twelve tribe form. They are many and they are different, which is the set of facts that inspired Noth et al. to develop a method for extracting representative historical data from those differences. But where Noth *imagined* a host of early oral traditions eventually written down, even he knew that what was *really* there was a series of late Judahite compositions. And even those tribal traditions in biblical literature that are older, or Israelite (or both), survive now only within the arc of historical narratives that are themselves late and Judahite in origin. They were chosen, arranged, introduced, and explained by Judahites who must have had their own reasons for doing what they did – even if some of those reasons may have included the weight of existing tradition.

The choice, then, to approach this voluminous corpus of twelve tribe descriptions mainly as a series of late Judahite efforts to redescribe Israelite identity has this extraordinary advantage: it allows us to take these traditions as they are, not as they have been imagined to be. And unlike the other methods, it allows us to address the four quadrants of explanations that need to be made, as I laid them out in the beginning – date, context, frequency, and variety. And if it were the actual Judahite authors of these compositions who were responsible for the differences between renditions of twelve tribe Israel, it would have been they who imbued these constructions of Israel with the realities of their world, their desires, their understandings, their hopes, and their fears – as we know peoples everywhere have gone on doing ever since. A method that can extract this information from biblical constructions of Israel can do the same everywhere else, too.

1.5 LEARNING TO CODE

In scholarship, as in life, way leads on to way. In 2017, I published a book called *The Sons of Jacob and the Sons of Herakles*, in which I argued that proponents of what I here call the preservative method were extracting the wrong kind of information from the differences between tribal lists. This insight had a number of different points of origin – including the late date of most tribal compositions – but the main point was this: Wilson, Malamat, and the like had simply been using the wrong comparisons.[91] Because of the assumptions they were working with, they compared the *linear, literary* genealogies of early second millennium Assyria and Babylon and the *segmented, oral* genealogies of African tribal cultures to what is really a large body of *segmented, literary* traditions.[92] And, as a number of scholars have now observed, there is an extensive body of segmented, literary genealogies roughly contemporaneous with the Hebrew Bible, and not too far away: the genealogical traditions of ancient Greece.[93] There, however, segmented literary traditions were used to do almost the opposite of what the preservative method suggests: they played a central role not in *preserving* a vision of early Greek realities, but in the ongoing construction and reconstruction of Greek identity more or less continuously, and among many different groups.[94]

---

[91] I have since explored this idea further, especially in Tobolowsky, "The Problem of Reubenite Primacy."

[92] Tobolowsky, *The Sons of Jacob*, 4–5; Tobolowsky, "The Problem of Reubenite Primacy," 30–31.

[93] For an early argument comparing biblical tribal genealogies to Greek literature, see Van Seters, *Prologue to History*, 197–98. For more recent discussions of the similarities between segmented biblical genealogies and Classical Greek myth, see Knoppers, "Greek Historiography and the Chronicler's History"; Darshan, "The Story of the Sons of God"; Tobolowsky, "Reading Genesis Through Chronicles"; Tobolowsky, *The Sons of Jacob*.

[94] See, for example, Konstan, "To Hellēnikon Ethnos"; McInerney, "Ethnos and Ethnicity in Early Greece"; Ulf, "The Development of Greek Ethnê."

Moreover, the comparative evidence of Greek mythological traditions (among others) suggests that it is specifically the era of the early ancestors that is most often manipulated for effect, which, in the biblical case, is the era of the tribal ancestors.[95] These traditions serve as a "mirror and projection of the present world," meaning the world of the authors themselves, and when "changes are wrought upon the past, as the names and relationships of the ancestors change ... it is really the present that is being described."[96] In these cases, the authority of inherited traditions is not so much a barrier to their adaptation as it is precisely the reason to adapt, in order to use that authority to new ends – as comparative examples clearly show.[97] Of course, the twelve tribes tradition, in other contexts besides the Hebrew Bible, is clearly used in just this way, to adopt and adapt, and to make claims and explain, by redescribing and reorganizing Israelite identity via new accounts of the twelve tribes of Israel.

Again, it must be said that the actual evidence of biblical tribal compositions, taken just as they are, already suggests nothing so much as the constant, dynamic reinvention of Israelite identity through the manipulation of the twelve tribes tradition by different Judahite authors. We have so many different late Judahite tribal descriptions, and they are different from each other in important and possibly telling ways. It is perfectly clear, whatever the history of the tradition, that there was an absolute explosion of interest in describing tribal Israel between the sixth and fifth centuries BCE, which cannot be explained by a simple desire to preserve a more ancient tradition. This boom is primarily responsible for the shape of biblical tribal discourse as we have it, and the possibility that there was

---

[95] Rutherford refers to a "panhellenic poetics," "the enterprise, through poetry, of reconciling and building connections between myths and genealogical traditions from different parts of Greece" generally towards the end of using those new connections in various ways (Rutherford, "Mestra at Athens," 101). Elizabeth Irwin describes Greek genealogical literature as an expression of "the dynamics underlying marriage exchange" and other issues, and thus "contested within the fluid and fragile grouping within the polis known as the *agathoi*," more or less elites. As she puts it, "because the elite of a given polis were not a well-defined group, but a loose group of contenders asserting their entitlement to this label, while attempting to exclude its application to others, poetic texts were a crucial instrument for these competitions over self-representation and self-definition of this group, for advancing a particular ideology amid contestations" (Irwin, "Gods among Men?," 83).

[96] Fowler, "Genealogical Thinking," 16.

[97] See especially Gruen, "Foundation Legends"; Fowler, "Genealogical Thinking"; Patterson, *Kinship Myth in Ancient Greece*.

some reason so many authors suddenly engaged in creating so many visions of tribal Israel, in Judah, at that time, should be hard to ignore.

The redescriptive method, then, is an approach that uses the likelihood that different biblical renditions of tribal arrangements and realities represent the efforts of different Judahite constituencies to tease out the ideological projects, and contextual realities, that inspired them. Here, too, the idea is that the differences between representations of tribal identity and history preserve a kind of "code," just as in the preservative method, but something is encoded besides the representative data of historical realities. Instead, we are likely to find preserved the traces of agendas, ambitions, and the needs of different historical moments.

In a recent article, I put an incipient form of this redescriptive method to work, with respect to an issue mentioned above: the curious "primacy" of the tribe of Reuben in a number of tribal traditions.[98] Again, Reuben is described as the eldest son of Jacob and is frequently the first tribe in tribal lists, but the Reubenites never seem to be an important tribe in the historical narratives. Where Noth – and Frank Moore Cross and many others – saw in this detail the echo of an era of Reubenite "primacy" too long ago to be otherwise preserved, I asked, instead, which Judahite projects might be served by the elevation of Reuben.[99]

In this case, there is a clear link between "Reubenite primacy" and the tribes more often associated with the region of Judah. While Reuben is indeed Jacob's eldest son, Simeon, Levi, and Judah – the prototypical Judahite tribes – are the next three eldest. In the fourteen lists in which Reuben appears as the first tribe, "one or more of Simeon, Levi, and Judah – and usually more – immediately follow Reuben ... in all but two cases."[100] Here, we can see the myopia of a preservative method that so thoroughly discounts the importance of the actual context in which tribal traditions emerged. For Noth et al., the elevation of these southern tribes revealed their importance in the formation of Israel itself, but there is obviously a more straightforward explanation for the prominence of Judahite tribes in Judahite tribal compositions from later periods.

What I argued is that the elevation of Reuben was part and parcel of the larger Judahite effort to appropriate an Israelite identity. Since Reuben is an Israelite tribe, rather than a Judahite one, placing it above the Judahite tribes made the hegemony of Judah seem like an ancient

[98] Tobolowsky, "The Problem of Reubenite Primacy."
[99] Cross, *From Epic to Canon*, 70; Tobolowsky, "The Problem of Reubenite Primacy," 28.
[100] Tobolowsky, "The Problem of Reubenite Primacy," 37.

Israelite idea, and the tradition that emerged an Israelite one. At the same time, Reuben, unlike Ephraim, Manasseh, and likely some others, had probably been destroyed in relatively early periods, something I will discuss in the next chapter. Thus, subordinating the Judahite tribes to Reuben, as opposed to one of the surviving Israelite tribes, achieved the ideological goal of its authors without empowering any surviving rivals.[101] And in a similar vein, a quick glance at other aspects of the Hebrew Bible's various depictions of tribal Israel reveals hints of many other agendas and potential agendas.

We might, for example, consider the Bible's treatment of the tribe of Levi. As I noted above, the conventional explanation for the fact that Levi is sometimes treated as one of the twelve tribes of Israel and sometimes not has usually been taken as a reflection of its early removal from the secular tribal organization in order to serve as the priestly tribe. When we scrutinize the texts that exclude Levi, however, we discover that Levi's exclusion is a largely priestly *idea*, which is to say it mostly appears in texts associated with the author of the Pentateuch referred to as the "Priestly" author, who we believe was active in sixth century BCE Judah and perhaps beyond.[102] In fact, in most of the relevant texts, Levi is still mentioned, but in a position of honor in relation to the other tribes. For example, in the Priestly lists of Numbers, Levi is not usually treated as just another tribe, but it is constantly featured in tribal descriptions; the other tribes gather to give Levi gifts, organize their camp around Levi, march with Levi at their center, and so on and so forth.[103] It is easy to

---

[101] Ibid., 43–45.

[102] Levi's absence is not *only* a Priestly idea; it is missing from accounts of the tribal conquest and settlement (Josh. 13:15–19:48, Josh. 21:4–40, Judg. 1:1–36). Various biblical authors seem to have agreed that Levi did not have a specific region of Israel to call their own, which is not very surprising given their constant association with the temple in Jerusalem. Yet besides that, it is absent from Priestly lists, or else in texts where special accommodations are being made for its settlement and welfare, especially with respect to "cities of the Levites" (Josh. 21:4–40, 1 Chron. 6:40–48, 1 Chron. 6:49–66). Indeed, Wilson observed that "the tradition underlying all of the twelve-tribe lists that omit Levi, divide the tribe of Joseph into Ephraim and Manasseh, and record the names of Naphtali and Asher in the order Asher-Naphtali" are "all the work of the Priestly writer" (Wilson, *Genealogy and History in the Biblical World*, 187). However, according to the norms of the period, he concluded that "there is no reason to doubt that the Priestly Writer and the Chronicler derived their genealogical information from the earlier Pentateuchal sources" (ibid., 189–90).

[103] The special status of Levi vis-à-vis the tribal lists in Num. 1:5–15 and 1:20–43 is enumerated in Num. 1:44–53. In Num. 2:3–33, where Levi is described along with the other tribes, it is to place it at the center of the arrangement of the Israelite camp in the wilderness. In Num. 7:12–83, the other tribes are listed in the process of giving special

imagine that, rather than a priestly fact, we have here a priestly *agenda* – a deliberate effort to enhance the status of Levi, by Levites, at the expense of other tribes.[104]

Or we can consider the tribe of Benjamin. Benjamin, most scholars believe, was originally part of the kingdom of Israel but became part of Judah at some point before the last eras of biblical composition.[105] This is not precisely certain, however, because of an oddity in the Primary History's presentation of tribal realities. For all the attention lavished on describing the details of tribal organization between the books of Genesis and Judges, there are in fact no lists of the tribes in the books concerned with the Israelite and Judah monarchies – and not even one complete account of which tribes were part of the kingdom of Israel. In the longer arc of history, the "Ten Lost Tribes of Israel" are proverbial, because 1 Kings 11–12 tells us there were ten of them and 2 Kings 17 that the entire population of the kingdom of Israel was taken away into Assyrian exile. But no biblical text tells us which tribes they were, let alone whether they once included Benjamin.

Additionally, the books of Kings are surprisingly unclear about even how many tribes were in the kingdom of Judah. The obvious answer would be two – ten plus two equals twelve – and at times the Primary History's account of the division of the kingdoms suggests just this. Ahijah, the Shilonite prophet, tears his cloak into twelve pieces, handing Jeroboam, the future king of Israel, ten, and keeping two for himself (1 Kgs. 11:30–31). In 1 Kings 12:21, Rehoboam, first king of Judah, is described explicitly as the ruler of the tribes of Judah and Benjamin. But other verses in 1 Kings 11–12 insist that the House of David kept only *one* tribe (1 Kgs. 11:13, 32, 36) – an idea that appears again even in 2 Kings

---

offerings to the Levites while Num. 10:14–27 repeats the conceit of Num. 2:3–33 but with Gershon, Merari, and Kohath, Levitical families, taking the place of Levi proper. Levi's genealogy is described in Num. 26:57–62, in Gershonite, Kohathite, and Merarite terms after the other tribes have been enumerated, while Levi is left out of the list of the spies sent from each tribe in Num. 13:4–15, and of the leaders for portioning out inheritance in Num. 34:14–28.

[104] Tobolowsky, *The Sons of Jacob*, 85.

[105] Some have argued that Benjamin was always Judahite, notably Nadav Na'aman and Omer Sergi. See Na'aman, "Saul, Benjamin and the Emergence of 'Biblical Israel' Part I"; Na'aman, "Saul, Benjamin and the Emergence of 'Biblical Israel' Part II"; Sergi, "The Emergence of Judah." For a counter-argument, see Finkelstein, "Saul, Benjamin and the Emergence of 'Biblical Israel'"; Finkelstein, *The Forgotten Kingdom*, 348–67. For a discussion of Benjamin as border territory, see Levin, "Joseph, Judah and the 'Benjamin Conundrum.'"

17's account of the Assyrian conquest, when, the text says, "none was left but the tribe of Judah alone" (2 Kgs. 17:18). And while 1 Kings 12:21 is explicit in one direction, 1 Kings 12:20 is explicit in the other: "no one followed the house of David except the tribe of Judah alone."[106]

What can explain all this? What I would suggest is that these details "preserve" and "encode" not the early history of Benjamin, but the ideological results of the transition of Benjamin from north to south sometime after the Assyrian conquest. In other words, a Benjaminite constituency would have made the tribe a part of Rehoboam's kingdom retroactively by introducing Benjamin into 1 Kings 12:21, thereby giving the Benjaminites roots in Judah as deep as the tribe of Judah's own. Simultaneously, to obscure Benjamin's original position, the ten tribes ruled by Jeroboam in Israel would have been anonymized. Meanwhile, the repeated insistence on one tribe of Judah throughout 1 Kings 11–12 might either reflect the original, pre-Benjamin state of affairs or a later Judahite effort to deny Benjaminites equal rights in Judah. In other words, this detail of the tradition might reflect a later competition over the legacy of Israel between Judah and Benjamin once the transition occurred.[107]

Likely, there are many such agendas in biblical tribal traditions, once we know how to look for them. For now, however, the main point is that the twelve tribes tradition was, even in ancient Judah, already a constant tool for redescribing Israelite identity in useful ways. There may well have been, as the proponents of the cultural invention method suggest, one major development in the history of these redescriptions, the one that made Judah into Israel and a smaller number of tribes into twelve – I think there likely was. But there would have been countless more minor redescriptions regardless, just as there have been ever since. And in them we can read the traces, not of the tribes in their original home, but of those who found meaning in the tradition and why.

---

[106] This idea that these references to the "one tribe" Rehoboam will receive might have been meant in addition to the tribe of Judah was suggested to me by Daniel Fleming at a conference. This may well be, but the 1 Kgs. 12:20 and 2 Kgs. 17:18 references are harder to explain away in this way.

[107] This ideological struggle between Judah and Benjamin in the south is visible in other ways in the text, including the fact that both are supposed to have conquered Jerusalem in different narratives. For Jerusalem as part of Benjamin's territory, see Josh. 18:28, Judg. 1:21. For Judahite Jerusalem, see Josh. 15:8, 63; Judg. 1:8. Both traditions lie uneasily alongside the narrative in which David conquers Jerusalem from the Jebusites in a later period (2 Sam. 5:6–9).

We can also see here that it was the segmented structure of the tradition that made the constant redescription of Israelite identity possible. I will have much more to say about how precisely segmented frameworks operate in the next chapter, and of course, throughout this book. But, the simple fact that Israelite identity is divided into twelve "segments," within the twelve tribes tradition, is what allows the contents of Israelite identity to be reshuffled and reinterpreted in various different ways. Above, we can see how the reorganization of the tradition to elevate Reuben and the three tribes of Judah within it makes meaning through redescription. We can see how the removal of Levi from the system, and its redefinition in relation to the system does the same, and how the movement of Benjamin between two different subgroups within Israelite identity does too. In other cases in the Hebrew Bible, we have efforts to make meaning not by rearranging details, but by reinterpreting what they mean through narrative interventions. The tradition that places Judah, Simeon, and Levi among Jacob's eldest children also makes Joseph and Benjamin his youngest – but the tradition that recounts the descent of Jacob and his family to Egypt also describes Joseph's youngest sons as his favorites. Generally, this kind of parry and riposte, couched in the language of twelve tribe stories, where familiar claims are frequently subverted, is characteristic of all efforts to "become Israel."

Ultimately, a redescriptive approach to the *data* of tribal narratives and descriptions fits much better than a preservative one with what we know about the development of traditions and identities over time. Similarly, the argument that redescribing Israelite identity via the twelve tribes tradition was a popular occupation in sixth through fourth century BCE Judah better explains the number and variety of biblical tribal depictions than an approach which focuses mainly on the *existence* of a singular act of cultural invention, or appropriation. And between these two points a conclusion emerges: the twelve tribes tradition was already a tool for "becoming Israel" – whether the Judahites had long understood themselves as Israelites or not, whether based on an early tradition or a later "invention." And this recognition opens the door to the comparisons to come.

1.6 CONCLUSION

The study of the construction of Israelite identity in the Hebrew Bible *and everywhere else* has historically been dominated by a pair of analytical habits. The first is a "historicist habit," which is to say a tendency to put too much emphasis on the question of whether a given tradition about the past is true or false.[108] Historians, obviously, want to know whether stories about the past are true, and this can be valuable in many cases. It is not, however, the only thing worth knowing about traditions, and historical description is not the only kind of historical information traditions can preserve.

The second is a "primordialist" habit, or perhaps I should say instinct.[109] Primordialism is an ethnic idea – the idea that ethnic identity has a stable, transhistorical core that defines what identity essentially is, going back to its moment of origin. The twelve tribes of Israel, to Noth et al., was precisely the primordialist core of Israelite identity, never lost or altered significantly. But primordialism has been emphatically rejected by scholars of ethnicity, so it no longer makes sense to even really consider the possibility that Israelite identity in relatively late Judah *was* essentially early Israelite identity, even if we could prove that the tradition itself was so ancient. It is, however, the fact that it tends to hang on, especially in the study of the ancient world, that makes primordialism a habit.[110] And together, these "habits" continue to reproduce the idea that, in scholarship, the main thing to do with traditions about the past is to discover whether they are telling the truth, and if not, how they can be used to reconstruct the periods they purport to describe regardless. And, they continue to suggest that reconstructing the history of very early periods – eras of supposed origins – is considerably more valuable than studying later realities even when, as with the Hebrew Bible, we know for sure that later eras are the ones that produced the traditions that we want to understand.

---

[108] "It does not help much how many times we say to ourselves that the old categories fact and fiction are not valid distinctions anymore. We are all nursed on historicist milk and weaning is hard. Our culture is obsessed with historical facts, and we are, obviously, unable to regain our 'innocence . . .' No 'post-modernist' thinker can stop this" (Barstad, "History and the Hebrew Bible," 15).

[109] Brubaker refers to "ethnic commonsense – the tendency to partition the world into putatively deeply constituted, quasi-natural intrinsic kinds" and notes that this is of course the most intuitive way for ethnic actors to think about their own identities (Brubaker, *Ethnicity Without Groups*, 9–10).

[110] As Carly L. Crouch observes, the "primordialist framework ... in the form of its emphasis on genetic or biological connections among group members, is probably the form of ethnic identity which has most frequently found its way into discussions of biblical texts" (Crouch, *The Making of Israel*, 99).

More than that, these internalized habits suggest that traditions about the past that are historically inaccurate are also, therefore, not very useful or interesting. Both of the existing methods of analyzing tribal traditions have something of this about them. Obviously, the preservative method's approach to tribal lists solely as sources of information about early tribal realities betrays a bias towards historicist concerns and a primordialist belief that later constructions of identity are likely to reflect the earliest constructions of the same identity to some considerable extent. But the cultural invention method is actually no less inspired by the belief that the main question to answer about the twelve tribes tradition is whether it reflects an early historical reality or not. Often enough, even those who conclude that the answer is "no" then immediately proceed to exploring what the original tribal tradition must have looked like, and how it reflects genuine historical realities.[111]

When we move past historicism and primordialism, however, we can see how limiting they have long been. We do not have to think there is nothing of historical reality about the twelve tribes tradition to recognize that there are other things to learn from how it was used than what really happened, when. Nor would this be an unparalleled recognition. Scholars in many other disciplines once avidly sought among the traditions that survive for "kernels of truth" from an earlier age. As soon, however, as we recognize that ethnic identity itself is constantly being reshaped – which, by this point in the history of scholarship, we are *obligated* to recognize – we must also realize that traditions *about* identity in different periods not only reflect and reveal these shifts in progress, but play a key role in authoring them in the first place – standing, as Jonathan M. Hall puts it, "among the very media through which such strategies operate."[112] These strategies are no less interesting or valuable to study

---

[111] Sometimes, once these scholars have reconstructed a hypothetical original Israelite tribal tradition, they use it to pursue a modified version of the "preservative method," as in Fleming, *The Legacy of Israel in Judah's Bible*; Finkelstein, *The Forgotten Kingdom*; Monroe and Fleming, "Earliest Israel in Highland Company." I consider this to be a more reasonable approach, since at least it is based on establishing what a supposedly early Israelite tribal concept looked like first, though it is important to remain attentive to what else shifts in the details of tribal traditions can reflect.

[112] Hall, *Ethnic Identity in Greek Antiquity*, 41. We will also see that "far from regarding mythical variants as the inevitable consequence of a genuine collective memory in decay, we should rather view them as indicating specific stages in the discursive construction of ethnicity" (ibid., 41).

than the particulars of early realities – in my view, they are much more.[113] And of course, the study of strategies can be the study of *strategists* and their world – what was wanted from Israel when, and what the "why" sheds light on.[114]

More than that, what the *essentially* discursive nature of ethnic articulations means for the study of any kind of identity, Israelite included, is that we can, very helpfully, avoid conflating the existence of ethnic "strategies" with inauthenticity, as if there were neutral, non-ideological accounts of identity to contrast "strategic" identity constructions with. Once we know cultural invention would have occurred whether or not the ancestors of the Judahites had thought of themselves as Israelites in early days, we must also realize that efforts to redescribe identity in order to use identity are not a feature only of identity constructions an earlier generation of scholars would have called "invented." They are simply a feature of identity.

Where the Hebrew Bible is concerned, then, our main conclusions are these. Noth and so many others, operating under a primordialist regime, believed that the same basic construction of Israelite identity survived from the earliest days of Israel to the last days of Judah. That is what made reconstructing earliest Israel so important to them in the first place – not the simple historiographical value of getting an accurate picture of early periods but the belief that the Hebrew Bible's various visions of Israel were *first and foremost* to be understood as descendants of the original, rich with ancient memory. Now we know, as Noth could not, that identity changes constantly, and especially in response to the exact kinds of experiences and challenges that were Judah's constant lot over the long eventful centuries of its independent history. So, we have to think of the Hebrew Bible's tribal traditions differently, especially because their number, variety, and typical dates of composition seem

---

[113] As Barstad notes, "the fact that the Bible has come much closer to literature, however, does not necessarily make it less historical ... Novels may provide us with some valuable insights here. No one, hopefully, would deny that from reading D. H. Lawrence, *Sons and Lovers* (1913) we learn a lot about what it is like to grow up in a mining village in Nottinghamshire around the turn of the century" (Barstad, "History and the Hebrew Bible," 22).

[114] Or, as Irad Malkin puts it, scholars have very often thought of myths in terms of "myth as history," meaning that a myth reflects or preserves history; a story about a Greek hero founding a cult site will reveal, through the right analysis, an event "originating in prehistorical (e.g. Mycenaean) contacts." As he argues, however, we need to turn "myth as history on its head" and "study myths as an integral part of the period in which they were told" (Malkin, *The Returns of Odysseus*, 22).

to *demand* as much, without a primordialist paradigm to defend their long-term stability.

We do not, then, have to conclude that the old questions have totally lost their value to recognize that they have been displaced by others that are more important, more interesting, and more relevant. In other words, we can certainly still want to know, say, what the early history of the tribe of Judah was like, or where the original settlement of the tribe of Benjamin was, if it is possible to discover these things from the information we have. But what we have to explain in the Hebrew Bible itself is not whether *the* or *a* vision of tribal Israel accurately describes early Israel, and to what extent, or whether the twelve tribes concept was originally an early Israelite reality or a Judahite invention.

Instead, what we have to explain in the book itself is the centrality of the twelve tribes of Israel in a narrative created by Judahite authors and editors long after all twelve likely even existed, and longer after any such institution could have functioned. We have to explain twenty-six different lists, largely late and Judahite, spanning the text from Genesis 29 to Ezekiel 48, and the many roles the tradition plays at many crucial junctures in the narrative – origin myth and land charter, identity framework and apocalyptic. No answer to the question of where the tradition originally comes from or what it was originally based on can explain how the twelve tribes tradition was used by so many biblical authors, in so many different ways, in such a late context – any more than we can explain a work of art by discovering where the potter got their clay, the painter their paint, the sculptor their marble. And if acknowledging as much compromises our ability to answer more purely historiographical questions like where Benjamin was, in exchange for new insights on what role Benjaminite agendas, and Benjaminite partisans, played in the late Judahite identity projects that ultimately produced one of the most consequential traditions in world history, we should be *glad* to make that trade.[115]

Of course, these recognitions, which amount to the conclusion that the twelve tribes tradition was used by a variety of different biblical authors towards a variety of different ends in a variety of different ways, wherever

---

[115] In Daniel Pioske's recent study of the biblical memory of David, he observes that "my analysis here is led by the conviction that the 'moment of inscription, on closer analysis, is itself a social moment,' and that both the historian and literary critic must be mindful of how a text mirrors and resists sociohistorical influences acting upon it as a historically contingent artifact" (Pioske, *David's Jerusalem*, 63–64). The quote within the quote is from Greenblatt, *Shakespearean Negotiations*, 5.

it came from or was based on, position the study of the twelve tribes tradition in the Hebrew Bible precisely where it belongs, and where it is found in this book – alongside the use of the same tradition, towards the same ends, in so many other places. Everywhere it happens, redescribing Israel – "becoming Israel," once or many times over – works in similar ways, serves similar purposes, and makes similar kinds of claims. In fact, an ancient tradition, stable in its details, but endlessly filtered through the prism of the needs of a hundred different constituencies, is fundamentally what "becoming Israel" is. That it should begin – that our long, unbroken story should begin – in the Hebrew Bible itself, because biblical authors were already doing what so many who came after would as well, need not be much of a surprise.

Thus, in the Hebrew Bible, a number of Judahite authors, standing at the far end of a long, eventful, independent history, used the twelve tribes tradition to explain how they were nevertheless part of "all Israel," and so have many who came after, and later on. Different groups of Judahites with different interests used the segmented structure of the twelve tribes tradition to redescribe the Israelite identity they claimed in useful ways, and so have those who have adopted it ever since. These various Judahites used the twelve tribes tradition to build a bridge to ancient Israel over a gap in time and space, and designed it to their liking, and there has never yet been an end to the building of bridges.

Thus, by sketching the sphere of the possible where "becoming Israel" is concerned over the next four chapters, we will gain a much greater appreciation for the actual – for the Israels there are, and how they came to be. And of course, as we go along, the evidence for the inherent, constant, and ongoing fluidity of constructions of Israelite identity will mount. After all, no one can reasonably deny the ongoing character of "becoming Israel," or the capabilities of the twelve tribes tradition as a medium for articulating it, when essentially the same set of traditions has been used to create so many different visions of Israel in so many different places over so long a period of time. No one can deny that those who inherit important and authoritative cultural traditions may well feel inclined to use them, but not always in the way we expect – not in view of all the different things Israel has become. As a result, no one can or should deny that what those who inherit Israel do with Israel is *best* understood as a mirror held up to themselves and to their world, from ancient Judah to the present day.

So as we turn our attention to the history of the Samaritans, we will see a little more of how precisely the segmented structure of the twelve tribes tradition serves to allow multiple heirs of Israel to claim to be the same and different at once – a recognition that has the potential to contribute significantly to some of the thornier debates in contemporary Samaritan studies while explaining more of how the twelve tribes tradition became the source for so many different visions of Israel later on. But, primarily, this discussion too will serve to underscore the point. Already in antiquity, the question is not what the twelve tribes tradition describes or does not describe, or what vision of Israel most reflects a historical reality. It was *what was done with the twelve tribes of Israel, how, by whom, and why.* Each answer adds to our store of answers, each gets us closer to understanding the myth of the twelve tribes of Israel – the beating heart of so many stories, all across the world.

2

The Tribes That Were Not Lost

The Samaritans

There are fifteen neat, white houses in the *Shikun Hashomronim*, with their centre, the synagogue, facing Mt. Gerizim (North-east). A deeply religious community inhabits them. Every night after work, but especially on Friday nights and holidays, the community changes into traditional garb. The little boys from the age of three are dressed exactly like their fathers and go with them to the synagogue to pray.

—Spector, "Samaritan Chant," 67.

Away in the north of the modern State of Israel, in what was once the kingdom of Israel, there lives another ancient Israel. The Samaritans, as they are generally known today, are "another ancient Israel" in the way of every group discussed in this book. They present another construction of Israelite identity and history, with their own traditions and practices, and their own account of what happened to Israel's tribes. In fact, they even have their own *Torah*, the so-called "Samaritan Pentateuch," which is similar in most respects, different in a few crucial ones.[1] They have their own holy mountain, Mt. Gerizim, which is to them what the Temple Mount in Jerusalem was to the Judahites and is, to some extent, to the Jewish people.[2] They have their own priests of the line of Aaron; their

[1] "... the MT and the SP are close to one another in many respects. This fact is obscured in many modern treatments of the SP, which speak of some 6,000 textual variations between them ... But the 6,000 figure is quite misleading, because most of the variants are rather minor in nature" (Knoppers, *Jews and Samaritans*, 179). See also Pummer, "Samaritan Studies – Recent Research Results."

[2] This is reflected in the Samaritan Pentateuch, if obliquely. Jerusalem is not in fact mentioned in either Pentateuch, but a reference in Deut. 27:4 which, in the Hebrew Bible, is to Mount Ebal – where Joshua is supposed to set up an altar upon entering the

own traditions of descent from Abraham, Isaac, and Jacob; and of course, their own claims to an identification with the twelve tribes of Israel.[3] In fact, the Samaritans are still organized by tribe even today. The last Benjaminite died in 1968, but Ephraimites, Manassites, and Levites remain.[4]

The Samaritans, however, are "another ancient Israel" in a second sense, too. They are, very probably, the descendants of the ancient Israelites, which is to say, of the Israelites as opposed to the Judahites who were the subject of the last chapter. Today, the Samaritan community is small in number, perhaps eight hundred strong, and about evenly split between a Samaritan enclave in the city of Holon, near Tel Aviv, and Kiryat Luza, their settlement on Gerizim.[5] But the simple fact that they exist – that they live where their ancestors lived, worship where they worshipped, and embrace another version of Israel and its history from the one that appears in the biblical account – raises fascinating and

---

land – is, in the Samaritan Pentateuch, to Gerizim, which is in fact a neighboring mountain (Jacobs, "Karaites, Samaritans, and Lost Tribes," 183). Also, in Exod. 20:17, in the Samaritan Pentateuch, one of the ten commandments includes building an altar on Gerizim.

[3] The line of Eleazar, son of Aaron, died out in 1624, but in the line of Ithamar, Aaron's younger son, the "Priests of the Aabta" continue to play their appointed role. See Tsedaka, "Families." For an early but influential treatment of the Samaritan high priesthood, see Gaster, "The Chain of Samaritan High Priests."

[4] According to the website of the Israelite Samaritan Information Institute, the Tsedaka Hassafari family of the tribe of Manasseh endures, and so do the Dinfi and Marchiv families of the tribe of Ephraim. The website further notes that the "House of Dinfi" separated into four branches in the eighteenth century – Sirrawi, Altif, Dar Imsallam, and Dar Elshalabi – but the last two lineages died out in the second half of the twentieth century. The Marchiv are divided between the branch still called Marchiv and the branch Yehoshua, with the Marchiv family split between Holon and Gerizim and the Yehoshua family in Holon. The Benjaminite family that died out in 1968 was known as "Matar." Again, see Tsedaka, "Families."

[5] Pummer, *The Samaritans: A Profile*, 170, 297; Knoppers, *Jews and Samaritans*, 1–2; Crown, "The Samaritan Diaspora," 196. Fascinatingly, there are now new Samaritan converts in Brazil, and in Sicily, testifying again to the popularity and variety of "becoming Israel" as a practice. This fact was pointed out to me by Matthew Chalmers, whose advice on this chapter has been invaluable, but new members in São Paulo, Brazil and Catania, Sicily are also mentioned on the website of the Israelite Samaritan institute (see *The Israelite Samaritan Institute*, "Israelite Samaritans in Brazil," www.israelite-samaritans .com/brazil/). See also Urien-Lefranc, "From Religious to Cultural and Back Again," 10–12. As for their numbers, things were quite different in antiquity when the Samaritans were "of immense cultural, religious and religio-political significance" (Hensel, "On the Relationship of Judah and Samaria," 35). In the late first millennium BCE, "there were probably ... more Samaritans than Judeans residing in Palestine" (Knoppers, *Jews and Samaritans*, 1–2).

difficult questions about the history of Israelite identity. And these questions have been sharpened to a razor's edge by recent developments in the scholarly study of Samaritan history and prehistory.

To be clear, the Samaritans have always claimed not only to descend from the ancient Israelites, but to still be them today. In fact, rather than "Samaritan," they prefer the name the "Keepers," because, they say, they and they alone have kept the true traditions and practices of ancient Israel, including Moses' original revelation, preserved in the Samaritan Pentateuch.[6] In their telling, it was the other Israelites who went away from them, already in the days of Eli, high priest of Shiloh. In the Hebrew Bible, Eli is tasked with raising the young Samuel, who would go on to anoint Saul and David, the first two kings of Israel. In Samaritan traditions, he is a betrayer and usurper who led the rest of the Israelite community astray – and away from Gerizim – perverting their traditions in the process.[7] Thus, the early Samaritans stood apart, not only from the Judahites, but from the rest of the people of Israel, even before there were kings in Israel. Later, they say, the scribe Ezra – who in Nehemiah 8:1 is supposed to have read a document called "the book of the *torah* of Moses" (ספר תורה משה) to the assembled community of the Persian period "return from Exile" – stole their *Torah* and corrupted its message, resulting in the inferior biblical version.[8]

Outside of the community, however, the origins of the Samaritans have most often been understood quite differently. Typically, their story has been told through the lens of a biblical text, 2 Kings 17, which describes the Assyrian conquest of the kingdom of Israel in 722 BCE. In this account, which is also the foundation myth for the "Ten Lost Tribes of

---

[6] Crown, "The Samaritan Diaspora," 196. From the Israelite Samaritan Institute: "We are not *Jews*; this is what the Assyrians called the people of Judaea. The Jews adopted the name the Assyrians gave them. We are not *Samaritans*; this is what the Assyrians called the people of Samaria. We, *The Keepers*, Sons of Israel, Keepers of the Word of the Torah, never adopted the name *Samaritans* ... through the ages we have referred to ourselves as *The Keepers*" (www.israelite-samaritans.com/history/keepers-israelite-samaritan-identity/). "The Samaritans are convinced that they are the original and true Israelites, whereas the Jews have gone astray. In their medieval chronicles, the Samaritans call the Jews, among other epithets, 'the sons of Israel the erroneous ones,' 'rebels,' 'heretics,' or 'the people of error'" (Pummer, *The Samaritans: A Profile*, 9).

[7] Pummer, *The Samaritans: A Profile*, 2, 9–10. This seems not to have been a particularly early Samaritan tradition.

[8] In fact, the Samaritans are not alone in treating Ezra as the corrupter of Moses' message. This was also a Muslim tradition and to some degree a Christian tradition. For discussions of these, see Fried, "Ezra among Christians, Samaritans, Muslims, and Jews"; Wollenberg, "The Book That Changed."

Israel," the entirety of the original population of that region was taken into Assyrian exile and "none was left but the tribe of Judah alone" (2 Kgs. 17:18). And after that, "the king of Assyria brought people from Babylon, Kuthah, Awwa, Hamath, and Sepharvaim, and he settled them in the cities of Samaria in place of the Israelites, and they possessed Samaria and lived in its cities" (2 Kgs. 17:24).

2 Kings 17 admits that these émigrés quickly embraced the local religion – in part because they kept being attacked by lions (2 Kgs. 17:25–28) – but they kept their foreign ways (2 Kgs. 17:29–34).[9] And it is these peoples, with their unfortunate hybrid practices, who have been understood as the true ancestors of the Samaritans. Indeed, "Kutheans" is how the first century CE Roman-Jewish historian Josephus, long a major scholarly source for reconstructing Samaritan history, refers to the Samaritans (Ant. 9.277–78). "Kutheans," or "Kuthim" in Hebrew, is what they are called in many rabbinic texts, including the extra-Talmudic tractate concerning the Samaritans, *Massekhet Kutim.*[10]

In recent years, however, scholarship has finally begun to acknowledge what the Samaritans have always claimed: that 2 Kings 17 is a quite inaccurate account of the Assyrian conquest, and presumably purpose-fully so. While the kingdom of Israel was indeed toppled between 722 and 720 BCE, and while there were deportations, they were not, and could not be, nearly so significant as the biblical text suggests. Nor, we now recognize, is there any evidence for what Gary Knoppers calls "two-way deportations," the movement in of massive quantities of foreigners as the Israelites were moved out.[11] And so, most likely, "the vast majority of those who endured the Assyrian invasions" – which is to say the Israelites themselves – "continued to reside in the land."[12] In fact, for many, life probably went back to normal fairly quickly – if under new manage-ment.[13] In a sense, if the big surprise in contemporary biblical scholarship is that the Judahites might have literally "become Israelite" sometime after 722 BCE, in Samaritan studies, the surprise is that their ancestors did not, because they did not have to. The contemporary community is, for the most part, genuinely the descendants of the tribes who were not lost.

[9] Indeed, the Samaritans were sometimes called "lion converts" (Schiffman, "The Samaritans in Amoraic Halakhah," 372).

[10] Schiffman, "The Samaritans in Tannaitic Halakhah," 327.

[11] Knoppers, *Jews and Samaritans*, 40–42. Knoppers additionally cites the studies of Oded, *Mass Deportations and Deportees in the Neo-Assyrian Empire*; Liverani, "Imperialism."

[12] Knoppers, *Jews and Samaritans*, 39.   [13] Knoppers, *Jews and Samaritans*, 9.

Still, this is not the same as saying that the Samaritans' own traditions of origin are now understood simply as *history*, which is part of the problem. Descendants of the Israelites they may be, but descent and identity aren't the same thing. Today, the best evidence suggests that a specifically Samaritan identity developed, in the north, only over the course of the last centuries BCE, much as a Jewish identity developed in the south – in part, through competition with the other. Both identities have significant continuities with older traditions and practices, but, very likely, neither can be said to have existed yet in the era in which biblical texts were still being written.

The end result of all of these developments is that there is a big new question in Samaritan studies: how precisely did most Judahites understand the people of Israel after the Assyrian conquest, and vice versa? If 2 Kings 17 is wrong, how were the people of Israel understood, and how did they understand themselves, between 722 BCE and the appearance of a distinct Samaritan community? After all, the Hebrew Bible insists on the survival of an "all Israel" identity between the kingdoms of Israel and Judah as long as both existed, and no matter what happened between them. If, after 722 BCE, the northerners were in fact still Israelites, whatever 2 Kings 17 says, *and* they were not yet Samaritans, why shouldn't "all Israel" have survived too, at least for many Israelites and Judahites? Indeed, many now wonder whether even the early Samaritans could be regarded as members of an enduring "all Israel" community, however hard and fast the distinction between Samaritan and Jew would eventually become. The inaccuracy of 2 Kings 17 – the fact that it is very likely propaganda – opens the door to the possibility that its otherizing of the post-conquest northerners also represents a minority view.

There is much to recommend in these new studies, and it does seem clear that northern Israelite and southern Judahite constructions of Israelite identity were, at the very least, more open to each other than 2 Kings 17 suggests, and for a lot longer. At the same time, there are significant problems with the course these discussions typically take, and in ways that can shed a lot of light on the phenomenon of "becoming Israel" more generally. First of all, many of the scholars engaged in rethinking the relationship between these two Israels throughout the first millennium BCE show the same uncritical approach to the concept of "all Israel" that we saw in the first chapter. They reinscribe the Bible's own problematic erasure of the long-term historical importance of the border between Judah and Israel, accepting the biblical notion of a universal "all Israel" identity that somehow spanned two quite different kingdoms.

In other words, the assumption that an "all Israel" identity actually survived the conquest if the deportation of the Israelites was not significant enough to break it is also the assumption that it really existed in so early a period – a biblical claim, rather than a demonstrated reality.

Likely enough, an "all Israel" discourse was, in fact, something that both southerners and northerners could participate in, from time to time, for far longer than 2 Kings 17 suggests they could. But it was *never* a simple reality. The Judahite construction of an "all Israel" identity would still be Judahite, and so, one presumes, would the Israelite version. This is a tension at the heart of "becoming Israel" writ large: every Israel presents itself as simply a part of a universal, and universally agreed upon Israelite identity, but every Israel is unique. Every Israel can claim to be one with the rest of Israel, and each one has its particular, irreconcilable features. And it is up to the scholar to look past the internal pretense of a broadly shared Israelite identity to see what makes each construction of Israel unique.

Second, also as in the last chapter, a great many re-evaluations of the relevant evidence for northern and southern similarity and difference take the traditions that present this "all Israel" identity at face value, without asking what the concept of "all Israel" is doing in a particular place. Specifically, contemporary scholarship tends to balance 2 Kings 17's description of the post-722 BCE northerners as foreigners with other descriptions that acknowledge they were still Israelites. These prominently include 2 Chronicles 30, a biblical account of a Passover celebration at Jerusalem, attended by the local Judahites and a selection of "those who escaped from the hand of the king of Assyria" (2 Chron. 30:6) – including certain Asherites, Ephraimites, Manassites, Zebulunites, and Issacharites (30:11, 18) – who in 2 Kings 17 are not supposed to exist. Josephus, too, acknowledges, despite himself, that there were Israelites in the north in the seventh century BCE.[14]

---

[14] In Josephus, in *Ant.* 10.68, Josiah, king of Judah, goes to the "other Israelites" who had "escaped" from the Assyrians and converts them to a more appropriate form of religious worship, abandoning their other gods. See Pummer, *The Samaritans in Flavius Josephus*, 77–78. See also Alon, "The Origin of the Samaritans in the Halakhic Tradition." As Chalmers observes, "contradictory elements of Samaritans characterize Josephus' works. On the one hand, Josephus attempts to classify Samaritans as absolute outsiders. On the other, as Alon noticed more than thirty years ago, Josephus also maintains at least three origin narratives of the Samaritans, each relating the group to Canaanites in different ways. His ethnicization is hardly decisive" (Chalmers, "Viewing Samaritans Jewishly," 342–43). Later in the article, Chalmers observes that Josephus "emerges not as a key witness to Samaritan difference, a stabilized point between Second Temple and Rabbinic

As logical as it may seem to treat these diverse acknowledgments of a shared identity after 722 BCE simply as the rhetorical opposite of 2 Kings 17's denial, this is a mistake, and it is especially a mistake when segmented identity traditions are involved.[15] From a comparative perspective, the fact that segmented systems preserve the independent existence of different entities within overarching expressions of similarity means that they are very often used as mediums for competitions between those entities.[16] And in fact, this does not only happen with segmented frameworks. In other cases, traditions aimed at furthering the competition between groups can begin with an acknowledgment of what they share, the better to explain why one is a better heir to land, legacy, or a similar quantity than the other.

In other words, even texts that describe an "all Israel" identity can be part of the competition between heirs to Israel, as are many of the relevant traditions concerning northern and southern Israelites, including 2 Chron. 30. As I have discussed throughout, even those peoples who did not have to literally "become Israel" in the first place still do "become," over and over again, because it is not specifically "invented" identities that are fluid and reinventive, era to era and context to context, but simply identity itself.[17] The twelve tribes tradition is constantly in use as tool for redescriptions, so it is precisely accounts of Israelite identity in

---

fluidity, but as a constructor. Josephus' works, similar to other texts of the time, actively construct Samaritan and Judean identities vis-à-vis specific theorization of belonging to Israel" (ibid., 359).

[15] The study of segmented identity traditions has played little role in the study of Israelite identity constructions anywhere, with the partial exception of my own previous studies of the twelve tribes tradition (Tobolowsky, "Reading Genesis Through Chronicles"; Tobolowsky, *The Sons of Jacob*; Tobolowsky, "The Problem of Reubenite Primacy").

[16] As Irad Malkin observes, the capacity for "differentiating and relating nations at the same time" – or in this case tribes – is the major characteristic of the segmented form (Malkin, *The Returns of Odysseus*, 61). See also Patterson, *Kinship Myth in Ancient Greece*, 28.

[17] "Indeed, as the space between culture (as a taken-for-granted order of symbols, institutions, structures, values, and/or beliefs) and identity (as a reflexive construct or experiential modality through which one knows oneself and claims recognition) has seemed to shrink, identity has become, in effect, a kind of metaculture: culture—to use the old Hegelian terminology—not just in itself but for itself" (Leve, "'Identity,'" 513–14). Or, as Michael Roy Hames-García puts it, "memberships in various social groups (or categories of social identity) combine with and mutually constitute one another. Membership in one group (for example, 'womanhood') thus means something different in the context of one simultaneously held group membership (for example, 'blackness') than in the context of another (for example, 'motherhood')" (Hames-García, *Identity Complex*, 5). See also Tabili, "Race Is a Relationship, and Not a Thing," 125.

tribal terms that must be scrutinized for dynamic efforts to redefine what Israel means, and to whom. In the case of the Samaritans and their ancestors, many key texts are less so passive descriptions of "all Israel," before it was finally broken, than they are active efforts to redescribe Israelite identity in order to elevate one claimant over another.

Ultimately, by revisiting the evidence for northern and southern constructions of Israelite identity while keeping in mind both the *generally* redescriptive quality of accounts of Israel and the *specific* capabilities of segmented identity systems, we will see much that is otherwise hidden, shining new light on increasingly thorny historical and literary problems. Meanwhile, in the context of the larger study of "becoming Israel" as a long-term historical practice, it will serve us well to discuss the articulation of similarity and difference between north and south already in the first millennium BCE.

As we will see, the way that Israelites and Judahites, Jews and Samaritans distinguish themselves from each other in the context of ethnic competitions is also how the other Israels of the world account for their unique features outside of them. The way that all these groups use the segmented structure of Israelite identity to their advantage is how they would be used ever since. And the simple fact that there was "another ancient Israel," even in ancient Israel itself, finishes laying the groundwork for where this study goes from here. The twelve tribes tradition was already a tool through which different claimants to an Israelite identity constructed and redescribed Israelite identity, in competition with each other and for their own purposes in antiquity. An approach aimed at understanding how construction, redescription, and the competition between Israels generally works can help us better understand each specific case.

2.1 THE SAMARITANS

In 722 BCE, the Neo-Assyrian empire, the indomitable war machine of its day, came down on the kingdom of Israel, in Byron's memorable phrase, like a "wolf on the fold."[18] This was neither the first nor the last incursion of the great Mesopotamian empires into the region, but this time the wolf carried away the kingdom in its jaws. In the "ninth year of Hosea," according to 2 Kings 17 – the only explicit biblical account of this epochal

---

[18] Byron was talking about the Assyrians, in this line from *The Destruction of Sennacherib* though he was actually referring to a slightly later, and less successful invasion of Judah.

event – "the king of Assyria captured Samaria," both the capital of the kingdom and another name for it, "and carried Israel into exile to Assyria. And he settled them in Halah, Habor, on the river Gozan, and in the cities of the Medes" (2 Kgs. 17:6). Supposedly, when the king – probably the emperor Shalmaneser V – was done, nothing of Israel was left in the region "but the tribe of Judah alone," and that in its separate kingdom, weakened but still standing (2 Kgs. 17:18). Never again would the twelve tribes of Israel live together in their native land.

This story is true, up to a point. There was a conquest, there were exiles, and not just in 722. A decade earlier, Tiglath-Pileser III, perhaps the most warlike of Assyria's abundance of warlike rulers, had devastated the region of Israel known as the Transjordan, removing a huge number of people to Assyria.[19] Shalmaneser, and his successor Sargon II, deported even more, by raw numbers.[20] Whole tribes of Israel likely were lost at this time, or even earlier. We never hear of Reuben, Gad, Dan, or Naphtali again. For that matter, Simeon is never mentioned again either, even though it was apparently a southern tribe, not a northern one.[21]

The heartlands of Samaria, however, were much larger and more populous than the Transjordan had been. Even if the emperors removed all thirty thousand Israelites they claim to have resettled – and they may well have been exaggerating – many would still have remained behind.[22] From an archaeological perspective, the conquest appears less prepossessing than its description in 2 Kings 17. Samaria itself – and Megiddo, another great city – appear to have been preserved largely intact, quickly

---

[19] For Tiglath-Pileser's claim and estimates of the population of the Transjordan – variously put between 18,000 and 22,500 – see Gal, *Lower Galilee During the Iron Age*, 109; Broshi and Finkelstein, "The Population of Palestine in Iron Age II," 50.

[20] See Knoppers, *Jews and Samaritans*, 33; Barmash, "At the Nexus of History and Memory," 207–8; Gal, *Lower Galilee During the Iron Age*, 109.

[21] Some of these tribes may have been destroyed even earlier. 2 Kgs. 10:32–33 claims that Hazael of Aram-Damascus conquered the regions where Reuben, Gad, and the Transjordanian part of Manasseh lived. In 1 Kings 15:20, Ben-Hadad of Aram-Damascus conquers "all the land of Naphtali," although in 2 Kgs. 15:29 it is Tiglath-Pileser III who does this.

[22] Estimates of the percentage of the population deported have ranged as low as 5 percent, but 20–25 percent around the region of central Samaria, and much less in other regions, is more common. See Yamauchi, "The Eastern Jewish Diaspora Under the Babylonians," 357; Zertal, "The Heart of the Monarchy," 44; Broshi and Finkelstein, "The Population of Palestine in Iron Age II," 50–51; Barmash, "At the Nexus of History and Memory," 216; Knoppers, *Jews and Samaritans*, 37–38; Na'aman and Zadok, "Sargon II's Deportations."

becoming centers of Assyrian administration in the region.[23] Rural settlements were largely left alone.[24] And as I said above, there is no evidence of the arrival in the region of a vast quantity of foreigners from Assyria or elsewhere. Thus, the Samaritans are almost certainly the descendants of Israelites, not outsiders, "Kutheans" or any others.

At the same time, it is indeed very unlikely that there were any "Samaritans" to speak of in the eighth century BCE. Some scholars have made the argument, long ago and fairly recently, that Samaritan practice is essentially ancient Israelite practice.[25] If, however, we consider the hallmarks of a distinctly Samaritan identity to include, for example, the Samaritan Pentateuch, that appears to have emerged in the second century BCE.[26] At Gerizim, one important development spurring re-evaluations is the recent recognition that Josephus' account of the construction of the Samaritan temple in the days of Alexander the Great is off by at least a century.[27] New excavations reveal there was something like a temple there already in the fifth century BCE, when the Second Temple in Jerusalem would have been fairly new.[28] But the fifth century BCE is not the tenth century BCE, or for that matter, the twelfth century BCE, the period that likely corresponds to the biblical account of the time of Eli.

---

[23] Knoppers, *Jews and Samaritans*, 36, 45–46; Dalley, "Foreign Chariotry and Cavalry," 31–38; Tappy, "The Final Years of Israelite Samaria"; Na'aman, "The Historical Background to the Conquest of Samaria (720 BCE)." As Hensel has recently observed, "it is mainly the works of Knoppers that should be acknowledged" for "highlighting" the cultural continuity in the north before and after the Assyrian conquest (Hensel, "On the Relationship of Judah and Samaria," 25).

[24] Bloch-Smith, "Assyrians Abet Israelite Cultic Reforms."

[25] In recent years, this argument has been made by Nodet (Nodet, *Samaritans, Juifs, Temples*; Nodet, "Israelites, Samaritans, Temples, Jews"). Long before Nodet, Moses Gaster made a similar argument (Gaster, *The Samaritans, Their History, Doctrines and Literature*). However, it is not a commonly held view.

[26] Eshel and Eshel, "Dating the Samaritan Pentateuch's Compilation"; Lim, "The Emergence of the Samaritan Pentateuch"; Anderson and Giles, *The Samaritan Pentateuch*. See especially Schorch, "The Samaritan Version of Deuteronomy"; Schorch, "A Critical Editio Maior of the Samaritan Pentateuch."

[27] For a comprehensive account of the flaws in Josephus' account of Samaritan history, long relied upon by scholars, see Pummer, *The Samaritans in Flavius Josephus*.

[28] Magen, "Mt. Gerizim: A Temple City"; Stern and Magen, "Archaeological Evidence for the First Stage"; Magen, Misgav, and Tsfania, "Mount Gerizim Excavations"; Magen, Misgav, and Tsfania, *Mount Gerizim Excavations*; Magen, "The Dating of the First Phase"; Dušek, "Mt. Gerizim Sanctuary."

Today, there are those who see the origins of the Samaritans writ large in the Gerizim temple's construction in the fifth century BCE.[29] Others argue there were no true Samaritans until the temple's violent destruction by John Hyrcanus, Hasmonean ruler of Judah, high priest, and nephew of Judah Maccabee, which, in these studies, is typically treated as the punctuation mark on an escalating series of north–south distinctions that also produced the first firm borders between Samaritans and Jews.[30] Some, not surprisingly, stress the likelihood that the development of a Samaritan identity was less a moment than a process, perhaps spanning the whole range from construction to destruction and beyond.[31] Still others argue that there may have been no Samaritans, in the sense of a distinct, self-identifying group, until the first century CE.[32]

Between these various proposals, my own preference for the era of Samaritan origins is the third and second centuries BCE, and likely more the second than the third. We know something like the Samaritan Pentateuch emerged at that time.[33] And we know, from a pair of inscriptions found as far afield as the island of Delos, that there were self-styled "Israelites" who defined themselves as those who worshipped at "hallowed Mt. Gerizim" in this period, whether they were also known

---

[29] Magnar Kartveit has made the case that the origins of the Gerizim temple and of Samaritanism were simultaneous (Kartveit, *The Origins of the Samaritans*, 351).

[30] Schwartz, "John Hyrcanus I's Destruction of the Gerizim Temple"; Bourgel, "The Destruction of the Samaritan Temple."

[31] Ingrid Hjelm calls this, somewhat disparagingly, the "two-episode paradigm," where the construction of the Temple began a process that its destruction finished (Hjelm, *The Samaritans and Early Judaism*, 45). For older studies, see Cross, "Papyri of the Fourth Century BC from Daliyeh"; Kippenberg, *Garizim und Synagogue*; Dexinger, "Der Ursprung der Samaritaner im Spiegel der frühen Quellen."

[32] For the argument that there were no Samaritans to speak of even until the first century CE, around the time of Jesus, which is indeed where we first see the term "Samaritan" used, see Crown, "Redating the Schism." For insightful discussions of the continued openness of one community to the other into later periods, see especially Hensel, "On the Relationship of Judah and Samaria"; Knoppers, *Jews and Samaritans*, 117–19. Schiffman notes that the two communities were largely separated by the early second century CE, but that processes of separation continued into the late third century CE with respect to issues such as intermarriage and eating and drinking together (Schiffman, "The Samaritans in Amoraic Halakhah," 388–89).

[33] Although, it is possible that the Samaritans took the distinctive features of their identity from the manuscript tradition that *became* known as the "Samaritan Pentateuch" rather than the other way around – or that the "Samaritan Pentateuch" is older than the Masoretic version. See Sanderson, *An Exodus Scroll from Qumran*, 319–20; Schorch, "A Critical editio maior of the Samaritan Pentateuch," 7; Schenker, "Le Seigneur choisira-t-Il le lieu de Son Nom ou l'a-t-Il choisi?"; Eshel and Eshel, "Dating the Samaritan Pentateuch's Compilation."

as Samaritans or not.[34] Any of the reconstructions mentioned above, however, would still raise the two significant questions about Samaritan history and prehistory that I mentioned in the introduction, and that would not, and could not, have featured in earlier scholarship. First, we want to know how the people of Israel understood themselves, and were understood by the people of Judah, between the fall of Samaria and the Samaritan horizon. Today, many new studies refer to the northerners after the conquest as "Samarians," a term borrowed from a name for the region both before and after the Assyrian conquest, but also an eloquent statement of scholarly uncertainty.[35] They certainly thought of themselves as Israelites.

Second, we would like to know when a hard and fast distinction between northern Israelites and southern Judahites first emerged, if not in 722 BCE. For at least most of the last two millennia, the Samaritans and the Jews have indeed regarded each other largely as an "other" to distinguish themselves from. But the possibility that "all Israel" survived 722 BCE raises the possibility that it survived even into the early days of the Samaritans, who might originally have been regarded as simply another species of Israelite or Jew. And in fact, a re-evaluation of the available evidence has revealed that early rabbinic texts from the first centuries CE are considerably less definitive about the "otherness" of the Samaritans than later rabbinic authorities would be.[36]

Older reconstructions, then, represent what Benedikt Hensel has called the "conflict" model in more ways than one – they envisage conflict between northerners and southerners after 722 BCE, and conflict between

---

[34] Bruneau and Bordreuil, "Les Israélites de Délos et la juiverie délienne"; White, "The Delos Synagogue Revisited."

[35] In the Assyrian imperial system, the province of "Sāmerīna" stood alongside two others that had been made out of Israel: *Dū'ru* (Dôr) and *Magidû* (Megiddo) (Lipschits, *The Fall and Rise of Jerusalem*, 6–7). See also Schneider, "Through Assyria's Eyes," 11.

[36] See especially Schiffman, "The Samaritans in Amoraic Halakhah," 349–50; Corinaldi, "The Personal Status of the Samaritans in Israel," 285–86. In a more recent treatment, Schiffman has observed that early rabbinic traditions show "a gradual separation of the two communities ... By the time of the Bar Kokhba Revolt (132–135 CE) the notion that the Samaritans were to be regarded as non-Jews was widespread and the schism was on the way to becoming more or less complete" (Schiffman, "The Samaritans in Amoraic Halakhah," 371). However, in this later study, he also observes the existence of a continuing ambivalence on the subject. See also Moshe Lavee, who describes a "gradual and prolonged process of halakhic exclusion of the Samaritans" *via* "the rise of a conceptual framework, supporting a binary and polar model of identity, in which there is no place for quasi-Jewish identities" (Lavee, "The Samaritan May Be Included," 147).

Samaritans and other self-described heirs of Israel as soon as there were Samaritans.[37] Newer models not only emerge from the sidelining of 2 Kings 17 in favor of other accounts but from the way a refusal to privilege it has opened our eyes to other kinds of evidence. The archaeological record also suggests significant continuities between post-conquest Israel and Judah more or less continuously.[38] There are, to be clear, evocative hints of north–south distinctions of various sorts too. There are names, like Jeroboam, which once belonged to important figures in northern history that so far have only been found in the north.[39] Northern coins and other similar kinds of material evidence show a more varied and international register of symbols, perhaps indicating a greater cosmopolitanism.[40] To be clear, the two cultures shared quite a lot with each other even *after* there were distinct Samaritan and Jewish communities, showing the limits of judging from similarities alone.[41] But the

---

[37] Hensel, "On the Relationship of Judah and Samaria."

[38] New evidence generally comes courtesy of new surveys of the northern region, and new publications of inscriptions from the ongoing excavations at Gerizim. See Zertal, *The Manasseh Hill Country Survey: The Shechem Syncline*; Zertal, *The Manasseh Hill Country Survey: The Eastern Valleys*; Dušek, *Les Manuscrits araméens du Wadi Daliyeh et la Samarie vers 450–332 av. J.-C.*; Dušek, *Aramaic and Hebrew Inscriptions from Mt. Gerizim and Samaria*. For older studies, see Cross, "The Discovery of the Samaria Papyri"; Cross, "Aspects of Samaritan and Jewish History"; Cross, "A Reconstruction of the Judean Restoration"; Leith, *Wadi Daliyeh I*; Gropp, *Wadi Daliyeh II*.

[39] For the significance of "Jeroboam" see Knoppers, *Jews and Samaritan*, 118. Giles and Anderson also note a number of divine names "common among the Moabites, Edomites, Canaanites, and several other population groups, possibly indicating a degree of religious syncretism among at least the Samarian aristocracy" (Anderson and Giles, *The Keepers*, 26). There are also quite a lot of *unique* northern names. At least at the time of one 1998 study, on sources from the end of the fifth century and the fourth century BCE, there were about 350 personal names collected overall, of which 90 were unique to northern documents and 200 to southern documents (Eph'al, "Changes in Palestine").

[40] For a study of the numismatic evidence, see Gerson, "Fractional Coins of Judea and Samaria," 108–9. As Gerson notes, Greek imagery appears on both sets of coins but is considerably more prominent in Samaria (ibid., 110). Similar scripts appear in both regions, but while Hebrew is relatively common on Judahite coins of the fifth through mid-third centuries BCE, no Samarian coins with Hebrew legends had yet turned up at least by the time of a 1998 study (Naveh, "Scripts and Inscriptions in Ancient Samaria," 91–92).

[41] Even after "interactions between Jews and Samaritans had become contentious by the 1st century CE ... the groups shared a belief in monotheism, an attachment to the land of Israel, and the same ancestral tongue (Hebrew). Both claimed descent from the same first progenitor (Adam), the same chain of ancestors (Abraham and Sarah, Isaac and Rebekah, Jacob ad Rachel and Leah), the same priestly tribe originating in the patriarch Levi, and the same priestly pedigree originating in the succession of Aaron, Eleazar, and Phinehas." Samaritans and Jews practiced a number of similar rituals, festivals, and feasts, and the

majority of the evidence suggests significant continuities between north and south throughout the first millennium BCE.[42]

In place of the conflict model, or models, then, it is hardly surprising that newer arguments stress the likelihood of continuity and commonality between Israel and Judah after 722 BCE instead. In one recent study, for example, Kristin Weingart suggests that an "inclusivist" view likely dominated relations between the regions for most of the period in question, in contrast to the "exclusivist" position of 2 Kings 17. In another, Ingrid Hjelm sees in texts like 2 Chron. 30 a "reconciliatory gesture towards the northern tribes," who are given "reason to identify with Jerusalem's surviving remnant."[43] Reinhard Pummer argues that "the Samaritans, together with the Jews of Judea, were part of the *common Israelite tradition*" – emphasis mine – "until the second century BCE" – again assuming that there must have been such a thing until whenever it was broken.[44] Other scholars, in my opinion more correctly, continue to stress the likelihood that the two Israels were recognizably *two* from very early periods, though they also stress the extent to which 2 Kings 17 was likely not representative.[45] But a paradigm shift is happening, usually to a more

---

groups shared an overlap in holy scriptures—the Pentateuch, or Five Books of Moses" (Knoppers, *Jews and Samaritans*, 2).

[42] Sometimes, two different well-qualified scholars will study the same evidence and come to different conclusions about whether it reveals similarity or difference – as, for example, in two recent studies of a body of votive inscriptions found at Gerizim. For a study stressing the existence of differences with southern forms, see Kartveit, "Samaritan Self-Consciousness." For the opposite argument, see Gudme, *Before the God in This Place*.

[43] Weingart, "What Makes an Israelite an Israelite?," 163; Hjelm, "The Hezekiah Narrative as a Foundation Myth," 663. Beyond these, Knoppers argues that this text reveals "a concession to the northern calendar" and suggests that, in it, "the devastating experiences of the past become a call to all Israelites to reunite, rally to the Jerusalem temple, and rededicate themselves to YHWH" (Knoppers, "Mt. Gerizim and Mt. Zion," 321–22). See also Dyck, "Ethnicity and the Bible."

[44] Pummer, *The Samaritans: A Profile*, 128. Pummer adds that the "split" that eventually occurred between Jew and Samaritan was "within the Israelite people," presuming the continued existence of such a thing (ibid., 22). Weingart adds that the position embodied by 2 Kings 17 was "highly polemical ... hard to maintain, and not really successful in the long run" (Weingart, "What Makes an Israelite an Israelite?," 171).

[45] Benedikt Hensel's and Gary Knoppers' treatments are, in my opinion, superior to the rest cited here, acknowledging the importance of the separate politics of Israel and Judah even if they were more open to each other than in the "conflict model." Knoppers especially notes that "cultic, historical, and political differences ... divided the two areas (Israel and Judah) for many centuries" before there were Jews and Samaritans (Hensel, "On the Relationship of Judah and Samaria," 34–35, 37; Knoppers, *Jews and Samaritans*, 119).

dramatic extent than in these latter studies, and it is happening because of the rejection of 2 Kings 17's account of what happened to Israel.

Certainly, the fact that the northerners both were and would have gone on understanding themselves as Israelites after the Assyrian conquest matters, and so does the evidence that suggests that Judahites and early Jewish authors could acknowledge as much, whatever certain texts say. Important too is the evidence for continuities, and even for potential cooperation. Not only, however, do some of these studies assume the existence of a "common Israelite tradition" that may never have existed – thereby assuming its survival by default rather than proving it by evidence – but replacing the "conflict" model with an "inclusivist" or "reconciliatory" one requires more than the presence of texts that offer inclusion and reconciliation at face value. We also have to understand what those texts are intended to do, and how they do it – both in terms of how ethnic competition generally works and the role segmented identity structures play within them.

2.2 THE VARIETIES OF ETHNIC COMPETITION

For whatever reason, the Hebrew Bible's "Secondary History" – the books of Chronicles – never quite describe the Assyrian conquest of Israel. They do, however, depict its immediate aftermath. In 2 Chronicles 30, King Hezekiah of Judah sends invitations to the north, to "the remnant of you who have escaped from the hand of the kings of Assyria," for a Passover celebration to be held in Jerusalem, Judah's capitol (2 Chron. 30:6). The tribes of Ephraim, Manasseh, Asher, Zebulun, and Issachar, all northern tribes, are mentioned by name (2 Chron. 30:11, 18). Not all come, but some do, and they eat together "with joy" (2 Chron. 30:23) – "all the assembly of Judah rejoiced, and the priests and the Levites and all the assembly of those who came from Israel" (2 Chron. 30:25). This was a gathering that had not been seen "since the days of Solomon, son of David, king of Israel" (2 Chron. 30:26). The days of Solomon, of course, were the last days of the great United Monarchy – the last moment when Israel and Judah had been ruled together, an evocative message for the future of north–south cooperation.

It is hardly surprising, then, that in recent years this text has been held to embody an "inclusivist" position in contrast to 2 Kings 17's "exclusivist" account, and to represent a celebration of the "common Israelite tradition" that still bound them all.[46] But consider this – how would a northern Israelite have read, for example, 2 Chron. 30:18, which claims that the northerners "were not ritually pure (טהר), because they ate the Passover in a way that was not written"? How would they respond to the idea that the (Judahite) Levites had to perform the sacrifices on their behalf, since it would not be appropriate to let them do this themselves, unclean as they were (30:17)? How would they feel about Hezekiah's prayer, in 2 Chron. 30:18–19, that YHWH should forgive those "from Ephraim, Manasseh, Issachar, and Zebulun" for eating without the appropriate rites because their hearts were in the right place: "pardon ... everyone who prepares his heart to seek YHWH, god of our fathers, though not according to the purity [regulations] of the holy place" (2 Chron. 30:18–19)? Would they think themselves to be particularly in need of forgiveness for, presumably, pursuing ritual purification in their own time-honored ways?

So, while in the world the text constructs, the gestures of the Levites and of Hezekiah are meant to seem very gracious, I suspect they would read in the north as masterpieces of passive aggression instead. Certainly, this narrative at once asserts the superiority of southern religious practices over northern and presents a rhetorical submission of the northerners to it. We can also note, with respect to the question of the "common Israelite tradition" that the authors of 2 Chron. 30 were already aware – likely in the fifth century BCE – that there were meaningful differences between northerners and southerners where their religious practices were concerned. This text's account of joyful reunion is explicitly built around the consciousness that there was such a thing as a northern Israelite, in contrast to a southern Israelite, and that more than a political border divided them. Practices did too, like how to celebrate Passover, and how to purify before observances.

If we choose to understand this text not in terms of the absence of a conflict paradigm – nor of inclusion, or reconciliation – but instead as an expression of competition in other terms, we will understand it better. Nor would this be very surprising when we consider the general shape of how groups compete with each other. Obviously, texts like 2 Kings 17, and Josephus' account of the same event, are more explicit expressions of competition, disqualifying the northerners from participation in an Israelite identity by denying their Israelite heritage altogether. But, the

---

[46] Weingart, "What Makes an Israelite an Israelite?," 163; Pummer, *The Samaritans: A Profile*, 128.

watchword of ethnic competition is variety, and as any sports fan knows, disqualification is only one way to win.[47] And especially when ethnic competitions are ongoing, the staccato rhythm of claim and counterclaim is a constant goad to creativity. Over centuries, there is no telling what must be countered, then countered again.

We will not go far wrong if we start by thinking of competitive discourses in terms of who their audiences are intended to be. Certainly, these can sometimes be the whole world. When Turkish nationalists, for example, claim a historical connection to the mighty Hittite empire that dominated the region in the second millennium BCE, this is an assertion of their world-historical importance.[48] Lebanon's "Maronites" play up their "Phoenician 'roots'" for similar reasons.[49] For the Third Reich, it was very important that they *were* third, in a sequence. The second Reich was the German empire between 1871 and the end of World War I, and the first was the Holy Roman empire itself.[50] Asserting a deep, historical continuity with widely recognized powers is a way of laying claim to an august historical significance. Organizing the past into what Eviatar Zerubavel calls "time maps" – "general orientational guides" to what matters in the past, and what is contiguous to the present – is a very common way of making meaning out of it.[51]

Often, however, "competitive" traditions operate on a much lower level. We might say that they are "relational," which is to say that they are aimed specifically at the claims of one other group. In Transylvania, for example, divided between Hungarian and Romanian interests, there is an ongoing debate about whether the invasion of the Magyars, the ancestors of modern Hungarians, occurred "in a region inhabited by a thriving 'indigenous Roman' population," which would support the claim

---

[47] As F. Allan Hanson notes, the desire to classify absolutely "provides people with confidence that the world that they inhabit has a stable form, and that the things and events found in it are ordered, meaningful, and, to one degree or another, predictable. However, the sheer fact that many different systems of classification exist indicates that while it may be natural for human intelligence to classify, there is nothing about either human intelligence or external reality that requires that the classification be done in any particular way. Classificatory schemes are products of culture." (Hanson, *The Trouble with Culture*, 49–50).

[48] Tanyeri-Erdemir discusses the "Turkish Historical Society," founded by Ataturk in 1930, whose "first assignment ... was to investigate the roots of Turkish history and to come up with an historical thesis that could be tested through future research." The conclusion, actually, was not that the Turks were the descendants of the Hittites, but that the Hittites were in some sense the descendants of the original Turks (Tanyeri-Erdemir, "Archaeology as a Source of National Pride," 382).

[49] Zerubavel, *Time Maps*, 104–5.   [50] Ibid., 104–5, 52.   [51] Ibid., 109.

of the Romanians, "or one already laid waste by Slavic invaders," conceptually clearing the field for Hungarian claims. The competition here is less over who has the earliest claim than the *earlier* one, compared to the other. Each group seeks what Patrick Geary calls "primary acquisition" over the other – the moment after which all "subsequent migrations, invasions, or political absorptions have been illegitimate."[52]

In another evocative case, this one from modern Israel, some Palestinian traditions recount the descent of this people from either the Jebusites, who held Jerusalem before David conquered it, or the Philistines.[53] At first glance, it might seem surprising that these Palestinians should refer to the same text that their rivals do, and which has so often been used to justify the existence of the modern State in the eyes of the world. Here, however, we see exactly the phenomenon that I am talking about. By acknowledging the validity of both the Jewish claim and the tradition it comes from, these Palestinian storytellers are able to subvert it, advancing their own as superior even according to the logic that was used to displace them. Additionally, they are able to connect their contemporary dispossession rhetorically to an ancient one, burnishing the Palestinian claim to indigeneity while implying that the Israelis not only are colonizers themselves, but the descendants of colonizers.[54]

It is this other, softer, more subtle form of competition we see in 2 Chron. 30, and in other similar texts, as we will see. That it should receive attention first because of its strong contrast to 2 Kings 17 is hardly

---

[52] That is, laying claim to the moment that "established once and for all the geographical limits of legitimate ownership of lands. After these ... similar subsequent migrations, invasions, or political absorptions have all been illegitimate" (Geary, *The Myth of Nations*, 8). He adds, "[i]mplicit in [ethnic] claims is that there was a moment of 'primary acquisition,' the first century for the Germans, the fifth for the Franks, the sixth and seventh centuries for the Croats, the ninth and tenth for the Hungarians, and so on" (ibid., 12).

[53] Zerubavel, *Time Maps*, 106.

[54] Today, indigeneity is a legal category which identifies groups around the world, a "globally circulating and rights-bearing concept" in some ways traceable "to the 1957 International Labour Organization's (ILO) Convention 107 on 'Indigenous and Tribal Populations,' which rendered indigenous peoples legible in international law by categorizing culturally and geographically diverse groups of people as 'indigenous'" (Skog, "Thinking with Indigeneity," 2). Yet it is also often used as a generic term for those claiming to be the original inhabitants of a land in contrast to those at the top of contemporary power structures. See, for example, Rata, "The Transformation of Indigeneity"; Shields, "Rehearsing Indigeneity"; Graham and Penny, "Performing Indigeneity"; Eubanks and Sherpa, "We Are (Are We?) All Indigenous Here."

surprising – but that contrast doesn't mean it is intended to achieve a totally different purpose. As we have just seen, sometimes the most effective form of ethnic competition involves playing the same game as your competitors – but playing the same game does not mean *becoming the other team*.[55] And between these forms of competition, the relational and the oppositional, the former most benefits from segmented identity systems like the twelve tribes tradition in ways that also presage how "Israels" elsewhere in the world account for their own unique characteristics even in the absence of competitions.

2.3 THE CAPABILITIES OF SEGMENTED SYSTEMS

Once again, segmented genealogical traditions are those that present identities in the form of a kind of family tree. The twelve tribes of Israel tradition is one, and there are many others. By their very nature, these traditions express the idea of a shared, overarching identity that nevertheless preserves the independent existence and special character of various sub-identities within it. As a result, members of those sub-identities can, and frequently do, compete with each other not by denying the right of the other sub-identities to participate in the overarching one, but by redescribing the nature and significance of the relationships between them.[56] Judah, for example, can claim to be one of Jacob's eldest sons in the birth narratives in Genesis 29–30, therefore being superior to younger ones. Joseph, a northern tribe, can explain in Genesis 37 that despite being Jacob's second youngest, he is his favorite. By such maneuvering do participants in segmented systems compete through the systems themselves.

---

[55] Indeed, as Jonathan Z. Smith observes: "Otherness is not a descriptive category, an artifact of the perception of difference or commonality. Nor is it the result of the determination of biological descent or affinity. It is a political and linguistic project, a matter of rhetoric and judgment ... 'otherness' is not some absolute state of being ... [it is] a situational category ... a transactional matter, an affair of the 'in between.'" As a result, "while the 'other' may be perceived as being either LIKE-US or NOT-LIKE-US, he is, in fact, most problematic when he is TOO-MUCH-LIKE-US, or when he claims to BE-US" (Smith, *Relating Religion*, 275).

[56] Again, "basic to the segmentary pattern is the principle of fission and fusion whereby members of a total social field can recombine at different levels of integration to form aggregates of varying size" (Lincoln, *Discourse and the Construction of Society*, 19). These patterns can present and justify "hierarchic order and ... differential rank and privileges," so they are "always subject to contestation" (ibid., 173). For the same reason, they are very useful.

The function, or functionality, of segmented systems has never played much role in considerations of the construction of Israelite identities in any context, to their great detriment, as I showed in the discussion in the first chapter. Segmented systems have not, however, been ignored everywhere, and scholars of ancient Greek myth especially are increasingly aware of the importance of understanding how they fundamentally work in order to understand the expressions of identity that are constructed through them.[57] In ancient Greece itself, "Panhellenic" constructions of Greek identity emerged largely over the course of the sixth and fifth centuries BCE, and in part through the construction of an embracing, segmented genealogical system based on descent from the eponymous Hellen, son of Deucalion.[58]

This Hellen, as I have argued before, has a place in ancient Greek traditions and identity constructions not too dissimilar to Jacob in the Hebrew Bible.[59] His relationship to the so-called "subethnicities" of ancient Greece – in reality, groups that, for the most part, pre-existed Panhellenism – is often mediated through eponymous descendants, just as it is with Jacob. There is, for example, Ion for the Ionians, Doros for the Dorians, Achaeus for the Achaeans, and so on.[60] Over time, as I discussed in the last chapter, the basic structure of this emerging tradition became a playground through which members of these constituencies pursued various aims, often against each other. The web of relationships provided the raw materials for all kinds of efforts to stake claims, justify wars, pursue trade relations, and so on, often by rearranging, reinterpreting, or adding to them.[61] In other words, in Lee E. Patterson's phrase, new claims were made "not by refuting the myth on which [they are] based qua

---

[57] Fowler, "Genealogical Thinking"; West, *The Hesiodic Catalogue of Women*; Rutherford, "Mestra at Athens"; Irwin, "Gods among Men?"; McInerney, "Ethnos and Ethnicity in Early Greece"; Finkelberg, *Greeks and Pre-Greeks*; Finkelberg, "The *Cypria*, the *Iliad* and the Problem of Multiformity."

[58] Hall, *Ethnic Identity in Greek Antiquity*, 42–43; Malkin, *The Returns of Odysseus*, 29; Rutherford, "Mestra at Athens," 101.

[59] Tobolowsky, *The Sons of Jacob*, 6–7.   [60] Hall, *Hellenicity*, 56.

[61] Lee E. Patterson's comprehensive study of "kinship myth" in ancient Greece contained, as a "surprising result," the "extent to which communities found ways to bridge their local myths through some Panhellenic stemma (usually one of the sons of Hellen) and even reconciled these accounts despite variations in the respective local traditions" (Patterson, *Kinship Myth in Ancient Greece*, 20). He describes, among others, the people of Magnesia using their purported kinship with the Sameans of Cephalonia to promote a local festival, the people of Lampascus asking for an alliance with Rome on the basis of their shared "putative Trojan origins," the Tegeans arguing for leadership of the right wing at Plataea on the basis of their descent from Echemus over Hyllus, son of Herakles, a

mythology ... but by adjusting the details of the myth itself as if a revision of history has been wrought."[62]

So, for example, in a typical version of the "Hellenic genealogy," the eponymous Ion is the son of the mortals Xouthos and Creusa, like his brother, the equally eponymous Achaeaus. In Euripides' play *Ion*, however, it turns out that his real father is Apollo.[63] Obviously, having a god for an ancestor burnishes the prestige of the Ionians, among whom Euripides' own Athenians were numbered – and not only absolutely, but in comparison to their now half-brothers, the Achaeans. Another example I have used before is the invention of a "Protogeneia," meaning "first-born," as a daughter of Hellen, in order to elevate the status of her Aetolian descendants, through her son Aethlios.[64]

It is easy to see not only how but why participants in segmented systems might choose to compete with each other through the system, rather than outside of it. Indeed, the appeal goes well beyond mere functionality. We might, for example, usefully think in terms of a concept pioneered by Arjun Appadurai in the early 1980s – the idea that the past is a "scarce resource." Basically, our awareness that those who do the work of redescribing identities are indeed quite creative might cause us to suspect that the past, in the hands of these individuals, is a "limitless and plastic symbolic resource, infinitely susceptible to the whims of contemporary interest."[65] In other words, we might think anyone can come up with any story they want, which might ultimately produce a lot of texts like 2 Kings 17. But in reality – and because ethnic claims do need to be legible to their intended audiences – individual storytellers who want their claims to be perceived as authoritative cannot tell any story at all about the past, but only those that will be intelligible in context. In any given case, there are only a few traditions – a "scarce" amount – that are likely to provide the necessary authority.[66]

---

sign of their people's military prowess, and many other such claims (ibid., 1–2, 7, 23–24). See also Tobolowsky, "The Problem of Reubenite Primacy," 31–32.

[62] Patterson, *Kinship Myth in Ancient Greece*, 8.

[63] West, *The Hesiodic Catalogue of Women*, 141; Tobolowsky, *The Sons of Jacob*, 101.

[64] West, *The Hesiodic Catalogue of Women*, 141; Tobolowsky, *The Sons of Jacob*, 179.

[65] Appadurai, "The Past as a Scarce Resource," 201, 203. He adds that the constraints which turn the past from universal to scarce resource involve "authority," a "cultural consensus as to the kinds of source, origin or guarantor of 'pasts' which are required for their credibility"; "continuity," "depth," and "interdependence" (ibid., 203).

[66] "... ethnic groups seeking to accentuate their social boundaries may represent themselves as separated by deeply incompatible cultures. But what I think has less often been noted is that processes of ethnic opposition and boundary-formation may be accompanied by

Where segmented frameworks are concerned, the mutual participation of different groups in what is ostensibly the same identity concept creates the *condition* of scarcity – only claims advanced through the system will be mutually intelligible. For the same reason, however, a shared system offers considerable advantages to its participants, since all already agree on the authority of a particular set of traditions which can be manipulated.[67] In other words, mutual participation means a mutual vocabulary for claim and counterclaim, especially when the parties involved agree that the others are members of a shared system.

Meanwhile, an underexplored peculiarity of the twelve tribes tradition makes competition through, rather than against, the system more likely. As I observed all the way back in this book's introduction, almost every claimant to an Israelite identity needs to acknowledge the continued validity of the entire structure to even be visible as Israel in the first place – meaning that the Judahites, the Mormons, the Beta Israel and so on would not necessarily appear to be Israelites at first glance, given where they are and how they construct what Israel is. At the same time, very few of the world's Israels claim to represent the entirety of Israel in and of themselves, and Israel and Judah are no exception. The end result is that most traditions about Israel actually function as an explicit assertion that there are other heirs to Israel out there somewhere. It should hardly be surprising, then, that some authors would choose to address the potential threat of counterclaims proactively.

Certainly, 2 Kings 17 is one way to address the threat of other Israels, while preserving the concept of "all Israel," by rhetorically sending the entire rest of Israel away. But 2 Chron. 30 represents another way that is both easier and likely more convincing. In it, there are still Israelites in the north after the conquest, but not only are their religious practices inferior to those of the Judahites, they know it. They troop down to Jerusalem not only to celebrate the holiday, but to acknowledge the spiritual leadership of Jerusalem's priests and the secular leadership of Hezekiah, both so gracefully offered despite their manifold faults.

---

inflated perceptions, not only of dissimilarity, but also of resemblance. In other words, ethnic groups may sometimes conceive themselves as in conflict not so much because they have irreconcilably different identities, but rather because they have irreconcilable claims or aspirations to the *same* identities" (Harrison, "Identity as a Scarce Resource," 239).

[67] More recently, Isabella Sandwell has argued that "because what it means to be a member of one religion can only be constructed in relation to what it means to be a member of another religion, religious interaction is always a prerequisite for the existence of religious identities" (Sandwell, *Religious Identity in Late Antiquity*, 3–4).

There is good reason why the biblical account of the division of the kingdoms is construed explicitly in tribal terms, ten and two, even though it is hardly clear what the twelve tribes of Israel could have meant in the Davidic monarchy, and certainly thereafter. There is good reason why 2 Kings 17 claims explicitly that it is the tribe of Judah that remains, not the kingdom or the people (2 Kgs. 17:18). And it is the same reason why 2 Chron. 30 is explicit that there were those from Ephraim, Manasseh, Zebulun, Asher, and Issachar that came, and those from these tribes that refused (2 Chron. 30:10–11, 18). In fact, there is a Samaritan account of this tradition that I will discuss in a moment, but it is even more explicit, describing the "eight tribes of Israel" and the "two and a half tribes" of the Samaritans along with the tribes of Judah.[68] "All Israel" can be divided into parts because it was born divided into parts. Being divided, it can have different experiences, different practices, even different *Torahs* and remain Israel. But some Israels, as the saying goes, might be more equal than others.

In short, the segmented structure of Israelite identity lends itself to just the sort of competition we see in 2 Chron. 30 for many different reasons – a form that begins with an acceptance, rather than a denial, of the other's claim to be Israel but goes on from there. And when we raise our eyes from these biblical accounts of the conquest and its aftermath, we see that it is this form that is broadly characteristic of many examples of the ongoing competition between Israelites and Judahites, Samaritans and Jews in different texts. So, for example, in *Massekhet Kutim*, the extra-Talmudic tractate dealing with the Samaritans, the rabbinical authors ask themselves "when shall we receive them back?"[69] They answer, "when they renounce Mt. Gerizim and confess Jerusalem," as well as when they accept the resurrection of the dead.[70] We could, if we wanted, see this as an example of an "inclusivist" approach too, since it asserts the common origins of Jews and Samaritans and suggests the possibility of future reconciliation, just as 2 Chron. 30 does. Since, however, this reconciliation would first require the Samaritans to *stop being Samaritans*, the rhetorical gesture is rather empty. Instead, the pretense of shared ancestry is used as a stage upon which to enact a criticism of Samaritan practices.

[68] Anderson and Giles, *Tradition Kept*, 251.

[69] Schiffman observes that "the process of separation of the two communities was completed in *Masekhet Kutim* and other 'post-talmudic' texts" (Schiffman, "The Samaritans in Amoraic Halakhah," 371).

[70] Hjelm, *The Samaritans and Early Judaism*, 11. I am grateful to Matthew Chalmers for his advice on this point.

Meanwhile, 2 Kings 17 is hardly the only time that biblical authors position their preferred community as the only true heirs of Israel by rhetorically sending other parts away, or by refusing to acknowledge them. When Judah is conquered by the Babylonians in 586 BCE, a number of biblical texts give the strong impression that anyone who was anyone was sent into Babylonian Exile, the so-called "myth of the empty land."[71] It isn't true; many Judahites remained behind just as many Israelites had in 722 BCE. Then, when the Persians conquered the Babylonians in 539 BCE, and supposedly allowed the Judahites to go back to the land of their ancestors, we get the impression that anyone who was anyone returned, as well, and that isn't true either. The Murashu family archives, the Elephantine papyri, and other pieces of evidence testify to a thriving Judahite diasporic experience, already and forever after.[72] But the cumulative effect of all of these divisions is that, as far as many biblical texts are concerned, the only remaining heirs of Israel by the time the biblical accounts end are the members of the Judahite "Returnee" community – who, presumably, were therefore responsible for giving them final shape.

As for Samaritan literature, the unfortunate fact is that besides the Samaritan Pentateuch, we have nothing that clearly survives from the era of Samaritan origins. And since the Samaritan Pentateuch ends with the death of Moses, as the biblical Pentateuch does, that means we do not have early Samaritan accounts of events like the Assyrian conquest. There are, however, quite a number of narrative collections, often called "chronicles," which have considerable status in Samaritan culture, prominently including *Asaṭir*, *Tūlida*, the Samaritan Book of Joshua, *Kitāb al-Tarikh* of Abu l-Fath, and *Shalshala*.[73] Most of these appear to be medieval in origin, if based on earlier traditions, while two, called the *New Chronicle* and *Chronicle II* or the *Sepher Ha-Yamim*, were continuously updated until the turn of the twentieth century.[74] Between them, there are a

---

[71] Barstad, *The Myth of the Empty Land*; Lipschits and Blenkinsopp, "After the 'Myth of the Empty Land'"; Middlemas, "Going Beyond the Myth of the Empty Land."

[72] The Murashu family was a family of bankers at Nippur, and the Elephantine papyri come from a Persian garrison of Judahites in the Nile Delta. See Clay, *Business Documents*; Coogan, "Life in the Diaspora"; Coogan, "More Yahwistic Names"; Porten, *The Elephantine Papyri in English*; Bolin, "The Temple of Yahu"; Rom-Shiloni, "The Untold Stories"; Granerød, "Canon and Archive."

[73] Pummer, *The Samaritans: A Profile*, 243–48. See, also Hjelm, *The Samaritans and Early Judaism*, 97–102.

[74] For important critical editions of the *Kitab al-Tarikh*, the *Samaritan Book of Joshua*, the *New Chronicle*, and *Chronicle II* see Crane, *The Samaritan Chronicle*; McDonald,

number of stories that resonate with 2 Chron. 30's treatment of north–
south relations, and with *Massekhet Kutim.*

One story, for example, appears in slightly different forms in the *New
Chronicle,* the Samaritan Book of Joshua, and *Kitāb al-Tarikh,* having to
do with the Babylonian Exile. In all probability, few if any northerners
actually went into Exile with the Judahites, but these traditions are
nevertheless set there.[75] In all three, when the time comes to return to
Israel, each group invites the other to come with them and become, in the
words of the Samaritan Book of Joshua, "one word and one soul."[76]
Here, too, there is an acknowledgment of shared ancestry, and at least a
rhetorical hope for reconciliation.

By this point, however, it should hardly be surprising that neither
group is interested in following the other's lead, and the result is a public
disputation before the Babylonian king between leaders of each community.[77] Neither should it be surprising that, in these Samaritan traditions,
it is the Samaritans who win this contest of scriptures, and then a miracle
occurs: the Samaritan leader allows the Samaritan Pentateuch to be
thrown into a fire where, of course, it does not burn. When Zerubbabel
does the same, his text burns to a crisp. Despite this miracle, the southerners fail to change their ways, and each group travels back to its
separate region, alone – and an "all Israel" premise is used to explain
why one part of it is better than another with just a hint of pathos. In this
tradition, the Judahites cannot accept the truth even in the face of
a miracle.

Above, I mentioned that there is even a Samaritan account of
Hezekiah's invitation to the northerners, which appears in *Chronicle II.*
In this remarkable text, Hezekiah sends letters to "all Israel, from Beer-
Sheba to Dan," an even more ambitious effort than in the Bible. They go to
the "cities of Samaria" where the "eight tribes . . . laughed them to scorn."

The Samaritan Chronicle II; Stenhouse, *The Kitab Al-Tarikh of Abu'l Fath*; Bowman,
Samaritan Documents; Anderson and Giles, *Tradition Kept*. See also Levy-Rubin, *The
Continuatio of the Samaritan Chronicle.*

[75] "As far as we know, Samaria did not participate in the rebellions against King
Nebuchadnezzar, and as a consequence most of its major towns did not experience the
serious losses that Jerusalem and other major Judean urban centers experienced in the
early 6th century" (Knoppers, *Jews and Samaritans,* 121).

[76] Crane, *The Samaritan Chronicle,* 113.

[77] In each version the Judahite champion is Zerubbabel, who, in Ezra 1–4, was the leader of
the first Judahite "Return." In the *New Chronicle,* the Samaritan champion is Abdiel the
High Priest, in the Book of Joshua and the *Kitab* it is "Sanballat the Levite," a common
figure of Samaritan lore.

Then they came to "Shechem, and handed the letters to the chiefs of the community of the Samaritan Israelites," who asked: "How can we substitute evil for good and forsake the chosen place Mount Gerizim" for Jerusalem? The narrative ends with the Samaritans sending their own messengers to Jerusalem, inviting Hezekiah to their Passover, but he refused, "and the people of Judah performed the Passover offering in the city of Jebis in the second month by themselves."[78] In this Samaritan version, Israel is divided into three parts, not two, and no northerners go to Jerusalem, but the incident provides the Samaritan authors an opportunity to assert the specific superiority of one site over another, and one set of practices over another – as the biblical version does.[79]

We can see how an awareness of more subtle forms of competition can help us understand the nature of the relationship between these two groups of self-identifying Israelites in various periods. We can also see how the existence of continuities in the material record, and even of outright expressions of commonality, does not mean an absence of crucial differences and awareness of them too – especially when mediated through segmented identity systems that are themselves statements of difference within similarity. In each of the stories just discussed, the inaugurating premise of an "all Israel" identity divided into parts is what lays the groundwork for an explanation of why one part is better than another and how it came to be this way, which is to say, competition, not communal identity. This is common both in competitions between groups generally and for segmented identity traditions specifically.

What we also see, however, is a crucial feature of how the machinery of "becoming Israel" works, everywhere in the world. That is, the ability to explain differences which emerge out of the segmented structure

---

[78] Anderson and Giles, *Tradition Kept*, 251.

[79] Other Samaritan chronicles have similar stories and details. In the *Kitab*, for example, Saul, first king of Israel, leads all but "the tribe of Phinehas and the tribe of Joseph, and ... a few others from among the tribes" from "the Holy Mountain," meaning Gerizim (ibid., 156). Interestingly, this chronicle also describes the Babylonian conquest under Nebuchadnezzar as a time when "the land ... became desolate of all ... the children of Israel, the children of Judah, and the community of Jehoiakim. And the king of Assyria brought in foreigners and settled them in the land of Canaan in place of the children of Israel" (ibid., 232). The complexity of this narrative – which translocates the "two-way" deportations of 2 Kings 17 to a considerably later period, includes both Judah and Israel in it, and apparently conflates Assyrians and Babylonians – is somewhat typical of Samaritan histories, but can also be read as a denial of the special status of the Judahites as those who escaped replacement.

of Israelite identity operates equally well in the absence of competitions. In other words, the ability to explain why something is better is also the ability to explain why something is simply different. And given how many different Israels there are in the world, this is an absolute necessity.

In each of the stories we have seen so far, the parts of the whole undergo different experiences and make different choices, taking on different characters as a result. The authors of all these texts, aside from 2 Kings 17, hold out hope that these changes can be reversed, and "all Israel" can be restored, but this hope is rhetorical only. The wish that the northerners will – supposedly once again, but actually for the first time – acknowledge the greater validity of southern practice, or vice versa, is also a way of staking a claim to greater validity. In this way, the separation of Israel into parts functions as a prompt for competitions and as a method of explaining the differences that make competition necessary.

In chapters to come, we will see many constructions of Israel that are much more obviously different from the biblical version thereof than the Samaritans' own. There, too, explanations will need to be given for how this came to be. In many of these cases, what I will call the "separable" structure of Israelite identity, conveyed by its segmented structure, will not always operate on the level of the individual tribe, as indeed it did not in all the examples described above. A broader "separability" will govern accounts of Israel in the next chapter, for example, where the separation of Israel between world Jewry and the "Lost Tribes of Israel" allowed descriptions of one to become a mirror of the other. Nevertheless, it will still be the fact that Israel was conceptually born divided into parts that simultaneously allows for one Israel to compete with another and for Israel to go on and on, in the words of John Milton, "to fresh woods, and pastures new."

2.4 THE INTERNAL LOGIC OF SEGMENTED SYSTEMS

On September 12, 1949, barely a year after the founding of the State of Israel, Yitzhak Ben-Zvi, then a member of the fledgling Knesset and soon to be President of Israel, rose in assembly to ask the foreign secretary a question. Was it "known to the government," he wondered, that there were people living in the vicinity of ancient Shechem who "are associated, according to their tradition, with the seed of Abraham, Isaac, and Jacob, and believe in the Torah of Moses, according to the special Samaritan version?" Would they be granted citizenship in the new Jewish state?

He was told that they would.[80] And why not? The State, whose founding mythology constructed it as the modern incarnation of ancient Israel, could be home to all of Israel's children.

Over the next two decades, however, the question of who precisely deserved the rights of Israeli citizenship by virtue of their descent gradually reached a crisis. The problem was that the 1950 "Law of Return," which codified the "Right of Return" to those of Jewish descent, did not offer a definition of what Jewish descent meant. So, in 1962, for example, one "Brother Daniel," a Carmelite monk, attempted to claim the Right on the basis of the fact that he had been born Shmuel Rufeisin, a Polish Jew. Ultimately, Israel's Supreme Court would refuse him, arguing that his conversion to another religion invalidated his Jewish descent, but similar issues kept being raised.[81] In the late 1960s, an Israeli Jew by the name of Benjamin Shalit sued to have his children registered as members of the "Jewish nation" because of their heritage alone: he was an atheist, his wife was not Jewish, and the children had not been raised in the faith.[82] Initially refused by the registering authorities, Shalit would eventually triumph at the Supreme Court, but by a bare 5–4 margin.[83]

In 1970, on the heels of the Shalit case, the Law of Return was amended to add the missing definition, and for the most part, this amendment greatly expanded access to the Right. In its new form, the Right now extended to "a child and a grandchild of a Jew, the spouse of a Jew, the spouse of a child of a Jew and the spouse of a grandchild of a Jew, except for a person who has been a Jew and has voluntarily changed his religion."[84] In other words, there were to be no more Brother Daniels, but even the grandchildren of a mixed marriage might hope to claim it otherwise.[85]

Whether intended or not, this more explicit effort to link the Right of Return to a specifically Jewish identity spelled trouble for the Samaritans, a problem which was not long in raising its head. In one case from the mid-1980s, two Samaritan women applied to be married to two Jewish men, a practice technically frowned upon in both sets of religious laws but

---

[80] Ben-Zvi, *The Book of the Samaritans*, 365; Schreiber, *The Comfort of Kin*, 57.

[81] Edelman, "Who Is an Israeli?," 95.

[82] "Religion: Who Is a Jew?," *Time*; Special, James Feron to the *New York Times*, "Israeli Court Rules a Jew Can Be One by Nationality" (Published 1970).

[83] Perez, "Israel's Law of Return," 61.

[84] *Jewish Virtual Library*, "Israel's Basic Laws," www.jewishvirtuallibrary.org/israel-s-law-of-return.

[85] Pummer, *The Samaritans: A Profile*, 296–97.

habitually permitted without issue nonetheless.[86] This time, however, a rabbinical court determined that if the sisters wished to have Jewish weddings, they needed first to convert to Judaism, which was to many Samaritans "a great insult and injustice."[87] Shortly thereafter, a trio of Samaritans who attempted to register as Israeli citizens – one from Kiryat Luza, two upon moving to Holon – were turned down unexpectedly.[88] Worse was to come.

The State of Israel has a complex dual court system which I will discuss at greater length in Chapter 5. For now, suffice it to say that there is a religious court system for matters of religious law and a secular court system for other matters. The two, naturally, sometimes overlap, and when they do the secular court's rulings take precedence. In 1985–86, in response to events like those just described, the Supreme Rabbinical Court officially ruled that "Samaritans are to be treated as Gentiles," countermanding the custom and practices established by Ben-Zvi and others.[89] In 1992, the secular courts followed suit, specifically on the basis of the fact that Samaritans are neither born to a Jewish mother nor, technically, of the Jewish religion.[90] And while the secular courts reversed themselves in 1994, restoring Samaritan access to the Right of Return, the rabbinic courts still have not, leaving this community in legal limbo and vulnerable to future changes in status.[91]

All else aside, the basic pattern we see here – of sporadic acceptance and rejection, and of acceptance in some quarters and not others – is likely a better reflection of the relationship between Judahite and Samarian "Israelites" and early Jews and Samaritans than any reconstruction that involves alternating phases of inclusion and exclusion. The reason is simple. Once we recognize that Israelite identity was constructed at least a little differently in Israel and Judah from the beginning – because they *were* Israel and Judah – there would have been grounds for emphasizing difference, whenever it was useful. And once we recognize that 2 Kings 17 likely does represent a minority view – meaning that most Judahites could, in fact, acknowledge the Israelite descent of the northerners after

---

[86] Schreiber, *The Comfort of Kin*, 58–59.   [87] Pummer, *The Samaritans: A Profile*, 296.
[88] Schreiber, *The Comfort of Kin*, 59–60.
[89] Corinaldi, "The Personal Status of the Samaritans in Israel," 287.
[90] Ibid., 290. See also Pummer, *The Samaritans: A Profile*, 296.
[91] Corinaldi, "The Personal Status of the Samaritans in Israel," 287; Pummer, *The Samaritans: A Profile*, 296. For details of the 1949, 1970, and 1994 rulings, see Corinaldi, "The Personal Status of the Samaritans in Israel," 290–91. For further discussion see Schreiber, *The Comfort of Kin*, 58–59.

722 BCE, whatever they did with that acknowledgment – we can see that there would have been grounds for emphasizing similarity as well. Likely, both could simply be used whenever it made sense to use them.

This is not to say that each era from ancient Israel to the present was lacking strong tendencies in one direction or the other. It is indeed likely that 2 Kings 17 represents a minority view, and that sometime in the first few centuries CE, Samaritans and Jews began to regard each other *as* other to an extent few had before. Still, the ability to push against tendency is inherent in the segmented structure of the tradition all of these Israels embrace – and which embraces them. In fact, segmented structures are useful in part because they allow their participants to stress their affinities or differences, depending on circumstances.[92] And it does seem as if expressions of genuine affinity sometimes appeared even after distinctions between Samaritans and Jews grew firmer. Reinhard Pummer mentions one instance, in a study of interactions in the city of Caesarea, in which certain Samaritans may have gone to live among the Jews in order to escape a Roman ban on circumcision.[93]

Another episode frequently cited by proponents of the "inclusivist" position in recent years involves the members of the Judahite garrison at Elephantine, in Egypt, serving the Persian empire. It turns out that, in the fifth century BCE, there were not two temples of YHWH in the region – Jerusalem and Gerizim – but at least three.[94] In 411 BCE, however, local Egyptian priests burned the Elephantine temple to the ground.[95] In response, certain members of the community there sent letters to both Israelite and Judahite authorities asking for their help in rebuilding. Many have seen in these letters, and in their apparent success, a sign that cooperation between the heirs of Israel in the region was a relatively common and natural occurrence at the time.[96]

---

[92] As Bruce Lincoln observes, "within segmentary systems, affinity in one set of circumstances can become estrangement in another, as when persons who had previously been encompassed within a single social formation redefine themselves as members of smaller, differentiated, and competing groups" (Lincoln, *Discourse and the Construction of Society*, 20).

[93] Pummer, "Religions in Contact and Conflict," 347.

[94] Bolin, "The Temple of Yahu," 130; Kratz, "The Second Temple of Jeb and of Jerusalem," 252–53; Lindenberger, "What Ever Happened to Vidranga?," 135; Dušek, "Archaeology and Texts in the Persian Period," 118; Porten, *Archives from Elephantine*, 278–98.

[95] Bolin, "The Temple of Yahu," 130.

[96] Knoppers, *Jews and Samaritans*, 119–20; Weingart, "What Makes an Israelite an Israelite?," 173; Pummer, *The Samaritans: A Profile*, 24.

Personally, I think it is most likely that if the Elephantine episode shows anything, it is the opposite: that already Samarian and Jerusalem authorities did *not* commonly work together. It is true that Bagohi, the governor of Judah, and Delaiah, a Samarian leader, pledged their mutual aid in a remarkable joint response combining north and south. But Bagohi himself, a Persian governor of the province, was likely neither a Judahite nor a Yahwist. Meanwhile, the letter writer from Elephantine, one Jedaniah, explicitly mentions that he wrote a letter, "to Jehohanan the High Priest and his colleagues the priests who are in Jerusalem and to Ostares the brother of Anani and the nobles of the Jews," that went unanswered.[97] The silence of the Jerusalem priesthood may well suggest that Judahites of a certain stripe did not understand the Yahwists of Elephantine as co-religionists, and perhaps by extension, not the northerners either, even in this early period. Nevertheless, the point remains that the destruction of a temple is precisely the sort of thing that would make someone appeal for help to anyone they think might listen – however they may have felt even the day before.

Here we reach a point of considerable importance for the rest of the book. This, of course, is a book about many Israels – ancient Israels and modern Israels; Israels in America, in Africa, and in the half-known lands, from the perspective of medieval Europeans, beyond the rim of the Crusades. It is about Israels in *terra incognito*, Israels across the Sambatyon or across the ocean, rumors of Israel, and ideas about Israel – Israels hurrying from parts unknown, to save, or to destroy. It is about a world as brimming with Israels as the fabled Argo was with heroes. And there is the rub. None of these Israels understand *themselves* as one of "many Israels." "Many" is just what it looks like from outside.

For those who lay claim to an Israelite identity, by contrast, there is only one Israel. Each claimant understands themselves as the living heirs of the original Israel – the protagonist of the biblical story wherever they are in the world and whatever they look like. The problem, for most of these claimants, is that every Israel is in fact constructed differently from all the rest, and sometimes quite a bit differently. This means that every self-proclaimed heir of Israel needs to explain, at once, how they came to be different while remaining part of *the* Israel, eternal and indissoluble.

The twelve tribes tradition is, above all, a wonderful tool for the making of just this kind of explanation. For one thing, as I said at the

---

[97] Albertz, "The Controversy about Judean versus Israelite Identity." Translation from Porten, *The Elephantine Papyri in English*, 142.

very beginning, it is already a statement that many different entities are all, somehow, Israel. If Reuben and Simeon can both be part of Israel, despite being different tribes, than the Judahites and the Samaritans, or the Mormons, or the Beta Israel can all be part of Israel. The framework itself says nothing, and prescribes nothing, about how different its constituent entities can be and remain Israel. Thus, the tradition very easily accommodates explanations of how part of Israel went from A to B, and changed shape in this or that way, while the rest did not.

Additionally, the twelve tribes tradition embodies what we might call a "primordialist premise." Primordialism, again, is the model of ethnicity that says we stay who are ancestors were, *ad infinitum*, and that identity, an inherent and intrinsic feature of who we are, survives anything history can throw at it.[98] If "all Israel" can survive separation into tribes, it can survive separation between kingdoms – and all the wars, kings, and different experiences that befell one and not the other. If it can survive the border between "Israels" intact, it can survive far greater separations still – once again, across oceans, continents, and great gulfs of time.

On the one hand, the twelve tribes tradition is extremely adept at making just the sorts of explanations that grease the wheels of "becoming Israel" as a historical practice. The arrangement of discrete elements within the segmented structure of the whole is what imbues it with the capacity to create new visions of Israel continually while costuming the fact that there is anything new about them. And these explanations can work better than we might think. Intuitively, it might seem as if one independently constructed Israel would always refuse to acknowledge the claims of the other, but in fact this is not even true in Israel today. As we will see in Chapter 5, the Beta Israel of Ethiopia were acknowledged by the Israeli courts, were granted access to the Right of Return, and ultimately came – and were brought – to Israel, where they are citizens to this day.

On the other hand, the weakness of the twelve tribes tradition as a means of making explanations is that there is only one kind of explanation it can make, without breaking the animating conceit of one Israel,

---

[98] As Anthony Smith observes, "early explanations of nationalism tended to be greatly influenced by organic varieties of nationalism. Nations were seen as the natural and primordial divisions of humanity ... What is now termed *primordialism* emerged from these widely accepted assumptions. For the primordialists, the key to the nature, power, and incidence of nations and nationalism lies in the rootedness of the nation in kinship, ethnicity, and the genetic bases of human existence" (Smith, *Myths and Memories of the Nation*, 3–4).

not many. These are what we might call "experiential" explanations: they attribute the differences that arise between claimants to Israel to the vagaries of experience – this part of Israel went to that place, had that experience as a result, and emerged with a new set of traditions, or similar. This capacity for experiential explanation can be a powerful tool. In the Samaritans' case, they explain their differences from the Israel described in the Hebrew Bible as a consequence of the perfidy of Eli and Ezra, which they evaded. Similarly, in 2 Kings 17, Judahite authors explain their difference from the post-722 BCE northerners, whom they acknowledge worship YHWH, by claiming that they are not really Israelites at all.

As we will see in later chapters, the same experiential logic is equally available, and for the same reasons, to explain how, say, members of the tribe of Manasseh made their way to America, experienced revelations that produced their holy book, and ultimately forgot their heritage – as in the Mormon tradition discussed in Chapter 4. Strange as it may seem, it is not really any more difficult to explain how a part of Israel ended up with Gerizim and the Samaritan Pentateuch, or Jerusalem and the biblical Torah, than it is to explain how another ended up with the Book of Mormon and the Hill Cumorah – the mountain upon which Joseph Smith Jr. discovered the golden plates from which he translated the Book. But that is the point: only the same kind of explanation is possible, in each case, whatever form it takes.

The problem this raises is that, despite the prominence of this experiential logic, the differences between constructions of Israel are not generally – and possibly never – actually the result of the different experiences of a primordialist Israelite entity. Even in these first two chapters, where we may be talking about two groups who actually do descend, biologically, from the original Israelites – or, in the case of the Judahites, perhaps not – experiential explanations are too deterministic. They suggest that later Judahite and Israelite visions of Israelite identity changed only *because* of historical experiences and otherwise would have stayed the same. Instead, it is simply the nature of identity to change, often unpredictably, through its continual application as a medium for the articulation of claims of all sorts, and for the making of claim and counterclaim.

Moreover, the ability of the twelve tribes tradition to explain is, in any given context, limited by another crucial detail: because there can be only one Israel in the world, no explanation can challenge the foundational premises of what Israel has come to mean in a given context. When, in later years, the restoration of Israel came to have an apocalyptic significance, for example, it would have been almost impossible to discover an Israel, or become an Israel, that was not on some level apocalyptic. Just so, the discovery of Israel in various places, throughout the last two thousand years, has always been shaped by how Israel was understood at the moment of discovery, which is another good reason to study "becoming Israel" diachronically.

In the case of the Samaritans in contemporary Israel, the combination of the rhetorical openness of twelve tribes constructions of Israel to other Israels with the actual impermeability of any given construction is a big part of the problem. It is hardly impossible, after all, that the Samaritans might receive the rights of citizenship in Israel not in spite of their Samaritan descent, but because of it – because, in the words of Michael Corinaldi, a lawyer who has often championed the Samaritan cause, of "their kinship to the tribes of Israel (as distinct from that of Judah)."[99] It would not be hard to explain that the descendants of different tribes of Israel had different historical experiences and emerged in the present as different, but equally valid heirs of Israel; in fact, this is more or less what seems to have happened.

The problem is that such an explanation would trespass against the need to preserve the conceptual unity of "all Israel" *as it is specifically constructed in Jewish tradition*. In that tradition, the Jewish people are not so much understood as the descendants of the people of Judah, as biblical figures are themselves supposed to be more or less Jewish. Of course, even the most conservative religious authority is aware that the bases of contemporary Jewish practices, especially the two Talmuds, were only composed long after the biblical canon was completed. They are, however, often supposed to be reflections of an oral law as old as the *Torah* itself – part of a "dual Torah" Moses received on Sinai.[100]

What this Jewish construction of a Jewish ancient Israel means, for both Jews and Samaritans, is that, as a matter of official policy, Israeli

---

[99] Corinaldi, "The Personal Status of the Samaritans in Israel," 291. The full quote is: "they hold themselves to be the true keepers of the law and the genuine representatives of the ancient people of Israel, affirming their kinship to the tribes of Israel (as distinct from that of Judah)."

[100] "The rabbinic view of the Sinaitic origin of the oral Torah naturally lets M [the Mishnah] begin at Sinai, too. Alongside this theory of a coexistence of oral and written Torah from the beginning, the other traditional opinion is that oral Torah derives from the written, and is the latter's consistent exegesis" (Strack and Stemberger, *Introduction to the Talmud and Midrash*, 142). See also Neusner, *Introduction to Rabbinic Literature*, xx.

authorities can only accommodate constructions of Israel that they can also characterize *as* Jewish. The Beta Israel, mentioned above, are a case in point. On the one hand, the Beta Israel community in Ethiopia originally had traditions and practices that were far more different from those of normative Judaism than the Samaritans' are. On the other, there is now a long Jewish tradition of regarding the Beta Israel as the practitioners of a pre-Talmudic form of Judaism.[101] As we will see in Chapter 5, this essentially discriminatory account of Beta Israel identity has had a great many negative consequences for this community in Israel, but it is a claim that can be accommodated within the matrix of the Jewish understanding of Israelite identity. By contrast, the Samaritans are non-Jewish Israelites, which, from the perspective of the internal logic of the Jewish construction of Israelite identity, are *not supposed to exist*. Hence the Samaritans' current precarity.

At the same time, it is less the capacity of the twelve tribes tradition to make explanations that has changed, than the fact that, in Israel today, it is Jewish authorities who have the power to accept or deny them. The Samaritans, of course, continue to press their claim on their terms, and have even had success.[102] The incompatibilities were always there, but what we can see here is something we will see again and again in chapters to come. Every Israel presents itself as part of *the* Israel, and every Israel is actually one of many Israels – but the latter reality is far more visible when Israels meet than it ever has to be when Israels stand apart. And even when Israels meet, their actual incompatibilities, in contrast to their claims to mutual intelligibility, only need to be dealt with when one needs something from the other. Then, as with the Beta Israel, the twelve tribes tradition can open its doors, or, as with the Samaritans, close them – but walking through them has its own challenges, as we will soon see.

---

[101] Kaplan, *The Beta Israel*, 156. Again, even this tradition does not necessarily claim that their ancestors never knew the oral law, but that they never had the Talmudic sages to interpret it for them. Yerushalmi mentions a Talmudic story in which Moses himself is transported to a rabbinic classroom and does not understand what is said: "That the whole of the Law, not only the written ... but also the oral ... had already been revealed to Moses at Sinai was an axion of rabbinic belief, nevertheless, were Moses transported to a second-century classroom, he would hardly understand the legal discussion. In the world of aggadah both propositions can coexist in a meaningful equilibrium without appearing anomalous or illogical" (Yerushalmi, *Zakhor*, 19).

[102] Indeed, as Julia Droeber notes, it is the "ambiguous position of the Samaritans—acknowledged as 'Jewish' by the Israel government, but not considering themselves 'Jews'" that has *reinforced* the need "to constantly draw religious boundaries, particularly against the Israeli 'Other'" (Droeber, *The Dynamics of Coexistence*, 85).

Where the history and prehistory of the Samaritans is concerned, the main points are these. More than likely, the Israelites of Israel and the Israelites of Judah constructed Israelite identity differently from each other as long as there was an Israel and Judah – or, at least, as long as the Judahites thought of themselves as Israelites, too. The twelve tribes tradition allowed the two Israels to acknowledge the validity of each other's claims or not, and both options were used at times, but the former did not erase the basis for the latter. The twelve tribes tradition is specifically adept at explaining how two different heirs to Israel are both part of an "all Israel" nonetheless. Then, towards the end of the first millennium BCE, the people of these two Israels do seem to have become different from each other in a new way, and before long, a more definitive way. This was not, however, an unprecedented way.

After all, it is again the case that at *every moment visible to the historian with anything like clarity*, the political realities of the people the Bible calls Israel were already divided, first between two kingdoms, then between imperial provinces of various sorts. As a result, the twelve tribes tradition is always, in every surviving instance, used to explain how a people outside or after ancient Israel – and generally both – are Israel, despite appearances. Nor does the possibility that Judahites and Jews might be descended from the original Israelites – or the virtual certainty that the Samaritans are – change things very much. In an example I have used before, if, after the American Revolution, the new Americans had gone on calling themselves British, or thinking of themselves as British, we could understand why that would happen.[103] We could even point to most of the things the Israelites and Judahites shared, the same language, the same basic religion, or religions, continued cultural ties and so on. Since, however, this is not what happened, we can recognize that if it had, that would still be something we would have to explain, not accept – and calling themselves British would not keep twenty-first century Americans from understanding themselves differently than the British in Britain.

Ultimately, every Israel has something to explain about the continued unity of "all Israel," despite its separations, and every Israel uses the same inherent features of the twelve tribes tradition to explain it. We should not regard these explanations as claims to be evaluated for their historical truth or fiction, but as part of their own internal acts of identity construction shaped by internal definitions of Israel. The rhetoric of explanation,

---

[103] Tobolowsky, *The Sons of Jacob*, 224.

in any particular case, is "a key part of what we want to explain, not what we want to explain things *with*."[104] And our ability to truly analyze this internal logic begins with refusing to substitute it for our own analytical logic – even to find it lacking, on historical grounds.

That is, when we begin with the arguments claimants to Israel make about the origins of their differences from each other, we constrain ourselves to exploring whether those arguments are historically correct. When we begin to ask, instead, how that logic is generated and used, we begin to understand how "becoming Israel" works. And again, "becoming Israel" is not only a process of creating new visions of Israel in new places, but of the constant adaptation of Israelite identities in any one place, too. It was used by Judahites to inscribe the priorities and prestige of their tribes over others, by Israelites to explain their superiority over the Judahites, by each, again and again, in the ongoing competition between them, and by many others, elsewhere, as well. A new vision of Israel is a new vision of Israel, whether it developed in direct continuity with earlier forms in ancient Israel itself or took root, for the first time, in the soil of a very different world.

2.5 CONCLUSION

Careful readers of this book will have already noticed that they are unlikely to find it on their bookstore's "Mysteries" shelf. There is, however, something of the *noir* about it, and it is this: my central premise is that the twelve tribes of Israel tradition is in disguise as a description of Israelite identity – a disguise that peoples all around the world have insistently put on. What we need to do is unmask it for what it really is: a tool for *redescribing* Israelite identity, and not once, but over and over again. It is the flexible fabric from which very different visions of Israelite identity can be built, in one place or in a hundred.[105] And this big reveal matters for a lot of reasons, but most especially because of the questions it invites. "Description" implies questions like "is it correct?" and "should

---

[104] Brubaker, *Ethnicity Without Groups*, 9.
[105] We might think of it in terms of Wendy Doniger's "micromyth," "the nonexistent, uninflected micromyth that the scholar constructs of the actually occurring, inflected myth confronted in any analysis of a text … like a condensed soup cube: the scholar confronts the soup (a particular variant of the myth) and boils it down to the soup cube, the basic stock (the micromyth), only to cook it up again into all sorts of soups (various detailed myths confronted in actual individual texts)" (Doniger, *The Implied Spider*, 105).

it be qualified?" "Redescription," by contrast, directs us to ask "what is being done, how, and why?"

So, in many studies of Judahites, Samaritans, and as we will see, all the rest, a lot of the big questions have been questions of description. Are the Judahites, "really" Israelites or not? Are the Samaritans? Are the Mormons? In the Samaritans' case, as we have seen, the fact that the answer is yes on biological grounds has sent scholarship in a new direction. But we still need to ask what *being* Israelite meant to them, and what they did with it. And the assumption that if they always understood themselves as Israelites, and the Judahites, despite 2 Kings 17, generally did as well, then they must have understood each other as equal parts of "all Israel" misses the functional qualities of "becoming Israel."

It misses the ongoing character of "becoming Israel" as well, where the flexibility of the twelve tribes tradition means that what one participant in the system meant to another can change on a dime. And it misses the most obvious lesson of the world history of "becoming Israel," where so many Israels can exist at once. As we saw in the last chapter, it may even be that it was the Judahites who did not originally understand themselves as Israelites, and certainly even 2 Chronicles 30 reveals that the two Israels of the ancient world always knew they did some things a bit differently, like purify before observances.

The question of what there is to say, in absolute terms, about the historical relationship between Israelites and (Israelite-identifying) Judahites in early periods is therefore an extremely complex one. One rather useful concept for thinking about constructions of Israelite identity not only in this chapter but in chapters to come, however, has recently emerged out of a more general concern in the study of identity. The concept in question is that of the "plural actor," pioneered by Bernard Lahire.[106] Broadly speaking, this idea developed as a response to what we might call identity's "Schrodinger's Cat" problem, the fact that it does and does not exist at once. On the one hand, the fact that identity is a tremendously important real-world phenomenon, shaping so much of how we think and interact with each other, requires that we talk about it.[107] On the other, the fact that identities change constantly, that they

---

[106] The phrase comes from Lahire, *The Plural Actor*. See also Rebillard, "Material Culture and Religious Identity," 427–28.

[107] This is what Jonathan M. Hall calls an "intersubjective reality." The "ethnic group is not a biological group but a social group" and contemporary scholarship "rejects the nineteenth-century view of ethnic groups as static monolithic categories with impermeable boundaries for a less restrictive model which recognizes the dynamic,

have no biological trace, and that they have a surprising capacity to go dormant or even disappear, keeps us from regarding them as we do permanent human attributes like height.

The concept of the plural actor cuts this Gordian knot by suggesting not only that we have many identities at once, as the name suggests, but that when one of these is dormant, it does not really exist.[108] The author of this book, for example, is a Jewish person from Texas, and of course both of these facts have left traces in my life and behaviors – in more ways, I imagine, than I know. At the same time, unless there is, say, a particularly Jewish way to watch a sitcom, it may be that I am not meaningfully Jewish while I am engaged in that particular business.[109] Of course, if someone asks me if I am Jewish at that time, I would say yes, but this is the point – someone would have to ask, which would have the effect of summoning my Jewish identity once more into being.

Where the Israelites and Judahites, Jews and Samaritans are concerned, one way to gloss some of the complexities discussed above is to suggest that "Israelite" was simply one of the plural identities available to the people of both regions. The people of the north would be Israelites *and* northerners, which is to say, possessed of certain characteristics that developed because Israel was a separate place, with separate experiences, from Judah. The people of Judah would have been Judahites *and* Israelites for the same reasons. The decision to connect with each other through their Israelite identities or refuse to connect because of their differences would be best understood less as phases in their relationship with each other than as constantly available options, especially before harder distinctions between Jews and Samaritans formed. Of course, internally, each would have understood their differences from each other, which always existed, as proof that one was Israel and one was not – when convenient. But, from the outside, we can think of the unique characteristics of any construction of Israel, which exist on top of broad consensuses

---

negotiable, and situationally constructed nature of ethnicity" (Hall, *Ethnic Identity in Greek Antiquity*, 2).

[108] "Not only are religious identities fluid, i.e. the boundaries between the different categories are permeable, but they are not necessarily activated in a given context, even when available" (Rebillard, "Material Culture and Religious Identity," 430).

[109] So, for example, "it is quite clear that the Christian clergy used burial to construct a Christian identity, but it was far from being the case that religious identity was the salient identity for all Christians when it comes to choosing a place of burial" (ibid., 432).

about who Israel is, where it came from, and to some extent, what happened when, as their "plural" features.

In this chapter, then, we might think of the various accounts of Israelite identity between Israel and Judah described above as redescriptive efforts to navigate pluralities. The twelve tribes tradition has always been a useful tool for these acts of navigation, with the tremendous capacity to explain difference within similarity that I described at length above. Biblical authors could explain that the northerners were not Israelites, by rhetorically sending the Israelites away, or that they were, but that they did not know how to wash themselves before meals. Samaritan authors, likewise, could explain that the people of Judah and their descendants were Israelites, but that thanks to Eli and Ezra, they had come to believe in the wrong *Torah* and the wrong holy place. These differences could be treated as fatal to the claim of the other to be a true heir of Israel any longer, or else, a relatively harmless quirk. But again, the paradigm of *description* forces us to ask largely whether these stories are true, and if not, what is. Awareness of *redescription* is what allows us to ask what each account of Israel is doing and why, which is the kind of thing that lets us see that not all acknowledgments of the Israelite identity of the other are made the same.

In chapters to come, however, the "plural" features of the various Israels will generally take on another significance because they will rarely appear between two Israels in direct competition over Israelite legacies. And, they will take on a different significance than they often have in studies of Israelite histories as descriptions of historical peoples. There, the existence of plural features is often taken as a sign of inauthenticity – if a differently constructed Israel appears in America or east Africa, it has seemed obvious to many that those differences are the sign that these are not really Israel at all. Yet to paraphrase Leo Tolstoy, all Israels are different in their own way – and not just once. All Israels change shape throughout their histories. And so, in this study, the plural characteristics of every construction of Israel are not red flags, but what we most want to know about. They are what reveals each Israel best, from ancient Israel and Judah to today. What is plural in every case – Israelite *and* northern, Israelite *and* Judahite, Israelite *and* Mormon, Israelite *and* Beta Israel – is not for us a problem to solve, but a window, and one we can look through. And on the other side is much that is worth seeing.

Finally, at the end of two chapters concerned with Israel in its original home, we might say that the particular value of the twelve tribes tradition as a lens through which to study the construction of Israelite identities everywhere comes from its use as a battering ram aimed at the heart of two commonsense but ultimately flawed distinctions. First, it connects the study of the internal manipulation of Israelite identities in one context to the external construction of new visions of Israel in different contexts. The same mechanisms, inherent to the same tradition, are responsible for both, so the way any Israel redescribes itself over time can shed light on how Israels suddenly appear where none was before.

Second, because the same mechanisms are at play, this book's focus on the twelve tribes tradition's capacity as a tool for redescription can diminish much of the importance of distinguishing between what we might think of – if a little too simplistically – as "genuine" and "invented" visions of Israelite identity.[110] Again, there are circumstances, contexts, and studies in which acknowledging that the subjects of these first two chapters have a better historical claim to connection with ancient Israel than the other peoples we will discuss will matter. But when we are attempting to study identity construction itself, and specifically how new visions of Israel are created and imbued with meaning, what matters most is the fact that these are all deeply felt identifications that are constructed and reconstructed in the same ways.

I started this book by talking about the silos that have separated the study of Israelite identity in the Hebrew Bible from the construction of Israelite identities elsewhere. In the first chapter, we saw that Judahite authors were already using the twelve tribes tradition to repeatedly rede-scribe Israelite identity. In this one, we see that the tradition was already used to allow different heirs to an Israelite identity to claim that identity at once, even in ancient Israel itself, and to explain what makes them special. And once we recognize that the twelve tribes tradition was indeed always a tool for redescription – and not simply a true description of Israel in some cases, a false description in others – we will begin to regard all attempts to redescribe Israel in a similar light. As a result, we can now move on from ancient Israel at last to other constructions of Israelite identity that we will take as seriously, studying them in the exact same way. We turn our attention, now, to the medieval age.

---

[110] Again, as I pointed out in the last chapter, contemporary approaches to cultural invention tend to regard all identities as to some degree invented.

3

Across the River Sambatyon

The Lost Tribes of Israel in Medieval Legends

Next to the desert between uninhabitable mountains, a certain stream flows beneath the earth, to which no entrance can be made unless by an accidental fall ... And this stream flows into another river of greater size, into which the men of our land enter and from which they carry out the greatest abundance of precious stones ... In that land, boys are also raised in water such that, on account of the stones found, they may live for a length of three or four months completely under the water. Truly, beyond the river of stones are the 10 tribes of the Jews, who although they contrive kings for themselves, they are in fact our servants and are tributaries to our excellency.

—Brewer, "Prester John," 75–76.

Between the end of the first millennium BCE and the beginning of the medieval age, the Hebrew Bible experienced one of the most profound transformations in literary history. Originally a collection of traditions created by and for the people of a small Levantine kingdom, the Bible had by the fifth century CE become a pan-Mediterranean phenomenon. Carried onwards by the Jewish diaspora, the rapid expansion of Christianity, and eventually the conversion of much of the Roman Empire to a biblical faith, biblical traditions spread and spread. By the early medieval period, they were poised to spread much further still. With them, the search for Israel spread too, and changed nearly as much. New audiences saw new things in Israel and wanted new things from it; "Israel" changed to meet them. A new era, or new eras, understood Israel in new ways.

Yet "becoming Israel" *is* a continuous story, as I insisted at the beginning – an ongoing process, internally and externally, that builds on itself, and at every instance, employs the same features of the twelve tribes tradition to redescribe Israel that already saw heavy use in the ancient world. Like water, visions of Israel take on the shape of the vessels that contain them, and like water, they remain the same nevertheless – that is why we can learn from them. A wider world surely meant new influences and new processes that had a tremendous effect on what Israel meant, to whom. But however "Israel" changed in the medieval age, the engines of its transformation – the machinery of "becoming Israel" – were still the pillars of our discussion all along.

Here, and for the rest of the book, three particular pillars stand out for their importance. First, the "separable" character of Israelite identity – what I described in the last chapter as the ability of different claimants to a conceptual "Israel" to go their separate ways and remain part of the whole – played a major role in medieval thought. In the medieval world, the twelve tribes tradition explained how Israel could be in multiple places at once and provided a medium within which multiple different traditions about Israel could co-exist, just as it had in ancient times. Second, the capacity of traditions about Israel to make explanations about who a people were, and why they had the characteristics they had, was in continual use throughout the medieval age, an era of nearly constant new encounters. In other words, the flexibility of Israelite identity continued to allow descriptions of Israel to account for the various characteristics of a given people. Finally, the primordialist premise embodied by the twelve tribes of Israel as a concept continued to create the expectation that all of Israel still existed *somewhere* – intrinsically whole, despite centuries of separation – even though only a small part of it was now visible in the form of world Jewry.

At the same time, each of these familiar features of the twelve tribes tradition was deployed in new ways that were shaped by the particular realities of the medieval world. Now, for example, the separability of Israelite identity would no longer be used mainly as a means of characterizing the experience of different tribes, individually or against each other. Instead, throughout the medieval period, Israel was largely understood to be divided between tribes and "Lost Tribes." That is, from a medieval perspective, there were the Jews on the one hand, and the Lost Tribes on the other. Often, descriptions of the Lost Tribes would serve as a mirror, or avatar, of the Jews of Europe, upon which Christian and Jewish commenters projected their hopes, fears, and expectations concerning the future of the Jewish people.

Next, the explanatory powers of the twelve tribes tradition were developed in two ways specific to the medieval period. First, as a conceptual "west" met a conceptual "east" on the middle ground of the Crusades, the idea of the Lost Tribes of Israel was often used to explain the character of peoples of the east and rumors about events even farther away, notably the Mongol invasions. Finally, the primordialist premise embodied in the idea of "all Israel" – an eternal and fundamentally indivisible Israel – would, in the medieval world, serve primarily to focus medieval thought on the problem of the future restoration of Israel. In Christian Europe especially, the return of the Lost Tribes was increasingly linked to the end of the world. This was not itself a medieval idea. Already in the Hebrew Bible, the restoration of Israel had been given an apocalyptic significance in biblical prophecy, and the same note is sounded in the New Testament.[1] However, in a world where the apocalypse was expected at any moment, this thread in the twelve tribe tapestry began to attract more and more attention.

Ultimately, visions of Israel in the medieval age remained just what they had been in previous periods: mediums for redescription and tools for expressing opinions, reflecting on realities, and advancing claims. At the same time, what needed to be redescribed, expressed, reflected upon, or advanced was particular to the age and to its understandings and requirements. Similarly, this chapter will simultaneously follow well-worn paths, where the major themes of this study are concerned, and embark on departures, in other respects. The nature of these departures, of course, are allied with this chapter's purposes in the larger scheme of the book.

Most of all, this chapter is meant as a transitional one. After two chapters on ancient Israel and its immediate heirs, this account of the tribes in the medieval world stands before a discussion of two "Israels" that still exist today. It is, correspondingly, transitional in time, filling in much of the necessary context between the distant past and the present, where the development of concepts of Israel is concerned. And it is

---

[1] The prophet Isaiah refers to some future day when "the wolf will dwell with the lamb" (Isa. 11:6), and when YHWH will also gather "the remnant of his people . . . from Assyria, Egypt, Patros, Cush, Elam, Shinar, Hamath, and from the islands of the sea" (Isa. 11:11). Jeremiah too foretells a time "when watchmen on the mountain of Ephraim will call out, 'arise, and let us go up to Zion, to YHWH our god'" (Jer. 31:6), and when the people of Israel will be brought "from the land of the north . . . from the ends of the earth . . . they will return here" (Jer. 31:8). In the New Testament, the restoration of Israel sometimes has a role to play in bringing about the end of the world. In Rev. 7, for example, there is a dramatic vision: four angels holding back the four winds from destruction until a fifth angel, holding "the seal of the living God," could seal, for their protection, 144,000 from Israel – twelve thousand from each of the tribes (Rev. 7:1–8).

transitional in space, explaining how "becoming Israel" developed from a limited Levantine phenomenon to a nearly global one – or at least, in this chapter, how visions of Israel acquired the features that would allow "becoming Israel" to become global in the end. And to provide these various transitions, this chapter will have to be unique in a number of ways.

First, while every other chapter is an account of one Israel, this chapter is about many Israels. It is about many self-identifying or other-identified Israelite individuals, or groups, who were discovered or presented themselves as Israel over the course of the period described in this chapter, which is roughly six and a half centuries – from the arrival of Eldad ha-Dani in Kairouan, in modern Tunisia around 893 CE, to the execution of David Reubeni in the 1530s. Second, while other chapters are about groups who "became" Israel themselves, this chapter is primarily about the discovery of Israel, and really, Israels – we might say, the external making of Israels. It is about the gradual proliferation of traditions about where the Lost Tribes of Israel had gotten to, and what was to be expected from them. It is about how understandings of who Israel was, and what Israel signified, were repeatedly reshaped over the course of the medieval age.

Finally, and more than anything else, this chapter is about the dramatic and escalating consequences of the launching of Israel onto a suddenly larger stage, of the new popularity traditions about Israel enjoyed among Jews and Christians alike, and of an increasingly global audience. One of the main results of the expanded scope of the search for Israel is the dynamic combination – and cross-pollination – of traditions about the tribes with other traditions, in ways that both expanded the ability of visions of Israel to reflect medieval perspectives and changed, fundamentally, what Israel seemed to mean, to whom. In other words, as links formed between traditions about the Lost Tribes and other traditions – especially those concerning Prester John, the legendary Priest King of the East, and Alexander the Great – the twelve tribes of Israel gained a new set of associations which would be crucial to the future development of the tradition.

As these links formed with other medieval legends, they would dramatically expand both the geography the tribes might be found in, from the perspective of European intellectuals, and the meanings Israel could have, which is to say, what the discovery of Israel could portend to whom. Generally, as we will see, rumors of the imminence of the Lost Tribes of Israel raised fears among Christian communities and hopes among Jewish ones. But in certain circumstances, the actual discovery of Israel could go against type, making Jewish communities deeply uncomfortable, and instilling a certain hope in Christian ones. And the inversion of these general trends not only results from the developments of the medieval era, but explains much about where "becoming Israel" goes from here.

I will begin, then, by describing how traditions about the tribes, the Prester, Alexander, and others came to form a rich interpretive framework for events to the east, especially in the context of the Crusades, that flexibly responded to new developments and were thus changed in turn. I will continue by demonstrating how descriptions of Israel were imbued with different perspectives on world Jewry by discussing the medieval tradition known as the *Letter of Prester John*. Then, I will show how the fluid repertoire of symbols produced by the combination of traditions allowed Jews and Christians alike to repeatedly redescribe the Mongol invasions as circumstances warranted. Finally, and through the story of three medieval travelers – one towards the Lost Tribes, and two supposedly from them – I will discuss typical Jewish and Christian responses to the lost of Israel, as well as circumstances in which these responses could change, sometimes turning on their heads.

This final investigation, of the ability of traditions about Israel to invert their typical meanings, will allow us to see how the appeal of Israel began to catch on among European Christian communities, despite the force of medieval antisemitism – which would also play a crucial role in the further expansion of "becoming Israel" as a practice. But this discussion will also allow us to see, as we saw in the last chapter, why restoring all of Israel was always easier to contemplate in practice than to attempt in reality. The twelve tribes of Israel tradition is, above all, best at allowing different peoples to claim, or discover, different Israels – different constructions of Israelite identity imbued with the particulars of context, expectation, and desire. At the same time, the whole point of "becoming Israel" is to lay claim to the same Israel as all the rest – ancient Israel, biblical Israel.

So, while the fundamental incompatibility between different visions of Israel is generally invisible at a distance, encounters between Israels tended, and still tend, to make the differences between traditions suddenly visible, often in dramatic ways. Here, as ever, the tensions between how many different visions of Israel there are – added to the fact that each Israel claims to represent a singular, universal version thereof – reveal the twelve tribes tradition anew for what it is. It is, again, not a tool for describing Israelite identities, but for constantly redescribing them according to the needs of the moment and the realities of different contexts. And in the busy medieval world, there was much to redescribe indeed.

3.1 AN INTERPRETIVE FRAMEWORK

Books (good books, anyhow), and sometimes even bookshelves, are well-organized. *Knowledge* is not. Knowledge is a fluid concoction of all the things we know and think, and not just us alone. Knowledge is social, and socially constructed.[2] Much that anyone knows in a given historical context is at least a partial expression of what passes for knowledge in their society.[3] And it is our knowledge, not our bookshelves, that we apply to the interpretation of new encounters and new developments, whether it is really "knowledge" or not. In this case, the Bible and extrabiblical traditions about the tribes of Israel, or even other legends about what is out there in the unknown, may belong on separate book-shelves while living together in our minds.

Historically speaking, the application of knowledge to experience has taken on aggressive, even imperialistic forms. In the study of the ancient world, for example, the ancient Greeks and Romans are well known for how readily they applied their own myths and legends to the foreign peoples and beliefs they encountered, without regard to how those peoples might feel. The scholarly terms for these interpretive acts are *interpretatio Graeca* and *interpretatio Romana* – interpretation in the manner of the Greeks and Romans, respectively. Herodotus, reporting from Egypt, refers to the Egyptian oracles of Apollo, Athena, Artemis, Ares, Zeus, and Leto, for example (Hdt. II.83). Julius Caesar character-ized the Gauls as especially devoted to the worship of Mercury, followed

---

[2] For useful studies of the social construction of knowledge in the medieval period, see Berkey, "Tradition, Innovation and the Social Construction of Knowledge"; Armstrong and Kay, "Textual Communities." For more general discussions, see Dawson, "Objectivism and the Social Construction of Knowledge"; Engeström, "Activity Theory and the Social Construction of Knowledge"; Wilson, "Instruments and Ideologies."

[3] Zerubavel refers to the "sociomental topography of the past," revealing the "pronouncedly social dimension of human memory" (Zerubavel, *Time Maps*, 2). Thus, "when asked to list the names that first come to mind in connection with U.S. history, young Americans often invoke the same historical figures – George Washington, Abraham Lincoln, Thomas Jefferson, Benjamin Franklin" (ibid., 3). It is not impossible to imagine a world where, in the same history, another cast of characters might be highlighted.

by Apollo, Mars, Jupiter, and Minerva (Caes. Gal. VI.17).[4] We can safely presume that the Egyptians and the Gauls did not share this opinion of who they worshipped – and initially had no idea who these gods even were. In other cases, acts of interpretation are neither so obvious nor so aggressive. Still, it is a historical constant to proceed to what we do not know through the prism of what we do know.

In the medieval world, we might speak of an *interpretatio in modo bibliorum* – interpretation in the mode of the Bible.[5] As we will see in the next chapter, too, the use of the Bible as an anthropological source text is, and was, quite common. We might think of it as a natural result of the belief in the Bible's infallibility. In other words, *naturally*, anyone who believes in the literal truth of the Bible will also believe – having learned it from Genesis 5–10 – that all of post-diluvian humanity is descended from the three sons of Noah: Shem, Ham, and Japheth.[6] As a result, any newly encountered people presented a problem to be solved with reference to the biblical account of human history. Who, among Noah's children, are these? The "Lost Tribes of Israel" was a frequent answer to the question from the medieval period on, but not the only one.

It is, however, important to stress that medieval frameworks of interpretation were not only biblical in origin. Even when they were biblical, they were undisciplined, which is to say that medieval authors saw nothing wrong with creatively combining elements of one biblical discourse with another – the Hebrew Bible with the New Testament, history with prophecy, and so forth. Medieval European "knowledge" about the world beyond the borders of reliable information was heavily leavened with a dynamic admixture of other traditions that were only tangentially related to the Bible, or not related at all. Jewish and Christian legends

---

[4] "From the ninth century B.C. on, Greeks sailed, explored, established guest-friendship (*xenia*) relations ... real people, doing concrete things ... but they perceived the reality that they encountered there through screens woven of both experience and myth. Myths ... were projected onto new lands, articulating landscapes, genealogies, ethnicities ... myth provided cultural and ethnic mediation with non-Greeks, and, once integrated, often came to provide the terms of self-perception for native populations" (Malkin, *The Returns of Odysseus*, 1).

[5] A term helpfully suggested by a colleague of mine at the College of William and Mary, Barbette Spaeth.

[6] As Romm observes, "since only Noah and his sons had survived the Flood, all the people of the earth had descended from them, according to the 'family tree' of humankind in Genesis 10" (Romm, "Biblical History and the Americas," 34). See also Katz, "The Wanderings of the Lost Ten Tribes," 107; Popkin, "The Rise and Fall of the Jewish Indian Theory," 64.

played a considerable role in the construction of European knowledge, including the common belief "that the Apostles had literally carried out the Lord's command and preached the Gospel to all nations."[7] So did books of the apocrypha. But so did other legends of various sorts. And often, despite the elevated status of biblical literature as holy scripture, biblical and nonbiblical traditions had roughly the same authority as sources of knowledge about the otherwise unknown. In fact, even the notion of the "Ten Lost Tribes of Israel" is not precisely a biblical idea.[8]

Similarly, it is Josephus, and not the Bible, who is responsible for introducing what would eventually become two fixtures of the medieval tribal imagination, if not precisely in the forms they would later have. He, as well as his contemporary Pliny, are the oldest surviving sources to mention the mystical Sambatyon, or "Sabbath River," which either roars impassably six days of the week and rests on the sabbath (Pliny) or vice versa (Josephus).[9] Josephus describes the "ten tribes" of Israel, now "beyond the Euphrates," in the aspect they would often have in medieval legends: "an immense multitude, not to be estimated by numbers" (*Ant.* 11.133). Both Jewish and Christian sources in the medieval world often imagined the Lost Tribes, wherever they were, as an invincibly large army. And already by the fourth century CE, if not earlier, the traditions concerning the Sambatyon and the armies of Israel had begun to merge.

In fact, the Jerusalem Talmud, likely from the late fourth century CE, and *Genesis Rabbah*, likely from the fifth, both describe the Lost Tribes as wholly or partly across the Sambatyon, where they lived removed from the rest of humanity until some future day of restoration.[10] In *Genesis Rabbah*, Rabbi Yehuda Ben-Simon is the first authority we see make the claim that would become so common in the medieval period, that all of

---

[7] Hamilton, "Continental Drift," 237.

[8] As Elizabeth Fenton observes, "the only use of the phrase 'ten tribes' in the Bible appears in 1 Kings," specifically in 1 Kings 11–12 (Fenton, *Old Canaan in a New World*, 6). As I mentioned in previous chapters, it is never clear which ten they are, and more than two seem to survive. More importantly, biblical authors do not seem to have considered them "lost" so much as gone; they knew where they were.

[9] Neither Josephus (*Jewish War* 7.96–99) nor Pliny (*Natural History* 31.18) connects the Sambatyon to the tribes.

[10] In the Jerusalem Talmud some of the tribes are across the Sambatyon, and some elsewhere (Yerushalmi Sanhedrin 53b). See Neubauer, "Where Are the Ten Tribes?," 75–76. For a trenchant brief discussion of the Jerusalem Talmud, see Strack and Stemberger, *Introduction to the Talmud and Midrash*, 188–89, 223–25. See also Neusner, *Introduction to Rabbinic Literature*, 9.

the Lost Tribes had gone across the Sambatyon, someday to return.[11] Other rabbinic traditions describe a more piecemeal exile, with some tribes across the Sambatyon and some elsewhere, which increased the range of where parts of Israel could be found by those who were looking.[12] All of these traditions had a role to play in shaping the medieval understanding of Israel.

As for the apocrypha, there is a work called 2 Esdras, likely from around the time of Josephus, that would prove influential in the medieval period and beyond, where visions of Israel's tribes are concerned. 2 Esdras describes the journey of the Lost Tribes from Assyrian exile, not across the Sambatyon but across the Euphrates, which YHWH obligingly stopped up for them as YHWH had once done with the Red Sea (2 Esdr. 13:41–42).[13] Passing through the Euphrates, the "lost" Israelites went on from the lands of their Assyrian exile, a year and a half's journey, to a country called "Arzareth" – probably a corruption of the Hebrew *eretz ahereth*, "another land" (2 Esdr. 13:40–45).[14] In the vision in which the pseudonymous author of the book – supposedly the scribe Ezra

---

[11] Genesis Rabbah 73:6. See Benite, *The Ten Lost Tribes*, 75; Neubauer, "Where Are the Ten Tribes?," 20. For Genesis Rabbah generally, see Neubauer, "Where Are the Ten Tribes?," 20; Ben-Eliyahu, Cohn, and Millar, *Handbook of Jewish Literature*, 81. It is typically dated to the early fifth century CE (Strack and Stemberger, *Introduction to the Talmud and Midrash*, 304).

[12] In the Pesiqta Rabbati, for example, probably from the eighth or ninth century CE, the tribes experience a tripartite exile, with two parts on either side of the Sambatyon, and other tribes elsewhere (Neubauer, "Where Are the Ten Tribes?," 21). The Jerusalem Talmud says much the same, describing the settlement of the tribes in three parts, "the one to the other side of the Sambatyon, another to Daphne in Antioch, and the third was covered by a cloud which descended upon them" (Yerushalmi Sanhedrin 53b) (Neubauer, "Where Are the Ten Tribes?," 20; Benite, *The Ten Lost Tribes*, 75–76). See also Cohen, "The London Manuscript of Midrash Pesiqta Rabbati," 210; Bamberger, "A Messianic Document of the Seventh Century"; Braude, *Pesikta Rabbati*, 21–26; Strack and Stemberger, *Introduction to the Talmud and Midrash*, 328–29.

[13] The history of 2 Esdras as a text is extremely complex. 2 Esdr. 3–14 is often called "4 Ezra," which exists as a book in Ethiopic scriptures. However, the likely Hebrew original no longer survives and the Greek manuscripts are not complete (Stone, *Fourth Ezra*, 1). As for the date, Stone notes that the early second century CE *Epistle of Barnabas* may cite 4 Ezra, but that the *Stromatis* of Clement of Alexandria certainly does; therefore, it was certainly in existence by the end of the second century. Stone argues that 4 Ezra was, however, earlier, since while it most likely appeared after the destruction of the Second Temple, it may reference Vespasian, Titus, and Domitian as contemporary figures (Stone, *Fourth* Ezra, 9–10).

[14] As Benite points out, William Aldis Wright was one of the first to realize this in the mid-nineteenth century (Wright, "Note on the Arzareth of 4 Esdr Xiii 45"; Benite, *The Ten Lost Tribes*, 63).

himself – learns of this journey, he also learns that these tribes would return at the end of days, again through the Euphrates when YHWH "destroys the multitude of nations" (2 Esdr. 13:49). As we will see in the next chapter, the duration of the journey of the Lost Tribes described here – a year and a half – sometimes played an important role in explaining how the tribes made it even so far as America. In this chapter, however, the explicit connection between the tribes and the end of the world that is such a prominent feature of Ezra's vision is more important in shaping the character of tribal discourse.

Still other traditions that fed European expectations where the Lost Tribes were concerned were not even so loosely related to biblical scriptures. In medieval Europe, traditions about the tribes mixed and matched with quite a number of others, and especially legends concerning Prester John and the conquests of Alexander the Great. Between the *Letter of Prester John*, which arrived – really, began to arrive – in the middle of the twelfth century CE, and versions of the *Alexander Romance*, which may have appeared as early as the third, Europeans "knew" a wide variety of things about the fantastic lands to the east. In medieval traditions, the tribes were often depicted alongside these worthies, in various arrangements.[15]

Together, this potent mix of symbols provided a profoundly expressive vocabulary for reflecting medieval perspectives on a range of subjects, and in response to a range of developments.[16] This interpretive framework also provided the knowledge basis for explaining what must have seemed

---

[15] Nowell, "The Historical Prester John," 436. The author to whom this work is often attributed, "Kallisthenes," is often supposed to be "Kallisthenes of Olynthos, the historian who accompanied Alexander the Great on his expedition," according to the *Oxford Dictionary of Byzantium*. This encyclopedia entry also notes that it is "based on an anonymous novel written originally in the 3rd C. and widely copied, with frequent accretions of fantastic episodes. Five recensions of the text, which can be dated from the 4th to 7th c., are identifiable." Reconstructions are based on "translations in Armenian (5th C.), Latin (by Julius Valerius Probus, 4th C., and the archpriest Leo, 9th C.), Syriac, Coptic, and Ethiopic" attesting to its widespread popularity (Jeffreys, Cutler, and Kazhdan, "Alexander Romance"). See also Nawotka, *The Alexander Romance*, 3–4; Stoneman, "Primary Sources from the Classical and Early Medieval Periods," 2–3; Stoneman, *The Greek Alexander Romance*.

[16] The idea of mythic traditions as a kind of expressive vocabulary has a heritage. More often, rather than "vocabulary" other studies have referred to the capacity of mythic narratives to serve as a "taxonomy," which is to say an organization system that, rearranged, makes new meaning. See Ballentine, *The Conflict Myth and the Biblical Tradition*, 3; Lincoln, *Theorizing Myth*, 147; McCutcheon, "Myth"; Smith, "What a Difference a Difference Makes"; Smith, *Map Is Not Territory*, xii. See also Tobolowsky, *The Sons of Jacob*, 203–9, 232–46.

like mysteries to many Europeans, including the large number of Christians and Jews who were then living in Asia. In addition, the advent of various Lost Tribe mythologies themselves made the whereabouts of Israel a mystery that needed solving. Since the Bible leaves the ultimate destiny of most of Israel unresolved, since it was now a pan-Mediterranean scripture, and since Israel's restoration was foretold in biblical prophecy, the return of Israel was not only expected by many medieval individuals, it was believed to be a certainty.[17] Thus, "Israels" were increasingly identified in the context of new encounters; after all, they had to be out there somewhere.

From a modern perspective, we might as well say that there was nothing much to explain in the existence of the Jews and Christians of the east, from the view of Europe. People have always moved farther and more often than we might expect, trade routes have always attracted travelers, and both Judaism and Christianity began in Asia. Thus, well before Western Europeans began seriously looking for Prester John, King of the Indies, there were likely Jews in what is today known as India.[18] There appear to have been Jewish traders along the Silk Road at least by the ninth century CE, if not much earlier, and settlement in Kaifeng likely happened not long after.[19] To many medieval authors, however, it was clear that here was the work of the apostles revealed, and there was the

---

[17] "In Benite's view, 'The Lostness represented by the ten tribes is, in Western historical consciousness, one of the most acute and oldest known instances of loss still "alive" today.' Global searching for the tribes is and will be ongoing, he suggests, because their 'lostness' is at once simple and profound. They are missing, and thus they should be sought" (Fenton, *Old Canaan in a New World*, 8; Benite, *The Ten Lost Tribes*, 8).

[18] Singh, *Being Indian, Being Israeli*; Asa-El, *The Diaspora and the Lost Tribes of Israel*, 205. As Asa-El notes, the Bene Israel believe themselves to have been "refugees fleeing the forced Hellenizing of King Antiochus in the second century B.C.E." Nathan Katz has argued that the first-century arrival claimed by the "Cochin Jews" at a place called Cranganore (or Shingly) is "entirely plausible" because of "Jewish participation in Greco-Egyptian and/or Roman expeditions to usurp Arab trade monopolies," Roman settlements at Cranganore, and the Jewish diaspora occasioned by the destruction of Jerusalem in 70 CE (Katz, *Who Are the Jews of India?*, 30). The major artifact associated with this group is a charter, inscribed on copper plates, supposedly given to Joseph Rabban by an Indian potentate in 379 CE, which probably actually dates from the tenth or eleventh century (ibid., 13). As for the Jewish settlement in Kerala, "Arabic travelers' diaries ... refer to the Jews of Kerala as early as the mid-ninth century, when Jewish merchants known as the Radanites reached the apex of their wealth and influence" (ibid., 30). Benjamin of Tudela, who traveled in the late mid-to-late twelfth century, also mentions Jewish settlements in India, whether by first-hand knowledge or otherwise (Adler, *The Itinerary of Benjamin of Tudela*, 57–59).

[19] See especially Xu, *The Jews of Kaifeng, China*, 1–32; Xu, "Jews in Kaifeng, China."

home, or a home, of the Lost Tribes of Israel. And, as always, in *describing* Israel, Jewish and Christian authors *redescribed* Israel, inflecting it with their own subjectivities and the realities of their context, revealing themselves and their worlds in how they went about the task.

As we turn our attention to depictions of the Lost Tribes in the *Letter of Prester John*, we will see immediately how these traditions worked together and reshaped each other, and how they can collectively reveal aspects of the medieval European imagination. In the following discussion of the various interpretations of the Mongol invasion, in its various phases, the ability of this heavily cross-pollinated body of traditions to express perspectives will be revealed even more clearly. In both cases, we will see the dynamism of this vocabulary at work, not just reflecting traditional European knowledge about the world, but at times reshaping it. The results would send the twelve tribes tradition across much of the known world, imbuing it with new meanings, and giving it a role in mediating encounters it has continued to play ever since.

3.2 THE ARMIES OF THE PRESTER

In 1144, the fall of the county of Edessa to the armies of Zengi, the Atabeg of Aleppo, shook the confidence of European Christianity.[20] Edessa had fallen many times before; it was a common target of countless struggles between Persians, Turks, and Arabs on the one hand and Byzantines on the other. In 1098, however, Edessa had become the first conquest, and thus the first tangible success, of the event known to history as the First Crusade.[21] Thus, to lose Edessa, "the first city to convert to Christianity and [...] the burial place of the apostles Thomas and Thaddeus," seemed an intimation of something truly dire.[22]

In the wake of this disaster, Bishop Hugh of the city of Jabala in Syria came hurrying to the Papal court at Viterbo, Italy bearing the terrible news, but also a strange and exciting rumor.[23] As the well-regarded German historian and monk Otto of Friesing put it:

---

[20] Phillips, *The Second Crusade*, xvii.

[21] "In July 1099 the armies of the First Crusade fought their way into the holy city of Jerusalem to achieve one of the most improbable victories of the medieval age" (ibid., xvii).

[22] Ibid., 52.

[23] Ibid., 88. Jabala is Byblos (Beckingham, "The Achievements of Prester John," 2).

He (that is, Bishop Hugh) ... related that not many years ago a certain Iohannes, a king and a priest, living in the Far East, in *extremo Oriente*, beyond Persia and Armenia, who like all his people was a Christian though a Nestorian, made war on the brothers, the kings of the Persians and Medes ... and stormed the capital of their kingdom, Egbattana ...

After "putting the Persians to flight," this "Prester John" – who, in Hugh's telling, was of the lineage of the Magi and intent on making the pilgrimage of his ancestors – "advanced to the help of the church of Jerusalem" but was unable to cross the Tigris.[24] Though he had failed, this time, it seemed reasonable to think that the Priest King might be induced to try again, and so come to the aid of the vulnerable crusader states.[25] However, the Second Crusade, begun in 1147, came and went with no sign of the Prester – a complete failure.[26] The effort to avenge Edessa, led primarily by the Holy Roman Emperor Conrad III and Louis VII, king of France, fell apart as the two armies suffered significant setbacks against the Turks in Anatolia, struggling to follow (literally) in the steps of the First Crusaders.[27] At that point, the legend of the Prester might well have faded away. But then something happened: the mythical king wrote a letter and sent it west.

Before we get to that, it is worth noting that Hugh's account of the career of Prester John gives us our first taste of the interpretive framework just described at work. Strange as it may seem, there actually was a great battle in the lands beyond Jerusalem; it just wasn't between the Prester and the Persians and the Medes. Instead, in 1141, the Seljuk Sultan Sanjar

---

[24] Translation and quote from Beckingham, "The Achievements of Prester John," 2.

[25] Some suggest that Prester John was actually known in Europe some decades earlier, referring to the apparent arrival at Rome of a representative of "patriarch John of India" in 1122 (Salvadore, "The Ethiopian Age of Exploration," 596; Lefevre, "Riflessi Etiopici nella Cultura Europea del Medioevo e del Rinascimento," 22; Barros e Sousa Santarém, *Recherches historiques*). This may be, although there are reasons to think this patriarch or "Archbishop" John was a different figure or only loosely connected to the main Prester John legend, John being a rather common name, and the Archbishop (or patriarch) certainly not being a king (Hamilton, "Continental Drift," 237).

[26] Frankopan, *The First Crusade*. As Frankopan reveals, Alexios' call to Urban, and Urban's answers, were part of a more complex political reality than they sometimes appear to be in contemporary studies. Urban was caught up in his own struggle with Clement III, an "antipope" backed by the Holy Roman Empire, and had been using his progress in breaking down the barriers between the Eastern and Western churches to gain ascendancy over his rival (ibid., 14–16).

[27] As Jonathan Phillips has shown, the Second Crusade is a great deal more complex and amorphous than this brief description suggests, and might properly be thought to encompass several spheres of action, including Spain and a campaign against the Wends (Phillips, *The Second Crusade*).

was defeated by a people known as the Qara Khitai, who had left China and settled to the west, under their ruler, the Gur-Khan.[28] This "Prester John," which is to say the Gur-Khan himself, was not a Christian, but there were many Christians in his kingdom.[29] And Hugh was even right that many of them were Nestorians, a Christian theological movement that was not in much favor in the West.[30] These half-known facts, jumbled together and filtered through the prism of European "knowledge," made the Gur-Khan into the Prester, and his soldiers into Christian avengers.

Where the Prester John Letter is concerned, however, the facts are these: sometime between 1165 and 1170, a letter addressed to the Byzantine emperor Manuel Comnenus arrived in the west.[31] This Manuel was the grandson of the emperor Alexios Comnenus, whose urgent request for aid, sent to Pope Urban II, played an important role in inspiring the First Crusade. That he, of all monarchs, should receive such a letter makes a good deal of sense. Before too long, however, the so-called *Letter* took on a life of its own. There are many manuscripts purporting to be *the Letter*, some very different from each other. Sometimes, they even have different addressees – Frederick Barbarossa, for example.[32]

---

[28] Beckingham, "The Achievements of Prester John," 2–3; Hamilton, "Continental Drift," 238; Richard, "The Relatio de Davide," 147.

[29] Biran, *The Empire of the Qara Khitai*, 176; Gillman and Klimkeit, *Christians in Asia before 1500*, 229.

[30] As one scholar put it, about a slightly later period: "Many of the core peoples of the vast Mongol Empire from the east identified themselves as part of the Nestorian or Assyrian Church of the East either in full or in part. These included the Kerait, Naiman, Merkit, Ongut, and Uighur tribes. Prominent Nestorian/Assyrian Christians in the bureaucracy at the Mongol Court included: Chinqai, minister to the early Khans Ögedei and Güyük; his colleague Qadaq, and Bulghar, the chief secretary to Möngke Khan ... many top-ranking Mongol women were Assyrian Christians, such as Sorqaqtani-Beki (d. 1252), the mother to Möngke Khan (1251–1259), Kublai Khan, and Hülegü Khan (d. 1265)" (Osipian, "Armenian Involvement," 83).

[31] Brewer, *Prester John*, 11. Brewer cites the two pieces of evidence for establishing a date for the arrival of the letter: a statement that the letter was sent in 1165 in the 1232 chronicle of Alberic de Trois-Fontaines, and "a scribal addition to a manuscript copy ... written in a thirteenth century hand, which holds that it was sent 'circa annum domini M.C.L.XX'" (ibid.).

[32] From this distance, we cannot say for certain even what language the original missive was composed in, although Latin seems a good bet; there are currently 469 surviving Latin manuscripts of it. For the language question, see Helleiner, "Prester John's Letter," 55–56. As Brewer notes, the best-known edition of the letter is Zarncke's 1879 translation, but "he knew of only 96 manuscripts and only made use of 74 of these for his edition" (Brewer, *Prester John*, 10; Zarncke, "Der Priester Johannes").

What they all have in common, however, is a lengthy description of John's fabulous realm. Generally, he is the overlord of many other kings – seventy-two, in what appears to be the original version of the *Letter* – and rules the "three Indies." The location of the land called "India" was often vaguely constructed in medieval Europe, but John's realm stretches from the "sepulcher of St. Thomas" – rumored to have died proselytizing in "India" – to the Tower of Babel. John is extraordinarily rich, and lives in a kind of paradise, full of sumptuous fruits and rivers running with precious jewels. John's realm is also fabulous in the literal sense of the word, featuring monstrous beasts and monstrous men, including the biblical Gog and Magog.

One crucial point here is that many of the more dramatic features of the *Letter*'s description are cribbed from the *Alexander Romance*, including running fights with elephants and cannibals, descriptions of the Amazons, rivers that flow from Eden, pygmies, fountains of youth – which John, who claims to have lived a very long time, often partakes of – and men without heads.[33] Thus, we see here another example of the cross-pollination of traditions just described. Another such example, and one with considerable relevance for our ongoing discussion, lies not within John's realm, but just across his borders. In many versions of the *Letter*, John's enormous kingdom is demarcated on one side by a mighty river, impassable much of the year: the fabled Sambatyon. Beyond it, there live the Lost Tribes of Israel in the enormous multitudes Josephus mentioned.

As John's realm was described and redescribed, as new versions of the *Letter* appeared, descriptions of the tribes became a vehicle through which European Christians expressed their views on, and fears about, the other part of Israel, the part that lived among them: the persecuted Jews of Europe. In other words, in these *Letters*, the ability of Israel to be in more places than one – conveyed by the segmented structure of the twelve tribes tradition – allowed lost Israel to be inscribed with European perspectives on the Israel they knew.

3.3 THE LOST TRIBES IN THE LANDS OF PRESTER JOHN

Whatever it was and was not for European Christians, there can be no doubt that the First Crusade was an absolute disaster for European Jewry.

---

[33] Bar-Ilan, "Prester John," 294.

The so-called "People's Crusade" of 1096, distinguished from the official "Prince's Crusade" that followed, was especially dire in this regard.[34] Between the Christian exceptionalism that was the calling card of the Crusades and the brutally antisemitic preaching of Peter the Hermit, it is hardly surprising, though deeply tragic, that the People's Crusade began with a slaughter of European Jews.[35] As one Jewish author of the period put it: "They said to one another: 'Behold we travel to a distant land to do battle with the kings of that land. [We take] our lives in our hands to kill or subjugate all the kingdoms which do not believe in the crucified. How much more should we subjugate or kill the Jews who killed and crucified him?'"[36] Ultimately, the violence across much of France and what is now Germany – a massacre at Worms; the "annihilation" of the community at Mainz; devastation in Cologne, Trier, and Metz; and forced baptism at Regensburg – was severe enough that it has sometimes been called the "first holocaust."[37]

Here, we see one extreme of European antisemitism, a thread not uncommon in the medieval era or after. However, not all influential Christians thought of the Jews in the same way, with respect to the Crusades or otherwise. For example, in the lead-up to the Second Crusade, another viciously antisemitic figure was active on its behalf: one Radulf, a Cistercian. This time, however, the impact of his preaching was at least softened by Bernard of Clairvaux, the driving oratorical force behind the Crusade. This is not to say that Bernard was a friend to the Jews by any measure, only that his approach was different. He argued, publicly, that the continued survival of the Jewish faith must have some larger divine purpose, else it would not have been possible.

---

[34] This abortive first effort has at least been perceived to be undisciplined, somewhat spontaneous, and operating in advance of the pope's plans – in part because it ended so poorly. The soldiers of the "People's Crusade," however, were much more professional than in some descriptions thereof, and their actions should not be taken as representative only of the opinions of less "civilized" Christians (Riley-Smith, *The First Crusade and the Idea of Crusading*, 51).

[35] Ibid., 50–51.

[36] Chazan, *European Jewry and the First Crusade*, 225. Quotation from Phillips, *The Second Crusade*, 84. Asbridge adds that the People's Crusade "set off for the Holy Land in spring 1096, months before any other army, making ill-disciplined progress towards Constantinople. Along the way, some of the crusaders concluded that they might as well combat the 'enemies of Christ' closer to home, and thus carried out terrible massacres of Rhineland Jews" (Asbridge, *The Crusades*, 41).

[37] Riley-Smith, *The First Crusade and the Idea of Crusading*, 50–51.

Indeed, Bernard thought he knew what that purpose was. He "indicated that the presence of the Jews was a living reminder of Christ's suffering and that one day 'all Israel shall be saved,' but those Jews who were killed before this would be lost to the faithful forever."[38] In other words, the Jews were to be preserved because God willed it "to remind us of what our Lord suffered. They are dispersed all over the world so that by expiating their crime they may be everywhere the living witness of our redemption ... if the Jews are utterly wiped out, what will become of our hope for their promised salvation, their eventual conversion?"[39] Moreover, Bernard argued, while the Muslims were "attacking the faithful," the Jews were at the moment "subjugated to the Christians."[40] In Bernard's view, in other words, the challenge European Jewry represented to Christian supremacy was not very important compared to the Muslim threat, and could safely be ignored for the moment. In the meantime, until their eventual conversion, the Jews should be protected as a reminder to Christians of the validity of their own faith.

Where our ongoing discussion is concerned, the most notable thing about the varieties of medieval antisemitism is how well they are reflected in different manuscripts of the *Letter of Prester John*, and specifically how different versions describe the Israelites who live near John's country. The original version of the *Letter* is not very useful in this respect – here, John says only that though they have kings for themselves, these Israelites are also his subjects.[41] But in a French manuscript from about 1500 we read:

There is a river full of precious stones and it descends so swiftly that nobody can cross it except on Saturday when it stands still; and whatever it encounters, it carries into the Sandy Sea. We have to protect this crossing, for we have on this frontier forty-two castles ... ten thousand knights, six thousand crossbowmen and fifteen thousand archers, and forty thousand troopers ... so that, if the great King of Israel would come with his men, he could not get across with his Jews, who are twice as numerous as the Christians, but not as the Saracens, for they hold two thirds of the world ... if the Jews could cross this passage, all the Christians and Saracens would be lost.[42]

Here, in a vision redolent of Josephus, and certainly more of Radulf than Bernard, "the Jews" – the distinction between Israelite and Jew has rarely been observed in the Common Era – are not just inhabitants of Prester

[38] Phillips, *The Second Crusade*, 74–75.   [39] Ibid., 85.

[40] From Bernard of Clairvaux's *Epistolae*, no. 363, translated in Phillips, *The Second Crusade*, 74–75.

[41] Uebel, *Ecstatic Transformation*, 157; Brewer, *Prester John*, 76.

[42] Brooks, "Prester John," 262.

John's realm, but a terrific threat, capable of overwhelming the Christians and Muslims together, even though the Muslims hold two-thirds of the world.[43] As a result, the passages must be guarded with a larger army than likely existed anywhere at that time. However, here a careful *entente* reigns, and no active conflict is necessary.

Another set of manuscripts are instructive in this same direction, and are written, of all things, in Hebrew. The first is addressed to "the Pope in Rome," and appears in a manuscript from Constantinople dated to 1519, though it may date from the twelfth century originally. The second is to "Emperor Frederick," from a manuscript dated to 1271, and the third to Pope Eugenius IV, from the middle of the fifteenth century.[44] Beckingham and Ullendorf, who published an edition of these *Letters* in 1982, supposed that they were written by Jewish authors, reasoning that few others would write in Hebrew, but the substance of the *Letters* – as well as the bad Hebrew – make this unlikely.[45] Regardless, in each letter, subtle differences in the relationship between John and the tribes are quite revealing.

In the Constantinople *Letter*, we see much the same thing as in the French manuscript, but the threat the tribes pose is even greater: "We are placing guards at the passages, for if the Jews were able to cross they would cause great damage in the whole world against Christians as well as Ishmaelites and against every nation and tongue under the heavens, for there is no nation or tongue which can stand up to them."[46] King Daniel rules "300 kings, all Jews," and much more besides, "and they have many

---

[43] The same Letter, it is worth noting, also speaks out against the "treacherous" Knights Hospitaller, an order who played a key role in the early Crusades. Michael E. Brooks, in his dissertation, repeats a suggestion of Vsevolod Slessarev that the Templars are actually meant here, who were devastated by Philip IV of France in the early fourteenth century (Brooks, "Prester John," 257; Slessarev, *Prester John*). Bernard Hamilton has also argued that the main text of the *Letter* was inspired by the contest between Pope Alexander III and Frederick Barbarossa for hegemony, an argument that Brewer finds convincing (Hamilton, "Prester John and the Three Kings of Cologne"; Brewer, *Prester John*, 12).

[44] Kaplan, "Review: The Hebrew Letters of Prester John," 283. As Beckingham and Ullendorf note, "we do not know on what earlier text the 1519 Constantinople version ... was based. But ... there is every reason to think that the original redaction ... of both letters belongs to the late 12th or early 13th centuries" (Ullendorf and Beckingham, *The Hebrew Letters of Prester John*, 18). These letters were earlier edited and published by Neubauer and Eisenstein (Neubauer, "Inyanai Aseret Haschevatim"; Eisenstein, *Ozar Midrashim*, 467–73).

[45] Roth, "Review: The Hebrew Letters of Prester John," 194.

[46] Translation from Ullendorf and Beckingham, *The Hebrew Letters of Prester John*, 56–58.

beautiful women and they are ardent by nature."[47] Here, Prester John goes to see King Daniel once a year accompanied by a great force, "to fight with our enemies if there is need to fight."[48] In this version of the *Letter*, violence is not only possible, but imminent.

The *Letter* to "Emperor Frederick," however, presents a less ominous vision of these armies of Israelites. Again they cannot cross, and again the border is absurdly garrisoned in case they try: "For if they were able to cross they would destroy the world."[49] Here, however, the Israelites pay Prester John tribute, "100 camels laden with gold and silver and precious stones and pearls," apparently to defray the cost to John of the towns the Israelites live in and the garrison, and to induce John's armies to protect the land that constitutes the border between them.[50] John goes to meet them annually, not to fight but to collect this tribute. In this version of the *Letter*, though the Israelites are frightening, they are still beholden to the Prester and his armies, and the two groups can conduct normal business from time to time. This, of course, is more Bernard than Radulf, or Peter.

Meanwhile, the Pope Eugenius *Letter* is the most virulently antisemitic of all. First, the Jews are not explicitly mentioned, but referred to only as "those accursed" – an omission explained in a gloss appended to the manuscript.[51] The author of this *Letter* also refers to the great number of Jews on Prester John's borders – "for they are so (numerous) that for every town we have they have ten" – and the letter-writer worries not that they will "destroy" the world, but instead "corrupt" it. Interestingly, the Eugenius author also refers to camels carrying gold, but this time the Israelites have no part in it. Instead, it is God himself who sends the gold to Prester John, presumably for his service in protecting the world from the Lost Tribes, cutting out the unsuitable middlemen.[52] Here, Radulf's and Peter's perspectives are much more apt comparisons than Bernard's for the tone of this version of the *Letter*.[53]

Throughout this and the last chapter, I have referred to the "separability" of Israelite identity, referring to the way the segmented structure of the twelve tribes tradition allows parts of Israel to be in many places at once, and to look differently from each other. While in previous chapters

---

[47] Ibid., 60.   [48] Ibid., 70.   [49] Ibid., 94.   [50] Ibid., 96.   [51] Ibid., 150.

[52] "And know that this king ... is not our favourite, for he is not a Christian" (ibid., 132).

[53] If the authors of these letters really were Jews, as Ullendorf and Beckingham suggest, it is not impossible to imagine Jewish authors enjoying the act of magnifying the threat they pose; however, they would still have taken their cues from Christian opinions of their day, as evident in the similarity between the Lost Tribes in these versions of the Letter and in other Christian traditions about them.

this "separability" was employed between claimants of Israel to compete with each other, from now on we will mainly see it used to explain the different destinies and characteristics of parts of Israel, and sometimes to create a mirroring other – especially against the best-known descendants of the Israelites, the Jews. Certainly, this is what the Lost Tribes in the Prester John *Letter* provide: a blank slate upon which European Christians could inscribe their views on the Jews of Europe, their understanding of the proper relationship between Jew and Gentile, and their apprehension of a millennial future. That they did not do so only once, but over and over again in a variety of different ways, sketching a representative range of opinions, demonstrates the point. The twelve tribes tradition is an extraordinarily flexible tool for imbuing a conceptual Israel with various kinds of significance. In the next section, we will begin to see that European Jews themselves could do much the same kind of inscribing, though with quite a different perspective.

Ultimately, the search for Prester John would peter out slowly, over the course of centuries. His realm of "the Indies," never very clearly defined in the medieval world, was originally thought to be in the regions east of Jerusalem, in the lands of the Khans, which likely played a role in the identification between the tribes and the Mongols discussed below.[54] Eventually, enough information filtered back to Europe – through the work of Marco Polo and others – to convince the era's scholars, kings, and pontiffs that Prester John was not there. In fact, Polo thought he had been killed in battle by Genghis Khan.[55]

Polo then went on to the "Second India" of John's three (which is to say, India itself), but found little that seemed to mirror the descriptions in the *Letter*. He found scattered Christian communities on the Malabar Coast, "but no great Christian ruler."[56] Eventually, "as the focus of Muslim power in the near east shifted from Iraq to Egypt, so ... did the Priest King's centre of power shift from Asia to Africa."[57] Specifically, the search shifted to Ethiopia and persisted into the sixteenth century,

---

[54] "The exact meaning of the term 'India' often varies in ancient and medieval sources. It was used not only to designate the Indian subcontinent, but also parts of China, North Africa, the Arabian Peninsula, or Ethiopia" (Valtrová, "Beyond the Horizons of Legend," 159 n.13).

[55] Hamilton, "Continental Drift," 248. Bar-Ilan notes that "Marco Polo identified Prester John with the khan of the Kereit, a tribe in Mongolia which was then Nestorian Christian. Others continued searching for him in China" (Bar-Ilan, "Prester John," 291).

[56] Hamilton, "Continental Drift," 249.   [57] Ibid., 237.

especially among the Portuguese.[58] Later, when an "Israel" in Ethiopia was discovered by Europeans it was in part because they were long believed to have been there already.[59]

For this chapter, however, the main point lies elsewhere. First, the ability of descriptions of the tribes in the *Letters* of Prester John to reflect not just *a* Christian perspective, but many, reveals anew the fundamental capacity of traditions of Israel to reflect the subjective perspectives of those describing it. The redescriptive capacities of the twelve tribes tradition is in evidence here as fully as anywhere else. Next, as far as the twelve tribes tradition is concerned, we see here the "separability" of Israel used to make the Lost Tribes a rhetorical proxy for the Tribes, which is to say, the Jews. In the next section, we will see the same thing from the other direction: when the Mongol invasions began in the thirteenth century – and they were naturally identified with the return of the Lost Tribes – many Jews would see in this a cause for hope, and deliverance from their present circumstances. Meanwhile, many Christians would see just what they saw in the tribes beyond the border of the kingdom of Prester John.

Yet we also see, in these versions of the *Letter*, the stirrings of the potent mix of symbols so characteristic of the medieval age generally. First, as we saw in the previous section, the legend of the tribes was connected to that of the Sambatyon. Next, the Sambatyon and the tribes both were placed in the lands of Prester John, amidst a geography that was also drawn in part from the *Alexander Romance*. In time, this cross-pollination would produce a surprising capacity for interchange that dramatically increased the capacity of legends about the Prester, the tribes, and Alexander to serve together as parts of the same descriptive

---

[58] Ibid., 257. As Matteo Salvadore notes, "in the late Middle Ages, Jerusalem was one of three contact zones between Europeans and Africans in general. It is in Jerusalem that Ethiopia encountered Europe, the city being – as Ernesta Cerulli put it – 'the clearing house of the Eastern Christian Cultures.' As the crusaders controlled the city – from 1099 to 1189 and later from 1229 to 1244 – they were exposed to various expressions of Christianity, including the Ethiopian one" (Salvadore, "The Ethiopian Age of Exploration," 599).

[59] Indeed, it would be the search for the Prester that would drive European exploration of Ethiopia in the first place, with results that we will later see. More than that, the various journeys after the Prester may have helped develop the concept of Europe itself in certain ways (Salvadore, "The Ethiopian Age of Exploration"). "The creation of a European identity was to a substantial degree in opposition to these 'others' … The immediate boundary between European Christian and Jew or Moor was endlessly duplicated through the world as Europe confronted hitherto unknown parts of the world" (Parfitt, *The Lost Tribes of Israel*, 24).

vocabulary. In the end, the existence of many different perspectives on the tribes, even among Christians, hints at a growing variety of opinion as to what the return of Israel might represent, for good and ill, but also a growing geography for the tribes to inhabit.

Thus, in the next section, we will see that when rumors of the Mongol invasions first arrived in the West, they were identified with the armies of the long-expected Prester. When their aspect turned more threatening, the referent became the tribes, or another legend concerning barbarian peoples supposedly shut up by Alexander beyond the Caspian mountains, or both together. By the thirteenth century, however, the swirl of traditions was such that the image of the Mongols could switch back again at a moment's notice, and even the tribes were not only to be feared. Before the end of the medieval age, Christian potentates would, in at least one instance, welcome the potential arrival not of Christian armies from the east, but a great Jewish one. It was likely Prester John, and the hope he had long engendered, that paved the way. And it was certainly the Prester, and others, who helped solidify the belief in Christian and Jewish Europe that the tribes were out there, perhaps imminently to be found.

3.4 THE GATES OF ALEXANDER

According to the *Alexander Romance* – according, in fact, to Josephus, even earlier – the great conqueror, weary of conquest, at last hit upon a different tactic. Having chased away a large army of barbarians, Alexander constructed a pair of enormous gates in the Caspian mountains to shut them inside the mountain range and keep them from troubling the world any longer.[60] These gates, if hastily constructed, were by no means a fly-by-night affair. According to the *Romance*, Alexander first prayed to bring the mountains closer together, then built the gates from bronze, then covered them with oil and surrounded them with brambles. Beyond the gates were "twenty-two kings with their subject nations," including Gog, Magog, and many others.[61]

Accounts of the gates of Alexander, like accounts of the Lost Tribes of Israel, have a long history of reflecting contemporary anxieties through different constructions of who was beyond them. During the Roman Empire, "fears over migrating peoples and the blurring of the traditional

---

[60] Perry, "The Imaginary War," 11. See also *Jewish War* 7.244–51, *Antiquities* 18.97.
[61] Stoneman, *The Greek Alexander Romance*, 185–86.

borders of the Roman Empire were mapped onto the myth of Alexander's gates."[62] Often, in literature, the gates serve as a boundary between civilization and barbarism – the world of the civilized Alexander on one side, horrors on the other.[63] In the medieval period, the gates remained a fixture of the European imagination of the dangers of Asia. The idea that the gates had been broken, or otherwise failed in some way, became relatively common – so, at certain points, a number of European commenters came to believe that the barbarian hordes that Alexander had shut up were now on their way to pillage the world.[64] Naturally, the Mongol invasions of the early thirteenth century more or less cried out for an explanation of this sort, from a European perspective.

Actually – and here we see the true fluidity of the repertoire of symbols that made up the interpretive framework described above – when rumors of the Mongols first reached the land of the Crusades, then Europe itself, many believed that here, at last, was Prester John making his move.[65] Hadn't the Khitai, from roughly the same region, already been identified with the Prester? And weren't the first targets of the Khans Muslim powers of the east, as befit the armies of the Christian king?[66] Thus, when "news of the turmoil caused by the Mongol invasion of Central Asia in 1218–1220, and the plight of the Muslim world, reached the crusaders ... [it] raised considerable hope among them."[67] In 1221, a certain James of Vitry reported it as fact, in Egypt, that a Christian king, whom he called David, was hurrying from "the two Indies ... to the help of the Christians, bringing with him a most ferocious people who will devour like beasts the sacrilegious Saracens."[68]

---

[62] Bond, "Building the Iron Gates of Alexander." As she observes, "those 'unclean' and 'wild' peoples that were kept out by the gates of Alexander regularly changed over time, depending on who and when the story was told." See also Boyle, "Alexander and the Mongols." Ambrose of Milan, writing in the fourth century CE, does not associate the Goths specifically with the gates, but he does describe them as Gog and Magog (Nawotka and Wojciechowska, *The Alexander Romance*, 203).

[63] Nawotka and Wojciechowska, *The Alexander Romance*, 205–13.

[64] The idea that the gates were broken was common in the medieval period. The Spanish Jewish traveler Benjamin of Tudela refers to the "lands of the Alans, which is a land surrounded by mountains and has no outlet except the iron gates which Alexander made, but which were afterwards broken," for example (Adler, *The Itinerary of Benjamin of Tudela*, 43–44).

[65] Brewer, *Prester John*, 2. See also DeWeese, "The Influence of the Mongols."

[66] Indeed, Genghis had attacked the Khitai in 1218 (Dashdondog, "A Brief Historical Background," 41).

[67] Osipian, "Armenian Involvement," 72.   [68] Ibid., 73.

Soon, however, the rumors from the east turned darker, and with them, the associations. When news arrived that the Mongols had defeated a Georgian (and Christian) army, for example, this surprising event caused doubt among some of those – though not James of Vitry – who had thought Prester John was on his way, and this doubt swelled as Mongol forces approached Russia and Hungary.[69] While some medieval chroniclers could not admit that they may have been mistaken, it was clear enough that something had gone wrong. In 1232, Alberic of Troisfontaines concluded, "sadly," that "Prester John ... had indeed been on his way" but simply gave up when he heard that the crusaders had lost the city of Damietta in Egypt. According to Alberic, the Prester's people had rebelled, assassinated him, and put a Mongol king on the throne – "a false Prester John in place of the real."[70] Now, rather than hastening to the help of Europe, the Prester's army was coming to destroy it.

From then on, the associations applied to the Mongols grew grimmer still. Some medieval commenters identified them as Gog and Magog, biblical harbingers of the apocalypse, or as "the fulfillment of Saint John's Apocalypse, and the revelation of Pseudo-Methodius."[71] For others, there were still more identifications available, showing both the reach and fluidity of medieval interpretive frameworks. For the Austrian poet Rudolf of Ems, in the thirteenth century, the Mongols were at once Gog and Magog and descendants of Abraham's first-born son, Ishmael.[72] Of course it was clear to many that whoever else they might be, these were the peoples Alexander had tried to protect the world from.[73] And, just as naturally, many European intellectuals thought that the Mongol armies were the armies of the Lost Tribes of Israel returning at last, and bringing with them the end of days – as they had long expected and feared.[74]

Generally, in European descriptions of the Mongol invasion, we see the interplay of the three great traditions we have discussed so far in this chapter – the Prester, and Alexander, and the Lost Tribes of Israel – and we see the ability of references to each to communicate perspectives.

---

[69] Bietenholz, *Historia and Fabula*, 133–34.   [70] Ibid.
[71] Osipian, "Armenian Involvement," 73–74.   [72] Bietenholz, *Historia and Fabula*, 134.
[73] This opinion was expressed, for example, in "the 12th century version of the *Iskandarnameh* written by the Persian poet Nizami Ganjavi" (Bond, "Building the Iron Gates of Alexander").
[74] Parfitt, *The Lost Tribes of Israel*, 20. See also Osipian, "Armenian Involvement," 73–74. It is also worth noting that there are Hebrew versions of the *Alexander Romance* where the conqueror meets the Lost Tribes (Dönitz, "Alexander the Great in Medieval Hebrew Traditions," 37).

We see fluidity – from the Prester when things seemed to be going well, from a European perspective, to Alexander's barbarians and the Lost Tribes when they were not. Each tradition communicated a different expectation with respect to what the Mongols were planning to do, and what they represented. And of course, the traditions involved continued to cross-pollinate with each other. Some – including the virulently anti-semitic thirteenth-century monk and chronicler Matthew of Paris, and the Holy Roman Emperor Frederick II – thought the Mongols were both the Israelites *and* the people beyond the gates.[75] One medieval chronicler identified them more specifically with the tribe of Reuben.[76] And as late as the late sixteenth century CE, Abraham Ortelius, a Dutch cartographer, included "the land of the *horda* of the Danites" and the "*horda* of the Naphtali" on "his map of Tartary in *Theatrum Orbis Terrarum* (Antwerp, 1573)."[77] Such was the swirl of myth in those days.[78]

The Mongol invasions also offer us our first glimpse at the other side of the coin, concerning the question of what the return of the Lost Tribes could represent or signify. As the Mongols struck deeper towards Europe, the fear engendered among Christian commenters was met by an enthusi-asm among some Jewish ones. Indeed, for many Jews, an avenging army of Israelites, headed for the heart of antisemitic Europe, seemed as if it could be for them what the Prester was to Christians.[79] Thus, for example,

---

[75] Parfitt, *The Lost Tribes of Israel*, 20. See also Salvadore, "The Ethiopian Age of Exploration," 597. See also Parfitt, *The Lost Tribes of Israel*, 14, 20. As Matthew wrote, "these *Saracens*, the memory of whom is detestable, are believed to have been of the ten tribes, who abandoned the law of Moses, and followed after the golden calves; and Alexander also endeavoured to shut them up in the precipitous Caspian mountains by walls cemented with bitumen." Translation from Menache, "Tartars, Jews, Saracens," 329. Menache notes that Richard of Sens also described the Mongols as "those Jews who were enclosed by the great king Alexander within the Caspian mountains" and so did Saturnina (ibid., 332–33).

[76] Bietenholz, *Historia and Fabula*, 134.   [77] Parfitt, *The Lost Tribes of Israel*, 20.

[78] As Menache puts it, "the ten tribes imagery thus provided a useful clue to understanding the Tartars' inhuman behaviour, while also incorporating an unknown, and therefore frightening, enemy into well-known patterns" – proceeding, as I said at the beginning of this chapter, from the known to the unknown (Menache, "Tartars, Jews, Saracens," 332). Menache also notes that Matthew's description of the Mongols "serves as a faithful mirror of the maturing image of the Mongols, which amalgamated both Saracen and Jewish stereotypes" (ibid., 329).

[79] "From the Jews' perspective, the timing of the Mongol invasion accorded it maximum importance, since according to ancestral traditions the year 1240 (5000 in the Jewish calendar) was expected to witness the coming of the Messiah" (ibid. 334).

A copious exchange of letters among the [Jewish] communities in Spain, Sicily and Germany indicates not only the intensity of messianic expectations at the time, but also the widespread belief that the Mongols had been sent by providence to save the sons of Israel from the lengthy tyranny of the gentiles.[80]

Matthew of Paris reports that, as the Mongols approached Europe, German Jews believed that the Mongols were the rest of Israel coming to save them at long last – and that some of them eagerly collaborated with the invaders.[81] Whether this was true or simply an antisemitic canard, it is a historical fact that the famous kabbalist, Abraham Abulafia, was disappointed to discover the Mongols were not Israelites – and he was not the only one.[82]

Most importantly, the consistent application of European interpretive frameworks to external events – and rumors of events – would have far more than merely rhetorical effects. In the medium-term, the thirteenth and fourteenth centuries would see a series of embassies and counter-embassies back and forth between European and Mongol courts. European potentates and pontiffs sought from the Mongols the help in prosecuting the Crusades they had long thought the Prester might supply, and the Mongols often found themselves facing enemies held in common.[83] Nor were they necessarily averse to deploying the Prester

---

[80] Ibid., 334.

[81] Perry, "The Imaginary War," 22. As Benite notes, "Matthew of Paris (c. 1200–1259) gives an account of a Hungarian bishop who interrogated captured warriors from the Mongol army" trying to figure out if they were Jews – it seems he came away feeling that they were not (Benite, *The Ten Lost Tribes*, 109). See, generally, Menache, "Tartars, Jews, Saracens."

[82] Benite, *The Ten Lost Tribes*, 111. "Genghis Khan and his successors, indeed, represented in the eyes of many Jews a powerful army sent by God to defeat the Christians who had oppressed European Jewry for generations" (Menache, "Tartars, Jews, Saracens," 337). However, for the likelihood that no such "plot" occurred, see ibid., "Tartars, Jews, Saracens," 340–41.

[83] In 1245 alone, Pope Innocent IV sent three or four different emissaries to the Mongols to ascertain their identity and ambitions, receiving two Mongol diplomats back in 1248 (Osipian, "Armenian Involvement," 75–80). At around the same time, Louis IX (1214–1270) sent an emissary into Mongol lands, seeking to establish relations. "In 1253, the Flemish Franciscan William of Rubruck (1215–1270) was originally only sent to Sartak Khan in the steppes of today's southern Russia, but in the end he travelled all the way to Great Khan Möngke (1209–1259) in Karakorum" (Valtrová, "Beyond the Horizons of Legend," 155–56). One John of Montecorvino, another Franciscan sent east, ended up archbishop of what is now Beijing (ibid., 155–56). The rulers of the Armenian kingdom of Cilicia proposed a joint Crusade between European powers and "the Tatar rulers – Īl-khāns – of Persia," and a later Il-khan, Oljaitu, sent emissaries to "the pope, Philip IV, and Edward I" (Osipian, "Armenian Involvement," 71). The Mongols sent other emissaries to the West, most famously Rabban Sawma, sent

John myth themselves. According to the French chronicler Jean de Joinville, a letter from the court of Guyuk Khan reached France in 1251, in which the Khan mentioned that the Mongols had killed Prester John and might do the same to Louis IX if he did not send a substantial annual tribute.[84]

Later on, the various associations between traditions, peoples, and places that developed over the medieval period would inspire still more dramatic real world effects. In 1541, the Portuguese soldier Christovão da Gama, son of Vasco da Gama, would land with four hundred muskets at Mitsiwa, in Ethiopia, in order to help the Ethiopian emperor Lebna Dengel in his war against the vicious, brilliant Ahmad Gran ("left-handed") – in large part, because the Portuguese believed that Dengel was Prester John.[85] In the twentieth century, the legend of Eldad ha-Dani, discussed below, would provide the key that would allow the Beta Israel of Ethiopia to become citizens of the modern State of Israel.

Yet of all the ramifications of twelve tribe speculation in the medieval period, the most unlikely, unexpected, and farthest-reaching came when the typical responses to the imminence of Israel gave way to atypical ones. These atypical developments are not just interesting and surprising in and of themselves, but explain a great deal about where "becoming Israel" goes from here. Specifically, a new Christian interest in the hope the return of Israel could represent would lay the groundwork for a later preoccupation with Israel among Christian communities, especially Western European Protestants – and even, at times, a desire to "become Israel." Meanwhile, the fear the return of Israel could sometimes stir in Jewish communities presages future challenges that a world full of Israels would raise – each different, but each understanding itself as *the* Israel nonetheless. We turn, then, to one more example of the common range, in the story of Benjamin of Tudela, the Spanish Jewish traveler who "discovered" the prosperous Lost Tribes in the reaches of Asia. We will then consider the destinies of two self-appointed emissaries from the Lost Tribes: Eldad ha-Dani and David Reubeni. In the receptions they received

---

from Khan Argun to the Pope in the thirteenth century (Coakley and Sterk, "Asian and African Christianity," 374–75).

[84] Bietenholz, *Historia and Fabula*, 136. As Bietenholtz notes, Joinville claimed to be "present at Caesarea in 1251" when this letter arrived, in response to Louis' own envoy to the Khan – though by that point, the letter came from Guyuk Khan's widow.

[85] Tamrat, *Church and State in Ethiopia 1270–1527*, 301; Marcus, *A History of Ethiopia*, 33; Kurt, "The Search for Prester John," 23; Pankhurst, *The Ethiopian Borderlands*, 170. For an eyewitness account, see Whiteway, *The Portuguese Expedition to Abyssinia*.

in the communities they visited, we see how complicated "becoming Israel" could be, and the portentous shape of developments to come.

3.5 HOPES AND FEARS OF ISRAEL

Sometime in the 1160s, Benjamin of Tudela, a Spanish Jew, set out from Spain for a journey that would last around thirteen years, largely through the Near and Middle East.[86] In the *Itinerary of Benjamin of Tudela*, which survives today, we learn that Benjamin left from Saragossa, and traveling through France, Italy, Greece, and Constantinople, crossed into Crusader territory at Antioch and Damascus. From Damascus he went on to Baghdad, to Basra, and "to Egypt by way of Aden and Assuan."[87] Something may have been in the air – it was in 1168 that Maimonides arrived in Egypt from Spain, there to settle for the rest of his life.[88] As for Benjamin, he would eventually make his way back west through Sicily, ending his narrative with his arrival in Paris.

In all likelihood, Benjamin's *Itinerary* spans a slightly wider geography than he actually traveled, including accounts of Persia, India, and even China – the "land of Zin" – that were presumably based on rumors he had heard, rather than experiences he had. But at least in the region of the Levant, Benjamin probably saw much of what he describes with his own eyes.[89] And what he saw, in place after place, was *Jews* – and not only that, but Jews whose situation in the east would have provided an extraordinary contrast to the weal of Europe's oppressed minority.

Recall if you will that, in the biblical visions of history, there are two great exiles – and in some ways, three. In 722 BCE, the Assyrians are supposed to have taken the people of the kingdom of Israel away into their lands, and in 586, the Babylonians are supposed to have done the same to the Judahites. As we know, neither of these events was quite as dramatic or complete as the biblical text describes, but something like both still happened, and so did another, similar event. Around 597, there was another Judahite exile: Nebuchadnezzar removed the Judahite king,

---

[86] Benite states that he began his journey in 1159, Shatzmiller in 1165, and Fauvelle-Aymar in the "mid-1160s" (Benite, *The Ten Lost Tribes*, 102–3; Shatzmiller, "Jews, Pilgrimage, and the Christian Cult of Saints," 338; Fauvelle-Aymar, "Desperately Seeking the Jewish Kingdom of Ethiopia," 385.

[87] Adler, "Introduction," 5.   [88] Man, *Saladin*, 71–72.

[89] As Benite puts it, "while most of the stories in his bestselling *Itinerario* are based on actual experiences, Benjamin incorporates numerous fictional anecdotes, traditions, and legends" (Benite, *The Ten Lost Tribes*, 103).

Jehoiachin, and a number of other Judahite dignitaries, including the prophet Ezekiel to Babylon. Apparently, this was a warning shot over Judah's bow, eleven years before Nebuchadnezzar destroyed the kingdom (2 Kgs. 24:10–16). He set Zedekiah on the throne in Jehoiachin's place, and it was Zedekiah's rebellion that eventually did Jerusalem in.

Throughout his journey, Benjamin of Tudela encounters legacies of all of these exiles in a wide variety of places. On the river Euphrates, he finds the Synagogue of Ezekiel "bearing an inscription of all those who accompanied the Judahites into exile, and the sepulcher of Ezekiel himself."[90] At Kufa, he tells us, the Judahite king Jeconiah is laid to rest, and on the river Raga, Zedekiah himself.[91] In Harran, once the home of Abraham, he finds a synagogue supposedly built by Ezra; in Mosul, one built by Jonah; and in Baghdad, one built by Daniel.[92] And as he goes further east, into the "cities of the Medes," one of the sites mentioned in 2 Kings 17:6's account of the Assyrian settlement of Israel, he finds those who "belong to the first captivity which King Shalmaneser led away; and they speak the language in which the Targum is written."[93] On the river Gozan, another reference to 2 Kings 17:6, he finds Israelites spread throughout several cities. And there he heard a rumor from farther east still: "there are men of Israel in the land of Persia who say that in the mountains of Nisabur four of the tribes of Israel dwell, namely, the tribe of Dan, the tribe of Zebulun, the tribe of Asher, and the tribe of Naphtali."[94] These were not part of the Jewish diaspora, but instead members of the Lost Tribes of Israel.

At a distance of nearly nine hundred years, the parts of Benjamin's narrative that still spark the imagination are the numbers of Jews and Israelites he discovers, and the circumstances of their station, which are so different from European realities. In the first case, Benjamin claims to have visited a city called Okbara, on the Tigris, hosting ten thousand Jews.[95] In Baghdad, he finds forty thousand Jews, ten academies, and twenty-eight synagogues.[96] As he goes on towards the lands of the Lost Tribes, as opposed to those of the exile of Judah, the numbers only increase – as befits the descriptions of Josephus, the *Letter of Prester John*, and much else besides. According to Benjamin, there are *hundreds of thousands of Jews* in the city of Teima, and fifty thousand in Kheibar alone: "learned men, and great warriors."[97] There are thirty thousand

[90] Translation in Adler, *The Itinerary of Benjamin of Tudela*, 45–46.   [91] Ibid., 47.
[92] Ibid., 38–39, 45.   [93] Ibid., 51.   [94] Ibid., 54.   [95] Ibid., 39.   [96] Ibid., 43.
[97] Ibid., 48–49.

"Israelites" near Hamadan, a "great city of Media," and one hundred thousand on the River Gozan.[98]

As for the status and social mobility of Asia's Jewry, Benjamin describes a Rabbi Joseph, at Mosul, who is astronomer to Nur ad-Din's brother, Sin ad-Din.[99] In Baghdad, there is a "Daniel, the son of Hisdai, who is styled 'Our Lord the Head of the Captivity of all Israel,'" a descendant of David, "and he has been invested with authority over all the congregations of Israel at the hands of the Emir al Muminin, the Lord of Islam."[100] And as for the Israelites of the old demesne of Assyria, they are just as they often were in the land of the Prester. They answer to nobody but themselves, a point Benjamin is quite insistent upon. The Jews of Nisabur are "not under the rule of the Gentiles, but they have a prince of their own, whose name is R. Joseph Amarkala the Levite," and they war as far as Kush.[101] The "yoke of the Gentiles" is also not on the Jews of Kheibar. And in the "land of the assassins" (*Hashishim*), "there are four communities of Israel who go forth with them in war-time" who are "not under the rule of the king of Persia, but reside in the high mountains ... and none can overcome them."[102]

Benjamin's vision of the powerful, free Jews of the east has rightly been called a "consolation for the Jewish people."[103] Another scholar describes it as "a compensatory *Imaginaire*," a strategy "for coping with harsh social realities ... an invincible Jewish kingdom."[104] It is also typical – and, like the Jewish responses to the Mongol invasions mentioned above, not terribly surprising. Just as Christian commenters exploited the "separability" of Israel to express their perspective on the present

---

[98] Ibid., 54. [99] Ibid., 38.
[100] "The authority of the Head of the Captivity extends over all the communities of Shinar, Persia, Khurasan and Sheba which is El-Yemen and Diyar Kalach (Bekr) and the land of Aram Naharaim (Mesopotamia), and over the dwellers in the mountains of Ararat and the lands of the Alans, which is a land surrounded by mountains and has no outlet except the iron gates which Alexander made, but which were afterwards broken" (ibid., 43–44).
[101] Ibid., 54. [102] Ibid., 48, 51.
[103] Cooper, "Conceptualizing Diaspora," 108. Here, Cooper quotes from Signer, *The Itinerary of Benjamin of Tudela*. Kim adds that "the Diaspora thematically framed the entire work, and Benjamin's detailed account of Jewish communities in the Mediterranean and eastward was rhetorically in the tradition of Consolation to his people in a time of suffering" – a "Consolation" that "does not only chronicle Jews past and present, but implicitly ... also looks to the future, to God's promise to his chosen people, and to the time when Jews will be restored to their land" (Kim, "The Itinerary of Benjamin of Tudela," 107).
[104] Perry, "The Imaginary War," 23.

and future of the Jews they knew, Jewish commenters could make the Lost Tribes a mirror held up to their hopes and desires for themselves. In Benjamin's vision, we see the *cri de coeur* of a person contemplating how different things could be in another world.

Yet for our purposes, it is important that Benjamin's vision of the Israelite east is on some level a fantasy. Not that there were no thriving Jewish communities of Asia, not that the experience of Jews under Muslim rule was never different from the experience of the Jews of Europe. There were, and they were. Still, the fact that Benjamin was able to observe the rest of Israel from a distance made all the difference here. In short, what the rest of the twelve tribes of Israel could represent, in theory – hope, consolation, aspiration – they could represent *only* in theory, because only in theory could the rest of Israel be whatever they were needed to be. In practice, which is to say whenever different "Israels" met, things would always be more complicated. As a result, *actual* encounters between claimants to Israel often went far differently than *imagined* encounters. In other words, Benjamin could use the Lost Tribes as a mirror – or consolation, or compensation – because he observed them at a distance, and in some cases, not at all. When different heirs to Israel actually met, the same would not be possible. And this brings us to the curious case of Eldad ha-Dani.

3.6 ELDAD HA-DANI AND THE JEWS OF KAIROUAN

In 883 CE, almost three hundred years before Benjamin of Tudela arrived in the Levant, a man calling himself Eldad ha-Dani – Eldad the Danite – appeared in Kairouan, in what is now Tunisia.[105] He presented himself as an emissary from the Lost Tribes. His Danites, he said, lived by the river "Kush," in East Africa, near a place named Havilah, "a kingdom of nomads under the leadership of King Addiel."[106] They had not, in fact, left Israel at the time of the Assyrian conquest, but, according to him, earlier.[107] They had risen in revolt against Jeroboam, first king of the

---

[105] Wasserstein, "Eldad Ha-Dani and Prester John," 214.

[106] Asa-El, *The Diaspora and the Lost Tribes of Israel*, 167. Havilah is mentioned in Genesis 2 in connection with the Garden of Eden (2:10–11) and in Genesis 25 as one of the lands settled by the sons of Ishmael "east of Egypt as one goes towards Assyria" (25:18).

[107] One of the reasons "Lost Tribe legends" is not a perfect catch-all designation for post-biblical myths about Israel is how many groups describe themselves as having left the rest of Israel before the Assyrian conquest, including the Samaritans.

independent northern kingdom of Israel, when he asked them to take up arms against the Davidic monarchy of Judah. Rather than allow them to spill Israelite blood, YHWH brought them to Egypt, and then to Kush. And "Eldad son of Mahli, son of Atiel, son of Yekutiel ... son of Hushim, son of Dan, son of Jacob" brought news to Kairouan not only of his own tribe, but of the rest of the Lost Tribes as well.[108]

Naphtali, Gad, and Asher, in the story he told the startled Kairouanis, had eventually joined the Danites in Africa, perhaps fleeing Tiglath-Pileser or Sennacherib, while Zebulun and Reuben lived on either side of the "mountains of Paran."[109] Ephraim and half of Manasseh were in Arabia, while Simeon and the other half were in the kingdom of the Khazars, a steppe people best known to history for their actual conversion to Judaism. The Issacharites lived in the mountains "near to the land of the Medes and Persians."[110] And here, as in the Prester John *Letter*, the Sambatyon has a role to play: Eldad's tribe of Dan – as well as Naphtali, Gad, and Asher – live near the river, but not across it. That honor is reserved for the "Sons of Moses" alone. As for Eldad himself, his wild tale of adventure still survives in a book called the *Sefer Eldad*, involving shipwreck, capture by cannibals, and finally, rescue by a member of the (lost) tribe of Issachar followed at last by his release.[111] He had come to Kairouan fresh from this rescue.

It is worth taking a moment here to note that the geography Eldad lays out for the rest of Israel is just such a mix of traditions as we have seen throughout this chapter. Many of the tribes live in or near biblical place names, although not always ones associated specifically with the Lost Tribes. These include Kush itself, and Paran. The settlement of the Issacharites near the land of the "Medes and Persians" probably reflects 2 Kings 17:6's account of the settlement of lost Israel in the "cities of the Medes." At the same time, the role of the "Sambatyon" is not biblical – the Sambatyon does not appear in the Bible – but echoes other legends, while the reference to the Khazars reflects legends of Jewish Khazars. The story of the "sons of Moses" is not biblical either, and it also appears in the *Targum of Pseudo-Jonathan* from roughly the same period as Eldad's

---

[108] Neubauer, "Where Are the Ten Tribes?," 99–100.
[109] Translations in this section are from Neubauer's 1889 edition. For this, see Neubauer, "Where Are the Ten Tribes?," 100–103. See also Perry, "The Imaginary War," 11.
[110] Neubauer, "Where Are the Ten Tribes?," 103.
[111] Benite, *The Ten Lost Tribes*, 86–87.

arrival.[112] According to the legend, this group – really priests of the line of Moses – had bitten off their fingers, while on their way to exile in Babylon, rather than play impious songs on their harps, as in the famous Psalm 137. As a result, they and they alone were rewarded with a mystical deliverance.[113]

The main point, however, is that given everything else we know about Jewish understandings of the Lost Tribes in the medieval period, we would naturally expect Eldad to inspire wild enthusiasm among the Kairouanis, and to be feted, honored, and pressed for news. In some ways he was, if not necessarily in Kairouan. The *Sefer Eldad*, his account of his adventures transcribed, would indeed become wildly popular among Jewish communities – what one nineteenth-century scholar called the "Arabian Nights of the Jews." It was "translated into Arabic, Latin, and German, and most probably there were also Spanish and Italian translations, now lost."[114] The enthusiasm, the hunger we see in Benjamin's story also extends to how eagerly Jews in other places consumed Eldad's history.

Yet the Kairouanis were quite concerned about Eldad's story because his Jewish practices were somewhat different from theirs and they shouldn't have been, no matter how long the tribe of Dan had been separated from the rest of Israel. It is true, as I pointed out in the last chapter, that Jewish tradition acknowledges that the major collections of Jewish law were composed much after the *Torah* itself was, but, typically, they are not supposed to be any less ancient. Again, the *Torah* and the Talmuds are often supposed to be part of the "Dual Torah" given to

---

[112] The exact date of the Targum of Pseudo-Jonathan appears to be impossible to establish. Like many similar texts, it includes traditions that may be quite old but also clear references to narratives that only emerged in later periods. There are some who suggest it emerged as early as the fourth century and some as late as the tenth. For the former, see Flesher and Chilton, *The Targums*, 178; Mortensen, *The Priesthood in Targum Pseudo-Jonathan*; Vermes, "The Targumic Versions of Genesis 4:3–16." For the latter, or rather for a reason to suspect a roughly eighth- through tenth-century date, see Kaufman, "Targum Pseudo-Jonathan"; Cook, "The 'Kaufman Effect.'" For the references to Islamic traditions, see Klein, *Michael Klein on the Targums*, 52. See also Benite, *The Ten Lost Tribes*, 79.

[113] This is apparently a take on Psalm 137, the famous song that begins "By the waters of Babylon" and includes the line "because there our captors asked of us songs ... sing to us of the songs of Zion" (Psalm 137:3). See Neubauer, "Where Are the Ten Tribes?," 101–2.

[114] Neubauer, "Where Are the Ten Tribes?," 99.

Moses on Sinai, one in written and one in oral form.[115] What this meant for Eldad is that even though his Danites were supposed to have left the company of other Israelites a thousand years or more before the Talmuds were finished, common Jewish practices should already have developed, since they really went back to Moses. The Jewish elders of Kairouan interviewed Eldad extensively and came away concerned.[116] They decided to call in an expert.

In those days, the highest Jewish authorities were the heads of the two great Jewish academies at Sura and Pumbedita – the *Gaons*, or presidents, of those academies. The Kairouanis wrote to the Gaon of Sura, Zemaḥ ben Ḥaim, whom we know to have been in office from 889–895, with a lengthy description of Eldad's practice – a document that survives today as *The Ritual of Eldad ha-Dani*.[117] After considering the matter, however, the Gaon wrote back with good news. The differences that existed between Eldad's practice and normative Judaism were adequately explained, he said, by the different modes through which the law had been transmitted in different places – "the Talmud is studied by the men of Babylon in Aramaic, and by the men of Palestine in *Targum*, and by the

---

[115] Strack and Stemberger, *Introduction to the Talmud and Midrash*, 142; Neusner, *Introduction to Rabbinic Literature*, xx.

[116] "... if the tribes were not part of biblical history, the covenant between God and Israel still bound them ... From a rabbinic point of view, just as Mosaic law developed 'here,' in the Jewish exile, so too it must have developed 'there,' ... Even if the ten tribes were removed from the rest of the children of Israel, they should have naturally or spontaneously developed the religious institutions and legal system of the Jews" (Benite, *The Ten Lost Tribes*, 96). In reality, Eldad may have been a Yemeni Jew, as Benite, following on the work of Schloessinger and Morag, argues, though there have been other answers over the centuries (Schloessinger, *The Ritual of Eldad Ha-Dani*, 8; Benite, *The Ten Lost Tribes*, 92; Morag, "A Linguistic Examination").

[117] Benite, *The Ten Lost Tribes*, 86; Perry, "The Imaginary War," 3. See also Epstein, *Eldad ha-Dani*, 6–10. The "Geonim," or heads of the academies (Gaons), generally, are understood, in the rabbinic chronology, to be the successors to the "Amoraim," spokesmen, whose efforts created the Talmud – the Jerusalem and Babylonian Talmuds – who themselves succeeded the "Tannaim," the teachers, whose thoughts are supposed to be encoded within them. The history of the rabbinical eras, as Strack and Stemberger warn, is of course "entirely in accordance with the perspectives and interest of the rabbis ... Thus the time of the *Tannaim* ... extends from Hillel and Shammai at the beginning of our era ... to Rabbi [Judah ha-Nasi] and his sons, i.e. to the early third century ... They are followed by the *Amoraim* ... up to c. 500. The time of the *Saboraim* ... found its continuation in the period of the *Geonim* ... until the eleventh century" (Strack and Stemberger, *Introduction to the Talmud and Midrash*, 7). The time of the *Geonim* is not the last rabbinic era either, but is followed by the *Rishonim* and *Acharonim* into the present.

sages exiled to Ethiopia" – historically identified with biblical "Kush" – "in Hebrew, which they understand."

Beyond that, the Gaon mused, perhaps the rigors of Eldad's own experiences caused him to misremember.[118] "The Mishna," he declared, with the full weight of his "geonic" authority, "is one law," and so, in a sense, were the people Israel.[119] After that, Eldad and his troubling story vanish from history. It would, however, have an extraordinary, and unexpected afterlife, which I will discuss in Chapter 5. As I noted above, not just the tradition of the Israelites of Kush, but the actual ruling of the Gaon would begin the process, and paper trail, that would ultimately result in the official recognition of the Beta Israel of Ethiopia as the tribe of Dan in the twentieth century.

For now, however, the point is this: if Benjamin's story represents the typical orientation of Jewish audiences to Lost Tribe traditions, as the stories of the Prester and Alexander represent the typical Christian perspective, then Eldad's story reveals another aspect of "becoming Israel." As opposed to aspirational encounters between different claimants to Israel, actual encounters would very often be a source of anxiety, as they brought into clear view how differently "Israels" could be constructed. The tension between Eldad and the Kairouanis, as opposed to the enthusiasm Benjamin had for the Lost Tribes, is an expression of this gap between discourse and reality where "becoming Israel" is concerned. Thus, Eldad's story could be an inspiring one at a distance, but up close and personal, it was a cause of genuine discomfort, even existential uncertainty. Every Israel claims to be *the* Israel, every Israel is really unique – so encounters, by revealing as much, raised questions that were difficult to answer.

Meanwhile, though Benjamin of Tudela's travelogue would be popular among Jewish communities, it would make its most enduring mark when it was rediscovered by European Christians, especially beginning in the early seventeenth century.[120] In this context, it would feed a suddenly voracious hunger to discover the whereabouts of the tribes, their role in

---

[118] From Benite, *The Ten Lost Tribes*, 98.   [119] Ibid.

[120] For the Jewish reception of Benjamin's work, see Marci Freedman's dissertation on the subject at the University of Manchester, Freedman, "The Transmission and Reception of Benjamin of Tudela's Book of Travels," 94–130. As she notes, the first Latin editions of the *Itinerary* – and thus, the first accessible to non-Hebrew readers – were published in 1575 and 1633 (ibid., 131). For an in-depth discussion of the Christian reception of the *Itinerary* in the context, especially, of the British exploration of America, see Kim, "The Itinerary of Benjamin of Tudela."

the course of sacred history, and whether or not they were on the verge of being discovered. For Christian audiences, since the Jews were already "other," there was no tension of identification to be had, but on the other hand, what a change from the existential fear the tribes engendered in the *Letter of Prester John*, and in the context of the Mongol invasion, to the hope the discovery of Israel would come to represent. The groundwork for this transition was laid by the compounding associations Israel gained during the medieval age, as indeed we have already seen – and will see, in a much more pronounced way, in the story of David Reubeni, the last in this chapter.

3.7 A JEWISH PRESTER JOHN

When it comes to David Reubeni, the question is, what are the odds? What are the odds that a man claiming to come, as an emissary, from an eastern army of Israelites – the very thing generations of European Christians had been taught to fear – would be taken seriously, let alone welcomed by some of the most august figures in Europe? But that is just what happened when David Reubeni first appeared in Italy, in the 1520s, claiming to be the son of one King Solomon, ruler of a kingdom called "Habor," in Arabia, and the general of Habor's armies, three hundred thousand strong.[121] In Habor, which is mentioned in 2 Kings 17:6 as one of the cities the Israelites were deported to, there dwelt, he claimed, the tribes of Gad, Manasseh, and his own tribe of Reuben.[122] David offered the crowned heads of Europe an alliance against the Muslims, in order to overthrow the Muslim kingdoms in Arabia and the Levant, just as Prester John supposedly had.[123] And in 1524, he was taken to see the Pope, Clement VII.

The Pope himself did not commit to work with David directly. He was, however, impressed: he paid David's expenses and sent him on to the king of Portugal, John III, with a letter of recommendation.[124] Nor was Clement merely fobbing off an inconvenient problem on someone else. The Portuguese were a canny target for David, as they were at that point as hot on the trail of Prester John as any people previously had been. If anyone would be interested in engaging the help of an army from the east,

---

[121] Cooper, "Conceptualizing Diaspora," 103; Benite, *The Ten Lost Tribes*, 113–14.
[122] Cooper, "Conceptualizing Diaspora," 103.   [123] Ibid., 104–5.
[124] Asa-El, *The Diaspora and the Lost Tribes of Israel*, 167–68; Cooper, "Conceptualizing Diaspora," 104–5.

even an Israelite one, it would be the Portuguese.[125] Beyond that, Clement wrote to the emperor of Ethiopia, who was a Christian, and whom many in Europe suspected to *be* Prester John.[126] As Clement put it in his letter, somewhat apologetically – and also hinting at things to come – "God sometimes uses enemies in order to punish enemies."[127]

In Portugal, too, David must have at first succeeded beyond his wildest dreams, especially given that Portugal "had recently expelled or forcibly converted its entire Jewish population."[128] Nevertheless, John III listened to David's proposal – and even promised David what he wanted. According to David, all his massive army lacked was munitions, and if given them, they would sweep the field clean of the enemies of Judaism and Christianity alike.[129] John said he would provide the munitions. But then something happened. David, of course, was not only playing to Christian audiences – no self-described emissary from the Lost Tribes could, whatever their intentions. And the *conversos* of Portugal – Jews forced into Christian conversion – responded with wild enthusiasm.

In the end, the arrival of this emissary from their hidden brethren – the mighty, free Jews of the east – touched off what one author described as a "messianic euphoria" among Portugal's own hidden Jews, something David may well have intended.[130] "Worst of all," as one author recently put it, "a high-ranking government official by the name of Dioguo Pirez became so impressed with Reubeni that he circumcised himself and fled the country (to become an adept of the Kabbalah and a messianic figure

[125] Benite, *The Ten Lost Tribes*, 125. In fact, as Eliav-Feldon notes, "when Reuveni arrived in Portugal, the court was still awaiting news from the delegation that had been sent to Ethiopia ten years earlier" (Eliav-Feldon, "Invented Identities," 222).

[126] Benite, *The Ten Lost Tribes*, 114.

[127] Quote from Eshkoli, *Sipur David Ha-Re'uveni*, 176–78, reproduced in Benite, *The Ten Lost Tribes*, 124.

[128] Eliav-Feldon, "Invented Identities," 210; Asa-El, *The Diaspora and the Lost Tribes of Israel*, 167; Cooper, "Conceptualizing Diaspora," 103–5. "The Pope ... suggested instead that Reuveni submit his plans and requests to the King of Portugal, who was then the monarch 'most involved in such matters'" (Eliav-Feldon, "Invented Identities," 210).

[129] Cooper, "Conceptualizing Diaspora," 104–5.

[130] Asa-El, *The Diaspora and the Lost Tribes of Israel*, 167–68. Eliav-Feldon observes that "in the Zohar, the most important medieval book of the Kabbalah, the tribe of Reuben is assigned an important role in the scheme of redemption: it would be the first of the tribes to arise and lead the Jews to a final confrontation with their enemies" (Eliav-Feldon, "Invented Identities," 219). Benite describes David's scheme, where Israel would be redeemed by the Ten Lost Tribes, as a species of what Abraham Abulafia called "natural redemption" (Benite, *The Ten Lost Tribes*, 114).

known as Solomon Molcho)."[131] As Jewish hope started bubbling to the surface, the Christian fear of Israel was reignited. David's warm reception abruptly turned chilly, and he was forced to leave.[132]

From there, David's story takes a tragic turn. Leaving Portugal, he barely escaped the Inquisition in Spain, then spent two years imprisoned by the Duke of Clermont. He appeared, at length, in Mantua, Italy, where after meeting with local dignitaries he was forced to flee again – though not before almost successfully making his case once more, this time to the powerful Gonzaga family.[133] At some point, he began to travel with Solomon Molcho, the transfigured Portuguese official, and ultimately, both met the same end. Molcho was burned at the stake in 1532.[134] David lasted another six years, dying in Spain in 1538 at the hands of the Inquisition he had previously escaped – and despite, it is said, "a last-minute conversion to Christianity."[135] How he got to Spain, and much of what he did after his flight from Mantua, is unknown.[136] His adventure in Europe, from a guest of kings to death at the stake, had lasted eight years.

In the story of David Reubeni, all the threads of this chapter meet. If he gained admission to the halls of European power, it was not only because of what he claimed to represent, but who he resembled – Prester John.[137] So long had European potentates been conditioned to hope for deliverance from mighty armies east of Jerusalem that they were willing to overlook the form these armies took. Besides, there *were* Jewish armies in the lands of Prester John, according to the *Letter* – supposedly, the greatest and most terrible army in the world. If this army was to pledge its services to Christian Europe, instead of threatening it, well, as the Pope had put it, "God sometimes uses enemies in order to punish enemies."

Meanwhile, for the *conversos* of Portugal, David meant simply what the Lost Tribes had long meant: a reason to hope that deliverance from their cruel persecution was at hand. In the end, the dynamic cross-pollination of traditions so characteristic of the medieval age could give each something of the flavor of the others. The fluid interpretive framework I have been discussing in this chapter proves that David could be, at

---

[131] Eliav-Feldon, "Invented Identities," 210.   [132] Ibid., 210–11.

[133] Ibid., 211. As Eliav-Feldon observes, he might have succeeded there "if he had not been caught forging letters" from his father. After that, he spent some time in Venice (ibid., 228).

[134] Hillelson, "David Reubeni, An Early Visitor to Sennar," 55.

[135] Eliav-Feldon, "Invented Identities," 212; Lipiner, *O sapateiro de Trancoso e o alfaiate de Setúbal.*

[136] Eliav-Feldon, "Invented Identities," 211.   [137] Benite, *The Ten Lost Tribes,* 114.

once, a Jewish Prester John for Christians and a crystallization of the hope of Europe's subjugated Jewry – at least for a while.

And in a way, "for a while" was David's tragedy – that he represented, in himself, the union of parts of a symbolic vocabulary that might well be used in sequence but could not stand to be unified long. In other words, by the early sixteenth century, Israel could represent hope to both Jews and Christians, but not at the same time. From another perspective, the most important thing about David's tragic fate is how unremarkable it was. It happened not because of who he claimed to be, but simply because of who he was: a Jew, and another victim of the virulent European antisemitism of the medieval age.[138]

For this study as a whole, the key aspect of David's story is how it foreshadows the shape of developments to come. In some ways, the initial Christian acceptance of David and his supposed army of Israelites reflects a problem at the heart of the European encounter with Christianity. Many European Christians were no less interested in the connection between the restoration of Israel and the fulfillment of biblical prophecy than many Jews were, and in some ways even more so. As a result, David's unusual proposal would not provide the only circumstance in which antisemitic Christian audiences would have to take seriously, and even attempt to bring about, the return and reunion of Israel's tribes. Did the role the return of Israel played in biblical schemes of redemption help David gain entrance into the halls of European power? It is hard to say. But certainly, by the time David arrived in Italy, the discovery of Israel had lost some of its horror among Christian audiences, as we will see in the next chapter.

Indeed, within less than a century of David's death, certain European Christian intellectuals were wondering whether the Lost Tribes might be European Christians themselves. When the early Mormons, who are the subject of the next chapter, not only began to look for Israel but to identify themselves with it – and when they made the restoration of Israel their chief goal – it was a response to the apocalyptic resonance the return of the rest of Israel had long represented, now turned from a source of fear to a source of hope. The hope the restoration of Israel could represent for Christian communities in later centuries is an evolved variety of the hope that had brought David to prominence, even for such a brief

---

[138] "David Reuveni did not die for his crimes as a liar and a forger; he died for his sins: for leading New Christians astray, and for contradicting the 'truth' of the Holy Catholic Church" (Eliav-Feldon, "Invented Identities," 232).

time. And the curious history of this Jewish Prester John, especially his initial successes, reveals that in some corners, Christian perspectives were already changing.

3.8 CONCLUSION

In the medieval period, the twelve tribes tradition blossomed. Far from its original home, the tradition's utility as a tool for creating new visions of Israelite history and identity saw constant use, especially by European Christians and Jews, as a way of mapping the unknown, interpreting events, and expressing hopes and fears about the present and future. Mingling with the legends of the Prester and Alexander, this already readily adaptable tradition became more adaptable still, forming part of a rich, symbolic vocabulary that carried visions of Israel into the depths of Asia and North Africa. Eventually, a kind of mimesis between the armies of the Lost Tribes and the armies of the Prester, allied with a growing Christian recognition of the role the return of the tribes plays in biblical prophecies of the endtimes, opened the door to new ways of thinking about Israel, and new identifications with Israel. Throughout the medieval period, it would not be Christians alone who could picture lost Israel as a massive, avenging army, poised to uproot European society. In the end, it was not only Jews who could hope that Israel would be restored some day, under the right circumstances – or even see themselves as Israel, on the brink of restoration.

Thus, there are many ways in which the developments of the medieval period lay the groundwork for future chapters, and for making "becoming Israel" a global phenomenon. The legends of the Prester and of Eldad ha-Dani would do this literally, directing the search for Israel towards Ethiopia. In the nineteenth century, Jewish authorities would encounter an Israel there, in the Beta Israel, and would identify them with Eldad's people. The history of David Reubeni reveals a growing Christian awareness that the role Israel was to play in Christian schemas of redemption was out of alignment with a complete Christian rejection of Israel. Down one branch of subsequent speculation, Christian efforts to convert both Jews and "Israelites" escalated, courtesy of the essentially biblical idea that the restoration of Israel was a prelude to the end of the world. Down another branch, certain Christian intellectuals began to wonder whether they might not be the chosen people themselves.

In all of these respects, it would indeed be the inherent features of the twelve tribes tradition at work, allowing Israel to be partitioned across an increasingly wider world, for one Israel to describe another, for different parts of Israel to look different from each other. The ability of Eldad ha-Dani and David Reubeni to lay claim to an Israelite identity came courtesy of the long trailing edges the twelve tribes framework provides. The ability to characterize Israel as a terror, or a hope, or a little of both comes courtesy of the almost blank slate the tradition of the Ten Lost Tribes of Israel provides. The "experiential logic" the tradition makes available gave the Jews of Kairouan the means to explain the differences between Eldad's practices and their own, while preserving the conceptual unity of all Israel – that Eldad's people had learned the Talmud from the oral teachings of the "sages exiled to Ethiopia," rather than the written Talmuds.[139] And of course, the "separability" of Israel saw constant use in the production of medieval maps of Israel, from the lands of Kush to inner Mongolia, from India to the Sambatyon.

In the next chapter, and in the story of Mormonism, all these threads of speculation about where Israel was and who Israel was would meet in the form of a new world religion, and of a people who simultaneously sought for Israel and came to identify as Israel. But the foundation of both species of endeavor are to be found in the history of "becoming Israel" in the medieval world – most especially in the increasingly common medieval habit of identifying newly discovered peoples with Israel and a new willingness, in Christian communities, to see the return of Israel as something to be anticipated. Before "becoming Israel" could circle the world, however, it would first have to cross the Atlantic Ocean.

[139] From Benite, *The Ten Lost Tribes*, 98.

4

Becoming Israel in America

The Mormons and the New Jerusalem

Ephraim has become mixed with all the nations of the earth, and it is Ephraim that is gathering together. It is Ephraim that I have been searching for all the days of my preaching, and that is the blood which ran in my veins when I embraced the Gospel. If there are any other tribes of Israel mixed with the Gentiles we are also searching for them... We want the blood of Jacob, and that of his father Isaac and Abraham, which runs in the veins of the people. There is a particle of it here, and another there, blessing the nations as predicted.

—Brigham Young, April 8, 1855[1]

When David Reubeni was led to the stake in 1538, Christopher Columbus was thirty-two years in the grave. Already, the "New World," with its almost unfathomable riches, its vast and varied landscapes, and its native peoples, was known in Europe as "America," a title it had received – in an homage to the explorer Amerigo Vespucci – in 1507.[2] Already, some European intellectuals and explorers suspected that Israel was to be found there at last, among the native peoples of the continent then being revealed. And already, many Europeans wished to convert the natives to Christianity, for this and other reasons. Some saw in these efforts at conversion the fulfillment of a sacred duty to restore the people Israel to themselves. And some had already begun to wonder – or at least not long after – whether their own ancestors might include Israel, and whether European Christians themselves might be the true subject of biblical prophecies about Israel.

---

[1] Young, "Preaching and Testimony."
[2] Johnson, "Renaissance German Cosmographers and the Naming of America," 3; Laubenberger and Rowan, "The Naming of America," 91–93.

All of these ideas would have a role to play in the construction and reconstruction of the Israelite-identifying people at the center of this chapter, the people known to the world as the Mormons.[3] But by the time there were Mormons, these ideas about Israel in America would no longer be new. In fact, it would be nearly three hundred years from David's death to the moment, in 1830, when E. B. Grandin's printshop in Palmyra, New York, first put a mysterious book up for sale. Called the *Book of Mormon*, its author claimed it was a translation of an ancient record, scrupulously kept and safeguarded by Israelites of the tribe of Manasseh, who had come to America almost 2,500 years before. The story of the Mormons is, therefore, a story of deep roots; of the interweaving of multiple threads of speculation; and of a long, complex, and unpredictable history of developments. It is precisely a story that the long view of this study can help illuminate.

Zooming out for a moment, we might start by reiterating that the power of the twelve tribes of Israel tradition as a tool for Israelite ethnogeneses – "becoming Israel" – and for identifying "Israels" around the world comes, first and foremost, from its tremendous adaptability. The segmented structure of the twelve tribes framework, its *e pluribus unum* character, allows multiple different traditions about Israel to co-exist by allowing, at least ostensibly, for different parts of Israel to be very different from each other. This is a book about "many Israels," but "many" is an etic, outsider appreciation of the phenomenon. Since the twelve tribes tradition has room for at least twelve different variants of Israel, this allows very different claimants to appear to be part of the larger whole.

Beyond that, the "primordialist premise" that the twelve tribes tradition embodies – the idea that Israel was always Israel, whatever else any part of it became, and that "all Israel" would always exist, however widely dispersed – gave the search for Israel and "becoming Israel" alike a flexibility that has allowed for the nearly constant exercise of each, as indeed we have seen. Because of this flexibility, different constructions of Israel can not only exist, but co-exist, as the number of different claimants to Israel that are supposed to be out there in the first place offers a ready explanation for their differences.

---

[3] In recent years, Russell M. Nelson, current president of the Church, has stressed a preference for the full name, "The Church of Jesus Christ of Latter-day Saints," over "Mormons" and "Mormonism" (Chiu, "Stop Calling the Mormon Church 'Mormon'"). I have kept the more common term for ease of understanding.

With all of these different threads in mind, the study of Mormon constructions of Israelite identity will be useful because, of all the case studies in this book, none demonstrate the capacity of the twelve tribes tradition for adaptation and coordination more clearly than the history of Mormonism. First and foremost, while there have been chapters about peoples who identified and re-identified as Israel over time, and chapters about peoples who sought and found Israel, the story of Mormonism is the story of both. If, in 1830, the Mormon effort to restore Israel was directed outwards towards the Native Americans who were supposed to be the descendants of the Book of Mormon's protagonists, by 1840 at the latest, it had turned inwards, when Mormons began to suspect that they too were descended from Israel. By that time, the Mormon search for Israel had begun to widen from local to global, as Mormon missionary work, everywhere in the world, was consistently characterized in terms of the recovery of the lost of Israel. These two Israels, so to speak, were to be united together in America to establish the New Jerusalem and bring about the Second Coming. And as "Israel" searched for "Israel," ideas about who Israel could be, and where it might be found, changed again and again.

Additionally, this chapter examines how dynamic combinations of ideas about Israel accumulate over time. Specifically, we will see how the strengthening association between the restoration of Israel and the fulfillment of biblical prophecy that developed over the medieval period – and the newly complicated Christian understanding of Israel revealed in the story of Reubeni and others – laid the foundations upon which Mormon constructions of Israel were built. The search for Israel would give Mormonism its sacred mission and the Mormon identification with Israel its role in that mission.

Finally, no other chapter, save perhaps the next one, will better demonstrate one of the main theses of this work: that the structure of the twelve tribes tradition allowed for the nearly constant internal adaptation of Israelite identity in a given context as readily as the construction of new visions of Israel in different contexts. In Mormonism, as in the story of the Beta Israel, we have crucial developments that occurred in a time close enough to our own to be well documented, revealing, in both cases, not Israelite ethnogenesis, but ethnogene*ses* – not just the construction of new understandings of Israel, but new ways of identifying as Israel. Fundamentally, Mormon ideas about who Israel was changed rapidly between 1830 and Joseph Smith Jr.'s death in 1844, and again after the Mormon trek to Utah under the leadership of Brigham Young in 1846.

These are changes we can trace, and, through analysis, use to solidify a number of threads of our discussion so far.

The central fact about the development of Mormon religion and identity, however, is still that it is a story of tangled roots. I have said throughout that a reason to investigate different constructions of Israel from a comparative perspective is that our awareness of the basic ingredients of "becoming Israel" is what helps us see what makes each use of these ingredients unique. Mormon constructions of Israel, as all others, are products of their time and place, in this case including the religious fervor that reigned in the region and era in which Mormonism was born, the "magic culture" of that region, existing ideas about ancient American wars, and many others. All of these traditions and practices would shape the Mormon construction of Israel, in the way that every "Israel" is fundamentally a product of the time and place in which it first appeared.

I will begin, therefore, by discussing the historical development of what is often called the "Jewish Indian Theory" – the idea that the Native Americans were Israelites – followed by analyses of the world into which the Book of Mormon was born at last. I will then analyze how the Mormon identification with Israel deepened and changed as the Mormons left their original homelands for the settlement in Utah.[4] From there, I will discuss the nature of the Mormon mission to Israel, as Mormons themselves have understood it, and two contexts in which the Mormon identification with and search for Israel are particularly felt. First, as we will see, Mormon missionary work has been profoundly shaped through the mental construction of these missions as a search for lost Israel. Second, the Mormon institution of the "patriarchal blessing" is a remarkable reflection of how literally Mormons today still identify with Israel. In it, members in good standing with the Church are typically told which tribe of Israel they descend from. Finally, I will revisit how the twelve tribes tradition allows claimants to Israel to adapt constructions of Israelite identity to contemporary contexts and changing

---

[4] Fenton calls it the "Hebraic Indian theory," observing quite accurately that "Assyria conquered the Kingdom of Israel before the development of the religion we now call Judaism. The lost tribes, in short, were not Jewish" (Fenton, *Old Canaan in a New World*, 3). She adds "the second reason I have opted not to use the word 'Jewish' with respect to this theory is that most – though, importantly – not all – of the authors associated with it had very little interest in and even less knowledge of actual Judaism and Jewish people" (ibid., 4). This is quite right, but again, I am using the common term for readability purposes.

circumstances, now with evidence from a period that, in the scope of this study, is very recent indeed.

4.1 THE "JEWISH INDIAN THEORY"

With everything we know from previous chapters, the speed with which Israel came to America, as Europeans began to explore it, will hardly come as a surprise. Again, the interpretation of new encounters through the lens of biblical traditions was often the product of a religious imperative. Since Genesis 10 describes all of humanity as the descendants of Noah's three children, any newly discovered peoples had to be identified within that biblical schema.[5] By the late medieval period, tradition had already made Europeans into the children of Japheth, "Shemites" of the people of Asia, and "Hamites" of the Africans – and the peoples of America inevitably begged a similar question.[6] Who were they, among the descendants of the children of Noah?

Columbus himself does not seem to have concerned himself much with who the natives he encountered were. He did not, after all, believe himself to have discovered a "New World" in the first place, but only another part of Asia. He did, however, wonder whether he might have landed in biblical Ophir, the source of Solomon's gold.[7] And he did send one Luis de Torres, "a converso who understood Hebrew and Chaldean and even some Arabic" along on various forays into the interior – just in case.[8] The so-called "Jewish Indian theory," however, might have occurred already to Bartolomé de las Casas, who arrived in the "New World" in 1502 and

[5] "To deny a biblical origin for the Indians was to see them, and their history, as outside of Scripture, and Scripture as incomplete and inadequate" (Popkin, "The Rise and Fall of the Jewish Indian Theory," 64). See also Parfitt, *The Lost Tribes of Israel*, 105–6; Katz, "The Wanderings of the Lost Ten Tribes." Those few that derived the natives from somewhere other than Noah, notably the seventeenth-century French theologian Isaac La Peyrère, stood out (Katz, "The Wanderings of the Lost Ten Tribes," 107).

[6] Jablonski, "Skin Color and the Establishment of Races," 137–38.

[7] Bernardini, "A Milder Colonization," 3–4. See also Romm, "Biblical History and the Americas," 33–34; Fenton, *Old Canaan in a New World*, 10. "He died in the belief that he had landed on the east coast of Asia: the Indians were Asiatics, and their presence was interesting but unremarkable" (Katz, "The Wanderings of the Lost Ten Tribes," 107).

[8] Katz, "The Wanderings of the Lost Ten Tribes," 107.

would eventually dedicate his life to decrying the injustices the Spanish committed against the natives.[9]

The Mormons, therefore, were hardly the first to discover Israel in America.[10] Nor were they the first to come to identify *themselves* – mainly the descendants of European settlers – with Israel, although that idea would develop a little later in the progress of Mormon thought. And Mormonism, a tapestry woven from many threads both local and international, was not the first system of thought to connect the conversion of America's native peoples to Christianity – even when they were understood as Israelites by descent – with bringing about the Second Coming. Indeed, by the 1820s, all three threads had been maturing for some time.

One of the trigger points for the development of European ideas about America came in 1644, when Antonio Montezinos – originally Aharon Levi – returned to Amsterdam with a wild story about a journey into the depths of South America. There, he said, a native named Francisco took him on a week's journey into the mountains. Upon arrival, Montezinos was introduced to a community that promptly revealed to the startled Portuguese traveler that it was indeed of the Lost Tribes of Israel.[11] This story, as with others like it, might well have been forgotten save that Antonio told it to a prominent rabbi and scholar named Menasseh Ben Israel, in Amsterdam. The rabbi, inspired, began to work on what would become the learned and tremendously influential tome, *Hope of Israel*, a compendium of speculation about the whereabouts of the Lost Tribes, published in 1650.[12]

Again, hope is what the Lost Tribes of Israel had long signified for medieval Jewry suffering under the thumb of Christian antisemitism.[13] By Menasseh's time, this struggle had already extended to the New World.

---

[9] As Parfitt notes, Juan de Torquemada names de las Casas as the first to identify the tribes with Israel (Parfitt, *The Lost Tribes of Israel*, 29–34). See also Casas, *Witness*, 72–79.

[10] A new book on the topic of the Lost Tribes in America, by Matthew W. Dougherty (*Lost Tribes Found: Israelite Indians and Religious Nationalism in Early America*), came out after the production of the present volume was well underway. The book adds a great deal of context to the fascinating story of Israel in America.

[11] This story is described in Benite, *The Ten Lost Tribes*, 135–38; Parfitt, *The Lost Tribes of Israel*, 76–90; Schmidt, "The Hope of the Netherlands."

[12] Ben Israel, *The Hope of Israel*. See, especially, the essays collected in Popkin, Qaplan, and Méchoulan, *Menasseh Ben Israel and His World*.

[13] This is roughly the argument, with some exceptions, in Efron, "Knowledge of Newly Discovered Lands." Into the eighteenth century, Efron argues, "when Jews were concerned about adventures overseas, it was typically because of what these adventures implied for the Jews of Europe themselves" (ibid., 49).

Menasseh was deeply concerned about the Jewish community of Recife, in what is now Brazil, where struggles with Portuguese authorities were growing more and more acute.[14] Beyond that, Menasseh had spent his life attempting to ease the weal of Europe's Jews. Britain had banned the Jews from the island all the way back in 1290, in the reign of Edward I, and the ban stood for nearly three and a half centuries. Late in life, Menasseh led a personal effort to convince Oliver Cromwell to reverse this ban, and while Menasseh died believing he had been unsuccessful, the ban was in fact lifted three years later, in 1657.[15] Not surprisingly, then, his book, as others before it, "may not quite have announced the arrival of a Jewish-Indian cavalry, but it did offer solace and impart optimism to Jews, in Europe and America, by suggesting that an age of miracles might soon be upon them."[16]

Here, however, we see the importance of the switch that was beginning to flip in the days of David Reubeni: the possibility that the discovery of Israel did not have to be terrible for European Christianity, but could, instead, mark the progress of Christian Europe into the next stage in a schema of redemption.[17] Menasseh's research brought him into contact with a number of Protestant intellectuals who were interested in Menasseh's discoveries for their own reasons, not his.[18] Thomas Thorowgood and the Calvinist John Durie showed special interest, and in their own thought, engaged deeply with the question of what the

---

[14] Schmidt, "The Hope of the Netherlands," 99. As Schmidt further notes, Ben Israel "had material and even familial interests in colonization projects. Using as an intermediary his brother Ephraim, who left for the West Indies in 1639, Menasseh invested in America in the late 1630s" (ibid., 95).

[15] Benite, *The Ten Lost Tribes*, 173–80; Parfitt, *The Lost Tribes of Israel*, 77–83. As Benite notes, Jews were readmitted to Britain in 1664, seven years after Ben Israel's death, perhaps in part because of his efforts (Benite, *The Ten Lost Tribes*, 175).

[16] Schmidt, "The Hope of the Netherlands," 99.

[17] As Benite observes, "some Christian theologies would develop" an "expectation for 'natural religious development,' except that, in the Christian version, the ten tribes were to possess the New Testament as well as the Old. In its most radical version, this theology is also the basis for Mormonism" (Benite, *The Ten Lost Tribes*, 96).

[18] Thus, Ben Israel's book was a smash hit in both Jewish and Christian communities, but it was its millennial message that would have the most enduring effect. It "ranks among the most influential documents of seventeenth-century Jewish history . . . In its day, it ignited a frenzy of messianic and millenarian speculation across the whole of Europe" (Schmidt, "The Hope of the Netherlands," 92). Or, as Katz put it, somewhat more cynically, "the discovery of the Lost Tribes enabled an unemployed and underpaid Dutch rabbi to connect with circles in London who hoped that by readmitting the Jews to England and converting them to true and pure English Protestant Christianity, the Second Coming of Christ would be brought closer" (Katz, "The Wanderings of the Lost Ten Tribes," 110).

reappearance of the tribes might mean in the cosmic scheme of things. Thorowgood's *Iewes in America, or, Probabilities That the Americans are of That Race*, which was published in the same year as Ben Israel's effort, suggested strongly that the end was near.[19]

Meanwhile, a speech Durie gave before the House of Commons in 1645 – entitled "Israel's call, to march out of Babylon unto Jerusalem" – shows something of the growing self-identification between white Europeans and Israel, or at least, the "new" Israel, which, supposedly unlike the old, would live in accordance with biblical scripture and be redeemed.[20] Ultimately, throughout the seventeenth century, an interest in Israel, and in its role in bringing about the end of the world, began to occupy many Protestant intellectuals.[21] Their new speculations, combined

[19] Thorowgood, *Iewes in America or Probabilities That the Americans Are of That Race* (1650). This book was republished in 1652 as *Digitus Dei: New Discoveries* and Thorowgood published a second study in 1660, *Jews in America, or Probabilities, that these Indians are Judaical, made more probable by some Additionals for the former Conjectures* (Cogley, "The Ancestry of the American Indians," 304). In some ways, John Durie was a somewhat hidden intermediary between Thorowgood and Ben Israel, and according to Fenton, introduced Thorowgood to Ben Israel's work (Benite, *The Ten Lost Tribes*, 174; Parfitt, *The Lost Tribes of Israel*, 77; Popkin, "The Rise and Fall of the Jewish Indian Theory," 66–68; Fenton, *Old Canaan in a New World*, 22. He was also, as Popkin observes, "perhaps the most active millenarian theoretician in the Puritan Revolution" (Popkin, "The Rise and Fall of the Jewish Indian Theory," 67). Durie also "wrote to Manasseh seeking confirmation of the story" – of de Montezinos – and "Manasseh responded in November of 1649, sharing with Dury a French translation" of de Montezinos' account (Fenton, *Old Canaan in a New World*, 27).

[20] For some of the text of the speech, including such lines as "God hath, since the beginning of the Reformation of His church from Popery and anti-Christian superstition, intended to bring his vessels out of Babylon unto Sion," see Nichols and Davids, *Calvinism and Arminianism Compared in Their Principles and Tendency*, 1. As Hill observes, "the close correspondence between England and Israel as elect nations made comparisons inevitable; and, in fact, it became a cardinal assumption of the Puritans that the Old Testament contained the blueprint for the required reconstruction of the English church and state. Israel's experience of election provided an invaluable guide and pattern for the nascent English theocracy," of which Durie's speech was a reflection (Hill, *John Milton*, 90). Indeed, Richard Popkin calls Durie "perhaps the most active millenarian theoretician in the Puritan Revolution" (Popkin, "The Rise and Fall of the Jewish Indian Theory," 67).

[21] Peter Toon notes that "the birth of Hebrew studies in Protestant universities" was "of tremendous importance for the development" of Protestant eschatology. The relevant scholars, including Paul Fagius and John Immanuel Tremelleius, a convert, not only studied the Hebrew Bible, but rabbinic commentaries as well (Toon, *Puritans, the Millennium and the Future of Israel*, 23). As Toon observes, a new interest in the study of the Hebrew Bible created certain specific effects including "the possibility of following Jewish exegesis and understanding the Old Testament prophecies (e.g. Ezek. 37) as meaning a future literal restoration of the Jews to Palestine" (ibid., 23–24). The

with the belief that "the conversion and restoration of the Twelve Tribes" would be an annunciatory event where the new millennium was concerned, and an ongoing set of rhetorical equivalences between Protestants and the New Israel, paved the way for many later literal identifications with Israel.[22]

For the future development of Mormonism specifically, the fact that these ideas were particularly prominent in Britain – where Thorowgood, and eventually Durie, lived – would ultimately play a decisive role, as Mormonism took root in America largely among people of British descent. Again, however, the history of Israel in America, even among the British, was growing long even by Ben Israel's time. Thorowgood himself corresponded with the early American explorer, the missionary John Eliot, on the subject of the tribes in America, and so did Cotton Mather, the prominent Puritan minister from Massachusetts.[23] William Penn, namesake of the state of Pennsylvania, was more forthright still, once declaring about his portion of the New World that "there were so many Jews around it was like being in a Jewish quarter in London."[24] The Anglican Bishop George Berkeley would be one of many, including the Mormons themselves, to begin with an aggressive outreach scheme towards converting the natives – he even considered opening a college in Bermuda to offer education in the Gospels to these "Israelites" – but to then alter his plans after a number of encounters with the natives went differently than he expected.[25]

Ultimately, the identification between the Native Americans and the Lost Tribes of Israel continued in force well past the American Revolution. Elias Boudinot, a delegate to the Continental Congress and later director of the US Mint, wrote a treatise on the subject.[26] Thomas Jefferson and John Adams debated the matter with each other, though

---

renewed interest in discovering "lost" Israel obviously goes hand in hand with this possibility.

[22] Ibid., 31. Toon also suggests that while some in the late sixteenth to mid-seventeenth centuries thought there would be a mass conversion of the Jews, "there were a few" who thought "Israel" in, for example, Romans 11:25, "referred to the whole New Testament Church of Gentile and Jew." Additionally, some already thought that the "lost" Jews would return to Israel, in the end, from America (ibid., 126).

[23] Mather, *The Triumph of the Reformed Religion in America*, 84; Cogley, "The Ancestry of the American Indians," 1; Toon, *Puritans, the Millennium and the Future of Israel*, 118.

[24] Parfitt, *The Lost Tribes of Israel*, 88–89.   [25] Ibid., 93.

[26] Boudinot, *A Star in the West*. For a discussion of Boudinot's work that places it in a historical context, see Fenton, *Old Canaan in a New World*, 88–100.

both were skeptical.[27] When Lewis and Clark, on their way to the west, visited the famed Dr. Benjamin Rush, he asked them personally to keep an eye out for any Israelites they might come across.[28]

As for the 1820s, which is when Joseph Smith Jr. began to receive his first visions, something of the flavor of the period can be felt in the newspapers of the day. To take just one example, a piece composed in the *Philadelphia Recorder* in 1826 describes a native chief's response to the effort by American authorities to establish schools in his region. The chief told the story of two brothers, one "red-skinned" and one white, whose old, blind father offered a book to whichever of them first killed a deer and prepared it for him. The white-skinned brother cheated and won the contest, and his father's blessing, while the red-skinned brother lost, trying to play by the rules. "If this cheat had not been practiced," the speech is supposed to have gone, "the red man would have been now as the white man is, and he as the red man ... if the Great Spirit had intended that the red man should know how to read, he would not have allowed the white man to take this advantage of us." Was there any doubt, the *Recorder* author wondered, that here was a native memory of the biblical story of Jacob and Esau, and therefore "circumstantial testimony in favour of the opinion, that the savages of our country are descendants of the Lost Tribes of Israel?"[29]

Similarly, just before the Book of Mormon itself appeared, a Massachusetts clergyman named Ethan Smith (unrelated to the soon-to-be prophet) published, in 1823, *A View of the Hebrews*, which Joseph

---

[27] Parfitt, *The Lost Tribes of Israel*, 99. See also Shalev, *American Zion*, 118–50.

[28] Woodger and Toropov, *Encyclopedia of the Lewis and Clark Expedition*, 217. Fenton adds that Rush gave Lewis and Clark a list of questions that included "What Affinity ... between [Native American] religious Ceremonies & those of the Jews?" – a question Clark rewrote a year later as "What affinity is there ... between their religious ceremonies and those of the ancient Jews?" suggesting "that he did not merely copy out Rush's questions, but revised them as he prepared his own guide for the expedition" (Fenton, *Old Canaan in a New World*, 1).

[29] "Descendants of Israel," *Philadelphia Recorder*. Another story about the "Jews of Bucharia," encountered at a fair in Leipzig, and their likely Lost Tribe lineage somehow reverberated across continents, becoming a subject of debate in several papers, from the Scottish *Caledonian Mercury* to the *Western Luminary* of Lexington, Kentucky; to the *Christian Watchman* of Boston, Massachusetts, to the *Christian Intelligencer and Eastern Chronicle* of Gardiner, Maine (*Caledonian Mercury*, "The Ten Lost Jewish Tribes"; "The Ten Lost Jewish Tribes," *Western Luminary*; "Ten Lost Tribes of Israel," *Christian Watchman*; "The Ten Lost Tribes," *The Christian Intelligencer and Eastern Chronicle*). As the author in the *Watchman* noted, "some have confidently argued that the Indians on our Continent are this ancient people; others have as confidently denied the opinion."

Smith Jr. was occasionally accused of cribbing from.[30] Ethan Smith claimed that he knew that the natives told tales of a great flood, and a god named "Ale, the old Hebrew name of God, and Yoheweah." He believed they did not eat "the hollow of the thigh of an animal," as the Israelites had not since Jacob's fight with the angel in Genesis 32, and that they were aware that, once upon a time, they had practiced circumcision.[31] He also pointed to the text of 2 Esdras, the work of the apocrypha discussed in the last chapter. This text describes the Ten Lost Tribes of Israel as having gone on to a place called "Arzareth" (2 Esdr. 13:45–46) "through the narrow passages of the Euphrates" (13:44), and from there, to a journey that took an entire year and a half to complete (13:45).

Where, Ethan Smith wondered, could the Israelites have gone that took so long, save for America itself? And hadn't the prophet Amos referred to some future day when the Israelites "shall wander from sea to sea," seeking the word of YHWH but without finding it?[32] With the discovery of America, Smith argued, the day when the "most High will begin to rescue those who are on the earth" (2 Esdras 13:29), "collecting to himself ... the ten tribes that were taken captive from their land in the days of King Hoshea, whom King Shalmaneser of the Assyrians took across the river as a captive" (2 Esdras 13:40), had begun, at last, to dawn.[33]

Thus, when the Book of Mormon appeared, with its account of an ancient Israelite voyage from Israel to America, it would have resonated with what many Americans of the day already believed.[34] At the same time, Mormon thought, which held that the restoration of Israel was the key to bringing about the Second Coming, has its roots in a Protestant

---

[30] Proponents of the theory that the Book of Mormon may have been based to some extent on Ethan Smith's "View of the Hebrews" include B. H. Roberts, in the early twentieth century, Fawn Brodie in the 1940s, and more recently David Persuitte (Roberts, *Studies of the Book of Mormon*; Brodie, *No Man Knows My History*; Persuitte, *Joseph Smith and the Origins of the Book of Mormon*). For a rebuttal, see Welch, "View of the Hebrews." As Parfitt notes, some nineteenth-century critics of Mormonism argued that Joseph Smith had come across an earlier study by Solomon Spaulding, and "on 24 April 1887, a somewhat convincing link was made in *The Cleveland Plain Dealer* between Spalding and Ethan Smith," who had both gone to Dartmouth and may have been friends (Parfitt, *The Lost Tribes of Israel*, 107). The evidence suggests that Lost Tribe speculation was so rife in the period under consideration that the Book of Mormon could be a natural outgrowth of it without depending on any other specific literary effort.

[31] Smith, *View of the Hebrews or The Tribes of Israel*, 47–48.   [32] Ibid., 52–53.

[33] Ibid..

[34] For another discussion of the relationship between early Mormonism and the "Jewish Indian Theory" see Fenton, *Old Canaan in a New World*, 113–24.

theological outlook dating back at least to the days of Thorowgood and Durie. And as we will see in a moment, there were other ways in which early Mormonism resembled its roots, much as every vision of Israel is a product of its own context. Then there were the ways in which early Mormonism was utterly unique, ways that would deeply trouble those the Mormons lived among. And within fifteen years of its founding, Mormonism's founder, Joseph Smith Jr., would be dead, murdered by a mob, and his flock would be in flight across the border of America.

4.2 THE BOOK OF MORMON

Joseph Smith Jr. was born in 1805 in Sharon, Vermont, and moved with his family to Palmyra, New York in 1816, as part of a general movement of Northeastern farmers seeking – but not really finding – better soil.[35] Growing up, Smith's family was often quite poor, and he seems to have performed a great deal of manual labor. Although the family farm was in nearby Manchester, it was in Palmyra, for better or worse, that he made his reputation.[36] He would receive his first vision, according to his own account, in 1820, when he would have been fourteen or fifteen. In the portion of his history preserved in a Mormon scripture called *The Pearl of Great Price*, he claims to have seen "two Personages, whose brightness and glory defy all description." They told him that he should not join any of the churches that existed in the area, a command he seems to have followed (Joseph Smith – *History* 1:16–18).[37]

---

[35] Engaging, more in-depth presentations of the history that follows can be found in Givens, *By the Hand of Mormon*, 3–61; Brodie, *No Man Knows My History*; Mauss, *All Abraham's Children*, 1–154; Bushman, *Joseph Smith: Rough Stone Rolling*. Smith's autobiographical account is available in various ways, including Smith, *History of Joseph Smith*. A large collection of Smith's papers can be found at www.josephsmith papers.org/articles/joseph-smith-and-his-papers-an-introduction. A portion of his autobiography is also available in the *Pearl of Great Price*, a Mormon scripture. For th is particular detail, as Bushman put it, speaking of the year 1815, "in the next two years nature conspired to drive them from Vermont" (Bushman, *Joseph Smith: Rough Stone Rolling*, 27). In the meantime, the Smith family had also lived for a little while in Lebanon, New Hampshire. He adds, of the region of New York they settled in, that it had "opened for settlement just twenty-five years earlier" (ibid., 30).

[36] "A strange book made its appearance in Palmyra, New York in March 1830. Its title page proclaimed it to be a history of Near Eastern Hebrews whom God had led to the Western hemisphere before the beginning of the Babylonian captivity in 587 B.C.E." (Shipps, "An Interpretive Framework," 7).

[37] Terryl Givens, in his study of the Book of Mormon and its history, notes that "it is both fitting and ironic that at a small crossroads in the town of Palmyra, New York, four

In September of 1823, Smith was visited for the first time by the personage known to history as the Angel Moroni.[38] He does not seem to have mentioned this vision, or the earlier one, to many people initially, but he later claimed that, upon receiving the second, he immediately rushed out to the famous "Hill Cumorah." He went there in search of the golden plates Moroni claimed were buried upon it – the record of Moroni's Israelite people.[39] But Moroni forbade him to begin his work at that time; he was still too young, too unworthy. Finally, in September of 1827, Joseph was allowed to take the plates home.

Over the next two years, Joseph said, he struggled to translate the plates – out of what he called "reformed Egyptian" – with the financial help of a man named Martin Harris, a friend of his father's, and the scribal help of his wife Emma and another friend named Oliver Cowdery.[40] Before the Book was published, by E. B. Grandin, in 1830 – and sold out of his Palmyra bookshop – the somewhat reluctant Grandin had to be convinced. Harris mortgaged his farm. The first printing did not do very much for Grandin – nor for Harris, who lost

churches occupy the four corner lots of the intersection. Fitting, because the four contiguous meeting houses ... aptly symbolize the hurly-burly of religious sects vigorously competing for new proselytes ... Ironic, because the embarrassment of denominational riches suggested by the intersection was not enough to provide a spiritual home for 14-year-old Joseph Smith himself" (Givens, *By the Hand of Mormon*, 8). Nevertheless, although most of the evidence suggests that Joseph was not much for organized religion before founding his own, at least one book of local history – written by an Orsamus Turner who was a resident of Palmyra from at least 1818 – called the future prophet a "very passable exhorter in evening meetings" of the Methodist persuasion (Turner, *History of the Pioneer Settlement*, 214). This same author referred to Joseph, whom he claims to remember "distinctly" as "lounging, idle ... of less than ordinary intellect" but also possessed of "a little ambition; and some very laudable aspirations." Orsamus Turner was quite impressed, at least, with the intellect of Joseph's mother (ibid., 214–15). John L. Brooke notes that Smith's mother, Lucy Mack, "moved from church to church searching for the true religion, while his father refused to join any denomination. The prophet's grandfather Asael Smith helped to form a Universalist Society in Tunbridge, Vermont, in the 1790s and advised his children to beware any formal creeds" (Brooke, *The Refiner's Fire*, 60).

[38] "Joseph Smith Jr. was seventeen years old when the Angel Moroni first appeared to him in the bedroom that he shared with his five brothers in their western New York log home" (Mueller, *Race and the Making of the Mormon People*, 1).

[39] Givens, *By the Hand of Mormon*, 15–16.

[40] Between 1823 and 1827, Joseph's brother Alvin died (in November of 1823), the family lost ownership of their farm (in 1825), Josiah Stowell asked Joseph to help him find a supposedly lost Spanish mine in Pennsylvania (also in 1825), and as a result of this trip, which Smith made with his father, Joseph met Emma Hale, whom he would marry in 1827 (Bushman, *Joseph Smith: Rough Stone Rolling*, 50–53).

his farm and perhaps also his wife in the bargain – but these initial struggles did not turn out to presage things to come.[41] By the next year, the initial branch of the church, in Kirtland, Ohio, would have over one hundred members. Today, the number of Mormons in the world is over fifteen million.[42]

The story that emerged laboriously under Smith's pen begins in Israel – or rather, without explanation, in Judah.[43] Their Judahite residence notwithstanding, the main protagonists and antagonists both are members of the northern tribe of Manasseh, descendants of Lehi, a prophet and patriarch. When the action of the book opens, however – around 600 BCE – Lehi and his family are living in the vicinity of Jerusalem when Lehi is warned of the coming Babylonian destruction. He moves with his family into the wilderness, and after a time, from there to America (1 Nephi 1–18). Quickly, his followers divide themselves into two camps: the Nephites, who follow Lehi's faithful son Nephi, and the Lamanites, the followers of Lehi's son Laman. The Lamanites would quickly descend into apostasy and error.[44]

The narrative that is told from that point on appears in two distinct types of material, often dealing with the worsening conflict between the two branches of the family. The first six of the fifteen books in the Book of Mormon are first-person accounts by a series of Nephite chroniclers who are also direct descendants of Nephi himself. After Nephi's own contribution, in 1 and 2 Nephi, these records grow increasingly short. The history

---

[41] Bushman states that "Mrs. Harris refused to be a party to the mortgage, and their marriage soon ended. In a sense she was right about the consequences of Martin's involvement with Joseph. Martin did sell his farm on April 7, 1831, even though Tucker judged that Harris could have paid the bill from other resources" (ibid., 80).

[42] Barlow, *Mormons and the Bible*, 49. The church website claims 16,118,169 members as of this writing (www.mormonnewsroom.org/facts-and-statistics).

[43] That is, the tribe of Manasseh is a northern tribe, which is to say a tribe of Israel, not Judah, but at the beginning of the Book of Mormon, the family of Lehi lives in Judah, and how it got there is never explained.

[44] As Terryl Givens puts it, "after incurring resentment and then persecution, [Lehi] is warned in a vision to gather his immediate family and depart into the wilderness ... Lehi finally departs southward through the Arabian Peninsula. After a wilderness sojourn of eight years, Lehi's righteous son Nephi is told in a vision to build a ship, and the group makes preparations for a lengthy journey ... Soon after landing, Lehi dies and conflict breaks out between Nephi, Lehi's successor as prophet, leader and record-keeper, and his brothers Laman and Lemuel. Nephi leads his people inland several days' journey, where they become established as a righteous, prosperous people ... and call themselves 'Nephites.' Meanwhile, their rivals, soon known by the name 'Lamanites' and cursed with darkness, become an 'idle people, full of mischief and subtlety' and 'a scourge unto [Nephi's] seed' (2 Nephi 5:24–25)" (Givens, *By the Hand of Mormon*, 44).

told by Nephi's son Jacob is seven chapters long; Enos' and Jarom's are one chapter long. The book of Omni is also one chapter; however, it includes not only Omni's account but those of his descendants Amaron, Chemish, Abinadom, and Amaleki.

At the end of the book of Omni, Amaleki, last of the Nephite chroniclers until Mormon himself, hands off the work to one King Benjamin. Benjamin is the ruler of a kingdom called Zarahemla, originally settled by other Israelites who had escaped from Jerusalem a little later than the Nephites, and were now joined by them there (Omni 1:12–15, 25). These are the records referred to as the "small plates of Nephi." The next set of materials in the book are presented as an abridgement from the "large plates of Nephi," and they are third-person accounts generally occupied with the lives and exploits of important Zarahemla individuals and other crucial developments. Five books – Mosiah, Alma, Helaman, 3 Nephi, and 4 Nephi – are of this sort. The book of 3 Nephi, named after Nephi, a grandson of Helaman, describes one of the central events of the Book of Mormon: the coming of Jesus to America (3 Nephi 8–30), with various important consequences discussed below.

Overall, the story the Book tells is not just the history of the Nephites and Lamanites, but that of its own composition. Moroni, who later appears to Joseph Smith Jr. in angelic form, is the one who, during his lifetime, received the finished record and buried it for Joseph to find. The most important figure in the Book of Mormon, however, is Mormon himself – Moroni's father, a Nephite, and a general. Around 385 CE, on the eve of the great final battle with the Lamanites, which destroys the Nephites entirely, Mormon completes his own great task.[45] Having been entrusted with the existing plates in much the way Joseph Smith Jr. would later be entrusted with them – Mormon is even directed to recover them from a hill called "Shim" by an elder named Ammaron (Mormon 1:3), just as Moroni directed Joseph to the Hill Cumorah – Mormon combines the small plates with his own abridgement of the large plates and

---

[45] "In A.D. 384, Mormon is old and tired. The last of the Nephite military generals finds himself in the land of Cumorah. There, once again, he is preparing to fight his bloodthirsty enemies and distant kin, the Lamanites. The seventy-four-year-old Mormon has spent a half century in continuous warfare with the Lamanites. These conflicts have reduced the once great Nephite people ... to refugees ... Mormon knows that the Nephites would make their last stand at Cumorah. Yet before this decisive battle, instead of sharpening his sword, Mormon sits down to write a history of both the Nephite and Lamanite people" (Mueller, *Race and the Making of the Mormon People*, 135).

produces the majority of the history, placing a statement of editorial intent between the parts (Words of Mormon).

After that, Mormon composes his own book, in the style of the old Nephite chroniclers, and hands the nearly completed text off to Moroni, his son, before the battle begins. Moroni takes over in Mormon 8, revealing his father's death – he was hunted down by the Lamanites after the battle – and creates two last entries. The first is the book of Ether, an apparently independent account of the Jaredites, who came to America shortly after the events of the Tower of Babel. Ether, the titular character, is a prophet of the Jaredites who foretells "that a New Jerusalem should be built up upon this land, unto the remnant of the seed of Joseph" and by "the remnant of the house of Joseph" (Ether 13:6–8). At the end of the book, the Jaredites are destroyed (Ether 15).

Finally, there is the book of Moroni himself: "I had supposed not to have written more, but I have not as yet perished; and I make not myself known to the Lamanites lest they should destroy me" (Moroni 1:1). Moroni's book is a miscellany: instructions for future days, a letter from Mormon to his son in which the Nephites are also condemned (Moroni 9), and finally, one last exhortation to the Lamanites (Mormon 10). Then, "in or about the year A.D. 421, Moroni, the last of the Nephite prophet-historians, sealed the sacred record, and hid it up unto the Lord … In A.D. 1823, this same Moroni, then a resurrected personage, visited the Prophet Joseph Smith and subsequently delivered the engraved plates to him."[46]

To call the Book of Mormon an expression of the Jewish Indian theory would be to deny what it purports to be: an ancient, first-person account of the experiences of Israel in America, delivered through Joseph Smith Jr. as translator. However, the story it tells would nevertheless have been familiar to audiences in the region because of the *longue durée* of similar ideas. Beyond that, the fact that Mormonism was a new religious movement would not have been particularly striking in the region, and time, in which it appeared.

Indeed, of all times and places, there could hardly be any more friendly to the appearance of this new revelation than upstate New York in the early nineteenth century. The region was already well on its way to earning the term "burned over district," meaning a region so passionate in its religious enthusiasms, it burned itself out. In fact – and here is why

---

[46] The quotes in these paragraphs are from "A Brief Explanation about the Book of Mormon," in the front matter of a 1999 printing of the Book (*The Book of Mormon*).

placing the appearance of Mormonism in time and place is so important – the term's coiner, Charles Grandison Finney, "Father of Modern Revivalism," held arguably the most famous revival of all time in Rochester, New York – not twenty-five miles away – in the exact same year the Book was published.[47] Nearby, in Dresden, NY – forty or so miles from Palmyra – William Miller, of "Millerite" fame, began to preach about the imminence of the Second Coming in 1833, three years after the Book was published, leading to the "Great Disappointment" in 1844.[48]

Meanwhile, six miles from Dresden, the little town called Jerusalem, New York, was still, in 1830, the settlement of the Society of Universal Friends, followers of the "Publick Universal Friend."[49] The Friend, initially from Rhode Island, had grown gravely ill in the year 1776. When the illness passed, the individual once known as Jemima Wilkinson claimed that Wilkinson had in fact died, and that her body now "housed a new spirit, sent from God with a special mission" – the Friend.[50] The Friend was, furthermore, genderless, a "heaven-sent spirit of truth."[51] The Society settled in Jerusalem, and in nearby Penn Yan, following the teachings of the Friend, who frequently preached their message in the surrounding area. The Friend passed on in 1819, but the Society survived them, at least for a time.

There were others. Mother Ann Lee, a founding leader of the Shakers, had settled in New York – though not particularly nearby – in the late eighteenth century, but in 1826, a Shaker community was established in Sodus Bay "only thirty miles from Palmyra."[52] Fawn Brodie, an early and controversial biographer of Joseph Smith Jr., mentions Isaac Bullard, a "champion of free love and communism" who "regarded washing as a sin and boasted that he had not changed clothes for seven years," and who "gathered a following of 'Pilgrims' in 1817 in Woodstock, Vermont, half

[47] Finney coined the term in his autobiography many years later (Finney, *Memoirs of Rev. Charles G. Finney*, 77–78). For the revival and its effects, see especially Johnson, *A Shopkeeper's Millennium*.

[48] Bliss, *Memoirs of William Miller*, 109–11.

[49] Brodie, *No Man Knows My History*, 13.   [50] Wisbey, *Pioneer Prophetess*, 7–16.

[51] Moyer, *The Public Universal Friend*, 8.

[52] Brodie, *No Man Knows My History*, 12–13. For other trenchant efforts to discuss the religious context in which Mormonism emerged, see Howe, "Emergent Mormonism in Context"; Bushman, "Joseph Smith and His Visions"; Hansen, "Joseph Smith, American Culture, and the Origins of Mormonism."

a dozen hills away from the old Smith Farm."[53] There were even other prophets, which is how Smith would come to understand himself, and how his followers would understand him.[54]

Other elements of the region's culture played a crucial role in laying the foundations for Mormonism. Today, Smith's claims to have "translated" the golden plates through special "seer stones" given to him by the Angel Moroni might strike non-Mormons as unlikely.[55] Yet well before he was a prophet, Joseph seems to have been a "money-digger," a sort of water-divining but for buried treasure. This popular occupation in that region, and other similar practices, involved magical stones (or sticks) that revealed what was otherwise hidden.[56] Not surprisingly, many of the early Mormons and their families had already dabbled in new religious

---

[53] Brodie, *No Man Knows My History*, 12. Brodie's biography is at once a seminal and controversial work. The quibbles have generally been not with its presentation of facts and events but with its harsh critique of Joseph Smith's motivations and its lack of interest in the religious origins and religious character of early Mormonism. For a recent reassessment of Brodie's work, exploring both its usefulness and flaws, see Bringhurst, *Reconsidering No Man Knows My History*. See in particular the chapters by Bringhurst, "Applause, Attack, and Ambivalence," and Hill, "Secular or Sectarian History?," in that volume.

[54] "While Joseph Smith prepared the Book of Mormon for publication, an elderly Quaker named Elias Hicks split the Society of Friends by declaring that the Inner Light, the inspiration of the individual, took precedence even over scriptures ... Theodore Parker, a radical antebellum Unitarian preacher, took the same line that the individual conscience superseded the authority of scripture, but based his argument on Transcendentalist romanticism rather than Quaker tradition ... Seventh-Day Adventist prophet Ellen G. White [born three years before the Book of Mormon was published] had visions containing revelations, and her prolific writings are still revered by her community" (Howe, "Emergent Mormonism in Context," 33–34). Bushman refers to the earlier study of Richard Brodhead who "lines up a number of the figures who seized a prophetic identity 'circa 1830,' including Nat Turner, Jemima Wilkinson, John Humphrey Noyes, Ralph Waldo Emerson, Handsome Lake, and George Rapp," and suggests that "prophethood was one of the 'repertoire of identities' waiting to be seized upon in this biblical culture 'as one idea of what a self can be'" (Bushman, "Joseph Smith and His Visions," 109; Brodhead, "Prophets in America circa 1830," 21, 18).

[55] An excellent, full-length study of the translation and publication of the Book of Mormon has recently appeared in MacKay and Dirkmaat, *From Darkness Unto Light*. For shorter treatments, see Ricks, "Translation of the Book of Mormon," 202–3; Skousen, "Towards a Critical Edition of the Book of Mormon," 41–69. Smith also seems to have worked by putting the stones and the plates in his hat (Skousen, "Towards a Critical Edition of the Book of Mormon," 51). See also Skousen and Jensen, *The Joseph Smith Papers, Manuscripts and Revelations, Vol. 3, Parts 1 and 2*.

[56] Brodie, *No Man Knows My History*; Quinn, *Early Mormonism and the Magic World View*; Givens, *By the Hand of Mormon*, 17. As Bushman put it, "money-digging was epidemic in upstate New York. Stories of spirits guarding buried treasure were deeply enmeshed in the regions' rural cultures ... Ordinary people apparently had no difficulty

movements.[57] They would have heard stories similar to the account in the Book of Mormon, and they would have been familiar with the practices Joseph used to "translate" it. They were well prepared to listen to his claims of prophecy and of ongoing revelation.

Finally, there were even local accounts of a great war between native peoples in the region, similar in many ways to the story the Book of Mormon unfolded. Indeed, Native American artifacts would often be interpreted as the legacy of such events by early nineteenth-century Americans, and far beyond New York. In Ohio, no less an old soldier than William Henry Harrison, two years away from his one month as President of the United States, would see in the native mounds on the Ohio River the remnants of a defensive fortification, and of a last great holding action that, once it failed, sent its survivors south to become the Aztecs:

That the crisis was met with fortitude, and sustained with valor, need not be doubted. The ancestors of Quitlavaca and Gautimosin, and their devoted followers, could not be cowards. But their efforts were vain ... Whatever might be their object in adopted [flight], whether, like the Trojan remnant, to seek another

blending Christianity with magic" (Bushman, *Joseph Smith: Rough Stone Rolling*, 50). Smith was supposedly tried in court for his involvement in activities of this sort. Bushman notes that the nephew of Josiah Stowell, who asked Joseph to find a Spanish mine for him, named Peter Bridgeman leveled a charge against Joseph for being a "disorderly person ... New York law specified that anyone pretending to have skill in discovering lost goods should be judged a disorderly person." Smith Sr. seems to have testified at the trial that he was embarrassed to have used Smith Jr.'s remarkable abilities only to search for gold, or "filthy lucre" (ibid., 52).

[57] As Brooke observes, in his effort to track down the deeper roots of "Mormon Cosmology," "Brigham Young's parents ... affiliated with the Reformed Methodists, a biblical primitivist group that practiced baptism by immersion, faith healing, and the laying on of hands ... The Kimballs joined the Shaker community at Enfield, New Hampshire, only to withdraw and move to northern Vermont in 1796 ... Wilford Woodruff, who joined the Mormons in Rhode Island in 1833, had been convinced by an 'old prophet' named Robert Mason to avoid the churches and await the restoration. And a host of important early Mormons, including Parley Pratt, Edward Partridge, Lyman Wight, Newell K. Whitney, and John Murdoc, were members of Sidney Rigdon's splinter Campbellite congregation in Mentor, Ohio, which was converted *en masse* to Mormonism in late 1830" (Brooke, *The Refiner's Fire*, 61). A similar point is made in Shipps, "An Interpretive Framework," 7–9. William Cowdery, father of Oliver, and Joseph Smith Sr. have even been linked with a group called the "Vermont Rodsmen," who proclaimed their own Israelite ancestry at the turn of the nineteenth century and performed other kinds of familiar rites with divining rods, although the evidence seems to be fairly thin, especially in Smith Sr.'s case (Shalev, *American Zion*, 118; Morris, "Oliver Cowdery's Vermont Years and the Origins of Mormonism").

country, "and happier walls," or like that of Ithome, to procure present safety and renovated strength ... we have no means of ascertaining.[58]

Here, and in other parts of the country, we see a reflection of anti-native sentiment. The theory of an older, more advanced native civilization developed from the idea that contemporary natives were too uncivilized to be responsible for the art and artifacts that were, of course, simply the remnants of previous native settlements.

As for Palmyra, there were indeed Native American mounds in that region too, occasionally disgorging skeletons and finely crafted artifacts, and they had long engendered similar stories of ancient war. Often, the nature of these finds suggested to their discoverers that this war had occurred between peoples "vast in number and greatly superior in civilization to the Iroquois."[59] Brodie refers to speculations appearing in Palmyra newspapers already in 1818 and 1823 that interpreted local discoveries precisely as evidence of a titanic ancient battle in the region, a theory whose adherents included then-New York governor DeWitt Clinton.[60] I have said throughout this book that the study of constructions of Israelite identity is perhaps most interesting because of the ways in which each construction reflects and responds to the context that gave it birth, and the history through which it developed. Seldom has that been more clearly the case than where the development of Mormonism is concerned.

Still, while in many respects the Book of Mormon was at home in its region of birth, there was one way in which it certainly was not – a way that explains the troubled early history of Mormonism. Prophets there were, and new revelations, and plenty of stories about Israel in America. Nobody else, however, claimed to have written, or discovered, or translated, what the Book of Mormon claims to be on its title page: "Another Testament of Jesus Christ."[61] In the 1830s and 1840s, the ambit of what

---

[58] Harrison, *A Discourse on the Aborigines of the Ohio Valley*, 11–12.

[59] Brodie, *No Man Knows My History*, 34–35.   [60] Ibid.

[61] This phraseology first appeared in a new edition of the Book in 1981, but it applies perfectly well to how it was previously understood (Shipps, "An Interpretive Framework," 21). For the editorial history of the Book of Mormon, see especially Matthews, "The New Publications of the Standard Works"; Gutjahr, *The Book of Mormon: A Biography*; Hardy, "The Book of Mormon." Thus, as Barlow observes, "the Book of Mormon remains the only important second Bible produced in this country" (Barlow, *Mormons and the Bible*, 43). After Smith's death, however, James J. Strang convinced a splinter group of Mormons – who did not go to Utah – that he had discovered brass plates, translated in the Joseph Smith fashion, that told the story of the "ancient civilization of Vorito" through the influence of "Rajah Manchou," followed by

counted as "Christian" practice was very large, and indeed, Mormons certainly understand themselves as Christians.[62] Yet there were no other new *scriptures*, and this was a big part of what made the new religion so controversial. It also made Smith, for the rest of his life, as much pariah as prophet.

Indeed, very quickly, the controversy kicked up by the publication of the Book of Mormon made upstate New York, for all its religious variety, an uncomfortable base of operations. In 1831, Smith chose to let his missionaries lead the way to two different settlements: Kirtland, Ohio and Jackson County, Missouri.[63] From there, after an arrest, and after a series of struggles with local and federal authorities, the Mormons resettled once again in 1839, this time in Illinois, in a town Joseph called Nauvoo (originally Commerce). Here, it seemed, was peace at last: before long, Nauvoo had become almost the size of Chicago. In 1844, Joseph Smith Jr. would even run for president.[64]

After five years in Nauvoo, however, certain Mormons were becoming disaffected with their leader. On June 7, 1844, a group of Mormon dissenters published "the one and only issue of the *Nauvoo Expositor*," containing seven essays arguing for a return to the original spirit of Mormonism – since corrupted by its leader and prophet – and a more conciliatory spirit towards non-Mormons in the region.[65] Joseph, in his capacity as mayor of Nauvoo, ordered the press destroyed, which resulted in a warrant for his arrest and an abortive flight in the direction of Washington, DC. On June 23, he returned to Nauvoo, and on June 24,

his discovery of the "Plates of Laban" which "enabled him to translate the Book of the Law of the Lord" (Beam, *American Crucifixion*, 246). Strang did attract something of a following, but of course this "scripture" did not catch on the way Smith's had.

[62] On the LDS website, the question "Are Mormons Christian?" is addressed explicitly, and answered: "Members of the Church of Jesus Christ of Latter-day Saints unequivocally affirm themselves to be Christians" ("Are Mormons Christian?," www.lds.org/topics/christians?lang=eng).

[63] "Elizabeth Ann Whitney, an early Mormon convert in Ohio, remembered when Joseph Smith strode into her husband's store in Kirtland in February 1831. 'I am Joseph the Prophet,' he said ... The declaration seemed natural when Whitney wrote almost fifty years later in Utah ... But in 1831, it was a startling claim for an unprepossessing young man of twenty-five. The title appalled the Palmyrans who thought of Joseph as a poor, rural visionary with pretensions to 'see' with a stone" (Bushman, *Joseph Smith: Rough Stone Rolling*, 127).

[64] Parfitt, *The Lost Tribes of Israel*, 110. For details on Smith's presidential campaign, see Robertson, "The Campaign and the Kingdom"; Wood, "The Prophet and the Presidency." See also the recent publication by Spencer W. McBride, *Joseph Smith for President*.

[65] Bushman, *Joseph Smith: Rough Stone Rolling*, 539–40.

surrendered himself to authorities. On June 27, an angry, anti-Mormon mob stormed the prison, killing Joseph and his brother Hyrum.[66] For the people Smith left behind, much still lay ahead: the great journey from Nauvoo west into the mountains, and with it, the founding of their New Jerusalem, and the creation of an Israelite people to live within it.

4.3 ON THE TRAIL OF ISRAEL

The Book of Mormon charges the Mormons with a sacred mission: to recover and restore the lost of Israel. Already in 1 Nephi 15, Nephi receives a vision of Israel as an olive tree with broken branches. He is told that in some future day, "the remnant of our seed" will "know that they are of the house of Israel, and that they are the covenant people." As a result, "they shall be grafted in, being a natural branch of the olive tree, into the true olive tree" (1 Nephi 15:12, 14, 16). When, in 3 Nephi, Jesus comes to America after his crucifixion, his message is much the same. Beyond that, he reveals that the discovery of the Book of Mormon will be the signal that the time of the ingathering of the tribes is at hand (3 Nephi 21:1–2, 26–29).[67] Once united, the Mormons and the Israelites would build "New Jerusalem," long an actual goal of Joseph Smith Jr. and the early Mormons:

And then shall the power of heaven come down ... And then shall the work of the Father commence at that day, even when this gospel shall be preached among the remnant of this people. Verily I say unto you, at that day shall the work of the Father commence among all the dispersed out of my people, yea, even the tribes which have been lost, which the Father hath led away out of Jerusalem. (3 Nephi 21:25–26)

Of course, it is to be the Mormons who, in the words of 3 Nephi 28:29–31, "shall minister unto all the scattered tribes of Israel ... great and marvelous works shall be wrought by them."[68]

---

[66] See especially ibid., 538–50. A dramatic and fantastically detailed account of Smith's last days can be found in Park, *Kingdom of Nauvoo*, 223–38.

[67] See also 3 Nephi 29:1: "When the Lord shall see fit, in his wisdom, that these sayings shall come unto the Gentiles according to his word, then ye may know that the covenant which the Father hath made with the children of Israel, concerning their restoration to the lands of their inheritance, is already beginning to be fulfilled."

[68] Thus, early Mormons already seem to have considered finding and redeeming Israel to be their "primary responsibility." It was their job, even their destiny, "to bring the newly restored gospel contained in the Book of Mormon to the Indian remnant of a lost branch of Israel in America. Together with these Lamanites, the white Mormons would build up

In 1842, just two years before his death, Smith produced a summary of Mormon beliefs that "was added to Latter-day Saints scripture in 1880 under the title of 'Articles of Faith.'"[69] The tenth article was: "We believe in the literal gathering of Israel and in the restoration of the Ten Tribes; that Zion (the New Jerusalem) will be built upon the American continent; that Christ will reign personally upon the earth; and, that the earth will be renewed and receive its paradisiacal glory." When, in the epigram that began this chapter, Brigham Young described himself as searching for Ephraim, this is what he meant; the restoration of Israel and the establishment of the New Jerusalem went hand-in-hand.

But who was Israel, and where was it to be found? These were already important questions in early Mormonism. Obviously, the Book of Mormon characterized the Native Americans – some or all – as the remnants of the tribe of Manasseh. In previous chapters, I referred to the "separability" of Israelite identity, via the twelve tribes tradition, and that is what we see here: it makes the possibility that part of Israel came to America, and remained Israel, seem plausible. Additionally, the identification of the natives with the tribe of Manasseh was something that was easily addressed by the twelve tribes tradition's ability to explain the existence of sometimes significant differences between the heirs to Israel via references to historical experience. The Book, however, acknowledged that there was more of Israel out there somewhere, as indeed anyone familiar with Lost Tribe mythology would suspect. In 1 Nephi 15:18, we read "our father hath not spoken of our seed alone, but also of all the house of Israel" (1 Nephi 15:18). So where were they? Before too long, early Mormons emerged with a surprising answer.

It is clear that the earliest Mormons, by and large, understood themselves as Gentiles tasked with the discovery of Israel. It is true enough that the Book of Mormon admits the possibility that Joseph himself might have a different heritage. In 2 Nephi 3:15, Lehi, the patriarch, has a vision of the biblical Joseph, who revealed that "a seer shall the Lord my God

---

a new Jerusalem in the New World" (Mueller, *Race and the Making of the Mormon People*, 4–5). As Howe notes, "restoration" was a "prominent theological feature common to several denominations of the Second Great Awakening ... that is, the effort to restore authentic New Testament Christianity. The goal of restoration went back at least as far as the Protestant Reformation of the sixteenth century ... Joseph Smith's revealed religion was avowedly restorationist, even while also presenting a whole new set of scriptures in the form of the Book of Mormon" (Howe, "Emergent Mormonism in Context," 27).

[69] Bushman, *Mormonism: A Very Short Introduction*, 117.

raise up, who shall be a choice seer unto the fruit of my loins," and "his name shall be called after me; and it shall be after the name of his father" (2 Nephi 3:15). But Joseph Smith Jr., here as elsewhere, seems to have been a special case.[70]

So, for example, in one early letter from Eliel Strong and Eleazar Miller, published in W. W. Phelps' *Evening Star and Morning Star* in 1833, the authors declare themselves most grateful "that we, as Gentiles, have the privilege of receiving the light manifested."[71] This is a message echoed in the scripture, where in the 1 Nephi text mentioned above, we read "this is what our father meaneth; and he meaneth that it will not come to pass until after they are scattered by the Gentiles; and he meaneth that it shall come by way of the Gentiles, that the Lord may show his power unto the Gentiles" (1 Nephi 15:17). Indeed, as Max Perry Mueller points out, whatever 2 Nephi 3:15 might say, the title page of the Book mentions that it has "come forth ... by way of the Gentile," meaning Joseph himself.[72] Here, of course, we may also see an echo of the theology of Durie and Thorowgood, who believed that Christian communities could themselves form a new Israel, not in terms of their biological descent, but in their obedience to what biblical scripture commanded.

Yet again, there had long been another strand of speculation about Israel, even in Europe. At the same time that Thorowgood, Durie, and Ben Israel were discussing the possibility that the natives might be members of the Lost Tribes, others were indeed wondering whether the British themselves, or their neighbors, might not be tribal descendants. Geoffrey Keating's early seventeenth-century *History of Ireland*, for example, described the descent of the Irish from the Israelites by way of Scythia.[73] Other books, including M. le Loyer's *The Ten Lost Tribes* (1590) and John Sadler's *The Rights of the Kingdom* (1649), made similar cases. The royal families of Europe had very often traced their descent back to the biblical world, sometimes all the way to Adam and Eve.[74]

The logic of these identifications is twelve tribe logic in a nutshell – who knew where the tribes might have gone, or what they looked like now? But I think it is also an expression of the conflict at the heart of the

[70] Mueller, *Race and the Making of the Mormon People*, 102–3.   [71] Ibid., 105–6.
[72] Ibid.   [73] Parfitt, *The Lost Tribes of Israel*, 49.
[74] Mauss, *All Abraham's Children*, 19; Katz, "The Wanderings of the Lost Ten Tribes," 107. A related possibility was entertained at least as early as the Welsh historian Nennius, who lived in the ninth century CE. In his *Historia Brittonum*, he describes how a Scythian, living in Egypt when the Israelites escaped, traveled from there through all of Europe, ultimately settling in Ireland. See also Bender, *Israelites in Erin*.

Christian regard for Israel discussed in the last chapter, in the story of David Reubeni. If Israel was YHWH's chosen people, if they had a special role to play in the schema of redemption, how could they simply be the accursed outsiders that European Christians so often imagined? Might they not be, literally rather than metaphorically, Europeans themselves? Certainly, it must have made little sense in, say, the early seventeenth century, for the subjugated Jews of Europe – or the banished Jews of England – to be members of an elect that their Christian betters could not hope to enter, however holy.[75]

Thus, in Joseph Smith Jr.'s own lifetime, so-called "British Israelism" got its start. John Wilson's *Our Israeliteish Origin*, a charter text for British Israelism, was published in 1840.[76] In 1925, the Mormon leader James E. Talmage would report back from his visit to a British Israelite meeting that he was quite surprised by their antisemitism. British-Israelite doctrine, in Talmage's rendition, "holds that the British nation is the Israel of the Old Testament, the designation 'Israel' being used in its distinctive sense apart from 'Judah'" and "this distinction ... is emphasized to such an extent as to make it appear that the Jews are opponents if not enemies to the cause."[77] With or without this particularly antisemitic strand of philosophizing, many Mormons would make similar historical arguments about how Israel had gotten to Europe.[78]

In the Mormon case, their openness to finding Israel elsewhere might have received a boost from an unexpected source. A number of excellent recent studies have made the case that the early Mormon search for Israel

---

[75] As a pseudonymous British author named "Oxonian" put it in 1881 "how can the unique position of the British Nation and Empire be accounted for, except on the supposition that it is the Nation and Empire of the seed of Abraham? Certain it is that this Nation fulfills at the present day the destined *role* of Israel. This can only be due to the fact that Israel is in Britain: no other nation can be stepped into the promises entailed by God on Israel, for God cannot lie" (Benite, *The Ten Lost Tribes*, 196; Oxonian, *Israel's Wanderings*, 4).

[76] Wilson, *Our Israelitish Origin*.

[77] In a letter to President Heber J. Grant, Mission Administration Files, CHL, generously shared with me by Ardis E. Parshall, operator of the Mormon history database "The Keepapitchinin" (www.keepapitchinin.org/).

[78] One 1883 publication, *Are We of Israel* – by George Reynolds, a Mormon who had long been involved in missionary work in England – makes "several specific claims: (1) the wandering of the lost ten tribes can be traced from Assyria to Europe; (2) ... numerous parallels ... suggest that the Anglo-Saxons and related people are Israelites ... (4) where descendants of Israel are found, they are especially responsive to the teachings of the gospel ... (6) LDS missionary success in the British Isles and Scandinavia is a natural consequence of these historical developments" (Mauss, *All Abraham's Children*, 26; Reynolds, *Are We of Israel?*).

widened in part because the Native Americans proved less interested in recovering their "heritage" than expected.[79] Meanwhile, and in sharp contrast, missionaries sent to Britain and Scandinavia exceeded expectations. It is hardly any wonder that early Mormons began to suspect that the true sign of hidden Israelite descent might be, after all, an openness to receiving the Mormon message.[80] And while this meant that there were parts of Israel hiding in Western Europe, who was more open to the Mormon message than the original Mormons themselves? Thus, the explicit Mormon identification with Israel began to take shape.

Already by the late 1830s, Joseph Smith Jr. had come to believe that the Mormons were connected "not only with the spirit but also in blood to the ancient Israelite patriarchs."[81] One inciting event came in the context of a new settlement in Clay County, Missouri, where perceived Mormon efforts to proselytize not just among Native Americans but African Americans – likely overstated – aroused the ire of the white settlers of the region.[82] On the heels of the occasionally violent conflict

---

[79] This basic shift, and its roots in the inability of early Mormons to attract much of a following among Native Americans, is a major topic of two excellent new publications in the study of Mormonism, both of which have already been cited here: Mauss' *All Abraham's Children* and Mueller's own *Race and the Making of the Mormon People*. As their titles suggest, both also deal, in an engaging and well-researched fashion, with the institutionalized racism of Mormon scriptures and the difficulties experienced by African American Mormons until very recently. See also Reeve, "The Mormon Church in Utah," 49; Reeve, *Religion of a Different Color*.

[80] Or, as Mueller puts it, "Mormons would come to believe that the converts' patrilineage made them naturally predisposed to receive the good news that the ancient Abrahamic covenant had been restored in the latter days" (Mueller, *Race and the Making of the Mormon People*, 94). Thus, from the mid-nineteenth century on, Mormons grew less interested in the Israelite identity of Native Americans and more in their own, and of "the common destiny of the northern Europeans and Latter-day Saints" (Mauss, *All Abraham's Children*, 26).

[81] Mueller, *Race and the Making of the Mormon People*, 94. There are ways in which Mormons continue to understand themselves as "Gentiles," but as Mueller observes, this seems to have become a "political designation," referring to their relationship to the (Gentile) political system of the United States (ibid., 102–3). See also Mauss, *All Abraham's Children*, 3.

[82] Mueller notes that in July 1833, W. W. Phelps published an "article entitled 'free People of Color' which largely restated existing Missouri statues re: the ability of African Americans who could document their freedom to settle in Missouri." This was taken by other white Missourians "as an attempt to agitate both free and enslaved blacks" by inviting them to join the Mormon community (Mueller, *Race and the Making of the Mormon People*, 81). Phelps quickly backtracked, but there does seem to have been some interest in converting African Americans to Mormonism, both generally and in Phelps' case. He "presents no theological objection to free blacks coming to Jackson County ... Christ's covenant, it seems, was open to all: to the Lamanite 'heathen,' to the white

that arose, Joseph Smith Jr. declared a need to scale back the Mormon redemptive vision. While contemplating the matter, he discovered that "the kingdom was organized around a network of family trees," which is to say that those who would be redeemed were already pre-selected via their descent from certain families that, generally, were also descended from ancient Israel.[83] This quite literal Mormon identification with Israel, through the tribes of Israel, would prove enduring. And after Smith died, and the Mormons began their great trek west – even out of what was then the borders of the United States of America – the official identification between the Mormons and Israel only became stronger still.

4.4 BECOMING ISRAEL

In the introduction, I described Mormonism as the meeting point of two otherwise separate threads of my analysis: those who seek for Israel, and those who identify as Israel. As we just saw, if the first concept developed earlier, the second was not far behind, and it would quickly strengthen as Mormonism entered a new phase. The possibility that life in Utah provided the staging ground for a *literal* Israelite ethnogenesis has recently been suggested by a number of scholars, and it is not hard to see why.

In 1846, two years after Joseph Smith Jr.'s death, Brigham Young led the majority of Mormons out of America altogether, into the Great Basin of Utah, then still one year shy of becoming the American Utah Territory. No doubt, after the difficult time the Mormons had had in America, this was part of the appeal. For somewhat obvious reasons, this difficult, dangerous trek into the unknown seemed to be another exodus, "led by a Moses figure ... [to] an arid homeland." So, for example, when the sojourners came across "a fresh lake and a salty lake, connected by a river" in their new homeland, they very naturally named it the Jordan.[84] And as they settled, they came to understand themselves as Israelites more than ever.

Isolation was key to this process: the "removal" of the Mormons from American society "was both geographic and spiritual, withdrawing into the isolation of the Great Basins and also into sacred time and space."[85]

Gentile, and even to the people the book of Moses names the 'seed of Cain,' as long as they were 'free people of color' and have the documentation to prove it" (Mueller, *Race and the Making of the Mormon People*, 90).

[83] Ibid., 94.   [84] Mauss, *All Abraham's Children*, 166.

[85] Reeve, "The Mormon Church in Utah," 39.

There, for the most part, they were able to worship and practice as they chose, a dramatic change from their first hunted years. In Utah, Mormon identity was "fashioned at the intersection of shared ethnic kinship, shared interpretation of sacred texts, shared participation in sacred rituals, and shared experiences – most notably persecution, exodus, and gathering to their new Zion."[86] This is not to say that Mormon separateness was only about becoming an Israelite people. For instance, the continued practice of polygamy likely deserves most of the blame for the fact that Utah became a territory in 1847 but would not become a state until 1896, six years after polygamy was outlawed in Mormonism.[87] Brigham Young himself was an enthusiastic polygamist, having more than fifty wives during his lifetime.[88]

Still, "ethnogenesis" seems to capture something of how early Mormon settlers in Utah saw what was happening. As one put it, "we found a Scotch party, a Welch party, an English party, and an American party, and we turned Iron Masters and undertook to put all these through the furnace, and run out a party of Saints for building up the Kingdom of God."[89] What was true for the first generation was even more true for the next: "Children born in the valleys or in the tops of the mountains did not remember the land from which their parents came" – and increasingly so as time went on.[90] When the Mormons crossed the Mississippi, "the members of the procession ... were by and large still New England or Southern or Canadian or British Saints." Their "Old Testament Exodus to the Promised Land ... so altered the way Mormons thought of

---

[86] Mueller, *Race and the Making of the Mormon People*, 109. See also Reeve, "The Mormon Church in Utah," 41–42.

[87] "In Joseph Smith's day, Mormons were best known for their extra-biblical scripture. In the era of Brigham Young, however, they gained their notoriety from the practice of polygamy. Until it was officially abandoned in 1890, many Mormon leaders defended the practice with scripture" (Barlow, *Mormons and the Bible*, 91). Reeve adds "over ... three decades, Congress proposed and sometimes passed legislation designed to force a Mormon surrender and ultimately to make the Latter-day Saints into acceptable Americans ... Congress maintained its role as gatekeeper, making it clear that Mormonism did not fit prevailing ideas about what it meant to be American" (Reeve, "The Mormon Church in Utah," 47). See also Shipps, "An Interpretive Framework," 19; Maffly-Kipp, "Mormons and the Bible," 126.

[88] The official number is apparently fifty-six, in terms of women "sealed" to Young, but there are certain gradations in what "sealing" meant, and the extent to which it meant "wife," that are important to observe (Johnson, "Determining and Defining 'Wife,'" 2).

[89] Snow, "To My Friend, 'The News,'" 2, quoted in Reeve, "The Mormon Church in Utah," 41.

[90] Shipps, "An Interpretive Framework," 18.

themselves that the pioneers were transformed into Saints first and foremost."[91] It might well be said that they were transformed into *Israelites* first and foremost. And this Israelite "ethnogenesis" shaped early Mormonism in profound ways and continues to shape Mormon practice today.

First, there is Mormon missionary work to consider, which has often been explicitly conceptualized in terms of the search for Israel. Already in Smith's *Doctrine and Covenants* (133:26–27), he draws a wider geography of Israelite identification than the Book of Mormon itself presents. He speaks, for example, of the return of the Lost Tribes from a northern region where they were believed to live. Various church elders at various points suspected that some had left this northern migration along the way, settling in Europe and other places.[92] Here, as in previous chapters, the grand "separability" of Israelite identity, embodied in what we might call the "twelveness" of the twelve tribes tradition, has a role to play – parts of Israel could separate; remain Israel; and appear all over Europe, Asia, and eventually the rest of the world. As a result, Mormon missionary work has long been explicitly conceptualized as a search for the rest of Israel.

Indeed, new studies have now investigated how patterns in Mormon missionizing were repeatedly reshaped, over time, by rumors of where the tribes of Israel might be found, or else, how consistently even early Mormon missions were described in terms of the hunt for Israel. So, Armand L. Mauss describes how the suspicions of George Q. Cannon, a crucial figure in late nineteenth-century Mormonism, directed Mormon attentions to Polynesia, as well as Germany, while in 1917, Serge F. Baliff assured the Saints "that the German people still had 'the blood of Israel in their veins.'"[93] Elsewhere, Reid L. Neilson describes a tendency among Mormon missionaries to discover new settlements of Israel just as old

[91] Ibid., 17.

[92] Thus, Samuel Bennion in a letter to James E. Talmage on January 12, 1933 (James E. Talmage collection, MS 1232 [Box 3, folder 21]), and John A. Widtsoe in a letter to J. W. Dunn, ca. February 15, 1938 (John A. Widtsoe papers, CR 712/2 [Box 45, folder 18]).

[93] Mauss, *All Abraham's Children*, 27. In another instance, Thomas E. McKay, one-time president of this mission, made remarks "at the General Conference in Salt Lake City, April 6, 1912," that were reported in a June 25, 1912 edition of *Liahona: The Elders' Journal*, concerning a mission to Hungary. In it, he reported on a woman in Hungary, "an 'Israelite,' as she called herself, a bright young woman who became interested in the gospel, attended our meetings, and attended our choir practice," who was instrumental, through her brother, in giving the Mormons the freedom of Hungary to do their work.

sources ran dry. Thus, in one telling example, "a major decline in missionary success in the Christian Atlantic world" produced an expansion of "traditional understandings of 'Lehite' blood ... to those of Latin descent" in the mid-twentieth century. Later still, Mormon missionaries would turn their attention to the Pacific Islands, using similar logic.[94]

A brief sampling of letters between Mormons from the late nineteenth and early twentieth century, typically between the members of the Church and its leaders, adds color to these general observations.[95] In 1897, Cannon, Wilford Woodruff, and Joseph F. Smith – members of the First Presidency, the highest authority in the Church – responded jointly to a series of letters from a mission to Turkey. They exhort the missionaries to be faithful in their work, since "Jerusalem must be rebuilt by the Jews, the ten tribes must return from the north, the American Indians, who are of the house of Israel must be converted and become workers in His cause. And many more of the different branches of the House of Israel must return to the promised lands."[96] Presumably, part of this task could be accomplished in Turkey.

Another, and more amusing, letter from 1920, from L. W. Bean to James E. Talmage, expresses the speculation that – in the early days of wireless radios – the stray radio waves that could be heard from time to

---

The woman supposedly asked whether her brother believed "all the stories that have been written about us as Jews?" (McKay, "The Gospel in Foreign Countries," 2–3).

[94] Neilson, "Mormon Mission Work," 191. He adds that "early Mormon evangelists were encouraged to search out the 'believing blood' of Israel, the elect, typically those with Anglo-Saxon heritage identified by many Christians as being connected with biblical lineages." Christopher Cannon Jones, professor at Brigham Young University, tells me that George Q. Cannon referred to Hawaiians as Israelites as early as 1851. Jones also shared with me a chapter in progress, describing an 1852 conference of Mormon missionaries, including this conviction that Hawaiians (and Tahitians) were possessed of the literal blood of Israel. While failures in Jamaica inspired a recourse to racist theorizing about African descendants, success in Tahiti caused one missionary, Addison Pratt, to declare that the Tahitians were in fact not just Israelites, but descendants of the Nephites themselves (Jones, "'A Necessary Book for Dark-Skinned People': Nineteenth-Century Missions, Race, and Scripture"). Here we see the equation between receptiveness to the Mormon message and an assumption of Israelite descent. Jones also mentions an 1865 letter from Brigham Young to King Kamehameha V referring to the "people of your Majesty's nation" as "of the House of Israel, and heirs of all promises made to the chosen seed" (Brigham Young to 'His Majesty, L. Kamehameha the Fifth, King of the Hawaiian Islands,' 24 March 1865, CHL). The chapter is to appear in *American Examples: New Conversations About Religion, Volume Two* in 2022.

[95] These letters were also generously supplied by Ardis E. Parshall, operator of the Mormon history database "The Keepapitchinin" (www.keepapitchinin.org/).

[96] Ibid.

time might be dispatches from the tribes.[97] A 1930 letter from Anthony W. Ivins to John A. Widtsoe observes that, given the success of a recent mission to Prague, the people of that region must be Israelites, and that it made sense they would be, since they were "exactly in the line of march followed by the ten tribes after they left Assyria, as outlined by the Prophet Ezra."[98] Here is meant not the book of Ezra, but 2 Esdras, which was of such interest to Ethan Smith as well.

Of course, in this as in all other things, Mormon thought was not monolithic. Thus, Talmage could declare, in a July 17, 1933 letter to Samuel O. Bennion, that

I venture to express a *personal opinion* to this effect: It appears to me improbable and indeed unreasonable to assume that "the blood of Israel" which has been spoken of as "the believing blood" is really the blood of the Tribe of Ephraim by literal, physical descent. Many of our people have been led to this assumption because in the great majority of patriarchal blessings the respective recipient is told that he is of Ephraim. I take this to mean an inheritance of privilege and blessing rather than a declaration of physical descent.[99]

Widtsoe, however, expressing himself in a letter to J. W. Dunn around February 15, 1938, believed that "modern historical research points clearly to a wide dispersion of the blood of Israel among the nations of earth, from China to Spain." He further ventures that "evidence from tradition, philology and archaeological discovery has been produced by the world's scholars to the effect that among the nations of northern Europe – Russia, Scandinavia, Northern Germany, the British Isles, etc., – there is a preponderance of the blood of Israel."[100] Today, this search for Israel has become more metaphorical in construction, but similar language is still used, and certainly a literal identification with Israel has not vanished from contemporary Mormonism altogether.[101]

---

[97] James E. Talmage collections, MS 1232 (Box 2, folder 12). This and all of the following letters were also supplied by Parshall.

[98] John A. Widtsoe papers CR 712/2 (Box 175, folder 6).

[99] James E. Talmage collection, MS 1232 (Box 7, folder 37).

[100] John A. Widtsoe papers, CR 712/2 (Box 45, folder 18). As Widtsoe noted in another letter from June 1931, in response to questions from missionaries, these were the two prevailing theories – that the Lost Tribes "are in the North shut off from civilization and will return with their records and with great rejoicing from this hidden country" or that "in going north ... they intermarried and mingled with other nations and that we're in the act of assembling them now" (John A. Widtsoe papers, CR 712/2 [Box 146, folder 4]).

[101] This note is also courtesy of Dr. Christopher Jones of BYU, who generously read a draft of this chapter.

At any rate, where early Mormons were concerned, it is the case that if future Mormons were prepared for their conversion by their previously unsuspected Israelite heritage, it is not much of a leap to the conclusion that those who were already Mormon had the same heritage. This brings us to a consideration of the "patriarchal blessing," where the specific identification, not just with Israel, but with particular tribes of Israel, is rendered explicit. As always, the dispersion of Israel across the world was mediated on the level of the tribe because different tribes can so naturally have different destinies and end up in different places from each other. But rarely, anywhere in the world, has this principle been made so clearly visible as in this Mormon ritual, which is almost as old as Mormonism itself.

4.5 ISRAEL IN THE MORMON PATRIARCHAL BLESSING

The Mormon patriarchal blessing, and the person who is deputized to perform it – the "patriarch of the church," until that office was discontinued, and "stake patriarchs" during and after – are both based on Genesis 49, the so-called "Blessing of Jacob." In this biblical text, Jacob, on his deathbed, pronounces a blessing for each of his twelve sons to carry on after his death. Indeed, Genesis 49 has other associations in Mormon thought:

Few ancient Jews or modern readers have taken that over-run well [of Gen. 49:1, 22, 26] to refer to the Pacific Ocean or the everlasting hills to evoke images of Utah's Wasatch Mountains. But to many Latter-day Saints, the Book of Mormon story that begins in Jerusalem and ends in the Western Hemisphere fulfills that very prophecy of Jacob.[102]

Mormons, then, both embody the promise of Jacob's blessing and continue to bless, with this biblical text as a model. And they have for a very long time – the office of the patriarch of the church appeared, at least in nascent form, in 1833, and blessings were already a part of it. Joseph Smith Jr. "revealed" that his father, Joseph Smith Sr., was to be "Patriarch," which "empowered the elder Joseph to bless individual Mormon converts and, if such a connection existed, proclaim their connection to the house of Israel."[103] After Joseph Smith Sr., his sons Hyrum

---

[102] Givens, *By the Hand of Mormon*, 43.
[103] Mueller, *Race and the Making of the Mormon People*, 103–4.

and William Smith held the office in turn, with William taking the reins after Hyrum's death in Carthage jail.[104]

In later days, Patriarch of the Church was a church-wide office that was always occupied by linear descendants of Joseph Smith Jr., and numerous blessings from church patriarchs have recently been published in a couple of weighty volumes.[105] However, the position was phased out in 1979, likely because of the political tensions that having a descendant of Joseph Smith Jr. around engendered.[106] Stake patriarchs – the world of Mormonism has long been organized into "stakes" – now bear the entire burden of the task, but the office of Stake Patriarch is itself nearly as old as that of Patriarch of the Church. Isaac Morley was appointed to the position in 1838, and the official justification for the dissolution of the church-wide office was a superabundance of these stake positions, which were sufficient to patriarchal needs.[107]

The fact that stake patriarchs have been blessing the members of their stakes for almost two centuries means, of course, that there are many more patriarchal blessings than could possibly be collected or analyzed. Adding to the difficulty, while early blessings were publicly pronounced and known, later blessings have been given in private and are meant to be kept private – which at least one author has claimed is a reflex of the declining force of a separate Mormon identity.[108] All blessings are still

---

[104] Ibid. See also Smith, "The Office of Presiding Patriarch."

[105] Marquardt, *Early Patriarchal Blessings of the Church of Jesus Christ of Latter-Day Saints*; Marquardt, *Later Patriarchal Blessings of the Church of Jesus Christ of Latter-Day Saints*.

[106] Marquardt, *Early Patriarchal Blessings of the Church of Jesus Christ of Latter-Day Saints*, xvi; Bates and Smith, *Lost Legacy*, 1–2. Another study, focused on the relationship between patriarchal blessings and the prophetic character of Mormonism more generally, can be found in Shepherd and Shepherd, *Binding Earth and Heaven*.

[107] For information on Morley, see Smith, "The Office of Presiding Patriarch." Marquardt adds "from the earliest years of the LDS Church, men besides the Presiding Patriarch or Patriarch to the Church have been ordained as local patriarchs in an effort to extend the opportunity to receive patriarchal blessings to as many Church members as possible. These local, or stake, patriarchs assisted the Church Patriarch in giving blessings to members of the stakes in which they resided" (Marquardt, *Later Patriarchal Blessings of the Church of Jesus Christ of Latter-Day Saints*, ix).

[108] Shepherd and Shepherd argue that the early patriarchal blessings were an expression of the need to "reinforce community bonds and shared commitments." "To be a devout Mormon in the nineteenth century meant to be at odds with the conventional secular and religious institutions of American society and, if necessary, to put at risk one's life, property, and family tranquility in defense of one's religious faith. Today, however, claiming LDS faith and affiliation is perfectly compatible with active involvement in both civil and religious arenas of American life and in most other countries around the

sent to the "LDS Church Historian," but they can only be accessed by blood relatives.[109] As a result, recent research relies heavily on blessings volunteered to scholars, and on the large collection of blessings at both stake and church-wide levels that survive from earlier eras.

Still, even this comparatively limited corpus is vast, and it is clear that revealing a person's tribe of origin was an early and common feature of the practice. Joseph Smith Sr., the first patriarch, was not very consistent on this score, and his early blessings rarely enough referred to the tribes of Israel, likely tracking the development of Mormon thought from Gentile to Israelite. Yet, as Mormon thought soon shifted, so did the character of these blessings, and it quickly becomes difficult to find any that do not identify the tribe the person being blessed descends from.[110] Then, the idea of explicit, identifiable descent from individual tribes continues to be a part of Mormonism today. As Apostle Bruce R. McConkie put it in 1958, "nearly every member of the Church is a literal descendant of Jacob who gave patriarchal blessings to his 12 sons."[111]

Within these blessings, the tribe of Ephraim has always predominated. "In 1929, Patriarch Hyrum G. Smith stated, 'At the present time in the Church the great majority of those receiving their blessings are declared to be of the house and lineage of Ephraim, while many others are designated

world." As a result, they argue, of the "declining need for resolute commitment in the face of powerful opposition," there has been a "decline in the solidarity function of patriarchal blessings in the lives of Latter-day Saints." That plus a decline in "historical conjunction with the rise of privacy norms in American culture ... provid[e] a plausible ex post facto rationale for changes in the institutional setting of modern patriarchal blessings" (Shepherd and Shepherd, *Binding Earth and Heaven*, 108).

[109] Bates, "Patriarchal Blessings and the Routinization of Charisma," 1.
[110] Although in Joseph Smith Sr.'s case, it was still at least as common to see him refer to the person being blessed as a descendant of Abraham – especially in the context of identifying members of the Melchizedek priesthood – as it was to see him identify descendants of Joseph. Thus, Samuel Rolfe was "blessed with the blessing of Abraham, and ... numbered with his seed," Joseph Putnam was "not of the seed of Joseph, but of the blood of Abraham" and so on (Marquardt, *Early Patriarchal Blessings of the Church of Jesus Christ of Latter-Day Saints*, 23, 136). Bates notes that "50 percent of Joseph Sr.'s blessings included in this study declared lineage. Such declarations became routine later" (Bates, "Patriarchal Blessings and the Routinization of Charisma," 6 n.21).
[111] McConkie, *Mormon Doctrine*, 504; Bates, "Patriarchal Blessings and the Routinization of Charisma," 5. Some have argued that, in recent years, the expansion of Mormonism around the globe has made the identification with the blood of Israel "more metaphorical than literal," but again this certainly does not seem to be universally the case (Shipps, "An Interpretive Framework," 21).

as members of the house of Manasseh.'"[112] However, a 1961 letter from Thomas G. Truitt to Eldred G. Smith, the last national patriarch, reveals that, by that time, blessings had been given "through ten of the twelve tribes of Israel, the two not mentioned being the tribes of Issachar and Asher."[113] So, to give something of the flavor of these, we can note that in Smith Sr.'s blessings, one Mathias Cowley had it revealed to him that he was of mingled Josephite and Judahite blood, and a Howard Egan, that he was "of the lineage of David of the tribe of Judah. Nevertheless, you have come to Zion, unto the Covenant, that shall be made with the House of Israel."[114] James Newberry, blessed by Hyrum on May 30, 1841, was "a descendant of Nathan that Prophet ... a descendant of Israel, in the lineage of Manasseh, which was remembered with the seed of Jacob."[115]

In more recent years, however, identifications with Ephraim seem to have become even more common. In the aforementioned volumes, the last blessings that have been published include some from the final Patriarch of the Church, Eldred G. Smith, even after the national patriarchate officially ended. In two blessings from 1989, he blessed two women "through the lineage of Ephraim, who was the son of Joseph who was sold into Egypt by his brethren."[116] The three blessings preserved in this collection from the previous patriarch, Joseph F. Smith, also all refer to descent from Ephraim, while a blessing by a stake patriarch named Saul Anderson Clark, given as recently as 1995, states, "you are of a choice lineage, even that of Joseph, who was sold into Egypt, through his son Ephraim."[117] In short, the patriarchal blessing in Mormonism has long been a main method of literally identifying with the tribes of Israel, and this institution is still going strong.

Today, the Mormon search for the blood of Israel, and for the tribes of Israel, is not limited to the living. Mormon doctrine is very concerned with the souls of the dead, and the not-yet-born as well. In the Mormon concept of "pre-existence," we see the idea that the souls of future

---

[112] Smith, "The Day of Ephraim," 123, found in Bates, "Patriarchal Blessings and the Routinization of Charisma," 4.
[113] "And fifteen other lineages had been named in blessings, including that of Cain." This is from a letter by Thomas G. Truitt to Eldred G. Smith in 1961, found in Bates, "Patriarchal Blessings and the Routinization of Charisma," 4.
[114] Marquardt, *Early Patriarchal Blessings of the Church of Jesus Christ of Latter-Day Saints*, 221, 236, 198.
[115] Ibid., 203.
[116] Marquardt, *Later Patriarchal Blessings of the Church of Jesus Christ of Latter-Day Saints*, 521–22.
[117] Ibid., 511–14, 499.

Mormons were chosen by God prior to creation, which is one reason why missionary work is so often conceived of as discovery rather than actual conversion.[118] On the other side, the current president of the Church as this book is in the process of being written, Russell M. Nelson, has frequently made speeches calling for Mormons to redouble their efforts to gather "scattered Israel" on "both sides of the veil."[119]

Here, we see a natural evolution of the belief that the mission of Mormonism is to gather "all Israel" to effect its complete restoration and bring about the New Jerusalem. As Tona J. Hangen puts it:

> Latter-day Saints orient themselves on a cosmic timeline, anchored in the idea that they live in the "latter days" ... History stretches backwards to draw upon elements of primitive Christianity and from Old Testament patriarchy, and extends even farther back to an imagined preexistence. Their sense of time also stretches forward to anticipate a millennial future and a triumphant family reunion in the eternities.[120]

This family is Israel, some part of it perhaps lost until some distant day of return from the north, other parts scattered throughout the known nations of the world, and some available to Israel through a kind of adoption, living or dead. From the time of the publication of the Book of Mormon, the inauguration of this "millennial future" is connected with the completion of the great task of Mormonism: the restoration of this Israel, begun with the discovery of the book on the Hill Cumorah and the announcement of its message to the world. And when Mormons look for Israel, they look for it in the form of its ever-present, ever-relevant tribes – lost, perhaps, but not gone.

---

[118] Indeed, as Mauss puts it, "by the 1850s, the Saints were beginning to learn that they had been identified and set aside in pre-mortal life to enter mortality through Israelite (especially Ephraimite) lineage as a people of 'royal' blood ... The doctrine that the Saints were a royal, Israelite people, chosen and foreordained in the preexistence, was developed most fully, however, by a later generation of LDS leaders, who brought the church into the twentieth century" (Mauss, *All Abraham's Children*, 24–25).

[119] In these addresses, Nelson states key points of contemporary Mormon doctrine, including the idea that "the Lord reaffirmed the Abrahamic covenant in our day through the Prophet Joseph Smith" and "in the temple we receive our ultimate blessings, as the seed of Abraham, Isaac, and Jacob." Nelson's interests were called to my attention by a colleague of mine at William and Mary, Evan Criddle. This quote is from a speech given by Nelson in October 2006, which can be found in Nelson, "The Gathering of Scattered Israel." See also The Church of Jesus Christ of Latter-Day Saints, "President Nelson Invites Record Crowd in Arizona to Help Gather Israel."

[120] Hangen, "Lived Religion Among Mormons," 213.

4.6 CONCLUSION

Throughout this book, we have seen *redescription* posing as *description*. Visions of Israel masquerade as simple accounts of Israelite identity – and are no doubt understood as such by their authors – because they derive their authority and efficacy from precisely this: appearing to describe Israel just as it actually is.[121] In a construction of Israelite identity where, say, Ephraim is superior to Simeon, or Judah to Joseph, the fact that this construction naturalizes a social or political order is a big part of how it works as a claim. In describing, it seeks to instantiate.[122]

With the larger study in view, the case of the Mormons is so useful for illuminating "becoming Israel" as a practice because, unlike in any of the previous chapters, the Mormon identification with Israel occurred "within the limits of some known" – and relatively recent – past.[123] This is what has allowed us to study the specifics of the process of Mormon "becoming Israel" in a way that we cannot do in the ancient world. More than that, an Israelite ethnogenesis occurred among people we know to have had no previous awareness of their own purported Israelite identity, but would, instead, generally have thought of themselves as of European descent. In other words, if, say, a future Mormon had joined another famous New York resident, Rip Van Winkle, for a nap in 1819 (the year Washington Irving's book was published, though it is set

---

[121] This framing of how ethnic identity works is not meant to imply that the "instrumentalist" operation of ethnic concepts is ever quite so explicit, or so conscious. As Max Perry Mueller observes, we "can understand Mormon identity as an 'invented' Israelite ethnicity without invoking, as Werner Sollers has written, 'a conspiratorial interpretation of a manipulative inventor who single-handedly made ethnics out of unsuspecting subjects'" (Mueller, *Race and the Making of the Mormon People*, 109; Sollors, *The Invention of Ethnicity*, xi–xii).

[122] Again, as Hall notes, while scholars often refer to the instrumentalist capacities of ethnic narratives, we must keep in mind that "the primordialist view of ethnicity" is the one "more likely to be held by members of an ethnic group." "Instrumentalism" is usually an outsider perspective – but there is still, today, "no doubt that ethnic identity is a cultural construct, perpetually renewed and renegotiated through discourse and social praxis" (Hall, *Ethnic Identity in Greek Antiquity*, 18–19). Thus, today, some speak of the *unconscious* inheritance of "an ethnic *habitus*" – in Pierre Bourdieu's phrase – coupled with the constant modification of "that *habitus* ... in the pursuit of various goals" (Hall, *Ethnic Identity in Greek Antiquity*, 18; Bentley, "Ethnicity and Practice"; Bourdieu, *Outline of a Theory of Practice*).

[123] Here, Malkin is referring to a study of Canadian Huron ethnogenesis by E. E. Roosens, another instance where we have a "primordialist myth ... 'invented' within the limits of some known past" (Malkin, *The Returns of Odysseus*, 57–58; Roosens, *Creating Ethnicity*).

in an earlier period), he or she would have fallen asleep a Gentile and woken up an Israelite.

So what, then, do Mormon processes of "becoming Israel" tell us about "becoming" itself? Really, the history narrated in this chapter is most useful as a way of solidifying aspects of our discussion so far. For example, we see how much the basic Mormon conception of Israel is shaped by what "Israel" itself had come to mean, to whom, by the time Joseph Smith Jr. was born, via the role the restoration of Israel had already assumed in certain Protestant theological approaches; its links with the Second Coming; and the literal and figurative Protestant identification with Israel that had begun in the days of Thorowgood and Durie.

At the same time, we see how the initial set of associations that shaped Mormon understandings of Israel and its whereabouts, as well as the Mormon sense of an eschatological mission, repeatedly responded to new developments throughout Mormonism's early history, including limited success in converting the natives; unexpected success in Britain and Scandinavia; and, eventually, Mormon separation and settlement in Utah, envisioned as a kind of Israelite enclave. Beyond that, we saw how heavily early Mormonism was informed by – or, more simply, how many continuities it had with – the specific beliefs, rituals, and practices of the world into which it was born. Between its enthusiasm for new religious movements, its openness to prophecy and new revelations, its seeing stones and divining rods, and even its local legends about ancient Native American wars, the early Mormon vision of Israel, its history, and its destiny was clearly forged in the fires of the culture of the region of New York state in which it emerged in the early nineteenth century.

More than anything else, however, the history of Mormon understandings of themselves and others as Israel continues to reveal the capacity of different versions of Israelite identity to be "particularized" – in the sense meant by Irad Malkin in a 1998 study of a specific kind of foundation myth centering on the return of various heroes from the Trojan War: *Nostoi* myths, of which *The Odyssey* is the most famous example.[124] Basically, because there were so many stories about heroes making their way home, and stopping at various points along the way – and because there could always be *more* if necessary – it was always plausible for

---

[124] "Since there was no 'Greece' in antiquity but only hundreds of discrete political communities, a particularized origins explanation was needed for each. The *Nostoi* were capable of particularizing history in a manner truer to the realities of Greek existence" (Malkin, *The Returns of Odysseus*, 3).

Greeks anywhere in the Mediterranean to claim descent from one of them, or cities their foundation, and so grant themselves or their settlements the prestige of a connection to this epochal event.[125] But, that same variety and multiplicity also meant that they could customize that connection in a way that suited their particular sense of their place in the world, their historical character, and their present ambitions.

In fact, so adaptable was this Trojan War framework that it, too, would have a considerable afterlife, just like the twelve tribes tradition. Certainly, the practice of claiming and repurposing heroic classical ancestors survived well into the medieval period. It is one Brutus, for example – a descendant of Aeneas certainly not mentioned in the *Iliad* or *Aeneid* – who, in the early medieval histories of Geoffrey of Monmouth, Wace, and Layamon, has the honor of founding Britain. And it was Francio, a hero of Troy who also somehow escaped Homer's notice, who went on to become the ancestor of the Frankish people, according to at least one seventh-century French chronicler.[126] There are many other such stories – all of them "particularized" to the realities of their contexts, all of them refashioning an inherited authority and prestige to new, and culturally *particular* ends.

In the case of the twelve tribes tradition, and its capacity for making Israels, the segmented structure of the tradition works in just the same way. Twelve is not so large a number as there are heroes who served in the armies of Greece and Troy. But, neither is it very few, nor does history suggest that anything stopped different groups in different places from claiming to be the same tribe. So, here too, anyone can tell a new story about one or more of the tribes that builds off of existing myths, but adapts them to local realities, and, through that story, lay claim to the august authority and sacred status biblical Israel enjoys in so many places in a *particular* way. And in Mormonism, we see Israel adapted into multiple different forms at different times, and at the same time – among the Native Americans, among the Mormons themselves, and among the nations visited by Mormon missionaries, all with different features and histories, but also a shared destiny.

---

[125] "Their main figures were heroes living long ago in never-never land, but with exploration, contact and settlement they came to be superimposed onto ethnic identities and territories ... The Nostoi mediated and informed cultural, ethnic, and political encounters among Greeks, in relation to non-Greeks, and in the relations of non-Greeks to Greeks" (ibid., 7).

[126] Patterson, *Kinship Myth in Ancient Greece*, 10.

More than anything else, the Mormon process of "becoming Israel" particularizes the twelve tribes tradition by creating it in the form of a mission statement. The twelve tribes framework, here as elsewhere, is incomplete – or, we might say, partially vacant – but in Mormonism it needs to be completed. By giving themselves the task, Mormons not only lay claim to a sacred purpose, but also inscribe themselves, as Thorowgood, Durie, and many others before them, within a particular epoch of history – an epoch drawing rapidly to a close, and which it is part of their mission to close.[127] Which means that, unlike Thorowgood, Durie, et al., who had viewed the role the restoration of the tribes would play in bringing about the Second Coming from the outside, Mormon theology makes the Mormons insiders.

Indeed, in Mormonism, the epoch was officially begun by the discovery and translation of the Book. The restoration of Israel is not only something the Mormons are to accomplish, but something they are already accomplishing merely by existing. Internally to the Mormon construction of Israel, the Mormons represent a partial fulfillment of the mission the Angel Moroni announced to Joseph Smith Jr., in his own words, in the words of Nephi, and in the words of Jesus. And completing that mission is the purpose Joseph Smith Jr. dutifully announced to his followers. The needs of this mission have shaped and reshaped Mormonism for almost two centuries, as pre-existing ideas about Israel helped give it shape in the first place.

Ultimately, then, the story of Mormonism reflects both the universal characteristics of "becoming Israel" as a phenomenon and the particular circumstances in which Mormonism took shape and developed. As a particular manifestation of general principles, Mormon constructions of Israel are open to the "redescriptive method" I have advocated throughout, where we ask not is this an accurate description of Mormon history, but what is being done with Israel in this case. And again, the history of Mormonism reveals as clearly as any case study possibly could how every construction of Israelite identity – from the biblical period to the present – is a particular product of the time and place that gave it birth, and the history it subsequently experienced.

At the same time, the unique features of Mormon visions of Israel – which I have previously called, with reference to the concept of "plural

---

[127] Again, there is a sense in which this may be too active a description of the construction and reconstruction of ethnic identities; they do operate instrumentally, but not always consciously so.

identity," the plural features of different Israels – hold the key to understanding this case study. In identifying Israel, developing Israel, and using Israel, every protagonist of this book reveals themselves, but only if we have enough of a sense of the universal features of "becoming Israel" as a practice to see the particulars of how they are being applied in a given instance. Here, Israel defines who the Mormons understand themselves to be, determines their role in history, and gives explicit shape to Mormon practices, including Mormon missionary work and the patriarchal blessing.

In the next and final chapter, even more than this one, we will see how the long history of "becoming Israel" shaped its development even into the present. We will also witness, once again, the sometimes unexpected results when different threads of Israelite identity discourse meet. In this case, we will be discussing the development of Israelite identities in Ethiopia over time, the challenges that shaped and reshaped "Beta Israel" identifications with Israel specifically, and finally, what happened when the Beta Israel came to the modern State of Israel and settled there, often uneasily. In the Beta Israel's story, the ongoing character of "becoming Israel" in one context and across contexts, the constructed nature of all visions of Israel, and the responsive character of Israelite identities to each other will all appear again, combining within one particularly complex historical problem, and provide a fitting capstone to this book's investigation.

5

A Lost Tribe Returns

The Beta Israel in Ethiopia and Israel

When we went out of Ethiopia, the haste in which the food was prepared reminded me of my father's stories of how the Israelites prepared their *matzot*. I said to my father: "This is like the Exodus out of Egypt." He replied: "This is true, and it is good that you recalled it. It is exactly the same"
—A Beta Israel named Brehanu, quoted in Ben Ezer, *The Ethiopian Jewish Exodus*, 152.

From a certain poetic perspective, the story of the Beta Israel of Ethiopia is the story of two brothers, sons of the wise King Solomon. One was named Rehoboam and he grew up in Israel. Upon Solomon's death, the people of the kingdom would come to him *en masse*, demanding that he promise to be a kinder, gentler king than his father. Rehoboam refused, with euphemistic scorn – "my little finger is thicker than my father's loins!" (1 Kgs. 12:10) – and ten tribes of Israel would leave him behind. Rehoboam would establish the kingdom of Judah and found a line of Davidic monarchs who would rule it for centuries.

The other brother was named Menelik, and the Bible does not mention him. He was the son of Solomon and the Queen of Sheba, whose meeting, though not its aftermath, is described in 1 Kings 10. He would grow up in Ethiopia, his mother's country, but he would visit his father when he came of age. He would be crowned in the Temple in Jerusalem, the great "First Temple" of Solomon. Then he would return home with an honor guard of Israelites drawn from all twelve of Israel's tribes. He, too, would found a Davidic monarchy, the great "Solomonic dynasty" of Ethiopia, and it, too, would rule for centuries.

The two brothers never met; they never got to know each other. They never took riding lessons together, or perhaps, under the circumstances, chariot riding lessons. In fact, they never even knew the other existed. But in time, the people of Rehoboam would become the Jewish people, spread by the winds of diaspora around the world, and the people of Menelik would become the Beta Israel of Ethiopia. And one day, their descendants would meet, and it would be something of a family reunion.

This, of course, is an entirely internal vision of the history of the Beta Israel, based on the traditions of the peoples involved rather than a historian's research. It does, however, capture some fundamental truths that would otherwise be difficult to see as clearly. The normative Jewish vision of Israelite identity and the Beta Israel version *were* born and raised separately from each other, at least for a while. That is, they developed independently, in different places in the world, and as the product of their separate experiences. They were at home in different contexts and they responded in different ways to the realities and challenges of these contexts. And they did meet, at last. In the mid-to-late nineteenth century, emissaries from the outside Jewish world encountered the Beta Israel in Ethiopia, kicking off decades of steady outreach that would culminate in the immigration of the Beta Israel to Israel, starting in the 1970s. This would occur, of course, because each "Israel" recognized the other as family – as part of the same people, however long separated.

Here, however, is where the history of the Beta Israel gets complicated. First, the story of Menelik, Solomon, and Sheba is not simply the origin story of the Beta Israel – or even first and foremost. Instead, it is the tradition of the *Kebra Nagast*, Ethiopia's "national epic," which was the charter myth of Ethiopia's *Christian* emperors and much of the Ethiopian Christian elite – who also understood themselves as Israelites.[1] The Solomonic dynasty would rule Ethiopia from the late thirteenth century CE until 1974, when its final emperor, the famous Haile Selassie, was deposed.[2] And when the Beta Israel first began to emerge in the fourteenth

---

[1] Quirin, *The Evolution of the Ethiopian Jews*, 18; Kaplan, *The Beta Israel*, 17–18; Parfitt, "The Construction of Jewish Identities in Africa," 33.

[2] Kaplan, *The Beta Israel*, 10. In 1955, Emperor Haile Selassie would encode his own descent from Solomon and Menelik, and that of his dynasty, into the Ethiopian constitution (Belcher, "African Rewritings of the Jewish and Islamic Solomonic Tradition," 442). "The Imperial dignity shall remain perpetually attached to the line of Haile Selassie I, descendant of King Sahle Selassie, whose line descends without interruption from the dynasty of Menelik I, son of the Queen of Ethiopia, the Queen of Sheba, and King Solomon of Jerusalem" ("1955 Revised Constitution of Ethiopia").

century, they would understand themselves not as part of the wider Jewish nation, but as *Jewish Israelites* among *Christian Israelites* in their own native land. Their traditions reflect this fact. Originally, the Beta Israel understood themselves, according to their version of the *Kebra*'s traditions, as the descendants of the people of Menelik who did not convert to Christianity, but instead preserved Solomon's original Jewish faith.[3] This is a fundamentally Ethiopian vision of Israel and a product of internal Ethiopian developments.

However, when the outside Jewish world came into contact with the Beta Israel at last, they would not understand them according to the traditions of the *Kebra*, or of the two brothers. Instead, in a stunning coincidence, Jewish authorities would view the Beta Israel through the lens of an altogether different tradition, but just as ancient, and of all things, also rooted in the days of Solomon. This was the story that Eldad ha-Dani told the Jewish community of Kairouan, in modern Tunisia, which I discussed in Chapter 3. According to Eldad, his Danite ancestors had left Israel for Kush, long associated with Ethiopia, when Jeroboam had ordered them to raise their swords against Rehoboam and the divinely ordained Davidic monarchy.[4] Discovering these Jews of Ethiopia in the nineteenth century, Jewish authorities would turn to this Danite legend, rather than native traditions, for explanations.

In fact, the Beta Israel had already been recognized as these Danite Jews by Jewish authorities in the early sixteenth century. Specifically, this was the ruling of David Ben Abi Zimra, the "Radbaz," a magisterial figure in Jewish law – only no one in Ethiopia likely knew it at the time, or would for centuries.[5] When, however, Ovadia Yosef, Chief Sephardi Rabbi of Israel, officially ruled that the Beta Israel were part of the Jewish people in 1973, it would be *because* he understood them to be "descendants of the Tribes of Israel that migrated south to Cush ... that they are of the Tribe of Dan ... [and] Jews whom we must save from assimilation and whose immigration to Israel is to be hastened."[6] In time, the Beta

---

Ethiopia's rulers had been Christian since the fourth century CE (Marcus, *A History of Ethiopia*, 7–8).

[3] Abbink, "The Enigma of Beta Esra'el Ethnogenesis," 417–18.

[4] Cooper, "Conceptualizing Diaspora," 113.

[5] Seeman, "Ethnographers, Rabbis and Jewish Epistemology," 15.

[6] Corinaldi, *Jewish Identity*, 198; Zegeye, *The Impossible Return*, xiv. To be precise, Yosef ruled that "there is no doubt that the aforementioned authorities" – including the Radbaz – "who ruled that they are of the Tribe of Dan carefully investigated and reached this conclusion on the basis of the most reliable testimony and evidence."

Israel would largely adopt this external myth of Danite origin as their own, leaving Menelik and the traditions of the *Kebra* behind.[7]

Thus, on one level, the story of the Beta Israel is remarkable because it is the story of how, for the first and only time in history, a Lost Tribe came home.[8] In theory, Jewish communities all over the world had been on the lookout for their lost brethren for millennia. In practice, however, the Beta Israel remain the only people ever brought to Israel, and ever recognized officially as part of the Jewish nation, by virtue of their perceived descent from an *Israelite* tribe, which is to say from a Lost Tribe as officially understood.[9] All other targets of Israel's so-called *kibuts hagaluyot*, the "ingathering of the exiles," have been members of the Jewish diaspora, who are by and large descended from the tribes of Judah, or otherwise identified in ways that leave the Lost Tribes *lost*.[10]

In this book, however, the Beta Israel are still more remarkable for the reasons just described: because, in short, they "became Israel" *twice*, in two fundamentally different ways, according to two quite distinct traditions. In Ethiopia, for many centuries, their vision of themselves as Israelites was built from Ethiopian traditions and rooted them in an Ethiopian context. It was shaped and reshaped, as all constructions of Israel are, by the particulars of their historical experience in their native land – in this case, especially their history of resistance to the Christian, Israelite emperors. Then, beginning in the late nineteenth century, as encounters with the outside Jewish world accelerated, they performed – and had performed upon them – a remarkable pivot, embracing the Danite legend that placed them, as Israelites, in relation to the history of normative, diasporic Judaism instead. Ultimately, the transition of this people from one place to another was encouraged, shaped, and made

---

[7] Kaplan, "Genealogies and Gene-Ideologies," 450.

[8] In recent years, "Lost Tribe" has taken on a more generic meaning, referring to any previously unsuspected Jewish community (Asa-El, *The Diaspora and the Lost Tribes of Israel*, 188). What I mean here is more specific: a group that understands itself, and is understood, as a descendant of one or more of the tribes of the northern kingdom of Israel, in this case the tribe of Dan.

[9] The Samaritans, of course, also claim descent from Israel and have sometimes been officially recognized by Israel's Jewish authorities. However, they were already in Israel when the modern State was founded, their history has been intertwined with that of the Jews for over two thousand years, and they explicitly understand themselves as the tribes who *were not lost*.

[10] Soroff, *The Maintenance and Transmission of Ethnic Identity*, 29.

possible by the substitution of one tradition for another – or, we might say, one Israel for another.[11]

Thus, for all its flaws as history, the story of the two brothers actually does capture the spirit of the history of interactions between the Beta Israel and the normative Jewish world remarkably well: two visions of Israel, related but raised apart, similar but different, at home in different worlds. It reflects the character of their efforts to get to know each other, beginning in the 1860s, as they explored their family resemblance and their different personalities. And thus, the lens of "becoming Israel" allows us to shed new light on a complex history of internal and external developments, cultural interactions, and dramatic shifts in fortunes.

Indeed, while the Beta Israel today identify simply as part of the wider Jewish world, the differences that existed between their construction of Israelite identity and the Jewish construction at the time of their first encounters continue to have ramifications into the present, for reasons that specifically have to do with the circumstances in which these two brothers met, on the one hand, and the limits of the twelve tribes tradition as a tool for accommodating other "Israels" on the other. The latter is at least as important as the former because the issue concerns what the tradition seems best able to do: explain the existence of multiple different heirs to Israel at once.

What the twelve tribes tradition is *used* to do, and what it is *supposed* to do, however, are a little bit different from each other. In other words, while it is used to explain the existence of so many different constructions of Israelite identity, what it is supposed to do, internally, is explain why there are so many different heirs to the same Israel – a universal Israel, biblical Israel. In this case, in order to account for the difference between Beta Israel and Jewish visions of Israelite identity, history, and practice, Jewish authorities constructed an image of this Ethiopian people, with their own time-honored traditions, as the practitioners of a "pre-Talmudic Judaism" that had left the ambit of the main streams of Jewish teaching and thought in such early periods.[12] In other words, they understood the Beta Israel as Jewish by descent, but primitive, rather than as the heirs of an independent tradition with its own proud history. Thus, the Danite framework would bring the Beta Israel to Israel, but only at the cost of defining them in discriminatory terms.

---

[11] Kaplan, "Genealogies and Gene-Ideologies," 447–51.
[12] Kaplan, *The Beta Israel*, 156–58.

Today, the Beta Israel still face an uphill struggle for equal rights and recognition that stems from the original framing of Beta Israel difference – which took the legacy of long centuries of internal Ethiopian development and explained it as a reflection of religious insufficiency and lack of education. The "Lost Tribe" explanation of their origins and difference has been stunningly effective in some ways, as the middle ground between the Beta Israel and the wider Jewish world, but it also represents a Jewish acknowledgment of a shared identity with the Beta Israel in a way that does not give them equal status as heirs to Israel.[13] The challenge the actuality of many Israels represents to the premise of one Israel is far from solely to blame for the issues the Beta Israel have faced in Israel but the discourse that redefined their history and identity in relation to the expectations of normative Jewish traditions certainly has a role to play, and a much underappreciated one.

Ultimately, then, the history of the Beta Israel offers us a tremendous opportunity to study the full extent of what the twelve tribes tradition can achieve as a tool for creating and adapting visions of Israel. That it could take one Israelite people and transform them to such an extent that it brought a Lost Tribe "home" is a truly remarkable development, unparalleled in the annals of history.[14] At the same time, the ongoing struggles of the Beta Israel *in* Israel reveal the fundamental limitations of "becoming Israel," via the twelve tribes tradition, since it could not secure the Beta Israel equal treatment as an heir to Israel, or equal status – only recognition. And as this gap between discourse and reality reveals so much of what the twelve tribes tradition can and cannot do, as a tool for "becoming Israel," this case study will provide a fitting conclusion to our discussion of this extraordinary transhistorical practice.

I will, therefore, begin this chapter by telling the story of the two brothers: how one vision of Israelite identity developed, over time, in Ethiopia, and how the other grew to maturity outside it. I will tell the story of how these visions of Israel came to meet, and how, in the end, one largely replaced the other. I will describe how the Danite legend achieved

---

[13] Hagar Salamon observes that "the warm and affectionate reception that greeted the Ethiopian immigrants on the level of media coverage, government slogans, and other popular expressions, and far exceeded the welcome enjoyed by any of the other immigrant groups to Israel," was in many ways in conflict with the "paternalism that greeted their arrival" (Salamon, "Ethiopian Jewry and New Self-Concepts," 235).

[14] Abbink also refers to the arrival of the Beta Israel in Israel as "one of the most remarkable episodes of Jewish history, showing a rare conflation of myths, legends, and modern political developments" (Abbink, "The Enigma of Beta Esra'el Ethnogenesis," 397–98).

what the traditions of the *Kebra* could not, how the Beta Israel came to Israel, and how they faced challenges while there. Throughout, I will focus my attention on how different versions of the twelve tribes tradition have placed the Beta Israel in relation to different realities, including what the twelve tribes tradition did in each context, and how the tradition's limitations continue to shape the Beta Israel's troubled present. In the end, I will connect the struggles of the Beta Israel in Israel to the general problem of many Israels all using the same tradition to present themselves as part of a universal Israel, so concluding this book's investigation.

5.1 ISRAELITES AMONG ISRAELITES IN ETHIOPIA

Of the various controversies over the history of the Beta Israel, the thorniest, as it often is, is the controversy over origins. In all of the stories that survive, the Beta Israel are supposed to be the descendants of a Jewish or Israelite group who came to Ethiopia well before Christianity took root. Indeed, both insiders and scholars have pursued arguments about their possible descent not just from Danites or the people of the *Kebra*, but from a group of Judahites who fled to Egypt with Jeremiah after the Babylonian conquest of Judah in 586 BCE; from the Persian-period garrison of Judahites at Elephantine, in the Nile Delta; from the first diaspora after the Roman destruction of the Second Temple; and even from the exodus itself, when their ancestors supposedly went their own separate way from the main body of Israelites.[15]

That something so close to the Beta Israel's own traditions continues to be found plausible in the scholarship of a skeptical age owes above all to certain aspects of the unusual religious history of Ethiopia. Basically,

---

[15] While many of these traditions appear to have become popular only in the twentieth century, the Beta Israel did tell the story of their descent from diasporic Jews – among others – to Samuel Gobat, who arrived as a Christian missionary in the middle of the nineteenth century, and as we will see below, a mid-nineteenth-century Beta Israel authority named Abba Ishaq mentioned the Jeremiah tradition to European investigators. The Beta Israel also told the scholar Wolf Leslau that their ancestors might have left Moses' exodus for Ethiopia (Gobat, *Journal of a Three Years' Residence in Abyssinia*, 467; Leslau, *Falasha Anthology*, xliii). See also Zegeye, *The Impossible Return*, 27–28. J. Martin Flad, in the mid-nineteenth century, heard that their ancestors were refugees from the Assyrian and Babylonian exiles, as well as that they might be part of the Jewish diaspora after the destruction of the Second Temple (Abbink, "The Enigma of Beta Esra'el Ethnogenesis," 412–13). The Elephantine argument was also popular among scholars for a time (Kaplan, *The Beta Israel*, 28; Leslau, *Falasha Anthology*, xliii).

Ethiopian Orthodox Christianity – which has its roots in the missionary work of the Syrian Frumentius in the fourth century, known as Abba Salama, beginning just before the reign of King Ezana, and a flowering in the sixth-century reign of King Kaleb, when the region was still known as Aksum – is ancient, but not so ancient as the tenure of these Jewish groups is supposed to be.[16] And it has a number of unusual characteristics that have sometimes read as Jewish, including Saturday sabbaths, circumcision, and dietary laws.[17] What, many have wondered, could be more obvious than that the early Jewish community described in these various traditions influenced the development of this surprisingly Jewish-seeming Christianity?[18] Indeed, in later years, additional Ethiopian Christian groups with seemingly Jewish features would form, including, in the mid-fourteenth century, the group following Abba Ewostatewos, who preached specifically and vociferously that "the people and the church ... must return to the great teachings of the Bible, including observance of the

---

[16] Kaplan, *The Beta Israel*, 34; Munro-Hay, *The Quest for the Ark of the Covenant*, 56–57. While in Ezana's reign Christianity seems to have co-existed with native religion, this was also a period in which "Ethiopia's destiny was set as a Christian power with a belief in a divinely mandated manifest destiny" (Hatke, "Holy Land and Sacred History," 261). Then, "by the sixth century, Ethiopia had become not merely a state ruled by Christians, but a Christian state" (Kaplan, *The Beta Israel*, 35). Another group credited with the appearance and nurturing of Christianity in Ethiopia is the "nine saints," who are supposed to have come from Syria toward the end of the fifth century CE (Marcus, *A History of Ethiopia*, 8).

[17] In Kaplan's words, "no church anywhere ... has remained as faithful to the letter and spirit of the Old Testament as the Ethiopian Orthodox Church" (Kaplan, *The Beta Israel*, 17–18). The relevant customs include circumcision "eight days after birth"; a sometimes preference for a "Saturday sabbath"; similarities in dietary laws; "the three-fold division of churches in Ethiopia," meant to mimic the biblical description of Solomon's temple; and others (Kaplan, *The Beta Israel*, 17–18). See also Piovanelli, "Jewish Christianity in Late Antique Aksum and Ḥimyar?," 177; Ullendorf, "Hebraic-Jewish Elements in Abyssinian (Monophysite) Christianity." As Quirin notes, "these Jewish practices were first explicitly mentioned in the eleventh century when the Egyptian bishops criticized the Ethiopian Church for observing 'customs of the Old Testament'" and have been steadily noted ever since (Quirin, *The Evolution of the Ethiopian Jews*, 16).

[18] As Steven Kaplan remarks, many believe that the religious history of Ethiopia preserves "in miniature ... the history of these two faiths in the world at large (Kaplan, "The Invention of Ethiopian Jews," 646). Thus, Zegeye, citing Wagaw, has recently argued that "the overwhelming impact of biblical and Hebraic patterns on early Ethiopian culture is undeniable" and that "archaeological evidence (which is still being disputed by some scholars) suggests that before the Axumite Kingdom of ancient Ethiopia accepted Christianity as the official religion in the fourth century CE, both Judaism and local pre-Christian forms of paganism ... existed alongside one another" (Zegeye, *The Impossible Return*, 15; Wagaw, *For Our Soul*, 7).

Sabbath to honor the Old Testament."[19] So the Jewish roots of Ethiopian Orthodox Christianity would seem to run deep.

No hard evidence of any such early Aksumite Jewish community has ever been found, however. Instead, the evidence strongly suggests that Beta Israel identity developed out of Ethiopian Orthodox Christianity.[20] Rather, it would be better to say that Beta Israel identity formed in opposition to the power of Ethiopia's Christian monarchs and its church, but in continuity with it, too. In other words, the early community seems to have formed as a rallying point for dissenters of all stripes, but in a way that was deeply influenced by Ethiopian Christianity.

So, for example, Ethiopian Christians and Jews shared, for quite a long time, not only a language for sacred scriptures – Ge'ez – but many institutions, especially monasticism, a self-evidently unusual feature for Jewish-identifying peoples worldwide. Beyond that, research into Beta Israel traditions has consistently turned up a number of direct borrowings from Ethiopian Christian materials.[21] Since the work of Kay Kaufman Shelemay in the late 1980s, scholars have observed the dependence of much Beta Israel music and liturgy on earlier Christian forms.

---

[19] Marcus, *A History of Ethiopia*, 22–23. Abbink observes that the Ewostatians were actually among three different groups that emerged in opposition to the Ethiopian orthodox church, including "the movement of the Shäwans" and the "Stephanites," all of whom "emphasized beliefs and customs of the Old Testament much more than the old Church was doing" (Abbink, "The Enigma of Beta Esra'el Ethnogenesis," 426–27).

[20] Abbink, "The Enigma of Beta Esra'el Ethnogenesis," 405; Piovanelli, "Jewish Christianity in Late Antique Aksum and Himyar?," 178–82; Quirin, *The Evolution of the Ethiopian Jews*, 15. There are scholarly histories of the Beta Israel that fully embrace their descent from early Ethiopian Jews, though these are generally too positivist in other ways as well; see, for example, Kessler, *The Falashas: The Forgotten Jews of Ethiopia*; Kessler, *The Falashas: A Short History*. While it is likely impossible to know whether there was a Jewish minority in early Axum, one problem is the common assumption that a literal community of Jews in the region is the only possible vector of Jewish influences, when many of the relevant traditions and practices simply come from the Hebrew Bible and associated legends, readily available in Christian cultures, and when we know there were Jews nearby, in Himyar for example. In any case, Kaplan is correct that the presence of a Jewish community in early Axum would not make Beta Israel identity and practice *simply* a descendant of it, as we can clearly see in the fact that other Jewish communities developed differently. "It is, moreover, even more problematic to claim that their religious system as it existed in the late nineteenth and early twentieth centuries was based on ancient Jewish practice. Immigration, intermarriage, acculturation, and major religious upheavals all played a part in the formation of the people" (Kaplan, *The Beta Israel*, 19–20, 32).

[21] Quirin, *The Evolution of the Ethiopian Jews*, 6; Shelemay, *Music, Ritual, and Falasha History*.

Other studies have revealed the relationship between many Beta Israel texts and Christian versions. Beta Israel "testaments," or *gadlat*, of important biblical figures follow the same arrangement as fourteenth- and fifteenth-century Christian manuscripts, while the *Te'ezaza Sanbat*, a crucially important Beta Israel text, draws on a Christian "homily of the Sabbath (*Dersana Sanbat*)" and "material from the homilies of Jacob of Sarug," a Christian theologian of the fifth and sixth centuries.[22] Even into the nineteenth century, as explorers and missionaries from outside of Ethiopia encountered the Beta Israel for the first time, they were often surprised to find texts such as *Fekkare Iyasus* (the "Teachings of Jesus") and a psalm called *Weddasse Maryam* (the "Praises of Mary") within this self-identifying Jewish community.[23] Thus, the evidence points to some extent in both directions, but is fairly clear on the point that the Beta Israel got many of their key practices and texts from Ethiopian Christians.

There is, however, a great irony in this ongoing debate which puts it into context, vis-à-vis our larger discussion. The fact is that the Beta Israel's *own traditions* assert both the importance of the fourteenth and fifteenth centuries to the emergence of a familiar form of Beta Israel identity *and* the role of Ethiopian Christians in its development.[24] Qozmos, a renegade Christian monk credited with giving the Beta Israel the *Orit* – the Beta Israel bible, in a sense – is supposed to have come to them in the days of Dawit I, in the late fourteenth and early fifteenth centuries.[25] The *Orit* is not quite the same thing as the *Torah*, although the term is used flexibly. Most often, it is an Octateuch that includes Genesis, Exodus, Leviticus, Numbers, Deuteronomy, Joshua, Judges, and Ruth.[26]

---

[22] Kaplan, *The Beta Israel*, 73–75. So do *Mashafa Mala'ekt* and *Mota Aaron*.

[23] James Bruce, discussed below, wondered why Beta Israel scriptures would be in Ge'ez, noting that "it is not probable that a Jew would receive the law and the prophets from a Christian, without absolute necessity" (Bruce, *Travels to Discover the Source of the Nile*, 491). Gobat, the early nineteenth-century missionary mentioned above, was shown a copy of the Psalms that included "*Weddasse Maryam* (The Praises of Mary)," while "Abba Yeshaq, the most learned of Beta Israel monks, included in his list of Beta Israel works, *Fekkare Iyasus* (the teachings of Jesus), a work whose Christian provenance and contents are undeniable" (Kaplan, *The Beta Israel*, 110–11).

[24] For a heated denunciation of contemporary trends in scholarship on the Beta Israel, see Teferi, "About the Jewish Identity of the Beta Israel."

[25] Kaplan, *The Beta Israel*, 56; Quirin, "Oral Traditions as Historical Sources in Ethiopia," 301.

[26] Delamarter, "The Content and Order of Books in Ethiopic Old Testament Manuscripts," 112; Pankhurst, "The Falashas," 568–69; Westheimer and Kaplan, *Surviving Salvation*, 14. Delamarter's investigation of the 332 manuscripts of "books of the Ethiopian Old Testament other than the Psalter, sixty-eight of which contain the Orit" is an invaluable

Abba Sabra, another Christian – and according to legend, both the founder of the crucial Beta Israel institution of monasticism and the composer of the *Te'ezaza Sanbat* – arrived among the Beta Israel, according to legend, in the days of the emperor Zar'a Ya'eqob in the middle of the fifteenth century, as did Sagga Amlak, who supposedly assisted Sabra in his work.[27]

Thus, we find that even from an internal perspective, the controversy is not really about "origins," which is to say when and how the Beta Israel took on something like their familiar form, but about *descent* – who the ancestors of the community that took shape at this time were. What we see here, of course, is the outsized role "primordialist" ways of thinking about ethnic identity continue to play even in contemporary studies where their presence would likely be denied. The question was there an early Jewish community in Ethiopia, and are the Beta Israel their biological descendants may remain, to some extent, despite an absence of evidence. But internal traditions and external evidence converge on the point that the Beta Israel *qua* Beta Israel emerged in the fourteenth and fifteenth centuries BCE, in conversation with Ethiopian Orthodox Christianity.

Today, increasingly, scholars tend to trace the origins of the Beta Israel not to any pre-Christian community, but to groups that formed in the

---

contribution to the study of Ethiopic traditions. In this case, see especially Delamarter, "The Content and Order of Books in Ethiopic Old Testament Manuscripts," 112–17. Here, we see that of the sixty-eight manuscripts, forty-two have just the *Orit*, while twenty-three more have the *Orit* in the same order and a few other books. From the stability of the order, and its inclusion as a whole in all these cases, we can conclude that "the Ethiopian Orit stood not just as a collection but as a distinct corpus with a clear unity, a distinct order, and an apparent priority." In the "final six manuscripts ... the book of Enoch came before the Orit, and in one case it was Enoch and Job that were prior to the Orit," while in the "twenty-three cases where other canonical books follow the Orit, nine of the manuscripts (39 percent) have the book of Jubilees following the Orit" (ibid., 116–17). The special status of Jubilees and Enoch in Ethiopia accounts for the fact that "the complete text of Enoch is extant only in Ethiopic. The most complete and accurate manuscript of Jubilees is also the Ethiopic version" (Quirin, *The Evolution of the Ethiopian Jews*, 69).

[27] According to Quirin, and Beta Israel tradition, "it is not known precisely when the Beta Israel acquired these books, but the *Orit* was 'copied' for them by Qozmos during the late fourteenth century. And in the mid-fifteenth century, *Abba* Sabra 'taught' the *Orit*" (Quirin, *The Evolution of the Ethiopian Jews*, 69). As for Amlak, "an alleged son of Zar'a Ya'eqob was influenced by the teaching of *abba* Sabra and joined him in the new monastery ... The son ... acquired the name Sagga Amlak ('Grace of God') among the Falasha. The king never did find him and he lived out his life assisting *abba* Sabra in teaching the Falasha religion" (Quirin, "Oral Traditions as Historical Sources in Ethiopia," 301).

vicinity of Lake Tana, beginning in the fourteenth century CE. Ethiopian chronicles refer to these groups as *ayhud* or *ayhudawi* – "Jew" and "Jews."[28] Even this evidence is not wholly straightforward: then, as now, "Jew" was sometimes used as a pejorative, and some of the members of this community were certainly non-Jewish dissenters with a variety of practices.[29] However, the areas where the *ayhudawi* flourished were, by and large, those that would become known as the Beta Israel homeland in later periods.[30]

From then on – we might say, simply, from the beginning – the history of the Beta Israel in Ethiopia is a history of conflict. We know little enough about these fledgling Beta Israel communities, and certainly not how they initially understood their own origins. However, we do know that this community, which became a focal point for resistance against royal and religious expansion, continued to be defined for centuries *by* resistance, which tended to strengthen social ties.[31] From the early fifteenth century through the late sixteenth, a series of wars with the Christian emperors pushed the Beta Israel back, but grudgingly, and not without successes.[32] By the turn of the seventeenth century, however,

---

[28] Kaplan, *The Beta Israel*, 52. As Kaplan puts it, "the earliest clear reference in any Ethiopic source to the Judaized groups in the Lake Tana region appears in the chronicles of the wars of Amda Seyon" where he attempted to subdue those who "were Christians but now ... denied the Christ like the Jews" (ibid., 55–56).

[29] Kaplan, "The Invention of Ethiopian Jews," 647 n.7; Quirin, *The Evolution of the Ethiopian Jews*, 14; Parfitt, *The Lost Tribes of Israel*, 240–42. Quirin observes, "small groups of *ayhud* ('Jews' or 'Jewish group') in the northwestern region resisted conversion and sporadically rebelled, while a few of their intellectual leaders joined anti-Trinitarian Christians in theological controversies with Orthodoxy" (Quirin, *The Evolution of the Ethiopian Jews*, 40). Kaplan suspects that there were somewhat earlier Jews in the region, likely "Agaw converts to Judaism or Jewish-Christianity," and that "in the fourteenth century, this group was also reinforced by dissident or rebelling Christians who joined them, bringing important new religious and literary elements" (Kaplan, *The Beta Israel*, 26–27).

[30] "In all the cases cited in our survey of sources above, the *ayhud* in question are associated with the area around Lake Tana, and in particular the regions of Semien, Sallamt, Dambey, and Wagara. In later years it is precisely in this area that we find the Falasha" (Kaplan, *The Beta Israel*, 61–62). And again, the nature of these events conforms in both character and chronology to what Beta Israel traditions themselves suggest. See especially Quirin, "Oral Traditions as Historical Sources in Ethiopia." Abbink adds "on the basis of oral and written sources, it is incontestable that, after the beginning of the 15th century, a Judaic group of Agäw origins ... lived in a region at the margins of the Solomonic empire" (Abbink, "The Enigma of Beta Esra'el Ethnogenesis," 408).

[31] Quirin, *The Evolution of the Ethiopian Jews*, 63.

[32] In the fifteenth century they "were obliged to defend themselves against the royal armies. A long period of wars starting with the reign of Dawit only ended in 1625 with the

these wars were almost over, and the Beta Israel would become a largely subjugated people.[33]

In the "Gondar era," beginning in the 1630s and named after the new capital the emperor Fasilides built – though really inaugurated by his father Susenyos, who completed the conquest of the Beta Israel, among other achievements – the Beta Israel lost many of their freedoms.[34] There would, however, be certain compensations. Under the emperor's protection, for example, the Beta Israel gained social status by taking on specialized trades, including "smithing, weaving, pottery, building, and soldiering."[35] In time, even the fact that they were outsiders became something of a professional qualification: emperors, then as ever, could prefer troops who did not owe allegiance to other noble houses.[36]

complete submission of the Beta Esra'el under king Susenyos (1605–1632)" (Abbink, "The Enigma of Beta Esra'el Ethnogenesis," 409). Still, "the Beta Esra'el were formidable opponents of the Amhara kings, as is evident from the latters' chronicles" (ibid., 409). Or, as Kaplan put it, "during the period from 1468 to 1632, the Beta Israel displayed their most sophisticated political-military organization, were involved in some of their most dramatic conflicts ... [and] suffered some of their most serious defeats." By the sixteenth century, "the area under their control had shrunk significantly. If in the past Semien, Sallamt, Dambeya, Sagade, Waldebba, Walqayit, and Wagara all had sizeable Beta Israel populations, by the middle of the sixteenth century only Semien and to a lesser extent Dembeya and Wagara still harbored an organized Jewish presence" (Kaplan, *The Beta Israel*, 79–80).

[33] They were "forcibly incorporated as part of the landless lower class within the Ethiopian empire" (Quirin, *The Evolution of the Ethiopian Jews*, 53, 72–73). Quirin adds that the "first major war in a two-hundred-year series of conflicts" began in the "reign of Yeshaq (1413–30)" and notes that the empire "completed its expansion in northwestern Ethiopia during the sixteenth century, despite the heroic and well-documented resistance of the Samen Beta Israel."

[34] Kaplan, *The Beta Israel*, 97. As Quirin observes, "the establishment of Gondar, the largest permanent urban center in highland Ethiopian since ancient Aksum, had a significant impact on Ethiopian social structure, relations among its peoples and classes, and on the continuing process of Beta Israel caste formation" (Quirin, *The Evolution of the Ethiopian Jews*, 89).

[35] Kaplan, *The Beta Israel*, 99–100. See Kaplan, *The Beta Israel*, 114–15; Wagaw, *For Our Soul*, 10–11.

[36] "Living in a special quarter were the Beta Israel, whose ancestral farms had been confiscated by Christian conquerors. Over the previous two centuries, they had survived by moving into such marginal occupations as weaving and smithing, the crafts that Christians avoided as the gift of the devil. The growth of Gonder and its need for workers allowed the Beta Israel to augment their skills ... Since the Beta Israel were far outside of the power structure, they were often recruited into the imperial guard and used in particularly delicate or confidential situations" (Marcus, *A History of Ethiopia*, 43). See also Kaplan, *The Beta Israel*, 101. It is worth noting, too, that at this time, the community began to be called by another name, "kayla," although the origins of the name are unclear (Quirin, *The Evolution of the Ethiopian Jews*, 72–73; Kaplan, *The Beta*

Next, however, would come the fearsome *Zamana Masafent*, the "era of the judges," beginning in the middle of the eighteenth century. The term, ominously and accurately, comes from a common refrain in the biblical book of Judges: "there was no king in Israel: every man did that which was right in his own eyes."[37] The power of the monarchy declined; the power of other Ethiopian elites increased correspondingly; and, as at other eras of instability, the Beta Israel, a marginalized people, suffered a great deal.[38] This difficult era would not end until 1855, when Dejazmach Kasa of Qwara was crowned King Tewodros II.[39] Exactly a century later, in 1955, the first Beta Israel would arrive in the State of Israel, at Kfar Batya, to connect – or from an internal perspective, reconnect – with their Israelite heritage.[40] Less than twenty years after that, Ovadia Yosef, Sephardi Chief Rabbi of Israel, would make his ruling that officialized the Jewish status of the Beta Israel – as Danite Jews – and open the door to their emigration to Israel. A century of rapid change was on the horizon.

5.2 THE CHILDREN OF SOLOMON AND SHEBA

In 1770, in the early days of the *Zamana Masafent*, James Bruce, the Laird of Kinnard in Scotland, made his way to Ethiopia, searching for the fabled source of the "Blue Nile." Upon his arrival, he was surprised to find a country full of Canaanites and Israelites. Rather, Bruce knew from his Bible that here was the ancient realm of the "Kushites," descendants of Kush, son of Ham, son of Noah (Gen. 10:6) – an important association in other ways, as we will soon see. But he described most of the people he

---

Israel, 14–15). It has been suggested it may have something to do with an Agaw word meaning metal-workers (Seeman, "Returning to Judaism," 97).

[37] Bekele, "Reflections on the Power Elite of the Wärä Seh Mäsfenate," 161. See, for more general discussion, Quirin, *The Evolution of the Ethiopian Jews*, 205; Kaplan, *The Beta Israel*, 105–7. Marcus describes the origins of this period in a civil war between "assimilated (Kwaran) and nonassimilated Oromo (Welo) into which the ras of Tigre, Mikail Sehul, intervened successfully, but was then opposed by the emperor Iyoas who feared his success." Sehul marched against the emperor, "whom he defeated and assassinated," beginning the *Zamana Masafent* in January 1769. It lasted until 1855 (Marcus, *A History of Ethiopia*, 47). Bekele's own account is more complex, arguing that rather than a dissolution of central authority, it was more of a replacement of the central authority of the emperor with that of the lords, who ruled in the name of the Solomonic dynasty. It was not "the era of independent princes who constantly fought each other," but rather one in which "the various regional ruling houses . . . retained tremendous local autonomy" (Bekele, "Reflections on the Power Elite of the Wärä Seh Mäsfenate," 161).

[38] Kaplan, *The Beta Israel*, 116–17.   [39] Ibid., 116.

[40] Semi, *Jacques Faitlovich and the Jews of Ethiopia*, 176; Kaplan, *The Beta Israel*, 116–17.

encountered there according to other biblical stories.[41] The Amhara, the Agaw, the Gafat – these, he said, had come from Palestine, fleeing the victorious armies of the biblical Joshua.[42]

Shortly thereafter, Bruce became perhaps the first European to spend a significant amount of time among the people then known as the "Falasha," a once-popular name for the Beta Israel now regarded as derogatory.[43] These, he said, were no Canaanites – "not any part of those nations who fled from Palestine on the *invasion* of Joshua." Instead, "they are now, and ever were, Jews."[44] Such was his first encounter with the people he understood to be – and who seem to have understood themselves as – the Jews of Ethiopia, the Beta Israel. But where had they come from? Obviously, these were neither Kushites nor the descendants of the targets of Joshua's wrath. Bruce asked, and the Beta Israel told.

The story Bruce heard from the Beta Israel was very nearly – and this is the point: *very nearly* – the story that is related in the *Kebra Nagast*, the Ethiopian "national epic."[45] In fact, he thought it agreed with the traditions of other Ethiopians – "Abyssinians" – "in every particular."[46] He was wrong, however, and the way he was wrong makes all the difference.

---

[41] "It is a tradition among the Abyssinians ... that almost immediately after the flood, Cush, grandson of Noah, with his family ... came to the ridge of mountains which still separates the flat country of Atbara from the more mountainous high-land of Abyssinia" (Bruce, *Travels to Discover the Source of the Nile*, 376).

[42] Ibid., 405. Bruce also refers to an inscription mentioned by Procopius of Caesarea in his *History of the Wars of Justinian*, which allegedly read in Phoenician, "We are Canaanites, flying from the face of Joshua, the son of Nun, the *robber*" in Mauritania (ibid., 400). See Procopius, *History of the Wars of Justinian*, 4.10.21–22. Procopius, who wrote in the sixth century CE, refers specifically to a city called Tigisis in Numidia, and one nineteenth-century article on the subject of this inscription notes the existence of a rabbinic legend, in the *Tosefta*, of Amorites in Africa (Bacher, "The Supposed Inscription upon 'Joshua the Robber,'" 354). While I find the existence of such an inscription extremely unlikely – and if extant, not relevant for the history of Ethiopia – not all biblical scholars have felt the same way. See Frendo, "Back to Basics," 55 n.29.

[43] In this chapter, as in Emanuela Trevisan Semi's biography of Jacques Faitlovich, "the term 'Falasha is used ... in order to be consistent with the sources, which refer to the period in question. This term began to take on negative connotations after the mass migrations to Israel in 1984–1985 (Operation Moses) and 1991 (Operation Solomon)" (Semi, *Jacques Faitlovich and the Jews of Ethiopia*, xv).

[44] Bruce, *Travels to Discover the Source of the Nile*, 404.

[45] Quirin, *The Evolution of the Ethiopian Jews*, 18.

[46] Bruce, *Travels to Discover the Source of the Nile*, 484. "The account they give of themselves ... is, that they came with Menelik from Jerusalem ... They agree also, in every particular, with the Abyssinians, about the remaining part of the story, the birth and inauguration of Menelik, who was their first king; also the coming of Azarias, and twelve elders from the twelve tribes."

As I noted above, the origin traditions of the Beta Israel at that time, in the late eighteenth century, were based on the *Kebra*, but they were also very much their own, much as every other tradition of Israel we have seen so far is based to some degree on long-extant traditions and to some degree its own.

Again, the *Kebra* – the "Glory of Kings" – tells the story, among a few others, of King Solomon, the Queen of Sheba, and their only son, Menelik, who would go on to found Ethiopia's royal dynasty. Historically, at least since the early fourteenth century, Ethiopia's monarchs claimed Israelite descent much as the Beta Israel did. In fact, "in most contexts, the term 'Esra'élawiyan' is most likely to be a reference to a member of the imperial dynasty... [rather] than to an 'Ethiopian Jew.'"[47] These are the two "Israels" of Ethiopia: one Jewish, one Christian, and in a nearly perpetual conflict with each other. The *Kebra* is the tradition of the latter.

Again, the jumping off point for the *Kebra*'s traditions is biblical: a story told in 1 Kings 10, where the Queen of Sheba comes to the court of Solomon to test his fabled wisdom (1 Kgs. 10:10). In the Bible, he passes the test and she goes home pleased, but in the *Kebra* she also goes home pregnant (KN 32).[48] Menelik, their son, is raised in the country he will eventually rule, but in time goes to visit his father and is crowned in a ceremony at the Temple in Jerusalem (KN 39).[49] Later, he would return home with two great gifts, one given and one taken, if with divine blessing. His father gifts him an honor guard of Israelites that, according to the version Bruce heard, included "a colony of Jews, among whom were many doctors of the law of Moses, particularly one of each tribe, to make judges in his kingdom." Menelik also takes, of all things, the Ark of the Covenant (KN 48).[50]

The precise origins of the *Kebra*'s version of this tradition, which is almost certainly older than the Beta Israel's own version, remain controversial, but not, in my opinion, for terribly good reasons. The *Kebra*

[47] Kaplan, *The Beta Israel*, 10.
[48] Munro-Hay, "A Sixth Century Kebra Nagast?," 44; Marcus, *A History of Ethiopia*, 16; Bruce, *Travels to Discover the Source of the Nile*, 475–76.
[49] Munro-Hay, "A Sixth Century Kebra Nagast ?," 44; Marcus, *A History of Ethiopia*, 16; Bruce, *Travels to Discover the Source of the Nile*, 475–76.
[50] Bruce, *Travels to Discover the Source of the Nile*, 476. Bruce's account actually does not mention the Ark, but the *Kebra* does (KN 48). The *Kebra* itself also describes this honor guard of Israelites but is less specific on the subject of twelve tribe representation than Ethiopian tradition in general seems to be (KN 38, 43, 45).

appears to have been composed in the days of the emperor Amda Seyon, in the early fourteenth century.[51] As with the Hebrew Bible, however, there are still many who argue that the literary version of the Menelik narrative is based to some considerable extent on oral traditions many centuries earlier.[52] Certainly this was believed in Ethiopia itself, and it does seem as if traditions of Israelite descent of some form or another pre-existed its composition. The Zagwe dynasty, which ruled parts of Ethiopia beginning around 900 CE and lasted until 1270, seems to have claimed descent from Moses, for example.[53] However, efforts to demonstrate the existence of a tradition of Solomonic descent in ancient Aksum, prior to the Zagwe, generally ignore much of the evidence and are based on some unlikely assumptions – for example, that references to David, or

---

[51] The written *Kebra* was produced, according to its colophon, by one Yishaq, "the leading ecclesiastical officer of the ancient city of Aksum, working with five orthodox monks" (Marcus, *A History of Ethiopia*, 19; Kaplan, *The Beta Israel*, 54. See also Quirin, *The Evolution of the Ethiopian Jews*, 18; Munro-Hay, "A Sixth Century Kebra Nagast?," 47; Kaplan, *The Beta Israel*, 22).

[52] D. W. Johnson has argued for a seventh-century date, and Kaplan has argued that it was "probably first composed sometime between the sixth and ninth centuries A.D. In the fourteenth century, it received its definitive form" (Johnson, "Dating the Kebra Nagast"; Kaplan, *The Beta Israel*, 22). Quirin notes that although "it did not receive its final written form until the early fourteenth-century reign of Amda Seyon, it has often been assumed that it was created in at least oral form soon after the Aksumite conversion of Christianity, and in written versions later" (Quirin, *The Evolution of the Ethiopian Jews*, 18). Belcher argues that "the Ethiopians have been continually expanding and altering this narrative over almost two millennia. A true palimpsest, it embodies the varying, sometimes contradictory, concerns of different times" (Belcher, "African Rewritings of the Jewish and Islamic Solomonic Tradition," 444–45). Though writing in the mid-twentieth century, Edward Ullendorf is characteristic of a number of scholars, today and for much of the twentieth century, when he observes that "the main components of the story must have had a very long period of gestation in Ethiopia and elsewhere and have possessed all the elements of a gigantic conflation of legendary cycles." But he presents as evidence only the fact that the Ethiopian Bible translates the biblical (Septuagint) text of 1 Kgs. 10:1, "she came to prove him with hard questions," to "with wisdom." In the same work, he describes Yeshaq of Aksum as "mainly redactor and interpreter of material which had long been known but had not until then found a co-ordinating hand, an expository mind, and a great national need," again without providing evidence, or explaining why "need" would have anything to do with producing a story that everyone already knew anyway (Ullendorf, *Ethiopia and the Bible*, 75). While it is of course likely that some of the Kebra's traditions are earlier, even much earlier, I find it hard to believe that the dynasty, which it is the charter myth of, would not have a substantial, active role in the production of the version that emerged in their early days. In general, I think there is a much greater difference between source traditions, existing in some vague form, and final products produced for particular reasons in particular contexts, than many other scholars do.

[53] Marcus, *A History of Ethiopia*, 12.

to the Bible, in royal inscriptions from early periods are evidence of an already extant claim to Solomonic descent.[54]

By contrast, Amda Seyon, whose reign saw the *Kebra*'s publication, was one of the first kings of a dynasty that would rule Ethiopia into the 1970s, and he *explicitly* claimed descent from Solomon and Menelik. It is this "Solomonic dynasty" that began in 1270, when Yekunno Amlak defeated and killed the last ruler of the Zagwe, and Seyon would be on the throne by 1314.[55] I would argue that the composition of a tradition glorifying the line of Solomon and Menelik, in the early days of a dynasty claiming descent from Solomon and Menelik, is not much of a mystery – and that there is no reason to assert a much earlier origin for the basic thread of this tradition when the evidence offers little support. Instead, I think we are in the presence of a common problem here, visible even in the first chapter, in which we see a certain confusion between the likelihood that aspects of a given narrative have deep roots and the possibility of attributing a greater antiquity to that narrative as a whole, in its familiar form.

At any rate, in Bruce's day, the Beta Israel's version of this tradition appears to have developed explicitly out of this Christian charter myth, and in a way, in response to it – perhaps because Amda Seyon's reign coincided with an attempted expansion of imperial power into the regions where "the Judaized groups around Lake Tana" dwelt.[56] According to the Beta Israel of Bruce's time, and perhaps much earlier, they shared descent with Ethiopia's royal house, but had parted ways already in the fourth century CE. Then, in the reigns of the kings "Abraha and Atsbaha," the rest of Ethiopia's Israelites had converted to Christianity, an event, the Beta Israel told Bruce, they called "the Apostacy."[57] Rather than accept the rule of Ethiopia's now Christian emperors, the Beta Israel appointed a king of their own, a "prince of the house of Judah," and ruled themselves as long as they were able.[58] In fact, they told Bruce that they

---

[54] Ibid.

[55] Ibid., 12–16, 19. In fact, Kaplan argues that while Yekunno Amlak is "the father" of the new dynasty, Seyon "is recognized as the founder of the Solomonic state" (Kaplan, *The Beta Israel*, 54).

[56] Kaplan, *The Beta Israel*, 54.

[57] Bruce, *Travels to Discover the Source of the Nile*, 485. According to Abbink, these kings are generally equated with the historical Ezana of Aksum, who does seem to have been king when Christianity took root in the region (Abbink, "The Enigma of Beta Esra'el Ethnogenesis," 416 n.22).

[58] Bruce, *Travels to Discover the Source of the Nile*, 485.

were still ruled by a king from the line of Judah even then.[59] For its part, the *Kebra* takes aim at the Beta Israel, at least by proxy, referring to "the Jews (in its last chapters 95 to 117), as a vanquished people, degraded and eternally subjected."[60]

In light of the history just discussed – from the hard-scrabble origins of the Beta Israel community, through the Gondar era, to the early days of the *Zamana Masafent* – we can see quite easily the functional appeal of the *Kebra*'s traditions among the Beta Israel. Indeed, if the rhetorical moves made by the Beta Israel's version of the *Kebra* tradition remind readers of the Samaritans of Chapter 2, they should. The Samaritans, too, claimed a shared ancestry with the Jewish people, but argued that the differences between them originated when the rest of the Israelite community was led away, first by the high priest Eli, then later by the corrupted *Torah* of Moses, produced by Ezra. Both stories account for the grand similarities between the practices of two different Israels, but also the key differences, and specifically in a way that asserts the cultural superiority of one or the other.[61] When the twelve tribes tradition is used between two different "Israels," this is how competitions are prosecuted.

In the Beta Israel's case, not only was this Ethiopic twelve tribes tradition a way of asserting and defending their own claim to an Israelite identity against other claims, but because of who the *Kebra* refers to – mainly the Ethiopian *elite* – it was also a way of asserting elite status, in comparison to other Ethiopian groups.[62] Indeed, as the members of Ethiopia's hereditary elite who, according to their traditions, had not abandoned their original faith, the Beta Israel were describing themselves as the elite of the elite, the best of the best. Such a claim may belie their historical status in the region – which is not unusual for cultural traditions – but it is quite explicable, given the role resisting the Solomonic monarchy played in the group's formation and how much that resistance

---

[59] Ibid., 488.   [60] Abbink, "The Enigma of Beta Esra'el Ethnogenesis," 410.

[61] "... we cannot also but emphasize the role of historical myths as *charters*. At historically crucial junctures, the mytho-legends can be utilized by certain groups as ideological mechanisms of defense and of justification, and as building blocks for self-identity or socio-political claims" (ibid., 400). See also ibid., 419.

[62] As Kaplan puts it, "by associating themselves with the Solomon-Sheba legend ... [they] were claiming to be part of Ethiopia's political-cultural elite" (Kaplan, "Genealogies and Gene-Ideologies," 449). The quote continues: "They were defining themselves in the most positive terms possible within the realm of that country's traditional religio-political categories. In a similar fashion, their self-designation as 'Israelites' or the 'House of Israel,' rather than Jews (*ayhud*), placed them alongside the Ethiopian royal family, which also depicted itself as belonging to *Daqiqa Esra'el* (The Children of Israel)."

gave shape to its subsequent history. In other words, here as ever, the Beta Israel vision of Israel reflects what the Beta Israel wanted it to do, consciously or not.

For our purposes, there are two main points to be made here. The first is that the *Kebra*-based account of the Beta Israel's origins continued to dominate within the community well into the nineteenth century. Samuel Gobat, a Protestant missionary and British Israelite who would eventually become the Anglican bishop of Jerusalem, heard it from the Beta Israel on his arrival in the 1830s.[63] So did the French explorer Antoine d'Abbadie in the 1840s.[64] In 1845, the Italian Filosseno Luzzato asked d'Abbadie, who had taken up residence in Ethiopia, to present Abba Ishaq, a Beta Israel authority, a series of questions, and d'Abbadie complied. The answers were ultimately published in both French and English newspapers in 1851. In them, Ishaq said that the Beta Israel had indeed come to Israel with Solomon – although he also said they came "after Jeremiah the prophet" – and that they "belong to a mixture of twelve tribes, of which each one sent an elder son to accompany Minylik."[65] There is, again, virtually no evidence that anyone in Ethiopia was yet aware of the Danite legend at that time.

The second main point is that, as it was birthed in Ethiopia and shaped by the demands of an internal Ethiopian history, this first tradition of Israelite origin that the Beta Israel embraced is profoundly Ethiopian in character. It orients the Beta Israel, historically and politically, to Ethiopian realities specifically, and it explains their relationship to

---

[63] Parfitt, "The Construction of Jewish Identities in Africa," 34; Quirin, *The Evolution of the Ethiopian Jews*, 179.

[64] See d'Abbadie, "Réponses des Falashas dit Juif d'Abyssinie aux questions faites par M. Luzzato," 183; Gobat, *Journal of a Three Years' Residence in Abyssinia*, 278, 331; Quirin, *The Evolution of the Ethiopian Jews*, 22.

[65] "Minylik" here is Menelik. See Luzzatto, "The Falashas or Jews of Abyssinia," September 26, 1851, 404–5; Luzzatto, "The Falashas or Jews of Abyssinia," October 10, 1851, 4. For further discussion, see Summerfield, *From Falashas to Ethiopian Jews*, 9–12. As recently as the 1930s, the Italian civil servant Giovanni Ellero discovered that some among the Falasha believed themselves to have come from Jerusalem at the time of Nebuchadnezzar's conquest and to be the descendants of all twelve of the tribes. This is according to a report on Ellero's unpublished notes by Irma Taddia. According to her, "the members of the original twelve groups (neghedè) would have come from Egypt to Ethiopia (the original groups were called Rabiel, Simon, Leuì, Yeudà, Sacòr, Zablòn, Dan, Neftalieu, Asisèr, Goad, Beniam, Yosief)" (Taddia, "Giovanni Ellero's Manuscript Notes on the Falasha of Walqayt," 48).

Ethiopian social structures.[66] Then, too, their traditions responded to the accidents of the Beta Israel's history, formed through a series of conflicts with Ethiopia's emperors and church. In Ethiopia, this version of the twelve tribes tradition provided a medium through which the two different "Israels" of Ethiopia, Jewish and Christian, competed with each other and expressed their relationship to each other as each understood it to be. Only when the Beta Israel would meet representatives from another Israel – a third Israel, an external Israel – would they begin to adopt a tradition fit for that set of encounters, as their original traditions were fit for their internal, Ethiopic realities. By that point, however, the tradition they would adopt would be over a thousand years old.

5.3 THE DANITE LEGEND

As I noted above, the legend of the Danite Jews of Ethiopia has its origins in an encounter described already in Chapter 3 – that moment, in roughly 893, when Eldad ha-Dani arrived in Kairouan, in North Africa. Eldad claimed to be a Danite – that is what ha-Dani means – and to have come from the land of Kush where his people were settled, along with a few other tribes, on the near side of the mighty Sambatyon. In the ninth century CE, Kush, a biblical place name, had already long been associated with Ethiopia.[67] In fact, in the Septuagint, a Greek translation of the Bible from the third century BCE, the place name Kush is rendered "Ethiopia," or rather, *Aethiopis*, a Greek word that means "burnt face."[68] Thus, the legend of the Danite Jews of Kush began.

Readers of Chapter 3 will recall that the Kairouanis, concerned about the differences between their Jewish observances and those Eldad described, wrote to the Gaon of Sura, a pre-eminent Jewish authority of the period. They sent him an account of Eldad's rituals – the "Ritual of Eldad ha-Dani" – and asked him to rule on Eldad's Jewish status.[69]

---

[66] The internal, Ethiopic legends, "form part of *one* domain of discourse. The significant oppositions and transformations to be found in the one (Beta Esra'el) vis-à-vis the other (Amhara-Tigray) have been formed in an historical dialectic of power struggle, in which differences of ethno-religious identification emerged" (Abbink, "The Enigma of Beta Esra'el Ethnogenesis," 399–400). Obviously, the legend of the Jews of Ethiopia is another such domain, and another site of struggle.

[67] Hidal, "The Land of Cush in the Old Testament"; Sadler, *Can a Cushite Change His Skin?*; Strawn, "What Is Cush Doing in Amos 9:7?"

[68] Hatke, *Aksum and Nubia*, 53 n. 211.

[69] Benite, *The Ten Lost Tribes*, 86; Perry, "The Imaginary War," 3.

The Gaon was not dismayed: "the *Mishna* is one law ... but the Talmud is studied by the men of Babylon in Aramaic and by the men of Palestine in Targum, and by the sages exiled to Ethiopia in Hebrew, which they understand."[70] Ultimately, when the Gaon's ruling confirmed not just Eldad's story, but the validity of his Jewish practices, he legitimated these supposed "Jews of Kush" as a whole. That is to say, they were officially Jewish in the eyes of the rabbinic authorities of normative Judaism.

With the benefit of hindsight, however, we can say that the Danite legend, born in this moment, is based not only on Eldad's unlikely story, but on a series of nearly as unlikely coincidences and misunderstandings. The first is that Eldad himself was almost certainly not an Ethiopian – which, in fairness, he did not necessarily claim to be – but perhaps, instead, a Yemeni Jew.[71] Of course he was also not a Beta Israel, since the Beta Israel did not yet exist. Beyond that, neither biblical "Kush" nor the Septuagint's *Aethiopis* – a term "applied by the Greeks and Romans to black Africans in general" – actually referred to Ethiopia itself, originally, but instead to a region of Africa that better corresponds to Nubia.[72] In fact, even by the time the Septuagint was written, Ethiopia was not yet called Ethiopia, a name it would not acquire until the fourth century CE reign of King Ezana.[73] Thus, the grandest coincidence of them all: an Israelite and Jewish identifying people appear to have developed right where Jewish legend long suspected they lived, long after those suspicions first developed, and quite independently of them. And thanks to the Gaon, these Jews of Ethiopia had been decreed Jewish by rabbinic authorities long before any rabbinic authorities actually met them – in fact, before the Beta Israel, as the Beta Israel, yet existed.

---

[70] Translation from Benite, *The Ten Lost Tribes*, 98.

[71] Benite, *The Ten Lost Tribes*, 92; Morag, "A Linguistic Examination." See also the earlier discussion in Schloessinger, *The Ritual of Eldad Ha-Dani*, 8. "Although most scholars are agreed that Eldad Ha-Dani ... did not come from Ethiopia, this has not prevented others from seeing his writings as the first reliable mention of Jews in Ethiopia" (Kaplan, "Genealogies and Gene-Ideologies," 449).

[72] Hatke, *Aksum and Nubia*, 53 n.21. For a discussion of this Septuagint issue, see Sadler, *Can a Cushite Change His Skin?*, 16–17. For general discussion of the identification of biblical Kush, usually against its identification with historical Ethiopia, see Strawn, "What Is Cush Doing in Amos 9:7?," 101–2; Holter, *Yahweh in Africa*, 109, 122; Levin, "Nimrod the Mighty"; Hidal, "The Land of Cush in the Old Testament."

[73] This was when "the Aksumites first identified themselves with the Ethiopians of Graeco-Roman parlance and came to be identified as such by foreigners" (Hatke, *Aksum and Nubia*, 53). For a discussion of this Septuagint issue, see Sadler, *Can a Cushite Change His Skin?*, 16–17.

Next, in another kind of coincidence, the Danite legend was first applied to the Beta Israel not in the nineteenth century, when Jewish authorities first arrived in the region, but in the early sixteenth. This was the work of Rabbi David Ben Abi Zimra – the "Radbaz."[74] What happened was that an Egyptian man wrote to the Radbaz with an unusual problem.[75] The Egyptian had purchased an enslaved man in the Cairo slave mart, only to find, to his great surprise, that the man claimed to be an Israelite. Exodus 21:2, the Egyptian knew, commanded that "if you buy a Hebrew servant, he will work six years, but on the seventh he shall go out a free person." Did he have to let him go free after seven years? The Radbaz responded by demanding the man release his slave immediately. Exodus 21:2, he said, only applies to those Israelites ordered enslaved by the courts, not taken as prisoners of war.[76]

For us, however, the main point is that the Radbaz was by no means surprised to hear about Israelites from Ethiopia, even though this was very nearly the first time a rabbinic authority heard, or could have heard, of the Beta Israel themselves. He knew well, from the Gaon's earlier ruling, that "those who have come from the land of Kush ... they are without doubt of the Tribe of Dan."[77] It is still likely enough that no one in Ethiopia was aware of these developments, and they would not be for centuries.[78] Nevertheless, these two rulings, nearly seven hundred years

---

[74] Seeman, "Ethnographers, Rabbis and Jewish Epistemology," 15. Shortly thereafter, the Radbaz would be seconded by his student, Jacob ben Abraham Castro, the "Maharikas," another step along the way (ibid., 16, 20).

[75] Corinaldi, *Jewish Identity*, 103–6; Seeman, "Ethnographers, Rabbis and Jewish Epistemology," 15.

[76] Seeman, "Ethnographers, Rabbis and Jewish Epistemology," 15.

[77] Kaplan, *The Beta Israel*, 25–26; Corinaldi, *Jewish Identity*, 104. "These *responsa* were certainly based on Eldad. The *responsa* now have the force of legal halakhic precedent" (Parfitt, "The Construction of Jewish Identities in Africa," 34).

[78] Rumors about Eldad's people may, at some point, have begun to be influenced by rumors about the actual Jews of Ethiopia, and likely around the time the Radbaz was making his ruling. Corinaldi notes that, in 1435, a rabbi named Elijah of Ferrera had written that "they have the Torah and an oral commentary on it, but they do not have the Talmud or our interpreters" (Corinaldi, *Jewish Identity*, 102). He also states that other well-known medieval rabbis were aware of them, including Abraham Halevy and Obadiah Bertinoro. Halevy wrote a letter in 1528 in which he claimed that "Falasa" – perhaps from "Falasha" – "is a strong kingdom of Jews who are valiant," while, closer to home, "the Arab chronicler of Ahmad Gragn's conquest of Ethiopia noted 'The Semien province was ruled by Jews of Abyssinia who are called Falashas in their own language'" (Kaplan, *The Beta Israel*, 66). Kaplan also notes that Bertinoro wrote a letter to his father, in 1488, where he reports that there are "Jews who live in the land of 'Prester John,' including two he met in Egypt ... 'And they say they belong to the tribe

apart, would form crucial parts of a paper trail that, in 1973, resulted in the official recognition, by Ovadia Yosef, Chief Sephardic Rabbi of Israel, of the Beta Israel as a Jewish people deserving of the rights of Israeli citizenship.

At that time, prompted by inquiries from the Beta Israel themselves, Yosef would note that "there is no doubt that the aforementioned authorities who ruled that they are of the Tribe of Dan carefully investigated and reached this conclusion on the basis of the most reliable testimony and evidence."[79] For this reason, he ruled, "the Falashas are Jews" and "brethren of the House of Israel."[80] In 1975, he would be seconded by the Ashkenazi chief, Shlomo Goren.[81] On April 25, 1975, the Jewish identity of the Beta Israel was officially enshrined in Israeli law, and the ingathering of the Beta Israel could begin.[82]

Ultimately, the Danite legend would not completely crowd out other traditions, and it has not done so even today. Though it has indeed become the preferred explanation of Beta Israel origins among the community itself, "many other Israelis continue to be enamoured of the romance of the Solomon and Sheba story."[83] Beyond that, as we will see in a moment, the first efforts at Jewish outreach to the Beta Israel, beginning in the mid-nineteenth century, seem not to have been inspired

---

of Dan.'" This observation, in Kaplan's opinion, "is unique in stating that the Ethiopians themselves put forward a claim to Danite origin," and no other evidence of this sort survives (ibid., 25). It also may be that "they" here does not refer to the Beta Israel themselves.

[79] Translation by Corinaldi, *Jewish Identity*, 198, quoted in Zegeye, *The Impossible Return*, xiv. Bard notes that Hezi Ovadia, a spokesman for the Beta Israel who had already made their way to Israel, "specifically asked Rabbi Ovadia Yosef ... for a ruling that would enable the Beta Israel to settle in Israel" (Bard, *From Tragedy to Triumph*, 20).

[80] Translation by Corinaldi, *Jewish Identity*, 198, quoted in Zegeye, *The Impossible Return*, xiv.

[81] Quirin, *The Evolution of the Ethiopian Jews*; Kaplan, *The Beta Israel*, 24–25; Parfitt, "The Construction of Jewish Identities in Africa," 34–35. According to Bard, Goren initially refused to accept Yosef's decision, but by 1977 was writing a "group of Beta Israel immigrants, 'you are our brothers, you are our blood and our flesh. You are true Jews'" (Bard, *From Tragedy to Triumph*, 21).

[82] Wagaw, *For Our Soul*, 57.

[83] Kaplan, "Genealogies and Gene-Ideologies," 450. However, Kaplan also notes that "even secular proponents of Ethiopian immigrants have enthusiastically adopted the Danite tradition, albeit with various caveats and creative elaborations." He also echoes some of the conclusions of earlier parts of this chapter: "the Solomon-Sheba story placed the Beta Israel in the mainstream of Ethiopian history and culture," but in Israel "the Danite traditions separate the Beta Israel from Christian Ethiopians, while simultaneously emphasizing their links to other Jews."

by any search for "Danites," but simply for Jews, and Jews who were, from the perspective of the Jewish world, increasingly under threat. Still, neither the Beta Israel's original traditions nor the impulses that inspired this early outreach could have succeeded in bringing the Beta Israel to Israel as the Danite legend did – which the last century and a half of Beta Israel history shows very well.

5.4 ISRAEL MEETS ISRAEL

Between the 1870s and the 1970s, Beta Israel identity, practices, traditions, and beliefs experienced a rapid transformation. Some of the causes were manmade, the products of dedicated efforts by Jewish institutions to connect the Beta Israel to the heritage they both believed were the Beta Israel's by right. Some were decidedly not. Tragically, between 1888 and 1892, the terrible *kifu-qen*, or "awful days," a combination of famine, pestilence, and even war with neighboring Sudan, would devastate the Beta Israel community, reducing its population by as much as half and destroying the integrity of certain long-treasured institutions.[84] Monasticism and animal sacrifice were especially difficult to maintain in such lean periods.[85] As a result, those Jewish emissaries who visited the region after 1892 would find a people that, quite by accident, more

[84] "No ... data [exists] with regard to the mortality rate among unconverted Beta Israel. On face value there seems to be no reason to assume that they were spared the enormous losses suffered by their Christian kinsmen and neighbors. Indeed, since they did not have access to either foreign money or assistance from Christian rulers in a manner comparable to the Falasha Christians, their losses may have been even greater. It appears probable that between half and two-thirds of all Beta Israel died in the famine and a larger number cannot be precluded. Craftsmen may well have been even more vulnerable to famine than agricultural laborers" (Kaplan, *The Beta Israel*, 147–48). Corinaldi also estimated that "between half and two-thirds of the Beta Israel population were wiped out; their settlements were decimated, survivors scattered and their religious system virtually destroyed" (Corinaldi, *Jewish Identity*, 124). Marcus adds "the social fabric unraveled ... People took to the roads, seeking survival by following the armies southward into newly conquered territory" (Marcus, *A History of Ethiopia*, 93–94).

[85] Kaplan, "Kifu-Qen"; Kaplan, *The Beta Israel*, 147–48; Corinaldi, *Jewish Identity*, 124; Marcus, *A History of Ethiopia*, 93–94. As Quirin notes, "although the Great Famine that affected Ethiopia in the late nineteenth century is usually said to have occurred between 1888 and 1892, local reports in the Begamder region refer to natural calamities as early as 1879, with reports of 'plague,' and seeds being eaten by insects, 'pestilence,' and 'great famine' in 1879, 1880, and 1882. In the north in general, famine had already begun by 1882. Foreign invaders, and the Ethiopian efforts to repel them, wrought more havoc on the countryside of northwestern Ethiopia between 1885 and 1892" (Quirin, *The Evolution of the Ethiopian Jews*, 167).

closely resembled the world of normative Judaism in its practices, because of what they had lost. They would also find a people who were far more open to receiving outside help and attention than would have been the case a few decades earlier.[86]

Yet in other respects, the transformation of the Beta Israel – from, some have said, "Beta Israel" to "Ethiopian Jews," a simplistic but not inaccurate framing – was planned and agonized over for decades.[87] Today, many new studies tell different parts of this story in detail. They relate, for example, how the attention of the Jewish world was first turned to Ethiopia not by the Danite legend, but by the activity of Protestant missionaries – beginning, for the most part, with the arrival of Samuel Gobat and Christian Kugler in 1830, followed by J. Martin Flad in 1855 – who threatened conversion.[88]

In fact, these missionaries had come, as so often in these cases, with the typically colonialist intention of converting not only non-Christian Ethiopians, but Ethiopian Christians to a supposedly more civilized form of Christianity.[89] Nevertheless, the Beta Israel quickly drew these missionaries' attention, no doubt in part because of evangelical beliefs about

---

[86] Kaplan, *The Beta Israel*, 153.

[87] The terms, as the authors of these studies generally know well, are a little misleading since the Beta Israel understood themselves as Jewish well before the arrival of Jewish emissaries in the region. However, insofar as "Jewish" here refers to *normative* Judaism, this simple framing is apt. See especially Summerfield, *From Falashas to Ethiopian Jews*; Kaplan, "The Invention of Ethiopian Jews"; Ben Ezer, "The Ethiopian Jewish Exodus."

[88] Parfitt, "The Construction of Jewish Identities in Africa," 34; Quirin, *The Evolution of the Ethiopian Jews*, 179. "While Kugler confined himself largely to Tigre, Gobat continued on to Gondar. During the next seven years, three of which he spent in Ethiopia, Gobat ... met on several occasions with Beta Israel, and strongly supported the establishment of a mission to them ... it was only in 1855 with the arrival of J. Martin Flad that the possibility of a mission to the Beta Israel appears to have been seriously considered" (Kaplan, *The Beta Israel*, 116–17).

[89] Eventually, their too-aggressive evangelizing would see a number of them arrested by Tewodros II. Tewodros II had demanded that the missionaries focus only on non-Christians and convert them only to the Ethiopian Orthodox Church itself, but "from the beginning, the dream of the Protestant missionaries ... had been not only to convert Jews to Christianity but to use the new converts to revive the Ethiopian Orthodox Church, which was uniformly seen as unenlightened and backward, if not corrupt and morally bankrupt" (Quirin, *The Evolution of the Ethiopian Jews*, 179). The British would respond to this imprisonment with the enormously expensive, enormously well-armed "Expedition to Abyssinia" under Sir Robert Napier – the quick success of which drove the emperor to suicide – and after that, Ethiopia would become more open to foreign intervention, whether it wanted to be or not (Marcus, *A History of Ethiopia*, 70–71).

the importance of converting the Jews, described in the previous chapters. In 1860, the London Society for Promoting Christianity Amongst the Jews sent a mission specifically to the Beta Israel community, one "headed by a converted German Jew, Henry Aaron Stern."[90] And now that this Lost Tribe looked like it would be lost *into Christianity*, numerous influential Jewish leaders – and certain fledgling Zionist organizations – published calls for action, and numerous individuals attempted to answer them.[91]

In 1867, Joseph Halévy, funded by the *Alliance Israélite Universelle*, finally succeeded in reaching the Beta Israel in Ethiopia, inaugurating the lengthy era of Jewish contacts in that region.[92] While Halévy's positive report on the Jewish identity of the Beta Israel would be largely ignored by the *Alliance*, and while no serious second effort would be made until the turn of the twentieth century, neither would the Jewish world ever completely disengage from the Beta Israel again.[93] The century between Halévy's visit and the official recognition of the Beta Israel by Israel was turbulent and eventful.

Here, we can only focus on part of the story. Other studies, and notably a fairly new biography by Emanuela Trevisan Semi, describe the fascinating life of Jacques Faitlovitch, once Halévy's student at the Sorbonne, who arrived in Ethiopia for the first time in 1904 and would work on behalf of the Beta Israel until his death in 1955.[94] They describe

---

[90] Kaplan, *The Beta Israel*, 116–17. "Even Flad did not arrive intending to work among the Jews. However, an extended period of inactivity in the Gondar region ... placed him in contact with the local Beta Israel and began a lifelong involvement with their evangelization. By May 1858, a school for Beta Israel had been established in Gondar and in 1860 the London Society for Promoting Christianity Amongst the Jews established a mission to the Falasha ... Within a short time, Flad's differences with his fellow missionaries ... led him to break company with them and devote himself completely to the Falasha mission" (ibid., 117).

[91] "Manifestos calling for material and spiritual aid to Ethiopian Jews were issued by leading lights including Rabbi Jacob Sapir of Jerusalem (1863), Rabbi Ezriel Hildesheimer of Hungary (1865), Rabbi Joseph Guggenheimer of Germany (1865), Rabbi Samuel Hirsch Margulies in France, and Chief Rabbi of Palestine, Abraham Isaac Kook (1921)" (Seeman, "Ethnographers, Rabbis and Jewish Epistemology," 16–17). See also Quirin, *The Evolution of the Ethiopian Jews*, 191–92; Kaplan, *The Beta Israel*, 142–45. Sohn discusses some of the articles published in German Jewish papers in the early twentieth century on this topic in Sohn, "The Falashas in the German Jewish Press." In later years, the fear that the Beta Israel would be converted would continue to drive Jewish outreach – even Ovadia Yosef's ruling would speak of the need to "save" them "from assimilation" (Corinaldi, *Jewish Identity*, 198).

[92] Kaplan, *The Beta Israel*, 140.   [93] Quirin, *The Evolution of the Ethiopian Jews*, 193.

[94] Semi, "Ethiopian Jews in Europe," 75.

the school he opened in Addis Ababa in 1923, which would eventually be run by his former student, Taamrat Emanuel, and other past pupils.[95] It was Faitlovitch who introduced a wide array of traditional Jewish practices to the Beta Israel for the first time, including lighting the sabbath lights, "*tefillin, mezuzot, kippot,* and *siddurim,*" while making efforts to stamp out what he saw as offensive "practices linked to codes of ritual purity" as well as the embers of monasticism and animal sacrifice.[96]

These studies recount how Faitlovitch earned the nickname the "father of the Falashas," or the "father of the Ethiopian Jews," while modern, more critical studies emphasize how these monikers express both the tremendous impact he had on shaping Ethiopian Jewish identity and the rank paternalism, and colonialist overtones, of his overall project.[97] Indeed, as Trevisan Semi notes, the Protestant missionaries and Faitlovitch were much alike in their plans to "regenerate" Ethiopia's native religious traditions, which, supposedly, were lacking much that Europeans could give them.[98] To Faitlovitch, the Beta Israel were an "*ever meduldal,* a dangling limb which urgently needed to be reattached to the rest of the Jewish body lest it break away for good."[99] This is not an encouraging image, and it often did not have encouraging results.

A few new studies have also delved into the most tragic aspects of Jewish outreach to the Beta Israel, including the unfortunate practice of sending Beta Israel children to fosterages in Europe and Israel, begun by Halévy. Often the places these young Beta Israel were sent to had little use for them, and they frequently came to bad ends.[100] Still others discuss the ongoing and faltering, but never completed nor abandoned, work of educating the Beta Israel, supposedly into the Jewish practices their ancestors had forgotten. In 1951, the Chief Ashkenazi Rabbi of Israel, Isaac Halevy Herzog, was sent by the Jewish Agency to "rule on the status of

---

[95] "In order to portray the results of Faitlovitch's programmes and their impact on Falasha society, it will first be useful to reiterate here its original aims: 1. To reform the Falashas' religion to make it conform with normative Judaism. 2. To improve the Falashas' religious and political situation. 3. To develop their economic, intellectual, and social position. 4. To combat Christian missionary activity and bring conversions to an end. 5. To educate Western Jewry about the Falashas and to encourage their assistance" (Summerfield, *From Falashas to Ethiopian Jews,* 73). Emmanuel would often find himself in conflict with Faitlovitch over what should be done or needed to be done (Semi, *Jacques Faitlovich and the Jews of Ethiopia,* 117).

[96] Semi, *Jacques Faitlovich and the Jews of Ethiopia,* xvi.   [97] Ibid., xvi.   [98] Ibid., 18.

[99] Ibid., 173.

[100] Semi, "Ethiopian Jews in Europe," 74–76; Kaplan, *The Beta Israel,* 141; Semi, "From Wolleqa to Florence."

Ethiopian Jews."[101] Unusually for such an authority, Herzog pursued the issue in part by interviewing secular scholars, as well as the aging Faitlovitch. His ruling would be disappointing. He did recommend that Israel bring the Beta Israel "near the wellsprings of Israel," which he characterized as an "act of salvation."[102] However, he did not believe that they were the heirs of the tribe of Dan, but instead were "the descendants of a non-Jewish race, which once converted."[103] While likely more historically accurate, Herzog's ruling would contribute to the long delay in bringing, or inviting, the Beta Israel to Israel, since legally this right was owed to the biological heirs of the Jewish world.

Nevertheless, efforts to "re-educate" the Beta Israel continued. In 1953, the Agency sent Rabbi Shmuel Be'eri and some of Faitlovitch's former students – notably Taddasa Yaqod and Yona Boggala – to open a school in Asmara, and Yehuda Sivan followed Be'eri in 1957.[104] Yet while Sivan and Boggala opened thirty-three schools in 1957, all but two closed almost immediately.[105] These kinds of efforts, sporadic and constant, whirlwind and lackadaisical, broadly characterize the shape of the relationship between the Jewish world and the Beta Israel from the time of Halévy's arrival in 1867 right up to the rabbinic rulings in favor of the Beta Israel's Jewish status in 1973 and 1975.

Thus, again, the period between 1867 and the 1973 was one of the most eventful in Beta Israel history. It saw the Beta Israel change from the practitioners of what Abbink calls "a form of indigenous Toranic Judaism ... [that] occurred within the specific conditions of Ethiopian socio-political formation" to a form of Judaism recognizable to the outside world.[106] It saw a remarkable transformation, from an Israel identified, defined, and shaped by its Ethiopian context to one oriented instead towards this external Israel, that of the outside Jewish world. It would, in

---

[101] Seeman, "Ethnographers, Rabbis and Jewish Epistemology," 19–20.

[102] See ibid., 20.

[103] Ibid., 19. See ibid., 17–19 generally. As Seeman observes, being converts would in fact alleviate the pressure of some questions regarding the Beta Israel's traditional practices, the validity of their marriages, and so on.

[104] Summerfield, *From Falashas to Ethiopian Jews*, 118–19, 121–22.   [105] Ibid., 121–22.

[106] Abbink, "The Enigma of Beta Esra'el Ethnogenesis," 436. He adds "their beliefs and group identity later (in the 20th century) evolved toward modern, contemporary Judaism, but not before the intensification of contacts with visiting groups of western Jews and travellers. During the long period of evolution of their religious culture, they neither had direct Jewish sources (Yemen or Egypt or the Holy Land) which could have inspired them, nor is there any documented immigration of Jewish groups to Northern Ethiopia."

the end, see the Beta Israel exchange one story for another, and finally, one home for another. Yet for us, strangely enough, in this study of the construction of Israelite identities, the ways that the Beta Israel did not change are more remarkable still, and perhaps even more interesting.

Of course, in 1850, nearly two decades before Joseph Halévy's journey, the Beta Israel already identified as Israelites, and they already identified as Jews. They already understood themselves in relation to a story about the twelve tribes of Israel, and how they had come from Israel to Ethiopia. Some of them even already wanted to come to Israel. In fact, in 1855, a Beta Israel named Daniel ben Hanina and his son Moses would make the journey, arriving in Jerusalem asking to study Torah.[107] In 1862, one Abba Mahari, guided by visions, would even lead a mass effort to reach the Holy Land, though ultimately he and his followers would not get very far – but they would try again in 1874 and 1879.[108] Later, when the Beta Israel finally began relocating to Israel *en masse*, some would wonder whether Mahari had simply misunderstood, from his visions, when their journey to Israel was supposed to begin.[109]

Thus, the Beta Israel already possessed all the ingredients for being recognized as part of Israel by Jewish authorities, and even the makings of a desire to be recognized. What they did not yet have was the right story, nor did these early Jewish emissaries give it to them, though it existed, and had been applied to them, for centuries. Indeed, writing in 1920, Faitlovitch could still report that other Ethiopians believed the Beta Israel had come "from Palestine to Ethiopia in the time of King Solomon and his alleged son Menilek I," and that this position was "partly shared also by the Falashas."[110] Instead, Halévy, Faitlovitch, Herzog and the rest were interested in the Beta Israel not as a Lost Tribe, but as a Jewish people far removed from the course of Jewish civilization for a very long time.

---

[107] Kaplan, *The Beta Israel*, 139; Quirin, *The Evolution of the Ethiopian Jews*, 192.

[108] Kaplan, *The Beta Israel*, 135–38. Ben Ezer adds "as far back as 1862, a distinguished Ethiopian Jew called Abba Mahari announced that the time had indeed arrived, meaning that they should go to Jerusalem. Thousands of Jews gathered around him in the Gondar region and started the long march toward Jerusalem ... The attempt failed. Most of the migrants died on the way ... Some continued until they arrived at a big river, probably in the Tigray area, where Abba Mahari ... pointed his walking stick towards the river waiting for God to part it so that the Jewish people could cross. When this did not happen, the remaining survivors turned and walked back to their villages" (Ben Ezer, *The Ethiopian Jewish Exodus*, 63).

[109] Ben Ezer, *The Ethiopian Jewish Exodus*, 63–64.   [110] Faitlovitch, *The Falashas*, 17.

Indeed, Faitlovitch himself was of the opinion that the Beta Israel descended from those Judahites who had fled to Egypt after the Babylonian conquest of Jerusalem; that they had entered Ethiopia upon the collapse of the Persian empire; and that they had later been augmented by the arrival of a population of Jews from Himyar, that Arabian Jewish kingdom, who had been transported as prisoners of war.[111] The rabbis might have known the Danite legend and believed it, but the early Jewish missionaries to the region seem not to have had much interest in it, whether they knew it or not.

Generally, then, we might think of the twentieth-century history of the Beta Israel partially as a product of the contest between two images – Danites, on the one hand, and the practitioners of a "pre-Talmudic" Judaism on the other.[112] The two are not inherently in conflict: if the Beta Israel missed out on the teachings of the Talmud, it would be because they had left the mainstream of Jewish tradition before it was codified. But – and no doubt because "pre-Talmudic" implies a lack that must be redressed before the Beta Israel could claim the heritage that was theirs by descent – which image was used, and when, shaped how the Beta Israel were treated by Jewish emissaries and officials.

Faitlovitch himself was not the inventor of the "pre-Talmudic" model, but he was "the most persistent and influential shaper" of this "mythic image," and he played a major role in transmitting it to the world.[113] Certainly, the pre-Talmudic paradigm is what sent Faitlovitch to Ethiopia in the first place, and after him all the others – all those who opened schools, investigated the Beta Israel's history, and hemmed and hawed about who they really were for decades. In theory, pre-Talmudic implies the possibility of *becoming* Talmudic, of a project that might someday be completed. In practice, no matter how many emissaries were sent, and no

---

[111] Ibid., 18–19.

[112] This is still a fairly common idea even in scholarship. Marcus, in his influential history, also refers to the "unique pre-Talmudic faith of the Beta Israel" (Marcus, *A History of Ethiopia*, 23). In her study of contemporary ethnic groups, Linda Begley Soroff describes the *Alliance* as having sent "Jacques Faitlovitch to rescue the Falasha ... and to introduce them to rabbinic Judaism. Faitlovitch was aware that in their two millennia of isolation ... the Falasha retained only the Old Testament in the Semitic language of Geez, but not the late oral rabbinic traditions of their Talmudic commentary" (Soroff, *The Maintenance and Transmission of Ethnic Identity*, 31–32). Wolf Leslau, in his much earlier study, argued that "one thing seems certain: their form of Judaism is primitive and might date from a time when the Mishnah and the Talmud were not yet compiled" (Leslau, *Falasha Anthology*, xli–xlii).

[113] Kaplan, *The Beta Israel*, 156.

matter how many schools were opened, all the way from 1867 right up to 1973, the proponents of the "pre-Talmudic" model could never bring themselves to declare victory and move on.

Indeed, nothing reveals the difference between these two models so well as the fact that the Danite identity of the Beta Israel, and therefore their status as Jews worthy of emigration to Israel, was confirmed by Ovadia Yosef one month after the Ministry of Absorption had finally concluded that "from a national-cultural perspective, the Falashas ... are completely foreign to the spirt of Israel, and therefore ineligible for automatic citizenship under Israel's 'Law of Return.'"[114] As a top religious authority, Yosef's judgment on religious matters superseded those of the Ministry, but it did not end the controversy, even among the rabbinate. For us, the main point is that each conclusion is a natural outgrowth of the thread of speculation leading up to it. According to the legal logic of Jewish immigration to Israel, the Beta Israel, as the descendants of Israelites, are entitled to rights that their Jewish practices might not entitle them to, but descent is generally the deciding factor in Jewish immigration to Israel, regardless of practice, in most other cases.[115]

At any rate, we best understand the final step in the process that brought the Beta Israel to Israel not when we think of it in terms of these re-education efforts, necessary or not, but in terms of the Beta Israel's own reorientation. The simplest way to put it is that a people who had long identified as both Israelite and Jewish, but in a way that placed them in relation to Ethiopian internal realities, substituted this inward-facing story for an outward-facing one that placed them in relation to the until-then-external world of normative Judaism instead. This did what no other efforts could do, and despite some negative judgments that had cropped up along the way – Rabbi Herzog's, for example.

Still, the official recognition of the Beta Israel as Danites, whether in the sixteenth century or the twentieth, did not change the fact that the original, native Beta Israel vision of Israelite identity was an Ethiopian construction of Israel, and that the Jewish vision of Israel was an external one – the story of the two brothers discussed above. The tensions generated by the efforts of Jewish authorities to interpret these differences from

---

[114] Seeman, "Ethnographers, Rabbis and Jewish Epistemology," 13.

[115] Corinaldi, "The Personal Status of the Samaritans in Israel," 290. As Soroff observes, "two major ideals dominated the *Yishuv*" – the settlement of Jews in Israel – "socialist equality and the Zionist rebirth of Israel. The Zionist vision stressed the establishment of a Jewish community along the lines of a modern secular nation" (Soroff, *The Maintenance and Transmission of Ethnic Identity*, 27).

a Jewish point of view continue to shape the experience of the Beta Israel in Israel even today. Nowhere are these tensions more visible than in how long it took Israel, after the State was founded, to recognize the Beta Israel compared to others among the Jewish peoples of the world, and in how the Beta Israel have been treated in Israel since they arrived. We now turn our attention to the struggles of the Beta Israel in Israel, and from there, the role the twelve tribes tradition played in creating ongoing challenges.

5.5 ISRAELITES AMONG ISRAELITES AGAIN

When the State of Israel was founded in 1948, its animating logic was to provide a homeland for the Jews of the world. In fact, so potent was this logic that, from the perspective of the Jewish state, Jewish immigrants to Israel were not – and are not – *considered immigrants at all.* Instead, they were already citizens, already part of the "constitutive community." For Jews, citizenship in Israel is not "an entitlement granted by the state, but ... a 'natural' right of every Jew in the world that precedes and constitutes the state."[116]

Very quickly, then, Israel developed a sophisticated bureaucratic apparatus for its "*kibuts hagaluyot*," the "ingathering of the exiles."[117] In 1950, the "Right of Return" was enshrined in Israel's "Law of Return," codifying the sentiment expressed above; another law, the "Law of Citizenship," was enacted in 1952, spelling out more of the particulars as to how the law was to be implemented; and the "World Zionist Organization/Jewish Agency (Status) Law" tasked the powerful "Jewish Agency" with its mission of "ingathering."[118] Even before then, the machinery of ingathering had clanked into motion. In 1949–50, there was "Operation Magic Carpet," which brought the Jews of Yemen to Israel, as well as the first immigrants from India's three Jewish communities – the Bene Israel, the Kerala Jews, and the Baghdadis, originally

---

[116] Shachar, "Citizenship and Membership in the Israeli Polity," 387; Joppke and Rosenhek, "Contesting Ethnic Immigration," 390. As Singh put it, "according to the Law of Return (1950) and the Law of Nationality (1952), every Jew has the right to settle in Israel and citizenship is automatically conferred upon arrival" (Singh, *Being Indian, Being Israeli*, 29). For a brief, readable history of immigration to Israel, see Soroff, *The Maintenance and Transmission of Ethnic Identity*, 25–46.

[117] Soroff, *The Maintenance and Transmission of Ethnic Identity*, 29.

[118] Tekiner, "Race and the Issue of National Identity in Israel," 48–51.

from Iraq.[119] In 1950–51, it was the turn of the Jews of Iraq, in "Operation Ezra and Nehemiah."[120]

Since by 1948, the Beta Israel not only possessed the rulings of two unimpeachable rabbinic authorities in favor of their claim to Jewish descent but had also been a target of Jewish outreach for eighty years, it certainly seems as if their own emigration to Israel should have swiftly followed. It did not, and for reasons just discussed: the dominance of the "pre-Talmudic" model over the Danite model, and a corresponding uncertainty about whether the Beta Israel really were who they said they were, or who the rabbis said they were. In 1951 had come Rabbi Herzog's ruling that, in fact, they were not Israelites. These doubts would plague the experience of the Beta Israel, in Israel, into the present. And while the Beta Israel's long wait for ingathering, compared to some other Jewish peoples of the world, was a symptom of these doubts, they lingered well after Ovadia Yosef weighed in, and after "ingathering" began.

Still, when Ovadia Yosef did make his ruling in 1973, and especially when it was seconded by Shlomo Goren and codified in 1975, the doors to Israel stood open at last. Now, however, there were new hurdles of a practical, political nature to consider. In 1974, the Solomonic monarchy, over seven hundred years old, suddenly fell, and its last emperor, Haile Selassie, was deposed and eventually assassinated. While Selassie had not wanted the Beta Israel to emigrate – particularly as so many had now received what he believed to be useful European-style educations – Israel at least had diplomatic relations with his Ethiopia.[121] The same was not true of the Derg government that succeeded Selassie, led by Mengistu Haile Mariam, and Israeli authorities struggled to find a way to get the Beta Israel out.[122] Nevertheless, by that point, neither Israel nor the Beta Israel were to be deterred.[123]

[119] Soroff, *The Maintenance and Transmission of Ethnic Identity*, 29; Meir-Glitzenstein, "Operation Magic Carpet"; Gould, Lavy, and Paserman, "Sixty Years after the Magic Carpet Ride"; Schectman, "The Repatriation of Yemenite Jewry"; Singh, *Being Indian, Being Israeli*, 28–30.
[120] Soroff, *The Maintenance and Transmission of Ethnic Identity*, 29; Katriel, "The Rhetoric of Rescue," 191.
[121] Spector, *Operation Solomon*, 9.   [122] Ibid., 11.
[123] In 1977, a tentative deal to allow some of the Beta Israel to emigrate was quickly dashed when Israel's Foreign Minister Moshe Dayan maladroitly revealed its existence at a press conference in Switzerland (Wagaw, *For Our Soul*, 61). Spector spends some time entertaining the question of whether Dayan made a mistake or spoke intentionally. An interview with an official in the Foreign Ministry and with former Prime Minister Yitzhak Shamir suggested that it was indeed simply a mistake, but others thought

Thus, in the absence of formal repatriation efforts, many Beta Israel began to make the perilous journey from Ethiopia to refugee camps in Kenya and Sudan by themselves.[124] Israel, for its part, began to facilitate the transfer of small groups of Beta Israel to Israel in efforts collectively referred to as "Operation Brothers," echoing the foundation myths described above.[125] Between November 1984 and January 1985, Operation Moses emptied out most of the camps, and in March, Operation Joshua finished the job.[126] For those Beta Israel still in Ethiopia, the wait continued, but soon history repeated itself. Starting in the late 1980s, many Beta Israel had made their way to a newly opened Israeli embassy in Addis Ababa.[127] On May 21, 1991, the Derg government fell and Israel jumped into action again. A massive airlift called "Operation Solomon" brought more than fourteen thousand Beta Israel to Israel, and by the end of the month, the vast majority of this community had been relocated.[128] Today, over eighty-five thousand Beta Israel have made Israel their home.[129]

Dayan was trying to get the arrangement canceled, or else trying to embarrass Ethiopia for receiving, as new-found allies, Soviet Russia (Spector, *Operation Solomon*, 11–12).

[124] As Wagaw observes, many Beta Israel were desperate to get out at that point because of the unrest in the early days of the Derg. This included "drought and ... famine ... civil strife" and other issues (Wagaw, *For Our Soul*, 57–59).

[125] Zegeye, *The Impossible Return*, 109.

[126] Ibid., 305. See Karadawi, "The Smuggling of the Ethiopian Falasha"; Rapoport, *Redemption Song*; Parfitt, *Operation Moses*.

[127] Ben Ezer, *The Ethiopian Jewish Exodus*, 33. "By the start of 1990, perhaps two thousand more of the Beta Israel in Ethiopia had put themselves at risk. They had sold their possessions, left their villages, and made their way south to Addis Ababa ... Ultimately, most of the remaining Jews of Ethiopia also traveled to Addis, which already was swollen with the refugees of a long civil war ... they could not know how much suffering awaited them before they would be allowed to leave Ethiopia" (Spector, *Operation Solomon*, 13).

[128] Zegeye, *The Impossible Return*, 112. See also Quirin, *The Evolution of the Ethiopian Jews*, 8–9. "Prior to 1977 all but a handful of Beta Israel lived in Ethiopia. During the 1980s almost half of them came on *aliyah* (immigration to Israel) ... In 1991 'Operation Solomon' put an end to the Beta Israel as an active and living Ethiopian community, and by the end of 1992 virtually all Beta Israel were in Israel" (Kaplan, "The Invention of Ethiopian Jews," 645).

[129] Ben Ezer, *The Ethiopian Jewish Exodus*, 33. Some who were still not considered Jewish – namely the Falash Mura, who were Beta Israel converts to Christianity, and even those who wished to convert back – were left behind, and roughly two thousand others had not been able to reach Addis Ababa on time (Wagaw, *For Our Soul*, 243). See also Kaplan and Salamon, "Ethiopian Jews in Israel," 122; Zegeye, *The Impossible Return*, 166–81.

Yet even after the rabbinic rulings had taken hold, doubts about the Jewish identity of the Beta Israel persisted in Israel.[130] In fact, the first Beta Israel immigrants to arrive from the refugee camps suffered the indignity of a kind of conversion ceremony, a legacy of Rabbi Herzog's ruling, and a practice that would continue into the mid-1980s.[131] In 1985, Ovadia Yosef, no longer chief rabbi, would harshly oppose Herzog's earlier conclusions: "I was wondrously amazed to see how the words of the world's *geonim*" – the plural of Gaon – "who established with certainty that they are descended from the Tribe of Dan, would be superseded by the words of researchers who cast doubt on their Judaism. Who should supersede whom?!"[132] However, "he did not do so as Chief Rabbi in 1973, nor did his successors to that office."[133] In the ensuing years, the Rabbinate would be as culpable in the mistreatment of the Beta Israel as any group.[134]

Not surprisingly, the last forty years of the Beta Israel's experience in Israel have been marked by controversy after controversy, and protest after protest. In the late 1980s, there was a major uproar over Beta Israel marriage and divorce. Traditional Beta Israel forms of both were performed by the Beta Israel's traditional religious leaders, the *Qessotch*, or *Qessim* in Hebrew. Israel's rabbinic authorities doubted the validity of either – which, in fact, the Radbaz had done long before.[135] As a result,

---

[130] Rather, while the 1973 and 1975 rulings had "recognized the 'Jewishness' of the Ethiopians as a community" the "personal status" of individual Beta Israel remained, and to some degree remains, in question, legally speaking (Kaplan and Salamon, "Ethiopian Jews in Israel," 131).

[131] It "included ritual immersion, the acceptance of rabbinic law and (in the case of men) symbolic recircumcision" (Kaplan and Salamon, "Ethiopian Jews in Israel," 131). "The last of these demands was dropped in late 1984" (ibid.). As Seeman notes "many Ethiopian Jews balked at what seemed a denial of the Jewish identity they had fought so hard to preserve, leading to a painful public protest against the Chief Rabbinate's position in 1985" (Seeman, "Ethnographers, Rabbis and Jewish Epistemology," 13–14).

[132] Seeman, "Ethnographers, Rabbis and Jewish Epistemology," 20. This is from a 1985 letter he wrote.

[133] Ibid., 13–14.

[134] "The ruling by Chief Rabbi Ovadia Yosef recognizing the Beta Israel as authentic Jews therefore did not merely open the doors of immigration. It also gave the chief rabbinate religious jurisdiction over the immigrants, planting the seed for future jurisdictional struggles. And indeed, despite having affirmed the Ethiopians' communal status as Jews, the rabbinate expressed reservations about the personal status of individuals" (Salamon, "Ethiopian Jewry and New Self-Concepts," 233).

[135] The Radbaz had actually made two rulings about the Beta Israel, both through the medium of the Cairo slave mart. In the second case, an Egyptian man had married an enslaved Beta Israel he had purchased in Cairo and had a son with her. The woman had

they called into question the legitimacy of many Beta Israel born from such marriages, and especially after remarriages that could not be considered remarriages because the divorces preceding them had not been halakhically legitimate.[136] Mass protests followed.

In the end, the solution was broadly typical of how Israel's religious courts have dealt with the differences between Beta Israel practices and normative Jewish ones.[137] The rabbis did not change their minds or issue a new ruling, but they found a kind of loophole. They made Beta Israel marriage the province of a rabbi, David Chelouche, the Sephardi Chief Rabbi of Netanya, who, on his personal authority, stated that Ethiopian Jewry did not require any conversion rituals to be halakhically viable.[138] In short, the ruling stood, but it no longer had to be applied. Since then, additional marriage registry offices have been opened for the Beta Israel to use.[139]

Shortly thereafter, an even greater protest erupted. In 1996, it was discovered that Israel's blood banks had been routinely dumping all Ethiopian blood for years. While the blood banks claimed this had been

been married before, in Ethiopia, though her husband had died, and in Jewish law, the death of a husband must be legally established for that marriage to be considered over, and this could not be done. As a result, the man worried that their son would be considered illegitimate. The Radbaz acknowledged that divorce could not be proven, but he thought that was immaterial. Since, in his opinion, the woman's previous marriage could not have been performed according to Jewish law in the first place, it was like it never happened – thus, no official divorce was necessary (Seeman, "Ethnographers, Rabbis and Jewish Epistemology," 15).

[136] "Although the Israeli chief rabbis had recognized the 'Jewishness' of the Ethiopians as a community, they continued to raise doubts regarding the personal status of individuals. Since the Ethiopians had not been familiar with *halakha* their religious leaders (*qessotch*) could not have performed valid divorces and conversions. Thus, virtually the entire community was suspect of being either (in the former case) illegitimate or (in the latter case) not fully Jewish" (Kaplan and Salamon, "Ethiopian Jews in Israel," 131).

[137] Initially the rabbis "ruled that the Beta Israel are Jewish by descent, as established by the Radbaz, but still require immersion ... prior to marriage because of a concern that improper conversions may have taken place in Ethiopia ... After the strike of 1985, the Rabbinate relented to the extent that 'renewal of the covenant would be required only for those individual Ethiopian Jews whose genealogy was called into question by testimony before a *bet din*, much as in the case for other immigrant groups ... This compromise solution, however, was never fully implemented" (Seeman, "Ethnographers, Rabbis and Jewish Epistemology," 27).

[138] Kaplan and Salamon, "Ethiopian Jews in Israel," 131.

[139] The final agreement "left final determination of the Jewishness of Ethiopian couples seeking marriage in the hands of a special rabbinic court which would be made up of rabbis who consider the whole Ethiopian community to be Jewish and in no need of symbolic conversions" (Wagaw, *For Our Soul*, 118).

done out of an abundance of caution regarding HIV/AIDS, in fact all donated Ethiopian blood had been disposed of, even the donations that had tested negative.[140] The protests around the "Blood Scandal" dwarfed any that had come before, ultimately including thousands of Ethiopian Israelis, allies, and civil authorities.[141] Indeed, the scandal became the focal point for Beta Israel frustrations more generally, as well it might. As one protestor put it: "We fight and die in the army, go on to study, but that is not enough. It's inconceivable that a person comes to donate blood and is tricked into thinking that he is saving another life ... and yet the minute he turns his head, they toss his blood in the garbage."[142]

Another Beta Israel, quoted in the *New York Times*, spoke of personal experiences: "I did two years in the army to become a citizen of Israel like everybody else ... When they tell me that since 1984 they've been spilling the blood, it feels like the army means nothing, that I'll never be part of Israel, because my color is black and my blood is contaminated. It really hurts."[143] A third notes: "It was after the Blood Scandal that Ethiopians had to wonder what their place was in Israeli society. As Ethiopians, you feel that you have to be the best to get the same treatment as a normal citizen."[144] For this and other reasons, many Beta Israel still wonder, as in the words of one newspaper headline, "When Will You Finally Allow Us to Feel That We Have Really Come Home?"[145]

Of course, the disenfranchisement – and the disenchantment – of the Beta Israel has many causes. Some issues are not specific to the Beta Israel, but the common lot of migrant and refugee communities around the world. For the most part, the Beta Israel arrived in Israel with little, and even a fairly robust social safety net has not consistently provided all they need to survive and thrive.[146] Older members of the community in

---

[140] Salamon, "Blackness in Transition," 17. For a discussion of the role of blood in marking identity, see Weil, "Religion, Blood and the Equality of Rights."

[141] Seeman, "One People, One Blood"; Seeman, *One People, One Blood*.

[142] Yasur-Beit Or, "Ethiopians Outraged Over Blood Disposal," 72.

[143] Schemann, "Ethiopians in Israel Riot Over Dumping of Donated Blood."

[144] Lyons, *The Ethiopian Jews of Israel*, 104.

[145] Katriel, "The Rhetoric of Rescue," 201.

[146] The Beta Israel tend to live in "distressed neighborhoods in concentrated Ethiopian pockets of Israeli society" (Zegeye, *The Impossible Return*, 241). Their children face issues of "juvenile delinquency, drug use, and school drop-outs," and "alcoholism is a serious issue among both young and old" (ibid., 242). See also Berhanu, "Normality, Deviance, Identity, Cultural Tracking and School Achievement." For a study of the Beta Israel and alcoholism, see Weiss, "Alcohol Use and Abuse." Suicide has sometimes been an issue as well (Arieli, Gilat, and Aycheh, "Suicide Among Ethiopian Jews"). As of 2008, the "vast majority of the Ethiopian community [was] living below the

particular have had a difficult time adapting to Israeli life, and often in a way that has produced significant divides between generations.[147] In some cases, with Ethiopian Jews whose children are born in Israel, there is even a language barrier between parent and child.[148]

Of course, racial discrimination has a significant role to play as well.[149] Especially in the context of the rising Black Lives Matter movement, there is something to be said, globally, about the difference between supposed equality under the law and the black experience in predominantly white communities.[150] Interestingly enough, some have connected Israel's legal recognition of the Beta Israel, after so long, to a desire to answer a

poverty line" while "their educational achievements are the lowest in Israel" (Weiss, "Alcohol Use and Abuse," 28). See also Benita and Noam, "The Absorption of Ethiopian Immigrants"; Chaklay, "Processes of Identity Consolidation among Ethiopian Adolescents"; Halper, "The Absorption of Ethiopian Immigrants"; Maart, "Crisis in Parent Authority among Ethiopian Newcomers."

[147] Eva Leitman and Elisabeth Weinbaum's study of Israeli women revealed that "younger informants ... often expressed feelings of satisfaction with life in Israel and became within a relatively short time what our Israeli informants called 'just another Israeli neighbour'" while "some of our older informants ... often revealed that 'life in Israel is harder than it was in Ethiopia'" (Leitman and Weinbaum, "Israeli Women of Ethiopian Descent," 129). Zegeye refers to the challenges faced by Beta Israel children who, in addition to contending with their own issues, had now to take over "some of the responsibilities and functions ... for their parents, who were often under-educated, poverty-stricken and slower to adapt to the more Westernised Israeli society than their children" (Zegeye, *The Impossible Return*, 195). Of course, this should not be considered a universal experience in either respect.

[148] "Family life used to be everything in our tradition. But here, it's the kids who are bringing the parents everywhere, to the doctors or translating for them wherever they go. They are very dependent on their kids. Instead of having someone who can show them the way, the children have become those who are showing and teaching ... People who came at my age, who remember Ethiopia, understand the adults. We do a lot better than the kids who were born here" (Lyons, *The Ethiopian Jews of Israel*, 86). "For the vast majority of Beta Israel, the departure from Ethiopia ... resulted in a traumatic separation of family members, loss of several thousand lives, and other experiences that will scar their memories for a long time to come" (Wagaw, *For Our Soul*, 216).

[149] On issues of race and skin color, see, among others, Chehata, "Israel: Promised Land for Jews"; Zegeye, *The Impossible Return*, 193–95; Shabtay, "Living with Threatening Identity"; Ojanuga, "The Ethiopian Jewish Experience as Blacks in Israel"; Ben-David and Ben-Ari, "The Experience of Being Different"; Mizrachi and Herzog, "Participatory Destigmatization Strategies"; Ben-Eliezer, "Multicultural Society and Everyday Cultural Racism." As one member of the community put it, "there I was a Jew; here I am black" (Salamon, "Ethiopian Jewry and New Self-Concepts," 237).

[150] In fact, the Beta Israel also protest what they see as consistently discriminatory treatment by members of Israel's police force (Halbfinger and Kershner, "After a Police Shooting").

1975 United Nations resolution equating Zionism with racism.[151] One scholar further suggests that American support for the Beta Israel, including material aid in the efforts to relocate them to Israel, emerged as a way of "making amends ... in particular for their role in preventing immigration by European Jews fleeing Hitler in the years before World War II," while another argues that "American Jews prided themselves on their support of their dark-skinned brethren, using it to signal their liberalism vis-à-vis the American local ethnic landscape."[152] That these kinds of gestures have not corresponded to markedly improved treatment is another familiar experience of the racial landscape in many places.

Indeed, it is difficult to observe the indignities the Beta Israel have endured in Israel and not suspect that skin color plays a prominent role, especially in a place that, from the beginning, has so aggressively sought the "ingathering" of immigrants from all over the world, often enough with their own unique customs, and without similar incidents. In the same vein, the challenges of the Beta Israel, as an African community in Israel, are reflected in the case of the Falash Mura, members of the Beta Israel community who converted to Christianity, in some cases under duress and social pressure. Many members of this community did make the move to Addis Ababa in the early 1990s with other Beta Israel to await what would turn out to be Operation Solomon, but they were excluded from the airlift.[153] Since then, the right of this community to emigrate has been a source of constant controversy, occasionally allowed in small numbers, then disallowed.

In fact, as recently as October 2020, an article appeared in the *New York Times* describing the anger that erupted when a November 2015 promise to bring the remaining ten thousand Falash Mura in Ethiopia to Israel "by the end of 2020" resulted instead in the arrival of just two thousand members of the community, supposedly "due to budget constraints," prompting impassioned outcries.[154] Even more recently, the "Abayudaya" community of Uganda, a Jewish community practicing in

[151] Spector, *Operation Solomon*, 11. Hagar Salamon adds, "the Beta Israel are the focus of attempts by Jews outside Israel, particularly those in the United States, to disprove allegations that Judaism is racist" (Salamon, "Ethiopian Jewry and New Self-Concepts," 234).

[152] Salamon, "Ethiopian Jewry and New Self-Concepts," 234; Katriel, "The Rhetoric of Rescue," 105.

[153] Kaplan, "Genealogies and Gene-Ideologies," 450–51; Spector, *Operation Solomon*, 89, 169–70.

[154] Rasgon, "Israel Accepts Ethiopians."

the Conservative tradition – which was officially recognized by the Jewish Agency in 2016 – has been refused access to the Right of Return by the Interior Ministry, and on February 4, 2021, by Israel's Supreme Court.[155] The case before the court was a complex one concerning not the community as a whole, but the specific rights of one Yosef Kibita to make Aliyah. It centers in part on the fact that Kibita's official conversion to Judaism in 2008 pre-dates the Jewish Agency's recognition.[156] But, as Nicole Maor observes, "the elephant in the room is that the Interior Ministry might have taken this position because of the fact that the Abayudaya community is a congregation in Africa."[157] Certainly, it is difficult not to see a pattern in the treatment of these various African communities by the state.

For our purposes, the main point is that the capacities of the twelve tribes tradition for constructing and accommodating Israelite identities – and especially its profound limitations in this direction – are not the best or even the most revealing way to think about the problems the Beta Israel have encountered in their new homeland. An account of what this tradition has done, has not done, can do, and cannot do for the community should not trivialize the other causes of their struggles in Israel. At the same time, the limits of the tradition as a tool for ethnogenesis are an underappreciated feature of the Beta Israel's experience with Israeli outreach, recognition, and the Right of Return, and in ways that solidify the basic conclusions of this book.

First of all, there is no denying that the identification of the Beta Israel with the tribe of Dan, and with it an accommodation into the Jewish vision of twelve tribe Israel, achieved some truly remarkable things for the community. It is because one account of "becoming Israel" was exchanged for another that an originally Ethiopian people, whose internal vision of themselves as Israel was home-grown, gained Israeli recognition, and it is what fueled truly massive efforts to bring them "home." It is what cleared at least the legal path towards integrating this community

---

[155] *The Times of Israel Liveblog*, "Interior Ministry Says It Doesn't Recognize Uganda's Abayudaya Community as Jews"; Zitser, "A Unique African Community"; Sacks, "Shall the State of Israel Recognize the Abayudaya Jews of Uganda?"

[156] "The State claimed that in order for conversions to be recognized by the State for purposes of Aliyah, under the Law of Return, they must be recognized by one of the major denominations and have taken place in a recognized Jewish community" (Sacks, "Shall the State of Israel Recognize the Abayudaya Jews of Uganda?"). As this author observes, an even larger issue is at stake: whether any conversions in any "emerging community" could be considered legitimate.

[157] Zitser, "A Unique African Community."

into Israeli society, and it played a big role in inspiring all the efforts to do right by them, however many issues remain. Without a doubt, seldom has any construction of Israelite identity enjoyed such recognition from another, and likely never has that recognition had such dramatic practical results.

At the same time, what the Danite legend, and by extension the twelve tribes tradition, did not do – and likely cannot do – is provide the Beta Israel with the actual acceptance, in Israel, that should have been theirs by right, and that was implied by these efforts. Again, there are many reasons for this, but at least one is inherent to the way the twelve tribes tradition constructs visions of Israel, and facilitates "becoming Israel." And these reasons bring together many threads of the study so far. Basically, the story of the Beta Israel expresses the tension that, on some level, has always existed between the twin premises embodied by twelve tribes tradition. The first is that there are many claimants to Israel, a claim built into the nature of the twelve tribes structure, which provided the rhetorical basis for the interaction between the Beta Israel and the normative Jewish world in the first place. The second, however, is that there is only one Israel, embracing them all.

Or, we might put it this way. Every construction of Israelite identity purports to be a vision of the universal Israel, and every vision of Israel, from the biblical vision on down, is actually particular – a particular product of a time, a place, and a history. When Israels meet, they must grapple with the particulars of the other, in a way that defends the right of their own construction to represent Israel in the present. In other words, while the first premise, that all Israels are part of the same universal Israel, has served all around the world, for several millennia, to allow many groups to claim to be Israel, full stop, the second premise has always done the work of explaining how each of these many groups is the *true* Israel, in comparison to others – what Israel was always intended to be. Yet Israel cannot be both many and one, and the interaction between Israel and Israel in this chapter reveals the tension that, for this reason, has always attended the act of "becoming Israel" plainly.

Ultimately, the profound gap between what the twelve tribes tradition appears to do and what it actually does has been visited on the Beta Israel in Israel in numerous ways. And that distinction is not only what connects the study in this chapter most powerfully to our larger set of discussions, but, where revealing the full shape of "becoming Israel" is concerned, is, to paraphrase Leonard Cohen, the crack that lets the light in.

5.6 CONCLUSION

In the story of the people who "became Israel" twice, the first thing we can notice is that, in Ethiopia, and for many centuries, the twelve tribes of Israel tradition did what it is best able to do. There *were* two different Israels, rather than one, in Ethiopia: one Jewish and one Christian. But that did not matter. The twelve tribes tradition allowed these two different Israelite-identifying peoples to explain themselves to *themselves*, and, secondarily, to each other – at least, it placed them in relation to each other. The two never had to become one, and so there was no problem. The premise of the twelve tribes tradition – the premise that allows it to serve as a means of claiming an Israelite identity in the first place – is that many different groups are all collectively Israel. So it was, in Ethiopia.

In Israel today, however, the twelve tribes tradition is used less to explain the differences between two constructions of Israel than why the two are actually one. Thus, it has been used to do what it really *cannot* do. Again, the premise – what in other chapters I call the "primordialist" premise – suggests that this explanation should be an easy one to make, and to live with. The idea that Dan and Judah are both Israel, despite being Dan and Judah, is what the tradition is all about. And in a way, this premise achieved a stunning success, where the Beta Israel are concerned. It is almost impossible to imagine any other Lost Tribe group in the world receiving the level of recognition from the State of Israel that the Beta Israel have.

Yet what the Beta Israel have enjoyed in legal and rhetorical terms has eluded them socially, politically, and practically, in large part because the form of Israelite identity they possess is actually in tension with the form of Israelite identity current in the Jewish world before their entrance into it. If Dan and Judah are different enough, they cannot both be Israel, but will be Dan and Judah instead – and that, more or less, is what has happened. The issue is not that one of these two Israels is real, and one is fake, nor that one set of traditions is true and the other false. It is that the Jewish explanation that the Beta Israel are a flawed Jewish Israel in need of correction, rather than a perfectly explicable Ethiopian Israel, is obviously prejudicial to the Beta Israel. And in Israel, where the Jewish "explainers" hold the reins of state and the power to grant and deny citizenship, that prejudice is expressed in the relationship between the state and the Beta Israel.

Of course, part of what makes the Beta Israel so interesting is that the incompatibility between the home-grown Beta Israel construction of

Israelite identity and that of the Jewish world by no means had to survive, and in many ways, it has not survived. Today's Beta Israel are Israeli, through and through. Many are born and raised in Israel, knowing no other life. Many wish only to be recognized as one of the Jewish peoples of the world, and to live Jewish lives.[158] In other words, Beta Israel identity is no less mutable than any other, and it has changed in response to circumstances. Now, they are in truth what Jewish authorities long believed them to be – a part of the normative Jewish world.

The real issues that give shape to discrimination against the Beta Israel into the present, then, have little to do with the construction of Beta Israel identity today, and much to do instead with the circumstances in which these two Israels encountered each other, and especially the inability of the twelve tribes tradition to serve as a *genuine* explanation of differences, as I have suggested throughout. Again, the tradition is most useful precisely when it is explaining how some Israel or another came to be different, either from some specific other Israel or simply from expectations. But it cannot explain why two Israels are different from each other in a way that preserves the essential unity of Israelite identity and preserves the equal right of both to represent Israel, even when precisely this is desired.

Indeed, what distinguishes the case of the Beta Israel from all the others discussed in this book is precisely that the modern desire of the Beta Israel, and the Jewish construction of Israel, to be recognized as part of the same Israelite people seems perfectly genuine on both sides. We might, by contrast, think of their experiences through the lens of our prior discussion of Jews and Samaritans, who are, after all, another "Israelite" group living in Israel today, with a fluctuating and often marginal status. As I argued in Chapter 2, scholars fundamentally misread the traditions that assert a shared origin for these two groups when they do not see that these are intended to serve as part of the competition between these two Israels. That competition is unavoidable, given fundamental incompatibilities. It cannot be the case at once that the *Torah* and the Samaritan Pentateuch are both the true revelation YHWH gave to Moses, or that both the Temple Mount and Mt. Gerizim are YHWH's only holy mountain.

---

[158] Although today, as Abbink observes, "a process of 'recasting' or reformulating the history of their community in Ethiopia has been going on ... In view of their somewhat precarious Jewish identity in the past (in the eyes of the above-mentioned religious authorities in Israel), an effort is made to retrospectively validate the Falasha traditions and religious ways, as well as their perseverance in the face of Christian assimilatory pressure of the past centuries" (Abbink, "The Enigma of Beta Esra'el Ethnogenesis," 398).

Thus, narratives that describe both groups as Israelites alike generally account for how one ended up with the right traditions and the other the wrong ones. In Ethiopia, the twelve tribes tradition does the same between the Beta Israel and the Solomonic House of Israel, and does it quite successfully.

In Israel today, however, no competition is intended between Jewish and Beta Israel "Israels" – and again, they no longer are even two different Israels, especially as far as the self-understanding of each is concerned. More than that, there is every indication that most everyone involved in the century of Jewish outreach to the Beta Israel was quite sincere in their intentions. Nor does the Danite legend, in and of itself, produce any incompatibilities. There is nothing incompatible in the idea that there are both a Jewish diaspora throughout the world *and* Danites in Africa – that there are tribes and Lost Tribes.

When, however, these two heirs of Israel – these two brothers, in the words of the introduction – encountered each other in Ethiopia between the late nineteenth century and the mid-twentieth, they were fundamentally different from each other. It had never been otherwise. They were the product of different histories, different experiences. They had been raised apart; they were at home in different worlds. At that point, these differences had to be explained somehow, and they were explained, as they are always explained, not in a way that put them on equal terms, but one that preserved the right of the one making the explanations to continue to regard themselves as the true heirs of Israel today. This state of affairs produced the explanation based on a deficiency on the part of the Beta Israel – the "pre-Talmudic" argument.[159] In this case, these explanations were apparently proffered in good faith, and followed up by a genuine effort to, from the Jewish perspective, correct the deficiency. But since the deficiency-based explanation is a discriminatory idea, discrimination has been the result.

---

[159] As I observed in a previous chapter, it would be technically possible for the descendants of the original members of a long-lost primordialist institution to have experienced different histories and emerged from them as different but equally valid heirs of that institution – and from time to time, arguments in this vein have even been made. During the protest surrounding Beta Israel marriage, the Israeli statesman Abba Eban pointed out that the Chief Rabbinate itself is of comparatively recent vintage, from the time of the Turkish administration of the region. Why, he wondered, should they exercise "coercive, executive power" over a people who claimed a much longer heritage? (Wagaw, *For Our Soul*, 117). See also Ben-Zvi, *The Book of the Samaritans*, 365; Schreiber, *The Comfort of Kin*, 57.

This is the sense in which the twelve tribes tradition cannot really do the main thing it has been *used* to do. It cannot really explain why there are so many different heirs to Israel in the world because there are not. There are, instead, a wide variety of different Israels – fundamentally different Israels, constructed differently from each other. The twelve tribes tradition is what provides the pretense that these many Israels are one Israel and is what has been consistently used to do just that for thousands of years. It even works, so long as the various Israels of the world remain apart, and so long as they need nothing from each other. But where the pretense falters – where the actual task of aggregating different Israels begins – analysis rushes in. And in this case, where no effort was spared to make two Israels one, the continuing ramifications of having once been two tell an eloquent story.

Thus, in many respects, the story of the Beta Israel allows us to close the circle of our discussion. The Beta Israel are, officially now, a Lost Tribe of Israel, but the Lost Tribes themselves are not a historical reality – they are a product of what makes the Bible a particular, rather than universal, vision of Israel. Those who have read Chapter 2 will know that 2 Kings 17, the biblical account of the conquest of Israel, claimed, falsely, that all the tribes of Israel were taken into Assyrian exile because its authors wanted to be able to claim the heritage of Israel entirely for themselves. Thus, the charter myth of Lost Tribe traditions *lost them on purpose* to disenfranchise the northern Israelites from the biblical vision of Israelite identity. It is little wonder that contemporary Jewish authorities have encountered issues in using, as a kind of field guide to "ingathering," a text by authors who actively did not want any other "Israels" to be found – even those that were never really lost.

And indeed, other parts of the Bible show the same kind of effort to preserve the concept of an overarching "all Israel" identity while winnowing down who it refers to, including among the Judahites themselves. Biblical accounts of the Babylonian Exile and the Persian period Return purposefully ignore all the Judahites who were not exiled and all those who did not return, in the same way that 2 Kings 17 ignores all the northern Israelites who remained in Israel after the Assyrians came through. The end result of these rhetorical narrowings is exactly what is intended: that, by the end of the biblical accounts of history, the biblical definition of Israel applies only to a circumscribed group of elite, Persian period returnees and the descendants of returnees.

It is in precisely the same vein that neither the Jewish nor Samaritan versions of who Israel is can be regarded simply *as* Israel, for all their historical (and biological) continuity with the earliest entity called by that name. Both are instead particular, post-biblical constructions of Israel fitted to the circumstances in which they were used. In the ways each group lays claim to an Israelite identity, and reshapes it for their purposes, the particular – and therefore explicitly non-universal – character of each vision of Israel is revealed. Thus, as we saw in Chapter 2, both of these Israels are able to acknowledge that the other might also descend from the original Israel, but only in the context of narratives that actually explain why they are inferior heirs nonetheless. In the Beta Israel's case, equality, rather than inferiority, is intended by the traditions that make these two Israels one. Since, however, the animating premise of "all Israel" is that all Israel is essentially indivisible, divisions can only be countenanced in ways that also explain why they exist. And because each Israel understands itself not as an heir to Israel, or one of many Israels, but *Israel*, it is not possible to explain the difference between one and another without explaining why the other got it wrong.

In fact, even if there really was a twelve tribes of Israel, once upon a time – even if this institution somehow survived intact all the developments of the first millennium BCE, even if some or all of its heirs genuinely preserved a sense of their own Israelite identity into the present – we would still find that all of these heirs of Israel were different from each other today. As I have discussed throughout this book, only outdated, primordialist models of ethnicity conflate origins with identity. In reality, all identities are reshaped by experiences over time. And since the authenticity and authority of any past-oriented vision of identity derives from its perceived fidelity to the past, "real" Israels – which is to say Israels with an empirical historical connection to ancient Israel – would have as many issues with each other as the Beta Israel and Jewish visions of Israel did at the time of their first encounter. The differences between them would raise the same sharp questions about which is really Israel – the answers would, of necessity, be no less discriminatory.

Here, then, is the final secret of the twelve tribes tradition. Every vision of Israelite identity is incompatible with every other – even when, as in this chapter, neither "Israel" really desires it – because every vision of Israel is unique. There are no tribes or Lost Tribes, which is to say, Israels that, through one or the other mechanism, are collectively the heirs of a supposedly universal, eternal, and unalterable Israelite identity formed long ago in earliest Israel. There are only different visions of Israel, developed in different periods, in different places, and for different reasons, but each a particular product *of* those periods, places, and reasons. All of them assert membership in this universal Israel, but in a way that expresses the unique situatedness of each. All of them, all alike, from biblical Israel to the present, take a prior generation's traditions about Israel and fashion them for their context. All of them refashion them over time, as they move through the course of their separate histories. Each is a unique construction of Israelite identity, built through those traditions in response to contexts. And in this, at least, all of them are alike.

The *particular* – and constantly renegotiated – character of every vision of twelve tribe Israel dooms what I called in the first chapter the "preservative" method of interrogating the world's "Israels." This is the method that treats accounts of Israel simply as descriptions of Israel, rather than dynamic efforts to redescribe Israelite identity in useful ways, and asks only whether those descriptions are true. Certainly, some Israelite histories have more historical truths in them than others. In every one, however, the twelve tribes tradition functions as a means of laying claim to an Israelite identity that did not have to be claimed, in a particular way that was not the only way it could have been claimed or shaped. As a result, Israelite histories are something more than description – something we cannot understand or appreciate if we focus simply on what traditions about Israel get right. We have to ask what gives each vision of Israel its shape, and why, even if it is based on historical truths.

Nevertheless, those who wish to investigate constructions of Israel, from the biblical to the Beta Israel, still have difficult choices to make. They can still choose what I call the "cultural invention" method, an approach that begins by acknowledging the inventive – or reinventive – character of every Israelite history. We might call it the truth or fiction method. Historians of a certain bent can focus on the fact that the Beta Israel are not, apparently, descended from an early Israelite Ethiopian settlement, or that none of the biblical, Jewish, or Samaritan visions of Israel are *precisely* early Israelite in origin, having developed either after or outside of early Israel, or both. They can study these constructions of Israel as inventions, where their invented character is a major object of interest – asking where, and when, and why.

I do not think these investigations are particularly fruitful in and of themselves, any more than I think it is fruitful to simply weigh in on whether an account of the Israelite past is true or false. But recognizing the post-Israel origins of the constructions that survive can be the *beginning* of fruitful inquiries. Today, for example, many scholars have begun to recognize that if biblical Israel is not precisely ancient Israel, then there are ways in which ancient Israel itself remains undiscovered. This, of course, is a surprising recognition: what place, ancient or modern, could feel more familiar than "ancient Israel" itself? But the more Judahite we suspect the Bible to be, the more unanswered questions about Israel *qua* Israel we will discover, and these questions deserve answers. At least, while there is room to rethink the ongoing scholarly preoccupation with Israel *over* Judah as a genuine rule, I think there is value to these efforts to pursue neglected historical truths as well.

Still, in this book, I have attempted to chart a third path – the path of redescription. By breaking down the barriers that have historically separated the study of traditions about Israel in different places, I have attempted to reveal how a single tradition, the twelve tribes tradition, has served continuously as a means of laying claim to an Israelite identity and as a source for the ongoing redescription of Israelite identities, internally and externally, across centuries and continents. I have attempted to analyze each construction of Israelite identity I presented, from the biblical period to the present, as conceptually identical efforts to redescribe Israelite identity. I asked what they do, how they do it, and what lessons we can draw for the rest. I have tried to narrow the gap, between how we perceive the adaptation of a given version of Israelite identity over time in one place and the invention of Israelite identities in multiple places, by pointing out that both species of activity exploit the same structural features of the twelve tribes tradition. I have tried to tell the history of "becoming Israel" as a continuous story, so that any given instance of redescribing Israel through the twelve tribes tradition can reveal to us universal lessons about the methods, the purposes, and the ramifications of "becoming Israel" – again and again and again.

Most of all, I have taken the fact that every vision of Israel is a particular product of a time, place, and history as a starting point for studying those times, places, and histories. I have used the way visions of Israel are marked and shaped, both by the circumstances of their birth and the accidents and incidents of their historical experience, to reconstruct a map of that historical experience. The way we might say that two directors reveal themselves by what they do with Hamlet, or two great chefs by how they make an omelet, that is how every Israel reveals itself by what it does with the traditions and legacy of Israel. In the making of many Israels, much is revealed – especially the makers themselves, and the worlds they called their own.

Conclusion

The Making of Many Israels

If you were lucky enough to be at Waterfront Park in St. Petersburg, Florida on March 26, 1931, you might have been treated to a most unusual spectacle: Babe Ruth putting on a big, fake beard before going out to play a game of baseball.[1] The Babe's opponent that day was also in the category of most unusual: a barnstorming outfit from the "House of David," or more properly, the "Israelite House of David." The House of David was famous for their stunts, like riding donkeys in the outfield, and yes, their prodigious side-whiskers.[2] They were also known for their genius for promotion; they were perhaps the only white outfit in those days that regularly played against the great Negro League teams of their era. They knew the power of celebrity. Satchel Paige pitched for them, and so did Jackie Mitchell, the famous woman who once struck out Babe Ruth and Lou Gehrig in an exhibition game. So did Babe Didrikson

[1] In this case, this is the date that seems most likely to me. There is a video clip which shows Babe wearing the beard, and even some highlights, purportedly from 1933. However, a Getty image of the bearded Babe is dated to March 28, 1931, and I was able to discover a ticket stub from the 1931 game, with the date and location mentioned above, on the auction site "Worthpoint" ("1933 Baseball"; *Getty Images*, "Babe Ruth Posing in Fake Beard"; *Worthpoint*, "1931 Babe Ruth"). For a general resource on the House of David baseball team, see Hawkins and Bertolino, *The House of David Baseball Team.*

[2] The "Israelite House of David" is in many ways significantly under researched. At the moment, the best resources for the House of David besides the book cited in the previous footnote seem to exist in online databases and periodicals. The following are especially good resources: Goodwillie, "Baseball, Beards, Bands, and the Babes"; Gates, "Giving the House a Home"; *Baseball Reference*, "House of David – BR Bullpen"; *Mary's City of David*, "'Jesus' Boys' Israelite House of David Baseball." For the games the House of David supposedly played on the backs of donkeys, including pictorial evidence, see Hawkins and Bertolino, *The House of David Baseball Team*, 95.

Zaharias, the most famous female athlete of her day, and so did some hall-of-famers, including Chief Bender and Grover Cleveland Alexander.[3] In fact, Alexander was the manager of a House of David team for a time.[4]

What was, and is, less known about the House of David is who they were, or perhaps, how they got their start – to some extent as the fundraising arm for the Israelite House of David community headquartered in Bentonville, Michigan. The Israelite House of David had among its major goals the "ingathering" and "restoration" of the twelve tribes of Israel, and specifically the 144,000 Israelites – 12,000 from each tribe – who are supposed to be saved at the end of days, according to the seventh chapter of the Book of Revelation.[5] In short, they were another "Israel," and another group seeking for Israel. And might there have been, among their fans that day, a British Israelite or two on holiday?[6] Might there have been a near ancestor of a future member of the Rastafarian movement, whose subdivisions include the "Twelve Tribes of Israel" "mansion"?[7] Or perhaps an ancestor of the "Twelve Tribes" community, "an international millenarian organization founded in Chattanooga, Tennessee in 1973?"[8] Perhaps there was.

In the twenty-first century, there are Israels around every corner. Many more showed up in my research for this book than in the book itself, and many more likely did not show up even there. I could not be comprehensive – I do not think anyone could – so I did not try to be. I did not try to tell the story of Israel around the world, except insofar as I discussed

---

[3] See Hawkins and Bertolino, *The House of David Baseball Team*, 41, 43; *Baseball Reference*, "Chief Bender."

[4] Hawkins and Bertolino, *The House of David Baseball Team*, 40.

[5] The House of David was founded by Benjamin and Mary Purnell. The Purnells understood themselves to be the seventh in a series of seven messengers whose task was to bring about this restoration and ingathering. The contemporary community is a divided one, including the Israelite House of David and Mary's City of David. After Benjamin Purnell's death – on the heels of a series of accusations of sexual misconduct with young women – Mary Purnell founded the latter in 1930. Information about the first community can be found at *Israelite House of David Benton Harbor Michigan*, "Israelite House of David Reading Materials." This is where my description of "ingathering" and "restoration" comes from. Mary's City of David maintains a website at www.maryscityofdavid.org/ (*Mary's City of David*, "Israelite House of David Church of the New Eve, Body of Christ"). The House of David "Little Book" and "The Key of the House of David" can be read in their entirety here (*Israelite House of David Benton Harbor, Michigan*, "Israelite House of David – Read It On-Line: 'The Little Book,'"; *Israelite House of David Benton Harbor, Michigan*, "Israelite House of David – Read It On-Line: 'The Key of the House of David'").

[6] For a charter text, see Wilson, *Our Israelitish Origin*.

[7] See especially Bedasse, "Rasta Evolution"; Barnett, "The Many Faces of Rasta."

[8] Palmer, "The Twelve Tribes," 59.

general developments in the global understanding of what Israel has meant, represented, or entitled different "Israelites" to over time. Instead, I have tried to tell the story of "becoming Israel" – the story of how peoples have adopted the mantle of Israel, exploiting the essential features of the twelve tribes tradition; how visions of Israel have been adapted to the contexts which gave them birth and to the histories they experienced; and why "becoming Israel" has been such a popular practice for so long. I have tried to tell this story, for the first time in a continuous fashion, linking nearly three thousand years of efforts to claim, describe, and adapt Israelite identities together.

Towards that end, I started with a simple insight: even in the Hebrew Bible itself, the twelve tribes tradition is more than a mere snapshot of a genuine tribal institution in its earliest days, if there even was such an institution – and more than the product of a singular Judahite effort to claim to *be* Israel in later periods, if there was not. The twenty-six different, largely late and Judahite visions of tribal Israel in biblical literature are, for the most part, engaged in using this tradition the same way it is used elsewhere: as a dynamic tool for the constant redescription of Israelite identity. And the dynamism of the tradition is the dynamism of "segmented" identity structures the world over: the ability to reorganize the contents of an identity concept and to reinterpret what those reorganizations can mean.[9] So, from the very beginning, authors were using the flexibility of the twelve tribes tradition, and the characteristics of this segmented structure, to imbue visions of Israel with meaning, and with various kinds of claims.

In the second chapter, I introduced a second basic principle of "becoming Israel." Through a case study of the Samaritans and their ancestors I showed that the twelve tribes tradition is not only a flexible fabric for the ongoing reconstruction of Israelite identities but one that can be used by multiple claimants to Israel at once. In fact, this was always the case; in the Bible, this principle explains how both Judahites and Israelites are Israelite, and in Samaritan contexts, Jews and Samaritans. Where the Samaritans themselves are concerned, I showed how its segmented structure allowed the twelve tribes tradition to serve as a medium for competitions between Israel's two oldest heirs. But I also demonstrated how the

---

[9] So, for example, in Genesis 49's "Blessing of Jacob," Reuben, Simeon, and Levi are all superior to Judah in the birth order, but each is disqualified from pre-eminence for various reasons – because Reuben slept with Jacob's maid (49:4), because Simeon and Levi are violent (49:5) and so on. The raw details are interpreted by the story.

features of the tradition that allow it to serve as such a medium could be used simply to allow any claimant to Israel to explain its own unique features. In other words, I described how the ability of one "Israel" to account for its cultural superiority, and the origins of its particular traditions and practices, against another Israel could be used just as easily to explain that superiority, and those origins, in isolation, anywhere in the world.

We might think of the rest of the chapters in this book as an exploration of how these two principles, once set in motion, operate – revealing the perpetually redescriptive quality of efforts to characterize an Israelite identity and the capacity of these to make explanations across a steadily wider world. In Chapter 3, the ability of the twelve tribes tradition to redescribe and explain combined with a number of external developments – the proliferation of legends concerning the Lost Tribes of Israel and the dynamic cross-pollination of tribal traditions with others – to dramatically expand the audience for Israel, and what Israel could mean to whom. In the medieval era, increased interest in "becoming" – and finding – Israel meant that traditions about Israel began to collide in ways that produced unexpected transformations. As both the geography and the meanings of Israel expanded, so did its audience, especially among European Christians. Still, the tradition that characterizes and defines Israel, the twelve tribes tradition, stayed the same, and these new developments exploited the same features that earlier accounts of Israel had.

Then, in the fourth chapter, we saw how a long-developing medieval "interpretive habit" of identifying newly-encountered peoples with lost Israel made the identification of Israel among the native peoples of America something of a *fait accompli*. But we also saw this habit combine with a growing Protestant interest in identifying with – and even as – Israel, especially in Britain, helping to produce a major new American religion. We saw a people who searched for Israel *and* became Israel – a people who still identify by tribe, still tell the story of a family out of the tribe of Manasseh who crossed the mighty Atlantic, and still look for Israel around the world. And in all these places, the ability to explain the existence of multiple different heirs to Israel in different places that helped place Jews and Samaritans in relation to each other did the same, again.

Finally, in the fifth chapter, we saw how two different sets of traditions about the Israelites of Ethiopia developed both inside and outside of that country, quite independently from each other and for a very long time. There, an ongoing series of encounters between three different constructions of Israel – Christian Ethiopian, Beta Israel, and normative

Jewish – continuously reshaped the nature of Beta Israel identity. From an Israel responsive to internal Ethiopian realities, the Beta Israel were remade, and remade themselves, into one acceptable to Jewish authorities, but in a way that kept the differences between Ethiopian and Jewish constructions of Israelite identity rebounding into the present. And in their move from one twelve tribe paradigm to another, both the incredible capacity of the twelve tribes tradition to make and remake visions of Israel stand totally revealed, and also, its specific limitations.

All of these cases of "becoming Israel" involve the same potent ethno-genetic tradition, and the same techniques for making explanations, that have been the centerpiece of our study all along. So, each of these case studies has its unique features, but all are also an expression of a circum-scribed set of narrative facts applied to a steadily widening world. Each case study, in turn, explores the build-up of meaning accomplished by the passing of a great deal of time. Outside and after Israel, the segmentation of Israelite identity into twelve different pieces formed a set of trailing edges that allowed many peoples, in different places and times, to lay claim to this identity and clothe themselves in its fabric. The particular contexts in which Israel was adopted and adapted made each vision of Israel unique, while the steady drumbeat of new ideas about Israel, audible on a global scale, gave new shape to what Israel could become, and to whom. Through it all, the flexible structure that is the permanent possession of the twelve tribes tradition is what allowed its claimants to respond to challenges, to justify themselves to the world, and to explain the origins of their unique characteristics from ancient Judah to America and Ethiopia.

Taken as a whole – which is to say, once we recognize it *as* a whole – "becoming Israel" emerges as something truly extraordinary: a steady, transhistorical phenomenon, with roots deep in the first millennium BCE, continuing into the present. We see the twelve tribes tradition as one of the most popular and enduring ethnogenetic traditions in history. Of course, "Israel" is not the only identity with a history of showing up unexpectedly. In Chapter 4, I mentioned the continued popularity of claiming descent from Trojan War heroes into the early medieval period.[10] Yet in the scope, intensity, and frequency of efforts to be, or find, a single historical people, "becoming Israel" must have nothing like a rival. Two thousand and six hundred years since Nebuchadnezzar

---

[10] Patterson, *Kinship Myth in Ancient Greece*, 8.

destroyed Solomon's Temple, the world is more full of Israels than ever before – and they have never stopped appearing.

Here in the conclusion, however, we can profit most by considering a few ways in which "becoming Israel" is *not* unique. First of all, while this particular species of identity manipulation, as a defined category of activity, is likely unparalleled in the annals of history, "becoming" itself is quite the opposite. Basically, we now know that in an important sense, all identities in the world are locked in continuous acts of "becoming" – French, Italian, or Chinese identities no less than "Israelite" ones. That is, the contemporary forms of these – and any other – identities are no less the product of the modern world, whatever their relationship to much earlier identity concepts, than any vision of Israel is a product of its world.[11] The twelve tribes tradition, in short, is simply a tool for a redescriptive identity activity that we see everywhere else.[12] And in the end, these aspects of "becoming Israel" that are perfectly common are the ones that give the final boost to the main arguments of this study.

As I said all the way back in the introduction, the simple reason no investigation of this sort has ever been attempted is that there is an intuitive distinction to be made between constructions of Israelite identity in the Bible and constructions of Israelite identity elsewhere. This distinction has formed a silo around this ancient act of "becoming," and the walls of the silo are strong. The question is whether this intuition is a sound one, and the answer begins with the fact that there is indeed not much difference between efforts to adapt an Israelite identity over time and efforts to create a new version of Israel.

Or we might put it this way: in recent years, there has been a tendency to view the problem of the Bible's many largely late and Judahite constructions of Israelite identity through the lens of recent studies that argue that early Judahites did not think of themselves as Israelites, but

---

[11] As Patrick Geary notes, "the real history of the nations that populated Europe in the early Middle Ages begins not in the sixth century but in the eighteenth ... the past two centuries of intellectual activity and political confrontation have so utterly changed the ways we think about social and political groups ... Not only is ethnic nationalism, as we currently understand it, in a certain sense an invention of this recent period, but as we shall see, the very tools of analysis by which we pretend to practice scientific history were invented and perfected within a wider climate of nationalism and nationalist preoccupations" (Geary, *The Myth of Nations*, 15–16).

[12] Lee E. Patterson, referring to Geary, observes that the problem contemporary "nationalistic claims" encounter is their inherent "assumptions about the supposedly immutable nature of religion, language, and custom" (Patterson, *Kinship Myth in Ancient Greece*, 9).

appropriated this identity only in later periods. This may well be. Centering this argument, however, means making the question of whether biblical visions of identity are *essentially* late and Judahite in character dependent on how ancient the basic idea of Judah as Israel is. In other words, the norm in biblical studies today is to explore the Judahite characteristics of the biblical presentation of Israel only if the scholar involved imagines that the idea itself is a Judahite cultural invention. But "becoming Israel" would have been perpetually ongoing, not just in Israel but everywhere it happens, no matter the origins of the tradition involved.

After all – and conclusions are the place for "after all" – the study just completed offers us numerous opportunities to question how much, precisely, biological descent matters, where the construction of identity is concerned.[13] This question need not be a flippant one. We can be open to the possibility that it *does* matter whether the people of a given "Israel" genuinely descend from the original Israelites. While the question of actual descent need not be as important for us, as scholars, as it is for ethnic actors – where it is generally the decisive one – it still has stakes.[14] Nor can, or should, the interests of scholars and those they study be totally divorced from one another.

Above all else, there is a pressing need to acknowledge that any study that undermines the perceived historicity of a people's traditions can have real life consequences for those peoples. In other words, marginalized minority groups around the world sometimes enjoy preciously few protections, when they enjoy them at all, by virtue of the fact that their claims have been accepted by the majority culture and enshrined into law.[15] The possibility that studies about ethnic claims can harm ethnic actors *must* be considered – even in studies like this, where one of the main points is that it is unfeasible to make consistent, sharp distinctions between "genuine" and "invented" traditions anywhere at all.[16]

---

[13] Thus, Steven Kaplan's observation about the Beta Israel reflects one of the main themes of this study: "in considering the question of historical continuity over the period of many centuries, it is important to avoid too heavy a concentration of the issue on physical-biological descent" (Kaplan, "The Invention of Ethiopian Jews," 55).

[14] Hall, *Ethnic Identity in Greek Antiquity*, 18.

[15] See, for example, Sutherland, "The Problematic Authority of (World) History."

[16] Again, this is not my own personal argument, but one that is increasingly common in the study of cultural invention. As Handler and Linnekin noted some time ago, "if genuine, naïve, or pristine traditions are difficult to discover empirically, they are even more difficult to justify theoretically ... for ... nationalist ideology depends on the notion of society bounded by objective tradition, with both society and tradition understood as

Still, let us consider our final case study once more, the story of the Beta Israel of Ethiopia. Again, the great irony of the debate about their history and origins is that there is little debate to be had. Contemporary scholarship and Beta Israel tradition agree that Beta Israel identity took on familiar shape only in the fourteenth and fifteenth centuries CE, that it continued to develop over the next several centuries, and that the Gondar era was formative for the creation of later Beta Israel self-understandings. They agree that the fundamental nature of Beta Israel practice was dramatically shaped by encounters with Ethiopian Christians in the early part of this history, and then once more through encounters with Jewish emissaries between the mid-nineteenth and mid-twentieth centuries. They agree, and there is no denying, that the 1980s and 1990s ushered in a new era in the history of these people because of the mass transfer of Beta Israel from Ethiopia to Israel.

Again, as I pointed out in the chapter itself, where tradition and scholarship disagree is really about whether this people, with this history, originally descended from Israelites or not. What we can ask in this conclusion is, what does it matter? From an analytical perspective, from the fourteenth century CE on, we genuinely would not understand the historical development of the Beta Israel any differently whatever the biological origins of the people who "became" this Israel. The transformations that demonstrably occurred between then and the twentieth century, in encounters between Ethiopia's Israels, would look the same whether the Beta Israel were descended from an ancient Ethiopian colony of Jews or not. The encounter between the Jewish and Beta Israel visions of Israel, beginning in the nineteenth century, would have proceeded along the same lines.

Similarly, in modern Israel, the tensions between these two visions of Israel emerge from the ways in which they were originally different from each other. The framework in which emissaries from the normative Jewish world met Jewish Ethiopians in Ethiopia was discriminatory towards the latter in order to preserve the status of the former as the

objects or sets of objects in the natural world. In other words, the social-scientific model of tradition, like the nationalistic, rests on a naturalistic and atomistic paradigm in which those aspects of social life that are considered traditional are endowed with (or reduced to) the status of natural things. But in our view, to posit a distinction between genuine and spurious traditions is to overlook the fact that social life is always symbolically constructed, never naturally given. All handing down, for example, depends upon the use of symbols and is thus constantly reinvented in the present" (Handler and Linnekin, "Tradition, Genuine or Spurious," 281).

supposedly more correct form of contemporary Israelite identity. Say, however, that both the Jewish people and the Beta Israel really were descended from the original Israelites, but still experienced, as in the *Kebra Nagast*, three thousand years of separation, and of separate historical experiences. Would they not still have emerged into the present quite a bit different from each other? And wouldn't those differences still beg the question which of the two were "really" Israel, according to the internal logic that makes each of these groups claim to represent not an heir to Israel, but Israel itself? For that matter, wouldn't Beta Israel identity be very different from what it now is if the outside Jewish world had encountered them in other periods, or not at all, regardless of the origins of Judaism in Ethiopia?

Or say that we were to discover something that proved once and for all that the Native Americans really did descend from the ancient Israelites, as the Book of Mormon claims.[17] Mormonism itself, obviously, would not have appeared any earlier, and its formative events would have charted the same course over time. The primordialist origins of Native Americans had no role to play in Joseph Smith Jr.'s untimely demise, nor in the Great Trek to Utah that followed. It did not shape Brigham Young's leadership or chart the course of Mormon missionary work. The Mormon gaze, the Mormon search for Israel, would not likely have turned inwards – or outwards and around the world – any faster. The same is true of biblical visions of Israel. It would be nice to know whether there was or was not a twelve tribes of Israel, but the question has little bearing on whether, how, or why Israelite identity took on different forms over time, aided and abetted by the redescriptive qualities inherent to the twelve tribes of Israel tradition. This is by no means to denigrate the clams of ethnic actors who emphatically deserve whatever respect and

---

[17] Various institutions have attempted to do this over the last few decades, notably the "Foundation for Ancient Research and Mormon Studies" (FARMS), founded in 1979, incorporated into Brigham Young University in 1997, into the Neal A. Maxwell Institute for Religious Scholarship in 2006, and finally dissolved in 2010. FARMS had as a general goal the use of modern scholarly tools to establish the historicity of the Book of Mormon and other Mormon texts. A truly excellent, comprehensive overview of developments in the history of efforts to prove the historicity of the Book of Mormon can be found in Duffy, "Mapping Book of Mormon Historicity Debates – Part I"; Duffy, "Mapping Book of Mormon Historicity Debates – Part II." Examples of "apologetic" pro-historicity arguments certainly include John L. Sorenson's massive tome, *Mormon's Codex: An Ancient American Book*, which explains the absence of evidence for the Book's events in the United States by suggesting it really refers to a Mesoamerican geography (Sorenson, *Mormon's Codex*). See also Tvedtnes, Gee, and Roper, "Book of Mormon Names."

protections they can be afforded. It is merely to say that change over time is not a hallmark of inauthenticity, but simply a constant. In all these counterfactuals, we see that the role historical experience plays in the ongoing development of identity is independent of questions of biological origin, and a good deal more important.

Once we put aside biological origin as a preoccupation – once we move past an obsessive concern for establishing or denying primordialist identity claims – the grand similarity between all efforts to claim and adapt an Israelite identity will emerge. Once we realize the typical character of so many aspects of "becoming Israel" – that the ongoing adaptation of Israelite identity, and Israelite identities, through historical experiences represents a species of identity activity that is going on everywhere else, too – it will emerge. Once we notice that the question of adaptation, or invention, and the question of origins are separate from each other – that the former occurs continually regardless of the latter – it will emerge.[18] Once, finally, we recognize that identities are shaped by the accidents of history – which is to say unpredictably, by unpredictable events, and no matter their origins – it will emerge, and the grand unity of "becoming Israel" across time and space will reveal itself anew. In the end, every Israel in the world is very literally adapting the same identity to new experiences and new contexts. We only think an identity cannot belong to multiple different peoples at once because of the primordialist preoccupations that have muddied the waters for so long.

---

[18] Here we encounter what Marc Bloch called the "idol of origins," which is to say a seemingly unavoidable concern for the true origins of a thing despite how little origins may actually explain (Bloch, *The Historian's Craft*, 29–35). As Steven Weitzman observes, echoing Bloch, there is a certain "confusion of beginnings with causes, ancestry with explanation" (Weitzman, *The Origin of the Jews*, 10; Bloch, *The Historian's Craft*, 32). Weitzman continues, "later generations of scholars—I have in mind figures like Roland Barthes, Maurice Blanchot, Jean Baudrillard, Judith Butler, and many other thinkers active in the second half of the twentieth century—went further in their critique, arguing variations of the idea of origin as something that isn't really there. For these and other scholars, the search to understand origins represents scholarly thinking gone astray. The curiosity at work seems deeply wired into how people think about things, and yet there is something misconceived or futile about it: it can never find what it is looking for; its vision is distorted by delusion" (Weitzman, *The Origin of the Jews*, 10). In Bloch's own words, "it is very like the illusion of certain old etymologists who thought they had said all when they set down the oldest known meaning of a word ... As if, above all, the meaning of any word were influenced more by its own past than by the contemporary state of the vocabulary which, in its turn, is determined by the social conditions of the moment" (Bloch, *The Historian's Craft*, 32–33).

Indeed, imagine if, rather than saying Israelite identity only belongs to its true genetic heirs, once we figure out which those are, we said that Israelite *literature* does. Imagine if we said that the Hebrew Bible – or the Old Testament, in Christian circles – could only be the property, the cultural patrimony, of biological descendants of the ancient Israelites. This, surely, would be an objectionable statement to many people around the world. Yet "Israel" itself is a global legacy too; it is part of our world heritage, and it is interpreted, in different places, as befits the contexts in which it appears. I have tried to investigate these acts of interpretation, the mechanisms involved, and what they all have in common.

In the end, we might put it this way. I have described the twelve tribes tradition as a bridge reaching back across a gap to ancient Israel from some other time and place. I began with the insight that, because Judah is not Israel, and because the Bible formed both after and outside of Israel *qua* Israel, here too is a gap, and here too is a bridge. Yet where other studies have focused on the question of bridges – which is to say, whether any claim to Israel descends in a direct line, without gaps, from ancient Israel itself – I have studied the *making* of bridges. Where another study might be satisfied with the conclusion that artifice is involved in the making of this or that Israel – that invention has occurred – I consider identifying the *existence* of artifice in identity constructions to be like saying the Louvre has paintings: it is a truth, but not by itself an illuminating one.

Instead, in constructing a fundamentally new set of comparisons, I have attempted to produce a course, in a sense, in art appreciation. After all, it is only when we come to understand something of the history of art – the development of techniques, the culturally contingent meaning of symbols, and the history of cultural trends – that we can begin to understand what an artist is trying to say and do. And as a canvas upon which Israels can be drawn, the twelve tribes tradition invites us to ask not "is this art?" but instead "what has the artist done?" When we realize that something was always being done – that the active nature of the construction of Israelite identities stands utterly apart, as a presence, from the validity or nonvalidity of their historical claims – we can begin to apply ourselves to these questions and find useful answers.

Of course, it is the privilege of conclusions to gesture towards a broader picture and, if possible, connect the topic of the book to more general issues and concerns. I would like to conclude, then, by pointing out two other ways that "becoming Israel" is less than unique as a historical phenomenon. First, the story of the twelve tribes tradition is a crash course in the fact that what we believe to be true about the past exerts a powerful influence on the present even when it is not really the past at all. That is, what we believe to be true works much the same as what is actually true, as a historical cause. And, even among true facts, we still make choices about what is important, and those choices shape what the past can do in the present. So, the "perceived past" is a term that applies to the past in the present – the past as it seems to be to individuals living in the historical present – both because a scholarly examination might reveal that it is not, in fact, the past after all *and* because other parts of the real past might have been emphasized and used instead of those we have been socialized into accepting.

In this book, we have seen many examples of how the perceived past has operated, with surprisingly long-term consequences. We saw how Eldad ha-Dani's wild confabulations paved the way for the actual Beta Israel to come to Israel; likewise, Prester John laid the groundwork for David Reubeni to become the unlikeliest visitor at the Papal court.[19] I mentioned, in Chapter 3, that the Portuguese sent the Ethiopian emperor Lebna Dengel military aid in 1541, believing him to be Prester John. The muskets of Mitsiwa, which is where Christovão da Gama landed his troops, are a paramount example of what a legend made flesh can do. The Portuguese sent an army to the aid of a king who never existed in the first place, but which nevertheless may have saved his kingdom.[20] And it is, certainly, the power the past continues to exert not just on our imaginations, but in practical reality, that explains why anyone would want to be Israel in the first place. If Israel had instead been forgotten by history, it would still have existed, and the archaeologist might still uncover something of it. But nobody would want to *be* it. It is the meaning, or meanings, of ancient Israel among later cultural groups,

---

[19] It is a staple of scholarship on Eldad ha-Dani, the mysterious traveler who showed up in Kairouan in the ninth century CE, to point out that he was a liar, or "trickster." Parfitt calls his claims "extravagant," his narrative a "work of the imagination," and likens him to a troubadour or novelist (Parfitt, *The Lost Tribes of Israel*, 9–11). Neubauer notes that he was "pretending to have communicated with members of four of the Ten Tribes" (Neubauer, "Where Are the Ten Tribes?," 98). Benite calls him a "clever trickster" (Benite, *The Ten Lost Tribes*, 91). David Reubeni might, or might not, have been a knowing "trickster," too. Yet for all the emphasis placed on this in scholarship, it would be wrong to attribute the influence of either story to this fact, when we know that so many other stories that are not true play an equivalent role even though no *intentional* misstatements were involved.

[20] Marcus, *A History of Ethiopia*, 33. For an eyewitness account, see Whiteway, *The Portuguese Expedition to Abyssinia*.

and not the reality of ancient Israel, that is the engine of "becoming Israel" – even, one presumes, among its true biological heirs.

The second and more complicated point is that the twelve tribes of Israel tradition represents an interaction between past and present that involves giving the past shape through organizational systems. In terms of numbered lists, we can think of the Five Good Emperors, the Third Reich, the Seven Wise Men of Greece, and so on.[21] But there are other ways of imposing organization on past data in a way that makes meaning. When, for example, Gutzon Borglum sculpted Mount Rushmore, he selected four presidents out of the many for certain reasons to express what he wanted to say in stone, and the monument that resulted has become a fixture of American cultural memory.[22] As a monument, it has to be reckoned with as a feature of American social memory whether one approves of or denigrates Borglum's choices, and for whatever reason. In other words, his choices create a particular group from within the larger category of presidents which, because of the prominence of the monument, thereafter seem natural to treat as a group, even if another sculptor might have made different decisions altogether.

Similarly, few even among biblical scholars have likely realized how arbitrary the concept of the twelve tribes of Israel is. As I touched on way back in the introduction, in the book of Genesis, Jacob's sons stand among a riot of genealogical information that doubles as a kind of anthropological charter. We have, for example, the vast and generally eponymic genealogies of Adam, Noah, and Noah's sons explaining the origins of so many of the peoples known to the ancient Israelites and

---

[21] "Like holidays and other anniversaries, historical analogies underscore the fact that our 'ties' to the past are not always physical or even iconic but quite often purely symbolic. That is certainly true of the ties between noncontemporary namesakes. The tremendous mnemonic significance of names as discursive tokens of 'sameness' help explain, for example, why the rebels in Chiapas would choose to adopt the name *Zapatistas* more than seventy years after the actual death of the revered hero of the Mexican Revolution, Emiliano Zapata ... A somewhat similar discursive form of bridging the historical gap between the past and the present is the subtle use of *consecutive, ordinal numbers* to imply temporal contiguity. The so-called Third Reich, for example, was thus featured by the Nazis as a *direct* successor to the 'second' (1871–1918) German empire, thereby tacitly glossing over the pronouncedly non-imperial fifteen-year-period actually separating them" (Zerubavel, *Time Maps*, 52).

[22] According to the National Park Service, "Gutzon Borglum selected these four presidents because from his perspective, they represented the most important events in the history of the United States," including its founding, its "growth" under Jefferson, its "development" under Teddy Roosevelt, and its "preservation" under Lincoln ("Why These Four Presidents?").

Judahites (Gen. 5, 10–11). After the flood, genealogy continues to function in the same way. Abraham's two sons with Sarah, Isaac and Ishmael, are the ancestors of different peoples – in Ishmael's case, the Ishmaelites (Gen. 17:20). So are the children of Abraham's nephew, Lot, who becomes the father of Ammon and Moab through an incestuous, if unwitting, liaison with his own daughters (Gen. 19:30–38). So, for that matter, are Jacob and Esau, who is the ancestor of the Edomites just as Jacob is of the Israelites (Gen. 36:9).

In the Hebrew Bible, then, the twelve tribes concept takes the messy data of biblical genealogy and borders off a subset to produce a definition: Israel is this, it is not that. But even now, it is easy to imagine other ways in which this data might be organized. In the early days, being a Reubenite or Simeonite might occasionally have meant more than being an Israelite. After Judah and Israel split – if they had ever been one – the tribes of Judah and the tribes of Israel might have been regarded as separate peoples in much the way the descendants of Jacob and Esau have been.[23] For all we know, there might have been moments when the Israelites and the Edomites – who, after all, are supposedly descended from twins – used their family connection the same way the Bible typically uses Reuben's and Simeon's. Yet the system of the twelve tribes of Israel makes meaning, and it has proved an enduring meaning. It is supposed to stand for all time, and so far, it has done a pretty good job of it.

I would describe the twelve tribes tradition, then, as a type of framework, which I would call a "system of meaning." I like the term because it has two parts, system *and* meaning, and these systems work on both levels. That is, the systematization provides a baseline meaning – this is Israel, and this is not. But it also provides the raw materials that, in the words of Debra Ballentine, are thereafter perpetually "available for

---

[23] In a previous study, I observed that two different Judahite prophets writing after the conquest of Judah use a stick metaphor to characterize the relationship between Israel and Judah. Ezekiel puts the "'stick of Judah' with the 'stick of Ephraim'" in Ezek. 37:16–22, and makes them one stick. Zechariah "cuts a stick in half and declares the brotherhood ... between Israel and Judah to be at an end" in Zech. 11:10–14 (Tobolowsky, *The Sons of Jacob*, 207). It is not too much to imagine that these authors are actually making different arguments about what the relationship between Judah and Israel *should* be, perhaps even against each other. In other words, Zechariah might be making a bid for abandoning the idea of "all Israel" in favor of something more Judah-centric, while Ezekiel might be insisting upon "all Israel."

innovative interpretations."[24] "Innovative interpretation" characterizes the continued use of inherited systems by explaining the details of familiar groupings in new and meaningful ways.

In Mount Rushmore's case, there is the intended meaning, a monument to American exceptionalism and national glory. Then there are a host of other meanings, from what a monument to four presidents, two of them slave-owners, represents to contemporary Americans, to the fact that the mountain the monument is carved into is itself sacred to the Lakota Sioux, as is the larger Black Hills region. Today, Mount Rushmore is often understood in terms of what it erases, obscures, and replaces, and what this says about who has mattered in our history and who has not.[25] Likewise, in many respects, it is the ability of narratives about the same set of facts to compete with others, to resist and subvert, that explains much of their enduring power.[26] But the systematization of the past, or pasts, provides a starting point from which interpretations spring.[27] Ultimately, the arbitrary and negotiable character of these systematizations is what reveals their essential similarity. And most of all, these systems work because, though they are arbitrary, their whole purpose is to seem to be natural and inevitable ways of thinking about the past. Similar borderings, similarly negotiable, are all around us, structuring our lives.

Of course, few traditions could present as clear a demonstration of the ability of the same system to be interpreted in many different ways as the twelve tribes of Israel tradition does. Nobody, to the best of my

---

[24] Here, Ballentine refers to myths that "elaborate sets of relationships among characters," which very generally make those "sets of relationships ... available for innovative interpretation" (Ballentine, *The Conflict Myth and the Biblical Tradition*, 3).

[25] As John Taliaferro observes "Native Americans regard it as a desecration of the sacred *Paha Sapa*, the 'hills of black.' Environmentalists regard Rushmore as a mutilation of Mother Earth ... to millions of others, Rushmore symbolizes all that is fine and noble in America" (Taliaferro, *Great White Fathers*, 2). See also Boime, "Patriarchy Fixed in Stone."

[26] See especially Lincoln, *Theorizing Myth*, 149–50.

[27] Jon Anderson observes of Trafalgar Square: "in fixing our attention on the traces which constitute a place, geographers are in effect interpreting and translating places. They do so by interpreting and translating the trace ... into the meanings intended by their 'trace-makers'. However, as we know in our own lives, there are many different opinions, thoughts and judgments about the meanings associated with any given trace ... We could ask ourselves, for example, whether the ideas of the nineteenth century trace-makers in Trafalgar Square still have currency and influence over us today? Do their ideas remain as strong and sturdy as Nelson's Column itself, or do they lurk in the shadows of the square which has been taken over by new trace-makers?" (Anderson, *Understanding Cultural Geography*, 6).

knowledge, has ever altered the twelve tribes tradition itself. Nobody has ever added a secret thirteenth tribe or subtracted one to make them eleven. Yet what this book shows over and over again is how many different things the same system can become. The same Israel can mean many things in many different stories, and the same details of Israelite identity can have many different significances, depending on how they are interpreted. The system defines who Israel is, now and for all time. And still, the stories about it tell us what Israel means, signifies, or portends. Meanwhile, the stability and adaptability of the twelve tribes tradition work together to produce the authority that makes "becoming Israel" worthwhile.

Still, when we think of the twelve tribes tradition not only as a historical phenomenon, but as a *type* of effort – we might say, a type of activity performed on the past – we realize that, however ambitious this book's comparisons already are, another set might be just as useful. We might compare the twelve tribes tradition with other similar efforts to organize and interpret the past that have nothing to do with Israel per se. We might think of the Round Table, or the Argo, or Greek and Roman pantheons – efforts to create stable structures that border and define complex myth systems, often out of a larger mass of traditions, to create "systems of meaning." Such a comparison between the historical use of the twelve tribes tradition and other efforts to systematize, connect to, and explain the relevance of the past in the present might prove very illuminating indeed.

For now, however, the final lesson of our discussion of the twelve tribes tradition is the absolutely essential one. True, false, or somewhere in between, we do not tell stories about the past for no reason, and we do not tell them merely because they are true, or because we believe they are true. When we *make* the past speak – by adapting it, organizing it, interpreting it, narrating it – it is because we want very much for others to hear what it has to say and to be persuaded by its arguments. Such is the power of giving the past meaning by connecting ourselves to it. Such is the power of the bridges we build, and the techniques we use to build them. Such, indeed, is the destiny of bridges: to take us where we want to go, to be used and used again, to be weathered by time and chance, and to endure as long as they can – or until they are replaced by something new.

Bibliography

"1933 Baseball: Yankees & House of David 220620-28 | Footage Farm."
YouTube video. Posted by "footagefarm." July 9, 2015. www.youtube
.com/watch?v=RYVcq4CrqPw.

"1955 Revised Constitution of Ethiopia." Accessed May 28, 2020. https://chilot
.files.wordpress.com/2011/04/1955-revised-constitution-of-ethiopia1.pdf.

Abbink, Jon G. "The Enigma of Beta Esra'el Ethnogenesis: An Ethno-Historical
Study." *Cahiers d'Études Africaines* 30, no. 120 (1990): 397–450.

Adler, Marcus Nathan. "Introduction." In *The Itinerary of Benjamin of Tudela*,
1–13. London: Philipp Feldheim, Inc, 1907.

trans. *The Itinerary of Benjamin of Tudela*. London: Philipp Feldheim, Inc,
1907.

Albertz, Rainer. "The Controversy about Judean versus Israelite Identity and the
Persian Government: A New Interpretation of the Bagoses Story (Jewish
Antiquities XI.297–301)." In *Judah and the Judeans in the Achaemenid
Period: Negotiating Identity in an International Context*, edited by Oded
Lipschits, Gary N. Knoppers, and Manfred Oeming, 483–504. Winona Lake,
IN: Eisenbrauns, 2011.

Alon, Gedaliah. "The Origin of the Samaritans in the Halakhic Tradition." In
*Jews, Judaism, and the Classical World: Studies in Jewish History in the
Times of the Second Temple and Talmud*, translated by J. Abrahams,
354–73. Jerusalem: Magnes Press, 1977.

Alt, Albrecht. "Das System der Stammesgrenzen im Buche Josua." In *Sellin-
Festschrift*, 13–24. Beiträge zur Religionsgeschichte und Archaologie Palästina,
1927.

Die Landnahme der Israeliten in Palästina; Territorialgeschichtliche Studien.
Leipzig: Druckerei dei Werkgemeinschaft, 1925.

Die Staatenbildung der Israeliten in Palästina; verfassungsgeschichtliche Studien.
Leipzig: Edelmann, 1930.

"Judas Gaue unter Josia." *Palästinajahrbuch* 21 (1925): 100–16.

Anderson, Jon. *Understanding Cultural Geography: Places and Traces*. London:
Routledge, 2010.

Anderson, Robert T., and Terry Giles. *The Keepers: An Introduction to the History and Culture of the Samaritans.* Peabody, MA: Hendrickson Publishers, 2002.

The Samaritan Pentateuch: An Introduction to Its Origin, History, and Significance for Biblical Studies. Society of Biblical Literature Resources for Biblical Study 72. Atlanta: Society of Biblical Literature, 2012.

Tradition Kept: The Literature of the Samaritans. Peabody, MA: Hendrickson Publishers, 2005.

Appadurai, Arjun. "The Past as a Scarce Resource." *Man* 16, no. 2 (1981): 201–19.

Arieli, Ariel, Itzhak Gilat, and Seffefe Aycheh. "Suicide Among Ethiopian Jews: A Survey Conducted by Means of a Psychological Autopsy." *Journal of Nervous and Mental Disease* 184, no. 5 (1996): 317–19.

Armstrong, Adrian, and Sarah Kay. "Textual Communities: Poetry and the Social Construction of Knowledge." In *Knowing Poetry: Verse in Medieval France from the "Rose" to the "Rhétoriqueurs,"* 165–96. Ithaca, NY: Cornell University Press, 2011.

Asa-El, Amotz. *The Diaspora and the Lost Tribes of Israel.* Berkeley, CA: Publishers Group West, 2004.

Asbridge, Thomas. *The Crusades: The Authoritative History of the War for the Holy Land.* New York: HarperCollins, 2010.

Bacher, W. "The Supposed Inscription upon 'Joshua the Robber.'" *The Jewish Quarterly Review* 3, no. 2 (1891): 354–57.

Ballentine, Debra Scoggins. *The Conflict Myth and the Biblical Tradition.* New York: Oxford University Press, 2015.

Bamberger, Bernard. "A Messianic Document of the Seventh Century." *Hebrew Union College Annual* 15 (1940): 425–31.

Bard, Mitchell Geoffrey. *From Tragedy to Triumph: The Politics Behind the Rescue of Ethiopian Jewry.* Westport, CT: Praeger, 2002.

Bar-Ilan, Meir. "Prester John: Fiction and History." *History of European Ideas* 20, no. 1–3 (1995): 291–98.

Barlow, Philip L. *Mormons and the Bible: The Place of the Latter-Day Saints in American Religion. Updated.* Oxford: Oxford University Press, 2013.

Barmash, Pamela. "At the Nexus of History and Memory: The Ten Lost Tribes." *AJS Review* 29, no. 2 (2005): 207–36.

Barnett, Michael. "The Many Faces of Rasta: Doctrinal Diversity within the Rastafari Movement." *Caribbean Quarterly* 51, no. 2 (2005): 67–78.

Barros e Sousa Santarém, Manuel Francisco de. *Recherches historiques, critiques et bibliographiques sur Améric Vespuce et ses voyages.* Paris: Arthur-Bertrand, 1842.

Barstad, Hans M. "History and the Hebrew Bible." In *Can a History of Israel Be Written?*, edited by Lester L. Grabbe, 37–64. Sheffield: Sheffield Academic Press, 1997.

The Myth of the Empty Land: A Study in the History and Archaeology of Judah During the "Exilic" Period. Symbolae Osloenses Fasciculus Suppletorius 28. Oslo: Scandinavian University Press, 1996.

Bartlett, F. C. "Some Experiments on the Reproduction of Folk Stories." *Folklore* 31 (1920): 30–47.

Baseball Reference. "Chief Bender." Accessed May 6, 2020. www.baseball-reference.com/players/b/bendecho1.shtml.

"House of David – BR Bullpen." Accessed April 22, 2020. www.baseball-reference.com/bullpen/House_of_David.

Bates, Irene M. "Patriarchal Blessings and the Routinization of Charisma." *Dialogue: A Journal of Mormon Thought* 26 (1993): 1–29.

Bates, Irene M., and E. Gary Smith. *Lost Legacy: The Mormon Office of Presiding Patriarch*. Urbana, IL: University of Illinois Press, 1996.

Bayart, Jean-François. *The Illusion of Cultural Identity*. Translated by Steven Rendall. Chicago: University of Chicago Press, 2005.

Beam, Alex. *American Crucifixion: The Murder of Joseph Smith and the Fate of the Mormon Church*. New York: Public Affairs, 2014.

Beckingham, Charles F. "The Achievements of Prester John." In *Prester John, the Mongols and the Ten Lost Tribes*, edited by Bernard Hamilton and Charles F. Beckingham, 1–22. Aldershot: Variorum, 1996.

Bedasse, Monique. "Rasta Evolution: The Theology of the Twelve Tribes of Israel." *Journal of Black Studies* 40, no. 5 (2010): 960–73.

Bekele, Shiferaw. "Reflections on the Power Elite of the Wärä Seh Mäsfenate (1786-1853)." *Annales d'Éthiopie* 15, no. 1 (1990): 157–79.

Belcher, Wendy Laura. "African Rewritings of the Jewish and Islamic Solomonic Tradition: The Triumph of the Queen of the Queen of Sheba in the Fourteenth-Century Text Kəbrä Nägäst." In *Sacred Tropes: Tanakh, New Testament, and Qur'an As Literature and Culture*, edited by Roberta Sterman Sabbath, 441–60. Leiden: Brill, 2009.

Ben Ezer, Gadi. "The Ethiopian Jewish Exodus: A Myth in Creation." In *Jews of Ethiopia: The Birth of an Elite*, edited by Tudor Parfitt and Emanuela Trevisan Semi, 122–30. London: Routledge, 2005.

The Ethiopian Jewish Exodus: Narratives of the Migration Journey to Israel 1977–1985. London: Routledge, 2002.

Ben Israel, Manasseh. *The Hope of Israel*. London, 1650.

Ben-David, Amith, and Adital Tirosh Ben-Ari. "The Experience of Being Different: Black Jews in Israel." *Journal of Black Studies* 27, no. 4 (1997): 510–27.

Bender, Abby. *Israelites in Erin: Exodus, Revolution, and the Irish Revival*. Syracuse, NY: Syracuse University Press, 2015.

Ben-Eliezer, Uri. "Multicultural Society and Everyday Cultural Racism: Second Generation of Ethiopian Jews in Israel's 'Crisis of Modernization.'" *Ethnic and Racial Studies* 31, no. 5 (2008): 935–61.

Ben-Eliyahu, Eyal, Yehudah Cohn, and Fergus Millar. *Handbook of Jewish Literature from Late Antiquity*. Oxford: Oxford University Press, 2012.

Benita, E., and G. Noam. "The Absorption of Ethiopian Immigrants: Selected Findings from Local Surveys." *Israel Social Science Research*, 10, no. 2 (1995): 81–96.

Benite, Zvi Ben-Dor. *The Ten Lost Tribes: A World History*. Oxford: Oxford University Press, 2009.

Bentley, G. Carter. "Ethnicity and Practice." *Comparative Studies in Society and History* 29 (1987): 24–55.

Ben-Zvi, Itzhak. *The Book of the Samaritans.* Jerusalem: Yad Itzhak Ben-Zvi, 1970.

Berhanu, Girma. "Normality, Deviance, Identity, Cultural Tracking and School Achievement: The Case of Ethiopian Jews in Israel." *Scandinavian Journal of Educational Research* 49, no. 1 (2005): 51–82.

Berkey, Jonathan P. "Tradition, Innovation and the Social Construction of Knowledge in the Medieval Islamic Near East." *Past & Present,* no. 146 (1995): 38–65.

Bernardini, Paolo. "A Milder Colonization: Jewish Expansion to the New World, and the New World in the Jewish Consciousness of the Early Modern Era." In *The Jews and the Expansion of Europe to the West, 1450 to 1800,* edited by Paolo Bernardini and Norman Fiering, 1–26. New York: Berghahn Books, 2001.

Beyerle, Stefan. *Der Mosesegen im Deuteronomium: Eine text-, kompositions- und formkritische Studie zu Deuteronomium 33. Beihefte zur Zeitschrift für die alttestamentliche Wissenschaft 250.* Berlin and New York: De Gruyter, 1997.

Bietenholz, Peter G. *Historia and Fabula: Myths and Legends in Historical Thought from Antiquity to the Modern Age.* Leiden: Brill, 1994.

Biran, Michael. *The Empire of the Qara Khitai in Eurasian History: Between China and the Islamic World.* Cambridge: Cambridge University Press, 2005.

Blenkinsopp, Joseph. "An Assessment of the Alleged Pre-Exilic Date of the Priestly Material in the Pentateuch." *Zeitschrift für die alttestamentliche Wissenschaft* 108, no. 4 (1996): 495–518.

Bliss, Sylvester. *Memoirs of William Miller: Generally Known as a Lecturer on the Prophecies and the Second Coming of Christ.* Boston: Joshua V. Himes, 1853.

Bloch, Marc. *The Historian's Craft.* Translated by Peter Putnam. New York: Vintage Books, 1964.

Bloch-Smith, Elizabeth. "Assyrians Abet Israelite Cultic Reforms." In *Exploring the Longue Durée: Essays in Honor of Lawrence E. Stager,* edited by J. D. Schloen. Winona Lake, IN: Eisenbrauns, 2009.

Blum, Erhard. "The Israelite Tribal System: Literary Fiction or Social Reality?" In *Saul, Benjamin, and the Emergence of Monarchy in Israel: Biblical and Archaeological Perspectives,* edited by Joachim J. Krause, Omer Sergi, and Kristin Weingart, 201–22. Atlanta: Society of Biblical Literature, 2020.

Boime, Albert. "Patriarchy Fixed in Stone: Gutzon Borglum's 'Mount Rushmore.'" *American Art* 5, no. 1/2 (1991): 143–67.

Bolin, Thomas. "The Temple of Yahu at Elephantine and Persian Religious Policy." In *The Triumph of Elohim: From Yahwisms to Judaisms,* edited by Diana Vikander Edelman, 127–42. Kampen: Kok Pharos, 1995.

Bond, Sarah E. "Building the Iron Gates of Alexander: The Migrant Caravan & Geographies of Fear." *History From Below: Musings on Daily Life in the Ancient and Early Medieval Mediterranean* (blog), November 25, 2018. https://sarahemilybond.com/2018/11/25/building-the-iron-gates-of-alexander-the-migrant-caravan-geographies-of-fear/.

Boudinot, Elias. *A Star in the West, or, A Humble Attempt to Discover the Long Lost Ten Tribes of Israel, Preparatory to Their Return to their Beloved City, Jerusalem.* Trenton, NJ: D. Fenton, S. Hutchinson, and J. Dunham, 1816.

Bourdieu, Pierre. *Outline of a Theory of Practice.* Cambridge: Cambridge University Press, 1977.

Bourgel, Jonathan. "The Destruction of the Samaritan Temple by John Hyrcanus: A Reconsideration." *Journal of Biblical Literature* 135, no. 3 (2016): 505–23.

Bowman, John. *Samaritan Documents Relating to Their History, Religion, and Life.* Pittsburgh: Pickwick, 1977.

Boyle, John Andrew. "Alexander and the Mongols." *Journal of the Royal Asiatic Society of Great Britain and Ireland*, no. 2 (1979): 123–36.

Braude, William. *Pesikta Rabbati.* New Haven, CT: Yale University Press, 1968.

Brewer, Keagan. *Prester John: The Legend and Its Sources.* Crusader Texts in Translation 27. Farnham: Ashgate, 2015.

Bright, John. *A History of Israel.* 4th ed. Louisville, KY: Westminster John Knox, 2000.

Bringhurst, Newell. "Applause, Attack, and Ambivalence: Varied Responses to *No Man Knows My History*." In *Reconsidering No Man Knows My History*, edited by Newell Bringhurst, 39–59. Logan, UT: Utah State University Press, 1996.

  ed. *Reconsidering No Man Knows My History.* Logan, UT: Utah State University Press, 1996.

Brodhead, Richard H. "Prophets in America circa 1830: Ralph Waldo Emerson, Nat Turner, Joseph Smith." In *Joseph Smith Jr.: Reappraisals after Two Centuries*, edited by Terryl L. Givens and Reid L. Neilson, 13–30. Oxford: Oxford University Press, 2009.

Brodie, Fawn M. *No Man Knows My History: The Life of Joseph Smith, the Mormon Prophet.* New York: Knopf, 1971.

Brooke, John L. *The Refiner's Fire: The Making of Mormon Cosmology, 1644–1844.* Cambridge: Cambridge University Press, 1996.

Brooks, Michael E. "*Prester John: A Reexamination and Compendium of the Mythical Figure Who Helped Spark European Expansion.*" PhD dissertation, University of Toledo, 2009.

Broshi, Magen, and Israel Finkelstein. "The Population of Palestine in Iron Age II." *Bulletin of the American Schools of Oriental Research* 287 (1992): 45–60.

Brubaker, Rogers. *Ethnicity Without Groups.* Cambridge, MA: Harvard University Press, 2004.

  Nationalist Politics and Everyday Ethnicity in a Transylvanian Town. Princeton, NJ: Princeton University Press, 2006.

Bruce, James. *Travels to Discover the Source of the Nile.* Vol. 1. Edinburgh: James Ruthven, 1790.

Bruneau, Phillippe, and Pierre Bordreuil. "Les Israélites de Délos et la juiverie délienne." *Bulletin de correspondance hellénique* 106, no. 1 (1982): 465–504.

Bushman, Richard Lyman. "Joseph Smith and His Visions." In *The Oxford Handbook of Mormonism*, edited by Terryl L. Givens and Philip L. Barlow, 109–20. Oxford: Oxford University Press, 2015.

Joseph Smith: Rough Stone Rolling. New York: Knopf, 2005.

Mormonism: A Very Short Introduction. Oxford: Oxford University Press, 2008.

Byron, George Gordon. "The Destruction of Sennacherib." Accessed March 1, 2021. www.poetryfoundation.org/poems/43827/the-destruction-of-sennacherib.

Caledonian Mercury. "The Ten Lost Jewish Tribes." *Religious Monitor and Evangelical Repository (1824–1842)*, January 1829.

Callender Jr., Dexter E., and William Scott Green. "Introduction: Scholarship Between Myth and Scripture." In *Myth and Scripture: Contemporary Perspectives on Religion, Language, and Imagination*, edited by Dexter E. Callender, Jr., 1–14. Atlanta: SBL Press, 2014.

Carr, David M. *The Formation of the Hebrew Bible: A New Reconstruction*. New York: Oxford University Press, 2011.

Casas, Bartolomé de las. *Witness: Writings of Bartolomé de Las Casas*. Edited by George Sanderlin. Maryknoll, NY: Orbis Books, 1992.

Chaklay, A. "Processes of Identity Consolidation among Ethiopian Adolescents, Theory and Group Intervention Model." *From Disconnection to Integration (Menituk Leshiluv)* 11 (2002): 8–21.

Chalmers, Matthew. "Viewing Samaritans Jewishly: Josephus, the Samaritans, and the Identification of Israel." *Journal for the Study of Judaism* 51, no. 3 (2020): 339–66.

Chazan, Robert. *European Jewry and the First Crusade*. Berkeley, CA: University of California Press, 1987.

Chehata, Hanan. "Israel: Promised Land for Jews … as Long as They're Not Black?" *Race & Class* 53, no. 4 (2012): 67–77.

Chiu, Allyson. "Stop Calling the Mormon Church 'Mormon,' Says Church Leader. 'LDS' Is Out, Too." *Washington Post*. August 17, 2018, Online edition.

Clay, Albert T. *Business Documents of Murashu Sons of Nippur Dated in the Reign of Darius II*. Philadelphia: University of Pennsylvania Press, 1912.

Coakley, John W., and Andrea Sterk, eds. "Asian and African Christianity in the Late Middle Ages." In *Readings in World Christian History*, 1:373–84. Maryknoll, NY: Orbis Books, 2004.

Cogley, Richard W. "The Ancestry of the American Indians: Thomas Thorowgood's Iewes in America (1650) and Jews in America (1660)." *English Literary Renaissance* 35, no. 2 (2005): 304–30.

Cohen, Norman J. "The London Manuscript of Midrash Pesiqta Rabbati: A Key Text-Witness Comes to Light." *The Jewish Quarterly Review* 73, no. 3 (1983): 209–37.

Coogan, Michael David. "Life in the Diaspora: Jews at Nippur in the Fifth Century B.C." *The Biblical Archaeologist* 37, no. 1 (1974): 6–12.

"More Yahwistic Names in the Murashu Documents." *Journal for the Study of Judaism in the Persian, Hellenistic, and Roman Period* 7, no. 2 (1976): 199–200.

Cook, Edward M. "The 'Kaufman Effect' in the Pseudo-Jonathan Targum." *Aramaic Studies* 4, no. 2 (2006): 123–32.

Cooper, Alanna E. "Conceptualizing Diaspora: Tales of Jewish Travelers in Search of the Lost Tribes." *AJS Review* 30, no. 1 (2006): 95–117.

Corinaldi, Michael. *Jewish Identity: The Case of Ethiopian Jewry*. Jerusalem: Magness Press, 1998.

"The Personal Status of the Samaritans in Israel." In *Samaritan Researches*, edited by Vittorio Morabito, Alan D. Crown, and Lucy Davey, 5:285–302. Studies in Judaica 10. Sydney: Mandelbaum Publishing, 2000.

Crane, Oliver Turnbull. *The Samaritan Chronicle or The Book of Joshua, The Son of Nun*. New York: John B. Alden, 1890.

Crielaard, J. P. "The Ionians in the Archaic Period: Shifting Identities in a Changing World." In *Ethnic Constructs in Antiquity: The Role of Power and Tradition*, edited by Ton Derks and Nico Royman, 37–84. Amsterdam Archaeological Studies 13. Amsterdam: Amsterdam University Press, 2009.

Cross, Frank Moore. "A Reconstruction of the Judean Restoration." *Journal of Biblical Literature* 94, no. 1 (1975): 4–18.

"Aspects of Samaritan and Jewish History in Late Persian and Hellenistic Times." *Harvard Theological Review* 59 (1966): 201–11.

From Epic to Canon: History and Literature in Ancient Israel. Baltimore: Johns Hopkins University Press, 1998.

"Papyri of the Fourth Century BC from Daliyeh." In *New Directions in Biblical Archaeology*, edited by David Noel Freedman and J. C. Greenfield, 41–62. Garden City, NY: Doubleday, 1969.

"The Discovery of the Samaria Papyri." *The Biblical Archaeologist* 26, no. 4 (1963): 109–21.

Cross, Frank Moore, and David Noel Freedman. "The Blessing of Moses." *Journal of Biblical Literature* 67, no. 3 (1948): 191–210.

Crouch, Carly L. *The Making of Israel: Cultural Diversity in the Southern Levant and the Formation of Ethnic Identity in Deuteronomy*. Leiden: Brill, 2014.

Crown, Alan D. "Redating the Schism Between the Judeans and the Samaritans." *Jewish Quarterly Review* 82 (1991): 17–50.

"The Samaritan Diaspora." In *The Samaritans*, edited by Alan D. Crown, 195–217. Tübingen: Mohr Siebeck, 1989.

Curtis, John Briggs. "Some Suggestions Concerning the History of the Tribe of Reuben." *Journal of the American Academy of Religion* 33, no. 3 (1965): 247–49.

D'Abbadie, Antoine. "Réponses des Falashas dit Juif d'Abyssinie aux questions faites par M. Luzzato." *Archives Israélites* 12 (1851–52): 179–85; 234–40; 259–69.

Dalley, Stephanie. "Foreign Chariotry and Cavalry in the Armies of Tiglath-Pileser III." *Iraq* 47 (1985): 31–48.

Darshan, Guy. "The Story of the Sons of God and the Daughters of Men (Gen 6:1–4) and the Hesiodic Catalogue of Women." *Shnaton, an Annual for Biblical and Ancient Near Eastern Studies* 23 (2014): 155–78.

Dashdondog, Bayarsaikhan. "A Brief Historical Background of the Armenians and the Mongols." In *The Mongols and the Armenians (1220–1335)*, 31–42. Leiden: Brill, 2011.

Davies, Philip R. *In Search of "Ancient Israel": A Study in Biblical Origins.* Journal for the Study of the Old Testament Supplement 148. Sheffield: JSOT Press, 1992.

In Search of "Ancient Israel": A Study in Biblical Origins. 2nd ed. Edinburgh: T&T Clark, 2004.

"The Origins of Biblical Israel." In *Enquire of the Former Age: Ancient Historiography and Writing the History of Israel,* edited by Lester L. Grabbe, 40–48. New York: T&T Clark, 2011.

Dawson, Graham. "Objectivism and the Social Construction of Knowledge." *Philosophy* 56, no. 217 (1981): 414–23.

De Geus, C. H. J. *The Tribes of Israel.* Studia Semitica Neerlandica 18. Assen: Van Gorcum, 1976.

Delamarter, Steve. "The Content and Order of Books in Ethiopic Old Testament Manuscripts." In *Reading the Bible in Ancient Traditions and Modern Editions: Studies in Memory of Peter W. Flint,* edited by Andrew B. Perrin, Kyung S. Baek, and Daniel K. Falk, 105–62. Atlanta: SBL Press, 2017.

"Descendants of Israel." *Philadelphia Recorder (1823–1831),* July 8, 1826.

DeWeese, Devin. "The Influence of the Mongols on the Religious Consciousness of Thirteenth Century Europe." *Mongolian Studies* 5 (1978): 41–78.

Dexinger, F. "Der Ursprung der Samaritaner im Spiegel der frühen Quellen." In *Die Samaritaner,* edited by F. Dexinger and Reinhard Pummer, 67–140. Wege der Forschung 604. Darmstadt: Wissenschäftliche Buchgesellschaft, 1992.

Dijkstra, Meindert. "Origins of Israel Between History and Ideology." In *Between Evidence and Ideology: Essays on the History of Ancient Israel Read at the Joint Meeting of the Society for Old Testament Study and the Oudtestamentisch Werkgezelschap, Lincoln, July 2009,* edited by Bob Becking and Lester L. Grabbe, 41–82. Oudtestamentische Studiën 59. Leiden: Brill, 2011.

Doniger, Wendy. *The Implied Spider: Politics and Theology in Myth.* New York: Columbia University Press, 2011.

Dönitz, Saskia. "Alexander the Great in Medieval Hebrew Traditions." In *A Companion to Alexander Literature in the Middle Ages,* edited by Z. David Zuwiyya, 21–40. Leiden: Brill, 2011.

Dougherty, Matthew W. *Lost Tribes Found: Israelite Indians and Religious Nationalism in Early America.* Norman, OK: University of Oklahoma Press, 2021.

Droeber, Julia. *The Dynamics of Coexistence in the Middle East: Negotiating Boundaries Between Christians, Muslims, Jews and Samaritans in Palestine.* Library of Modern Middle East Studies 135. London: I.B. Tauris, 2014.

Duffy, John-Charles. "Mapping Book of Mormon Historicity Debates – Part I: A Guide for the Overwhelmed." *Sunstone,* 151 (2008): 36–62.

"Mapping Book of Mormon Historicity Debates – Part II: Perspectives from the Sociology of Knowledge." *Sunstone,* 152 (2008), 46–61.

Dušek, Jan. *Aramaic and Hebrew Inscriptions from Mt. Gerizim and Samaria Between Antiochus III and Antiochus IV Epiphanes.* Culture and History of the Ancient Near East 54. Leiden: Brill, 2012.

"Archaeology and Texts in the Persian Period: Focus on Sanballat." In *Congress Volume Helsinki 2010*, edited by Martti Nissinen, 117–32. Leiden: Brill, 2012.

Les Manuscrits araméens du Wadi Daliyeh et la Samarie vers 450–332 av. J.-C. Culture and History of the Ancient Near East 30. Leiden: Brill, 2007.

"Mt. Gerizim Sanctuary, Its History and Enigma of Origin." *Hebrew Bible and Ancient Israel* 3, no. 1 (2014): 111–33.

Dyck, Jonathan E. "Ethnicity and the Bible." In *Ethnicity and the Bible*, edited by Mark G. Brett, 89–116. Leiden: Brill, 1996.

Edelman, Martin. "Who Is An Israeli? 'Halakhah' and Citizenship in the Jewish State." *Jewish Political Studies Review* 10, no. 3/4 (1998): 87–115.

Efron, Noah J. "Knowledge of Newly Discovered Lands among Jewish Communities of Europe (from 1492 to the Thirty Years' War)." In *The Jews and the Expansion of Europe to the West, 1450 to 1800*, edited by Paolo Bernardini and Norman Fiering, 47–72. New York: Berghahn Books, 2001.

Eisenstein, Judah David. *Ozar Midrashim*. Vol. II. New York: J. D. Eisenstein, 1915.

Eliav-Feldon, Miriam. "Invented Identities: Credulity in the Age of Prophecy and Exploration." *Journal of Early Modern History* 3, no. 3 (1999): 203–32.

Engeström, Yrjo. "Activity Theory and the Social Construction of Knowledge: A Story of Four Umpires." *Organization* 7, no. 2 (2000): 301–10.

Eph'al, Israel. "Changes in Palestine during the Persian Period in Light of Epigraphic Sources." *Israel Exploration Journal* 48, no. 1/2 (1998): 106–19.

Epstein, Abraham. *Eldad ha-Dani: Seine Berichte über die X Stämme und deren Ritus*. Pressburg: Adolf Alkalay, 1891.

Erll, Astrid. "Cultural Memory Studies: An Introduction." In *Cultural Memory Studies: An International and Interdisciplinary Handbook*, edited by Astrid Erll and Ansgar Nünning, 1–16. Berlin: De Gruyter, 2010.

Eshel, Esther, and Hanan Eshel. "Dating the Samaritan Pentateuch's Compilation in Light of the Qumran Biblical Scrolls." In *Emanuel: Studies in the Hebrew Bible, Septuagint, and Dead Sea Scrolls in Honor of Emanuel Tov*, edited by Shalom M. Paul, 215–40. Vetus Testamentum Supplement 94. Leiden: Brill, 2003.

Eshkoli, A. Z. *Sipur Dayid Ha-Re'uveni: 'al-Pi Ketav-Yad Oksford : Be-Tseruf Ketavim Ve-'eduyot Mi-Bene Ha-Dor, 'im Mavo Ve-He'arot*. Jerusalem: Mosad Byalik, 1993.

Eubanks, Charlotte, and Pasang Yangjee Sherpa. "We Are (Are We?) All Indigenous Here, and Other Claims About Space, Place, and Belonging in Asia." *Verge: Studies in Global Asias* 4, no. 2 (2018): vi–xiv.

Evans-Pritchard, E. E. *The Nuer*. Oxford: Clarendon Press, 1940.

Faitlovitch, Jacques. *The Falashas*. London: Forgotten Books, 2012.

Fauvelle-Aymar, François-Xavier. "Desperately Seeking the Jewish Kingdom of Ethiopia: Benjamin of Tudela and the Horn of Africa (Twelfth Century)." *Speculum* 88, no. 2 (2013): 383–404.

Fenton, Elizabeth. *Old Canaan in a New World: Native Americans and the Lost Tribes of Israel*. North American Religions. New York: New York University Press, 2020.

Finkelberg, Margalit. *Greeks and Pre-Greeks: Aegean Prehistory and Greek Heroic Tradition.* Cambridge: Cambridge University Press, 2005.

"The *Cypria,* the *Iliad* and the Problem of Multiformity in Oral and Written Tradition." *Classical Philology* 95, no. 1 (2000): 1–11.

Finkelstein, Israel. "A Great United Monarchy? Archaeological and Historical Perspectives." In *One God, One Cult, One Nation: Archaeological and Biblical Perspectives,* edited by Reinhard G. Kratz and Hermann Spieckermann, 3–28. Berlin: De Gruyter, 2010.

"King Solomon's Golden Age? History or Myth?" In *The Quest for the Historical Israel: Debating Archaeology and the History of Israel,* edited by Brian B. Schmidt, 107–16. Atlanta: Society of Biblical Literature, 2007.

"Saul, Benjamin and the Emergence of 'Biblical Israel': An Alternative View." *Zeitschrift für die alttestamentliche Wissenschaft* 123, no. 3 (2011): 348–67.

The Forgotten Kingdom: The Archaeology and History of Northern Israel. Ancient Near East Monographs 5. Atlanta: Society of Biblical Literature, 2013.

Finkelstein, Israel, and Neil A. Silberman. *David and Solomon: In Search of the Bible's Sacred Kings and the Roots of the Western Tradition.* New York: Free Press, 2006.

The Bible Unearthed: Archaeology's New Vision of Ancient Israel and the Origin of Its Sacred Texts. New York: Free Press, 2001.

Finkelstein, Jacob J. "The Genealogy of the Hammurapi Dynasty." *Journal of Cuneiform Studies* 20, no. 3/4 (1966): 95–118.

Finney, Charles Grandison. *Memoirs of Rev. Charles G. Finney.* New York: Fleming H. Revell Company, 1876.

Fleming, Daniel. *The Legacy of Israel in Judah's Bible.* New York: Cambridge University Press, 2012.

Flesher, Paul V. M., and Bruce Chilton. *The Targums: A Critical Introduction.* Waco, TX: Baylor University Press, 2011.

Fowler, Robert L. "Genealogical Thinking, Hesiod's Catalogue and the Creation of the Hellenes." *Proceedings of the Cambridge Philological Society* 44 (1999): 1–19.

Frankopan, Peter. *The First Crusade: The Call from the East.* Cambridge, MA: Harvard University Press, 2012.

Freedman, Marci. "*The Transmission and Reception of Benjamin of Tudela's Book of Travels from the Twelfth Century to 1633.*" PhD dissertation, University of Manchester, 2016.

Frendo, Anthony J. "Back to Basics: A Holistic Approach to the Problem of the Emergence of Ancient Israel." In *In Search of Pre-Exilic Israel,* edited by John Day, 41–64. London: T&T Clark International, 2006.

Fried, Lisbeth S. "Ezra among Christians, Samaritans, Muslims, and Jews of Late Antiquity." In *Ezra and the Law in History and Tradition,* 118–47. Columbia, SC: University of South Carolina Press, 2014.

Gal, Zvi. *Lower Galilee During the Iron Age.* Winona Lake, IN: Eisenbrauns, 1992.

Gaster, Moses. "The Chain of Samaritan High Priests: A Synchronistic Synopsis: Published for the First Time." *Journal of the Royal Asiatic Society of Great Britain and Ireland* 41 (1909): 393–420.

The Samaritans, Their History, Doctrines and Literature. London: Oxford University Press, 1925.

Gates, Jim. "Giving the House a Home." *Baseball Hall of Fame*. Accessed April 22, 2020. https://baseballhall.org/house-of-david-donation.

Geary, Patrick J. *The Myth of Nations: The Medieval Origins of Europe*. Princeton, NJ: Princeton University Press, 2002.

Gelb, Ignace J. "Two Assyrian King Lists." *Journal of Near Eastern Studies* 13, no. 4 (1954): 209–30.

Gerson, Stephen N. "Fractional Coins of Judea and Samaria in the Fourth Century BCE." *Near Eastern Archaeology* 64, no. 3 (2001): 106–21.

Getty Images. "Babe Ruth Posing in Fake Beard," *March* 28, 1931. www.gettyimages.com/detail/news-photo/the-new-babe-ruth-at-the-house-of-david-brought-baseball-news-photo/515513766.

Gillman, Ian, and Hans-Joachim Klimkeit. *Christians in Asia before 1500*. Abingdon: Routledge, 1999.

Gil-White, Francisco. "How Thick Is Blood? The Plot Thickens ... If Ethnic Actors Are Primordialists, What Remains of the Circumstantialist/Primordialist Controversy?" *Ethnic and Racial Studies* 22, no. 5 (1999): 789–820.

Givens, Terryl L. *By the Hand of Mormon: The American Scripture that Launched a New World Religion*. Oxford: Oxford University Press, 2002.

Gobat, Samuel. *Journal of a Three Years' Residence in Abyssinia*. 2nd ed. London, 1850.

Goodwillie, Christian. "Baseball, Beards, Bands, and the Babes: Michigan's House of David Religious Community." *The Ephemera Journal* 18, no. 3 (2016): 1, 4–9.

Gould, Eric D., Victor Lavy, and M. Daniele Paserman. "Sixty Years after the Magic Carpet Ride: The Long-Run Effect of the Early Child Environment on Social and Economic Outcomes." *The Review of Economic Studies* 78, no. 3 (2011): 938–73.

Grabbe, Lester L. "The Case of the Corrupting Consensus." In *Between Evidence and Ideology: Essays on the History of Ancient Israel Read at the Joint Meeting of the Society for Old Testament Study and the Oudtestamentisch Werkgezelschap, Lincoln, July 2009*, edited by Bob Becking and Lester L. Grabbe, 83–92. Oudtestamentische Studiën 59. Leiden: Brill, 2011.

Graham, Laura R., and H. Glenn Penny. "Performing Indigeneity: Emergent Identity, Self-Determination, and Sovereignty." In *Performing Indigeneity: Global Histories and Contemporary Experiences*, edited by Laura R. Graham and H. Glenn Penny, 1–31. Lincoln, NE: University of Nebraska Press, 2014.

Granerød, Gard. "Canon and Archive: Yahwism in Elephantine and Āl-Yāḫūdu as a Challenge to the Canonical History of Judean Religion in the Persian Period." *Journal of Biblical Literature* 138, no. 2 (2019): 345–64.

Greenblatt, Stephen. *Shakespearean Negotiations: The Circulation of Social Energy in Renaissance England*. Berkeley, CA: University of California Press, 1988.

Gropp, Douglas M. *Wadi Daliyeh II: The Samaria Papyri from Wadi Daliyeh*. Discoveries in the Judaean Desert 28. Oxford: Oxford University Press, 2001.

Gruen, Erich S. "Foundation Legends." In *Rethinking the Other in Antiquity*, 223–52. Princeton, NJ: Princeton University Press, 2011.

Gudme, Anne Katrine de Hemmer. *Before the God in This Place for Good Remembrance: A Comparative Analysis of the Aramaic Votive Inscriptions from Mount Gerizim*. Berlin: De Gruyter, 2013.

Gunkel, Hermann. *The Legends of Genesis*. Translated by W. H. Carruth. Handkommentar zum Alten Testament 1. Chicago: Open Court Publishing, 1901.

Gutjahr, Paul C. *The Book of Mormon: A Biography*. Princeton, NJ: Princeton University Press, 2012.

Halbfinger, David M., and Isabel Kershner. "After a Police Shooting, Ethiopian Israelis Seek a 'Black Lives Matter' Reckoning." *The New York Times*, July 13, 2019, sec. *World*.

Hall, Jonathan M. *Ethnic Identity in Greek Antiquity*. Cambridge: Cambridge University Press, 1997.

Hellenicity: Between Ethnicity and Culture. Chicago: University of Chicago Press, 2002.

Halper, J. "The Absorption of Ethiopian Immigrants: A Return to the Fifties." *Israel Social Science Research* 1–2 (1985): 112–39.

Hames-García, Michael Roy. *Identity Complex: Making the Case for Multiplicity*. Minneapolis: University of Minnesota Press, 2011.

Hamilton, Bernard. "Continental Drift: Prester John's Progress through the Indies." In *Prester John, the Mongols and the Ten Lost Tribes*, edited by Bernard Hamilton and Charles F. Beckingham, 237–70. Aldershot: Variorum, 1996.

"Prester John and the Three Kings of Cologne." In *Studies in Medieval History Presented to R.H.C. Davis*, edited by Henry Mayr-Harting and R. I. Moore, 177–91. London: Hambledon Press, 1985.

Handler, Richard. "Reinventing the Invention of Culture." *Social Analysis: The International Journal of Social and Cultural Practice* 46, no. 1 (2002): 26–34.

Handler, Richard, and Jocelyn Linnekin. "Tradition, Genuine or Spurious." *Journal of American Folklore* 97, no. 385 (1984): 273–90.

Hangen, Tona J. "Lived Religion Among Mormons." In *The Oxford Handbook of Mormonism*, edited by Terryl L. Givens and Philip L. Barlow, 209–26. Oxford: Oxford University Press, 2015.

Hansen, Klaus J. "Joseph Smith, American Culture, and the Origins of Mormonism." In *Joseph Smith Jr.: Reappraisals after Two Centuries*, edited by Terryl L. Givens and Reid L. Neilson, 31–47. Oxford: Oxford University Press, 2009.

Hanson, F. Allan. *The Trouble with Culture: How Computers Are Calming the Culture Wars*. Albany, NY: State University of New York Press, 2007.

Hardy, Grant. "The Book of Mormon." In *The Oxford Handbook of Mormonism*, edited by Terryl L. Givens and Philip L. Barlow, 134–48. Oxford: Oxford University Press, 2015.

Harrison, Simon. "Identity as a Scarce Resource." *Social Anthropology* 7, no. 3 (1999): 239–51.

Harrison, William Henry. *A Discourse on the Aborigines of the Ohio Valley, in Which the Opinions of Its Conquest in the Seventeenth Century by the*

Iroquois Or Six Nations, Supported by Cadwallader Colden … Gov. Thomas Pownall … Dr. Benjamin Franklin … Hon. De Witt Clinton … and Judge John Haywood … Are Examined and Contested; to Which Are Prefixed Some Remarks on the Study of History. Chicago: Fergus Printing Company, 1883.

Hatke, George. *Aksum and Nubia*. New York: New York University Press and the Institute for the Study of the Ancient World, 2013.

"Holy Land and Sacred History: A View from Early Ethiopia." In *Visions of Community in the Post-Roman World: The West, Byzantium and the Islamic World, 300–1100*, edited by Walter Pohl, Clemens Gantner, and Richard Payne. Farnham: Ashgate, 2012.

Hawkins, Joel, and Terry Bertolino. *The House of David Baseball Team*. Chicago: Arcadia Publishing, 2000.

Helleiner, Karl F. "Prester John's Letter: A Mediaeval Utopia." *Phoenix* 13, no. 2 (1959): 47–57.

Hendel, Ronald. "The Exodus in Biblical Memory." *Journal of Biblical Literature* 120, no. 4 (2001): 601–22.

Hensel, Benedikt. "On the Relationship of Judah and Samaria in Post-Exilic Times: A Farewell to the Conflict Paradigm." *Journal for the Study of the Old Testament* 44, no. 1 (2019): 19–42.

Hidal, Sten. "The Land of Cush in the Old Testament." *Svensk Exegetisk Årsbok* 41 (1977): 97–106.

Hill, John Spencer. *John Milton: Poet, Priest and Prophet; A Study of Divine Vocation in Milton's Poetry and Prose*. London: Macmillan, 1979.

Hill, Marvin S. "Secular or Sectarian History? A Critique of *No Man Knows My History*." In *Reconsidering No Man Knows My History*, edited by Newell Bringhurst, 60–93. Logan, UT: Utah State University Press, 1996.

Hillelson, S. "David Reubeni, An Early Visitor to Sennar." *Sudan Notes and Records* 16, no. 1 (1933): 55–66.

Hjelm, Ingrid. "The Hezekiah Narrative as a Foundation Myth for Jerusalem's Rise to Sovereignty." *Islamic Studies* 40, no. 3/4 (2001): 661–74.

The Samaritans and Early Judaism. Journal for the Study of the Old Testament Supplement 303. Sheffield: Sheffield Academic Press, 2000.

"Tribes, Genealogies and the Composition of the Hebrew Bible." In *The Politics of Israel's Past: The Bible, Archaeology, and Nation-Building*, edited by Emanuel Pfoh and Keith W. Whitelam, 18–27. Sheffield: Sheffield Phoenix, 2013.

Hobsbawm, Eric. "Introduction: Inventing Traditions." In *The Invention of Tradition*, edited by Eric Hobsbawm and Terence Ranger, 1–14. Cambridge: Cambridge University Press, 1983.

Hobsbawm, Eric, and Terence Ranger, eds. *The Invention of Tradition*. Cambridge: Cambridge University Press, 1983.

Høgenhaven, Jesper. *Gott und Volk bei Jesaja: Eine Untersuchung zur biblischen Theologie*. Acta Theologica Danica 24. Leiden: Brill, 1988.

Holmes, J. Teresa. "When Blood Matters: Making Kinship in Colonial Kenya." In *Kinship and Beyond: The Genealogical Model Reconsidered*, edited by

Sandra Bamford and James Leach, 50–83. New York: Berghahn Books, 2009.

Holter, Knut. *Yahweh in Africa: Essays on Africa and the Old Testament.* Bible and Theology in Africa 1. New York: Peter Lang, 2000.

Hong, Koog P. "Once Again: The Emergence of 'Biblical Israel.'" *Zeitschrift für die alttestamentliche Wissenschaft* 125, no. 2 (2013): 278–88.

"The Deceptive Pen of Scribes: Judean Reworking of the Bethel Tradition as a Program for Assuming Israelite Identity." *Biblica* 92, no. 3 (2011): 427–41.

Howe, Daniel Walker. "Emergent Mormonism in Context." In *The Oxford Handbook of Mormonism,* edited by Terryl L. Givens and Philip L. Barlow, 23–37. Oxford: Oxford University Press, 2015.

Irwin, Elizabeth. "Gods among Men? The Social and Political Dynamics of the Hesiodic Catalogue of Women." In *The Hesiodic Catalogue of Women,* edited by Richard L. Hunter, 35–84. Cambridge: Cambridge University Press, 2005.

Israelite House of David Benton Harbor, Michigan. "Israelite House of David – Read It On-Line: 'The Key of the House of David.'" Accessed April 23, 2020. https://m.israelitehouseofdavid.com/the_key.html.

"Israelite House of David – Read It On-Line: 'The Little Book.'" Accessed April 23, 2020. https://m.israelitehouseofdavid.com/the_little_book.html.

"Israelite House of David Reading Materials." Accessed April 23, 2020. https://m.israelitehouseofdavid.com/reading_materials.html.

Jablonski, Nina G. "Skin Color and the Establishment of Races." In *Living Color: The Biological and Social Meaning of Skin Color,* 134–41. Berkeley, CA: University of California Press, 2012.

Jacobs, Martin. "Karaites, Samaritans, and Lost Tribes." In *Reorienting the East: Jewish Travelers to the Medieval Muslim World,* 180–90. Philadelphia: University of Pennsylvania Press, 2014.

Jeffreys, Elizabeth M., Anthony Cutler, and Alexander Kazhdan. "Alexander Romance." In *The Oxford Dictionary of Byzantium.* Oxford: Oxford University Press, 2005. www.oxfordreference.com/view/10.1093/acref/9780195046526.001.0001/acref-9780195046526-e-0163.

Jewish Virtual Library. "Israel's Basic Laws: The Law of Return (July 5, 1950)." Accessed January 19, 2021. www.jewishvirtuallibrary.org/israel-s-law-of-return.

Johnson, Christine R. "Renaissance German Cosmographers and the Naming of America." *Past & Present,* no. 191 (2006): 3–43.

Johnson, David W. "Dating the Kebra Nagast: Another Look." In *Peace and War in Byzantium,* edited by T. S. Miller and J. Nesbitt, 197–208. Washington, DC: The Catholic University of America Press, 1995.

Johnson, Jeffery Ogden. "Determining and Defining 'Wife': The Brigham Young Households." In *Brigham Young's Homes,* edited by Sandra Dawn Brimhall, Marianne Harding Burgoyne, Mark D. Curtis, Randall Dixon, Judy Dykman, Elinor Hyde, Kari K. Robinson, and Colleen Whitley, 1–12. Boulder, CO: University Press of Colorado, 2002.

Johnson, Marshall D. *The Purpose of the Biblical Genealogies with Special Reference to the Setting of the Genealogies of Jesus.* London: Cambridge University Press, 1969.

Johnson, Paul E. *A Shopkeeper's Millennium: Society and Revivals in Rochester, New York, 1815–1837.* New York: Farrar, Straus & Giroux, 2004.

Jones, Christopher Cannon. "'A Necessary Book for Dark-Skinned People': Nineteenth-Century Missions, Race, and Scripture." In *American Examples: New Conversations about Religion, Volume Two,* edited by Samah Choudhury and Prea Persaud. Tuscaloosa: The University of Alabama Press, 2022.

Joppke, Christian, and Zeev Rosenhek. "Contesting Ethnic Immigration." *European Journal of Sociology* 43, no. 3 (2002): 301–35.

Joyce, James. *Finnegans Wake.* Edited by Robert-Jan Henkes, Erik Bindervoet, and Finn Fordham. Oxford: Oxford University Press, 2012.

Kallai, Zecharia. "A Note on the Twelve-Tribe Systems of Israel." *Vetus Testamentum* 49, no. 1 (1999): 125–27.

"The Beginnings of Israel: A Methodological Working Hypothesis." *Israel Exploration Journal* 59, no. 2 (2009): 194–203.

"The Twelve-Tribe Systems of Israel." *Vetus Testamentum* 47, no. 1 (1997): 53–90.

Kaplan, Steven B. "Genealogies and Gene-Ideologies: The Legitimacy of the Beta Israel: (Falasha)." *Social Identities* 12, no. 4 (2006): 447–55.

"Kifu-Qen: The Great Famine of 1888–1892 and the Beta Israel (Falasha)." *Paideuma: Mitteilungen zur Kulturkunde* 36 (1990): 67–77.

"Review: The Hebrew Letters of Prester John by Edward Ullendorf, C.F. Beckingham." *Numen* 32, no. 2 (1985): 282–84.

The Beta Israel: Falasha in Ethiopia – From Earliest Times to the Twentieth Century. New York: New York University Press, 1992.

"The Invention of Ethiopian Jews: Three Models." *Cahiers d'Études Africaines* 132 (1993): 645–58.

Kaplan, Steven B., and Hagar Salamon. "Ethiopian Jews in Israel: A Part of the People or Apart from the People?" In *Jews in Israel: Contemporary Social and Cultural Patterns,* edited by Uzi Rebhun and Chaim Isaac Waxman, 118–50. Lebanon, NH: Brandeis University Press, 2004.

Karadawi, Ahmed. "The Smuggling of the Ethiopian Falasha to Israel Through Sudan." *African Affairs* 90 (1991): 23–50.

Kartveit, Magnar. "Samaritan Self-Consciousness in the First Half of the Second Century B.C.E. in Light of the Inscriptions from Mount Gerizim and Delos." *Journal for the Study of Judaism in the Persian, Hellenistic, and Roman Period* 45, no. 4/5 (2014): 449–70.

The Origins of the Samaritans. Vetus Testamentum Supplement 128. Leiden: Brill, 2009.

Katriel, Tamar. "The Rhetoric of Rescue: 'Salvage Immigration' Narratives in Israeli Culture." In *Jewish Studies at the Crossroads of Anthropology and Literature: Authority, Diaspora, Tradition,* edited by Ra'anan S. Boustan, Oren Kosansky, and Marina Rustow, 185–203. Philadelphia: University of Pennsylvania Press, 2011.

Katz, David. "The Wanderings of the Lost Ten Tribes from 'Mikveigh Yisrael' to Timothy McVeigh." In *The Jews and the Expansion of Europe to the West, 1450–1800*, edited by Paolo Bernardini and Norman Fiering. New York: Berghahn Books, 2001.

Katz, Nathan. *Who Are the Jews of India?* Berkeley, CA: University of California Press, 2000.

Kaufman, Stephen A. "Targum Pseudo-Jonathan and Late Jewish Literary Aramaic." *Aramaic Studies* 11, no. 1 (2013): 1–26.

Kawashima, Robert S. *Biblical Narrative and the Death of the Rhapsode.* Bloomington, IN: Indiana University Press, 2004.

Kessler, David. *The Falashas: A Short History.* 2nd ed. London: Frank Cass, 1996.

The Falashas: The Forgotten Jews of Ethiopia. New York: Africana, 1982.

Kessler, Rainer. *The Social History of Ancient Israel.* Translated by Linda M. Maloney. Minneapolis: Fortress Press, 2008.

Kim, Margaret. "The Itinerary of Benjamin of Tudela, Lost Israelites, and Vanishing Indians: Trans-Atlantic English Reception of the Medieval Past in the Seventeenth Century." *EurAmerica* 40, no. 1 (2010): 103–31.

Kippenberg, H. G. *Garizim und Synagogue: Traditionsgeschichtliche Untersuchungen zur samaritanischen religion der aramäischen Periode.* Religionsgeschichtliche Versuche und Vorarbeiten 30. Berlin: De Gruyter, 1971.

Kirkpatrick, Patricia G. *The Old Testament and Folklore Study.* Journal for the Study of the Old Testament Supplement 62. Sheffield: JSOT Press, 1988.

Klawans, Jonathan. *Impurity and Sin in Ancient Judaism.* New York: Oxford University Press, 2000.

Klein, Michael L. *Michael Klein on the Targums: Collected Essays, 1972–2002.* Edited by Rimon Kasher, Michael Marmur, and Avigdor Shinan. Leiden: Brill, 2011.

Knauf, Ernst Axel. "Bethel: The Israelite Impact on Judean Language and Literature. In *Judah and the Judeans in the Persian Period*, edited by Oded Lipschits and Manfred Oeming, 291–359. Winona Lake, IN: Eisenbrauns, 2006

Knauf, Ernst Axel, and Philippe Guillaume. *A History of Biblical Israel: The Fate of the Tribes and Kingdoms from Merenptah to Bar Kochba.* Sheffield: Equinox, 2016.

Knoppers, Gary N. "Greek Historiography and the Chronicler's History: A Reexamination." *Journal of Biblical Literature* 122, no. 4 (2003): 627–50.

Jews and Samaritans: The Origins and History of Their Early Relations. Oxford: Oxford University Press, 2013.

"Mt. Gerizim and Mt. Zion: A Study in the Early History of the Samaritans and Jews." *Studies in Religion/Sciences Religieuses* 34, no. 3–4 (2005): 309–38.

Koiv, Mait. *Ancient Tradition and Early Greek History: The Origins of States in Early Archaic Sparta, Argos and Corinth.* Tallinn: Avita, 2003.

Konstan, David. "To Hellēnikon Ethnos: Ethnicity and the Construction of Ancient Greek Identity." In *Ancient Perceptions of Greek Ethnicity*, edited by Irad Malkin, 29–35. Washington, DC: Center for Hellenic Studies, 2001.

Kratz, Reinhard G. *Historical and Biblical Israel: The History, Tradition, and Archives of Israel and Judah*. Translated by Paul Michael Kurtz. Oxford: Oxford University Press, 2016.

"Israel in the Book of Isaiah." *Journal for the Study of the Old Testament* 31, no. 1 (2006): 103–28.

"The Second Temple of Jeb and of Jerusalem." In *Judah and the Judeans in the Persian Period*, edited by Oded Lipschits and Manfred Oeming, 247–64. Winona Lake, IN: Eisenbrauns, 2006.

Kurt, Andrew. "The Search for Prester John, a Projected Crusade, and the Eroding Prestige of Ethiopian Kings c. 1200–c. 1540." *Journal of Medieval History* 39, no. 3 (2013): 297–320.

Labuschagne, Casper J. "The Tribes in the Blessing of Moses." *Oudtestamentische Studiën* 19 (1974): 97–112.

Lahire, Bernard. *The Plural Actor*. Translated by David Fernbach. Cambridge: Cambridge University Press, 2011.

Laubenberger, Franz, and Steven Rowan. "The Naming of America." *The Sixteenth Century Journal* 13, no. 4 (1982): 91–113.

Lavee, Moshe. "The Samaritan May Be Included: Another Look at the Samaritan in Talmudic Literature." In *Samaritans: Past and Present*, edited by Menachem Mor and Friedrich V. Reiterer, 147–73. Studia Samaritana 5. Berlin: De Gruyter, 2010.

Lefevre, Renato. "Riflessi etiopici nella cultura europea del Medioevo e del Rinascimento." *Annali Lateranensi* 8 (1944): 9–89.

Leith, Mary Joan Winn. *Wadi Daliyeh I: The Seal Impressions*. Oxford: Oxford University Press, 1997.

Leitman, Eva, and Elisabeth Weinbaum. "Israeli Women of Ethiopian Descent: The Strengths, Conflicts, and Successes." In *The Beta Israel in Ethiopia and Israel: Studies on the Ethiopian Jews*, edited by Tudor Parfitt and Emanuela Trevisan Semi, 128–36. Richmond: Curzon, 2013.

Leonard-Fleckman, Mahri. *The House of David*. Minneapolis: Fortress Press, 2016.

Leslau, Wolf. *Falasha Anthology*. New Haven, CT: Yale University Press, 1951.

Leve, Lauren. "Identity." *Current Anthropology* 52, no. 4 (2011): 513–35.

Levin, Yigal. "Joseph, Judah and the 'Benjamin Conundrum.'" *Zeitschrift für die alttestamentliche Wissenschaft* 116, no. 2 (2004): 223–41.

"Nimrod the Mighty, King of Kish, King of Sumer and Akkad." *Vetus Testamentum* 52, no. 3 (2002): 350–66.

Levy-Rubin, Mika. *The Continuatio of the Samaritan Chronicle of Abu L-Fath Al-Samiri Al-Danafi*. Princeton, NJ: The Darwin Press, 2002.

Lim, Timothy H. "The Emergence of the Samaritan Pentateuch." In *Reading the Bible in Ancient Traditions and Modern Editions: Studies in Memory of Peter W. Flint*, edited by Andrew B. Perrin, Kyung S. Baek, and Daniel K. Falk, 89–104. Atlanta: SBL Press, 2017.

Lincoln, Bruce. *Discourse and the Construction of Society: Comparative Studies of Myth, Ritual and Classification*. New York: Oxford University Press, 1989.

Theorizing Myth: Narrative, Ideology and Scholarship. Chicago: University of Chicago Press, 1999.

Lindenberger, James M. "What Ever Happened to Vidranga? A Jewish Liturgy of Cursing from Elephantine." In *The World of the Aramaeans: Studies in Honour of Paul-Eugène Dion*, edited by P. M. Michèle Daviau, John W. Wevers, Michael Weigl, and Paul-Eugène Dion, 134–57. *Journal for the Study of the Old Testament Supplement* 326. Sheffield: Sheffield Academic Press, 2001.

Linnekin, Jocelyn. "Cultural Invention and the Dilemma of Authority." *American Anthropologist* 93, no. 2 (1991): 446–49.

Lipiner, Elias. *O sapateiro de Trancoso e o alfaiate de Setúbal*. Rio de Janeiro: Imago Editora, 1993.

Lipschits, Oded. *The Fall and Rise of Jerusalem: The History of Judah under Babylonian Rule*. Winona Lake, IN: Eisenbrauns, 2005.

Lipschits, Oded, and Joseph Blenkinsopp. "After the 'Myth of the Empty Land': Major Challenges in the Study of Neo-Babylonian Judah." In *Judah and the Judeans in the Neo-Babylonian Period*, 3–20. Winona Lake, IN: Eisenbrauns, 2003.

Liverani, Mario. "Imperialism." In *Archaeologies of the Middle East: Critical Perspectives*, edited by S. Pollack and R. Bernbeck, 223–44. Malden, MA: Blackwell, 2005.

Israel's History and the History of Israel. London: Routledge, 2005.

Lowie, Robert H. "Oral Tradition and History." *Journal of American Folklore* 30 (1917): 161–67.

Luzzatto, Filosseno. "The Falashas or Jews of Abyssinia." *Jewish Chronicle*, September 26, 1851.

"The Falashas or Jews of Abyssinia." *Jewish Chronicle*, October 10, 1851.

Lyons, Len. *The Ethiopian Jews of Israel*. Woodstock, VT: Jewish Lights Publishing, 2007.

Maart, D. "Crisis in Parent Authority among Ethiopian Newcomers and the Way of Its Repair." *Gadish: Bulletin of Adult Education* 10 (2006): 98–103.

Macchi, Jean-Daniel. *Israël et ses tribus selon Genèse 49*. Orbis biblicus et orientalis 171. Göttingen: Vandenhoeck & Ruprecht, 1999.

MacKay, Michael Hubbard, and Gerrit J. Dirkmaat. *From Darkness Unto Light: Joseph Smith's Translation and Publication of the Book of Mormon*. Provo, UT: Brigham Young University Press, 2015.

Maffly-Kipp, Laurie F. "Mormons and the Bible." In *The Oxford Handbook of Mormonism*, edited by Terryl L. Givens and Philip L. Barlow, 121–33. Oxford: Oxford University Press, 2015.

Magen, Yitzhak. "Mt. Gerizim: A Temple City." *Qadmoniot* 120 (2000): 74–118.

"The Dating of the First Phase of the Samaritan Temple on Mount Gerizim in Light of the Archaeological Evidence." In *Judah and the Judeans in the Fourth Century B.C.E.*, edited by Oded Lipschits, Manfred Oeming, and Rainer Albertz, 157–212. Winona Lake, IN: Eisenbrauns, 2007.

Magen, Yitzhak, Y. Misgav, and L. Tsfania. *Mount Gerizim Excavations*. Judea and Samaria Publications 2. Jerusalem: Israel Exploration Society, 2004.

"Mount Gerizim Excavations: Vol. 1, The Aramaic, Hebrew and Samaritan Inscriptions." *Qadmoniot* 33, no. 2 (2000): 125–32.

Malamat, Abraham. *History of Biblical Israel*. Leiden: Brill, 2001.
"King Lists of the Old Babylonian Period and Biblical Genealogies." *Journal of the American Oriental Society* 88, no. 1 (1968): 163–73.
"Tribal Societies: Biblical Genealogies and African Lineage Systems." *European Journal of Sociology* 14, no. 1 (1973): 126–36.
Malešević, Siniša. *The Sociology of Ethnicity*. London: Sage Publications, 2004.
Malkin, Irad. *The Returns of Odysseus*. Berkeley, CA: University of California Press, 1998.
Man, John. *Saladin*. Philadelphia: DA Capo Press, 2016.
Marcus, Harold G. *A History of Ethiopia*. Berkeley, CA: University of California Press, 1994.
Marquardt, H. Michael. *Early Patriarchal Blessings of the Church of Jesus Christ of Latter-Day Saints*. Salt Lake City: The Smith-Pettit Foundation, 2007.
Later Patriarchal Blessings of the Church of Jesus Christ of Latter-Day Saints. Salt Lake City: The Smith-Pettit Foundation, 2012.
Mary's City of David. "Israelite House of David Church of the New Eve, Body of Christ." Accessed April 23, 2020. www.maryscityofdavid.org/.
"'Jesus' Boys' Israelite House of David Baseball." Accessed April 22, 2020. www.maryscityofdavid.org/html/baseball.html.
Mather, Cotton. *The Triumph of the Reformed Religion in America: The Life of the Renowned John Eliot*. London, 1691.
Matthews, Robert J. "The New Publications of the Standard Works—1979, 1981." *Brigham Young University Studies* 22, no. 4 (1982): 387–424.
Matthews, Victor Harold. *A Brief History of Ancient Israel*. Louisville, KY: Westminster John Knox Press, 2002.
Mauss, Armand L. *All Abraham's Children: Changing Mormon Concepts of Race and Lineage*. Champaign, IL: University of Illinois Press, 2010.
Mayes, Andrew D. H. *Deuteronomy*. New Century Bible Commentary. Grand Rapids, MI: Eerdmans, 1979.
Mazar, Amihai. "Archaeology and the Biblical Narrative: The Case of the United Monarchy." In *One God, One Cult, One Nation: Archaeological and Biblical Perspectives*, edited by Reinhard G. Kratz and Hermann Spieckermann, 29–58. Beihefte zur Zeitschrift für die alttestamentliche Wissenschaft 405. Berlin: De Gruyter, 2010.
"Jerusalem and Its Vicinity in Iron Age I." In *From Nomadism to Monarchy: Archaeological and Historical Aspects of Early Israel*, edited by Israel Finkelstein and Nadav Na'aman, 70–91. Jerusalem: Yad Izhak Ben-Zvi, 1994.
"The Search for David and Solomon: An Archaeological Perspective." In *The Quest for the Historical Israel: Debating Archaeology and the History of Israel*, edited by Brian B. Schmidt, 117–40. Archaeology and Biblical Studies 17. Atlanta: Society of Biblical Literature, 2007.
McBride, Spencer W. *Joseph Smith for President: The Prophet, the Assassins, and the Fight for American Religious Freedom*. New York: Oxford University Press, 2021.
McConkie, Bruce R. *Mormon Doctrine*. Salt Lake City: Bookcraft, 1958.

McCutcheon, Russell T. "Myth." In *Guide to the Study of Religion*, edited by Willi Braun and Russell T. McCutcheon, 190–208. London: Cassell, 2000.

McDonald, John. *The Samaritan Chronicle II (or: Sepher Ha-Yamim). From Joshua to Nebuchadnezzar*. Beihefte zur Zeitschrift für die alttestamentliche Wissenschaft 107. Berlin: De Gruyter, 1969.

McInerney, Jeremy. "Ethnos and Ethnicity in Early Greece." In *Ancient Perceptions of Greek Ethnicity*, edited by Irad Malkin, 51–74. Washington, DC: Center for Hellenic Studies, 2001.

McKay, Thomas E. "The Gospel in Foreign Countries." *Liahona: The Elder's Journal*. June 25, 1912, 10, 1 edition.

Meir-Glitzenstein, Esther. "Operation Magic Carpet: Constructing the Myth of the Magical Immigration of Yemenite Jews to Israel." *Israel Studies* 16, no. 3 (2011): 149–73.

Menache, Sophia. "Tartars, Jews, Saracens and the Jewish–Mongol 'Plot' of 1241." *History* 81, no. 263 (1996): 319–42.

Middlemas, Jill A. "Going Beyond the Myth of the Empty Land: A Reassessment of the Early Persian Period." In *Exile and Restoration Revisited: Essays on the Babylonian and Persian Periods in Memory of Peter R. Ackroyd*, edited by Gary N. Knoppers, Lester L. Grabbe, and Dierdre N. Fulton, 174–94. London: T&T Clark, 2009.

Middleton, John. *Lugbara Religion*. London: Oxford University Press, 1960.

Miller, J. Maxwell, and John H. Hayes. *A History of Ancient Israel and Judah*. 2nd ed. Louisville, KY: Westminster John Knox Press, 2006.

Miller, James C. "Ethnicity and the Hebrew Bible: Problems and Prospects." *Currents in Biblical Research* 6, no. 2 (2008): 170–213.

Mizrachi, Nissim, and Hanna Herzog. "Participatory Destigmatization Strategies among Palestinian Citizens, Ethiopian Jews and Mizrahi Jews in Israel." In *Responses to Stigmatization in Comparative Perspective*, edited by Michèle Lamont and Nissim Mizrachi, 54–71. London: Routledge, 2012.

Monroe, Lauren A. S., and Daniel Fleming. "Earliest Israel in Highland Company." *Near Eastern Archaeology* 82, no. 1 (2019): 16–23.

Moore, Megan Bishop. *Philosophy and Practice in Writing a History of Ancient Israel*. New York: T&T Clark, 2006.

Morag, Shlomo. "A Linguistic Examination of Eldad the Danite's Origin." *Tarbiz* 66 (1997): 223–46.

Morris, Larry E. "Oliver Cowdery's Vermont Years and the Origins of Mormonism." *BYU Studies Quarterly* 39, no. 1 (2000): 107–29.

Mortensen, Beverley. *The Priesthood in Targum Pseudo-Jonathan*. Leiden: Brill, 2006.

Moyer, Paul B. *The Public Universal Friend: Jemima Wilkinson and Religious Enthusiasm in Revolutionary America*. Ithaca, NY: Cornell University Press, 2015.

Mroczek, Eva. "The Hegemony of the Biblical in the Study of Second Temple Literature." *Journal of Ancient Judaism* 6, no. 1 (2015): 2–35.

   The Literary Imagination in Jewish Antiquity. Oxford: Oxford University Press, 2016.

Mueller, Max Perry. *Race and the Making of the Mormon People*. Chapel Hill, NC: University of North Carolina Press, 2017.

Munro-Hay, Stuart. "A Sixth Century Kebra Nagast?" *Annales d'Éthiopie* 17, no. 1 (2001): 43–58.

The Quest for the Ark of the Covenant: The True History of the Tablets of Moses. London: I.B. Tauris, 2007.

Na'aman, Nadav. "Dismissing the Myth of a Flood of Israelite Refugees in the Late Eighth Century BCE." *Zeitschrift für die alttestamentliche Wissenschaft* 126, no. 1 (2014): 1–14.

"Saul, Benjamin and the Emergence of 'Biblical Israel' Part I." *Zeitschrift für die alttestamentliche Wissenschaft* 121, no. 2 (2009): 211–24.

"Saul, Benjamin and the Emergence of 'Biblical Israel' Part II." *Zeitschrift für die alttestamentliche Wissenschaft* 121, no. 3 (2009): 335–49.

"The Historical Background to the Conquest of Samaria (720 BCE)." *Biblica* 71 (1990): 206–25.

"The Israelite-Judahite Struggle for the Patrimony of Ancient Israel." *Biblica* 91, no. 1 (2010): 1–23.

"The Jacob Story and the Formation of Biblical Israel." *Tel Aviv* 41, no. 1 (2014): 95–125.

Na'aman, Nadav, and Ran Zadok. "Sargon II's Deportations to Israel and Philistia (716–708 B.C.E.)." *Journal of Cuneiform Studies* 40, no. 1 (1988): 36–46.

Naveh, Joseph. "Scripts and Inscriptions in Ancient Samaria." *Israel Exploration Journal* 48, no. 1/2 (1998): 91–100.

Nawotka, Krzysztof. *The Alexander Romance by Ps.-Callisthenes*. Mnemosyne Supplements 399. Leiden: Brill, 2017.

Nawotka, Krzysztof, and Agnieszka Wojciechowska. *The Alexander Romance: History and Literature*. Eelde: Barkhuis, 2018.

Neilson, Reid L. "Mormon Mission Work." In *The Oxford Handbook of Mormonism*, edited by Terryl L. Givens and Philip L. Barlow, 182–95. Oxford: Oxford University Press, 2015.

Nelson, Russell M. "The Gathering of Scattered Israel." *The Church of Latter-Day Saints* (blog), October 2016. www.lds.org/general-conference/2006/10/the-gathering-of-scattered-israel?lang=eng.

Neubauer, Adolf. "Inyanai Aseret Haschevatim." *Sammelband* 4 (1888): 10.

"Where Are the Ten Tribes? I. Bible, Talmud, and Midrashic Literature." *The Jewish Quarterly Review* 1, no. 1 (1888): 14–28.

"Where Are the Ten Tribes? II. Eldad the Danite." *Jewish Quarterly Review* 1, no. 2 (1889): 95–114.

Neusner, Jacob. *Introduction to Rabbinic Literature*. Anchor Bible Reference Library. New York: Doubleday, 1994.

Nichols, James, and Laurence Womock Davids. *Calvinism and Arminianism Compared in Their Principles and Tendency*. London: Longman, Hurst, Rees, Orme, Brown, and Green, 1824.

Niditch, Susan. *Folklore and the Hebrew Bible*. 2nd ed. Eugene, OR: Wipf & Stock, 2004.

Nodet, Etienne. "Israelites, Samaritans, Temples, Jews." In *Samaria, Samarians, Samaritans: Studies on Bible, History, and Linguistics*, edited by József Zsengellér, 121–72. Studia Samaritana 6. Berlin: De Gruyter, 2011.

Samaritans, Juifs, Temples. Cahiers de la Revue Biblique 74. Paris: Gabalda, 2010.

Noth, Martin. *A History of the Pentateuchal Traditions*. Translated by Bernhard W. Anderson. Chico, CA: Scholars Press, 1981.

Das System der zwölf Stämme Israels. Stuttgart, Germany: Kohlhammer, 1930.

Geschichte Israels. Göttingen, Germany: Vandenhoeck & Ruprecht, 1950.

The History of Israel. Translated by P. R. Ackroyd. 2nd ed. New York: Harper, 1960.

Überlieferungsgeschichte des Pentateuch. Stuttgart: Kohlhammer, 1948.

Nowell, Charles E. "The Historical Prester John." *Speculum* 28, no. 3 (1953): 435–45.

O'Brien, Flann. *At Swim-Two-Birds*. London: Dalkey Archive Press, 1998.

Oded, B. *Mass Deportations and Deportees in the Neo-Assyrian Empire*. Wiesbaden: Reichert, 1979.

Ojanuga, Durrenda. "The Ethiopian Jewish Experience as Blacks in Israel." *Journal of Black Studies* 24, no. 2 (1993): 147–58.

Olick, Jeffrey K., and Joyce Robbins. "Social Memory Studies: From 'Collective Memory' to the Historical Sociology of Mnemonic Practices." *Annual Review of Sociology* 24 (1998): 105–40.

Olyan, Saul M. *Rites and Rank: Hierarchy in Biblical Representations of Cult*. Princeton, NJ: Princeton University Press, 2000.

Osipian, Alexandr. "Armenian Involvement in the Latin-Mongol Crusade: Uses of the Magi and Prester John in Constable Smbat's Letter and Hayton of Corycus's 'Flos Historiarum Terre Orientis,' 1248–1307." *Medieval Encounters* 20 (2014): 66–100.

Oxonian. *Israel's Wanderings, or, The Scüths, the Saxons, and the Kymry: A Connected Account, Tracing the Lost Tribes of Israel into the British Isles*. London: British Israel Identity Corporation, 1881.

Palmer, Susan J. "The Twelve Tribes: Preparing the Bride for Yahshua's Return." *Nova Religio: The Journal of Alternative and Emergent Religions* 13, no. 3 (2010): 59–80.

Pankhurst, Richard. *The Ethiopian Borderlands: Essays in Regional History from Ancient Times to the End of the Eighteenth Century*. Lewisville, NJ: The Red Sea Press, 1997.

"The Falashas, or Judaic Ethiopians in Their Christian Ethiopian Setting." *African Affairs* 91, no. 365 (1992): 567–82.

Parfitt, Tudor. *Operation Moses*. London: Weidenfeld & Nicolson, 1985.

"The Construction of Jewish Identities in Africa." In *Jews of Ethiopia: The Birth of an Elite*, edited by Tudor Parfitt and Emanuela Trevisan Semi, 1–42. London: Routledge, 2005.

The Lost Tribes of Israel: The History of a Myth. London: Phoenix, 2003.

Park, Benjamin E. *Kingdom of Nauvoo: The Rise and Fall of a Religious Empire on the American Frontier*. New York: Liveright Publishing, 2020.

Patterson, Lee E. *Kinship Myth in Ancient Greece.* Austin, TX: University of Texas Press, 2010.

Perez, Nahshon. "Israel's Law of Return: A Qualified Justification." *Modern Judaism* 31, no. 1 (2011): 59–84.

Perry, Micha. "The Imaginary War Between Prester John and Eldad the Danite and Its Real Implications." *Viator* 41, no. 1 (2010): 1–23.

Persuitte, David. *Joseph Smith and the Origins of the Book of Mormon.* 2nd ed. Jefferson, NC: McFarland & Company, 2000.

Phillips, Jonathan. *The Second Crusade: Extending the Frontiers of Christianity.* New Haven, CT: Yale University Press, 2010.

Pioske, Daniel. *David's Jerusalem: Between Memory and History.* New York: Routledge, 2015.

Memory in a Time of Prose: Studies in Epistemology, Hebrew Scribalism, and the Biblical Past. Oxford: Oxford University Press, 2018.

Piovanelli, Pierluigi. "Jewish Christianity in Late Antique Aksum and Ḥimyar? A Reassessment of the Evidence and a New Proposal." *Judaïsme ancien – Ancient Judaism: Revue internationale d'histoire et de philologie – International Journal of History and Philology* 6 (2018): 175–202.

Popkin, Richard H. "The Rise and Fall of the Jewish Indian Theory." In *Menasseh Ben Israel and His World,* edited by Yôsēf Qaplan, Henry Méchoulan, and Richard H. Popkin, 63–82. Leiden: Brill, 1989.

Yôsēf Qaplan, and Henry Méchoulan, eds. *Menasseh Ben Israel and His World.* Leiden: Brill, 1989.

Porten, Bezalel. *Archives from Elephantine.* Berkeley, CA: University of California Press, 1968.

The Elephantine Papyri in English: Three Millennia of Cross-Cultural Continuity and Change. Leiden: Brill, 1996.

Provan, Iain, V. Philips Long, and Tremper Longman III. *A Biblical History of Israel.* Louisville, KY: Westminster John Knox Press, 2003.

Pummer, Reinhard. "Religions in Contact and Conflict: The Samaritans of Caesarea Among 'Pagans,' Jews and Christians." In *Samaritan Researches,* edited by Vittorio Morabito, Alan D. Crown, and Lucy Davey, 5:329–53. Studies in Judaica 10. Sydney: Mandelbaum Publishing, 2000.

"Samaritan Studies – Recent Research Results." In *The Bible, Qumran, and the Samaritans,* edited by Magnar Kartveit and Gary N. Knoppers, 57–78. Studia Samaritana 10. Berlin: De Gruyter, 2018.

The Samaritans: A Profile. Grand Rapids, MI: Eerdmans, 2016.

The Samaritans in Flavius Josephus. Texts and Studies in Ancient Judaism 129. Tübingen: Mohr Siebeck, 2009.

Quine, Cat. "Reading 'House of Jacob' in Isaiah 48:1–11 in Light of Benjamin." *Journal of Biblical Literature* 137, no. 2 (2018): 339–57.

Quinn, Michael D. *Early Mormonism and the Magic World View.* 2nd ed. Salt Lake City: Signature Books, 1999.

Quirin, James. "Oral Traditions as Historical Sources in Ethiopia: The Case of the Beta Israel (Falasha)." *History in Africa* 20 (1993): 297–312.

The Evolution of the Ethiopian Jews: A History of the Beta Israel (Falasha) to 1920. Philadelphia: University of Pennsylvania Press, 1992.

Rapoport, Louis. *Redemption Song: The Story of Operation Moses.* New York: Harcourt Brace Jovanovich, 1986.

Rasgon, Adam. "Israel Accepts Ethiopians of Jewish Descent, but Fewer Than Promised." *The New York Times,* October 12, 2020, sec. World.

Rata, Elizabeth. "The Transformation of Indigeneity." *Review (Fernand Braudel Center)* 25, no. 2 (2002): 173–95.

Rebillard, Eric. "Material Culture and Religious Identity in Late Antiquity." In *A Companion to the Archaeology of Religion in the Ancient World,* edited by Rubina Raja and Jörg Rüpke, 427–36. Chichester: Wiley Blackwell, 2015.

Reeve, W. Paul. *Religion of a Different Color: Race and the Mormon Struggle for Whiteness.* Oxford: Oxford University Press, 2015.

"The Mormon Church in Utah." In *The Oxford Handbook of Mormonism,* edited by Terryl L. Givens and Philip L. Barlow, 38–54. Oxford: Oxford University Press, 2015.

"Religion: Who Is a Jew?" *Time,* February 2, 1970. http://content.time.com/time/magazine/article/0,9171,878177,00.html.

Rendsburg, Gary A. "The Internal Consistency and Historical Reliability of the Biblical Genealogies." *Vetus Testamentum* 40, no. 2 (1990): 185–206.

Reynolds, George. *Are We of Israel?* Salt Lake City: Perry, 1883.

Richard, J. "The Relatio de Davide as a Source for Mongol History and the Legend of Prester John." In *Prester John, the Mongols and the Ten Lost Tribes,* edited by Bernard Hamilton and Charles F. Beckingham, 139–58. Aldershot: Variorum, 1996.

Ricks, Stephen D. "Translation of the Book of Mormon: Interpreting the Evidence." *Journal of Book of Mormon Studies (1992–2007)* 2, no. 2 (1993): 201–6.

Riley-Smith, Jonathan. *The First Crusade and the Idea of Crusading.* London: Continuum, 2003.

Roberts, B. H. *Studies of the Book of Mormon.* Edited by Brigham D. Madsen. Urbana, IL: University of Illinois Press, 1985.

Robertson, Margaret C. "The Campaign and the Kingdom: The Activities of the Electioneers in Joseph Smith's Presidential Campaign." *Brigham Young University Studies* 39, no. 3 (2000): 147–80.

Romm, James. "Biblical History and the Americas: The Legend of Solomon's Ophir, 1492–1591." In *The Jews and the Expansion of Europe to the West, 1450 to 1800,* edited by Paolo Bernardini and Norman Fiering, 27–46. New York: Berghahn Books, 2001.

Rom-Shiloni, Dalit. "The Untold Stories: Al-Yahūdu *and* or *versus* Hebrew Bible Babylonian Compositions." *Die Welt des Orients* 47, no. 1 (2017): 124–34.

Roosens, Eugeen E. *Creating Ethnicity: The Process of Ethnogenesis.* Frontiers of Anthropology 5. Newbury Park, CA: Sage, 1989.

Roth, Norman. "Review: The Hebrew Letters of Prester John by Edward Ullendorf, C. F. Beckingham." *Hebrew Studies* 25 (1984): 192–95.

Rutherford, Ian. "Mestra at Athens: Hesiod Fr. 43 and the Poetics of Panhellenism." In *The Hesiodic Catalogue of Women,* edited by Richard L. Hunter, 99–117. Cambridge: Cambridge University Press, 2005.

Sacks, Andrew. "Shall the State of Israel Recognize the Abayudaya Jews of Uganda? A Summary of the Hearing before Israel's High Court of Justice |

The Rabbinical Assembly," *February* 4, 2021. www.rabbinicalassembly.org/
story/shall-state-israel-recognize-abayudaya-jews-uganda-summary-hearing-
israels-high-court-justice.

Sadler Jr., Rodney Steven. *Can a Cushite Change His Skin? An Examination of
Race, Ethnicity, and Othering in the Hebrew Bible*. New York: T&T Clark,
2009.

Salamon, Hagar. "Blackness in Transition: Decoding Racial Constructs through
Stories of Ethiopian Jews." *Journal of Folklore Research* 40, no. 1 (2003):
3–32.

"Ethiopian Jewry and New Self-Concepts." In *The Life of Judaism*, edited by
Harvey E. Goldberg, 227–40. Berkeley, CA: University of California Press,
2001.

Salvadore, Matteo. "The Ethiopian Age of Exploration: Prester John's Discovery
of Europe 1306–1458." *Journal of World History* 21, no. 4 (2010):
593–627.

Sanders, Seth l. "What If There Aren't Any Empirical Models for Pentateuchal
Criticism?" In *Contextualizing Israel's Sacred Writing: Ancient Literacy,
Orality, and Literary Production*, edited by Brian Schmidt, 281–304. Atlanta:
Society of Biblical Literature, 2014.

Sanderson, Judith E. *An Exodus Scroll from Qumran: 4QpaleoExodm and the
Samaritan Tradition*. Atlanta: Scholars Press, 1986.

Sandwell, Isabella. *Religious Identity in Late Antiquity: Greeks, Jews and
Christians in Antioch*. Cambridge: Cambridge University Press, 2011.

Schectman, Joseph B. "The Repatriation of Yemenite Jewry." *Jewish Social
Studies* 14, no. 3 (1952): 209–24.

Schemann, Serge. "Ethiopians in Israel Riot Over Dumping of Donated Blood."
New York Times, January 29, 1996. www.nytimes.com/1996/01/29/world/
ethiopian-in-israeli-riot-over-dumping-of-donated-blood.html?mtrref=www
.google.com.

Schenker, Adrian. "Le Seigneur choisira-t-Il le lieu de Son Nom ou l'a-t-Il choisi?
L'apport de la Bible Grecque ancienne à l'histoire du texte Samaritain et
Massorétique." In *Scripture in Transition: Essays on Septuagint, Hebrew
Bible, and Dead Sea Scrolls in Honour of Raija Sollamo*, edited by Anssi
Voitila and Jutta Jokiranta, 339–51. Journal for the Study of Judaism
Supplement 126. Leiden: Brill, 2008.

Schiffman, Lawrence H. "The Samaritans in Amoraic Halakhah." In *Shoshannat
Yaakov: Jewish and Iranian Studies in Honor of Yaakov Elman*, edited by
Shai Secunda and Steven Fine, 371–89. Leiden: Brill, 2012.

"The Samaritans in Tannaitic Halakhah." *The Jewish Quarterly Review* 75,
no. 4 (1985): 323–50.

Schloessinger, Max, trans. *The Ritual of Eldad Ha-Dani*. Leipzig: Rudolf Haupt
Verlag, 1908.

Schmidt, Benjamin. "The Hope of the Netherlands: Menasseh Ben Israel and the
Dutch Idea of America." In *The Jews and the Expansion of Europe to the
West, 1450 to 1800*, edited by Paolo Bernardini and Norman Fiering,
86–106. New York: Berghahn Books, 2001.

Schneider, Tammi J. "Through Assyria's Eyes: Israel's Relationship with Judah." *Expedition* 44, no. 3 (2002): 9–15.

Schorch, Stefan. "A Critical Editio Maior of the Samaritan Pentateuch: State of Research, Principles, and Problems." *Hebrew Bible and Ancient Israel* 2 (2013): 1–21.

"The Samaritan Version of Deuteronomy and the Origin of Deuteronomy." In *Samaria, Samarians, Samaritans: Studies on Bible, History and Linguistics*, edited by József Zsengellér, 23–37. Studia Samaritana 6. Berlin: De Gruyter, 2011.

Schorn, Ulrike. *Ruben und das System der zwölf Stämme Israels: Redaktionsgeschichtliche Untersuchungen zur Bedeutung des Erstgeborenen Jakobs*. Beihefte zur Zeitschrift für die alttestamentliche Wissenschaft 248. Berlin: De Gruyter, 1997.

Schreiber, Monika. *The Comfort of Kin: Samaritan Community, Kinship, and Marriage*. Leiden: Brill, 2014.

Schwartz, Seth. "John Hyrcanus I's Destruction of the Gerizim Temple and Judean-Samaritan Relations." *Jewish History* 7, no. 1 (1993): 9–25.

Seeman, Don. "Ethnographers, Rabbis and Jewish Epistemology: The Case of the Ethiopian Jews." *Tradition: A Journal of Orthodox Jewish Thought* 25, no. 4 (1991): 13–29.

One People, One Blood: Ethiopian-Israelis and the Return to Judaism. New Brunswick, NJ: Rutgers University Press, 2010.

"One People, One Blood: Public Health, Political Violence, and HIV in an Ethiopian-Israeli Setting." *Culture, Medicine and Psychiatry* 23 (1999): 159–95.

"Returning to Judaism." In *One People, One Blood: Ethiopian-Israelis and the Return to Judaism*, 84–108. New Brunswick, NJ: Rutgers University Press, 2009.

Semi, Emanuela Trevisan. "Ethiopian Jews in Europe: Taamrat Emmanuel in Italy and Makonnen Levi in England." In *Jews of Ethiopia: The Birth of an Elite*, edited by Tudor Parfitt and Emanuela Trevisan Semi, 74–100. London: Routledge, 2005.

"From Wolleqa to Florence: The Tragic Story of Faitlovitch's Pupil Hizkiahu Finkas." In *The Beta Israel in Ethiopia and Israel: Studies on the Ethiopian Jews*, edited by Tudor Parfitt and Emanuela Trevisan Semi, 1–14. Richmond: Curzon, 2013.

Jacques Faitlovich and the Jews of Ethiopia. London: Valentine Mitchell, 2007.

Sergi, Omer. "The Emergence of Judah as a Political Entity between Jerusalem and Benjamin." *Zeitschrift des Deutschen Palästina-Vereins* 133, no. 1 (2017): 1–23.

Shabtay, Malka. "Living with Threatening Identity: Life Experiences with Skin Color Difference among Youth and Adult Ethiopians in Israel." *Trends (Megamot)* 1–2 (2001): 97–112.

Shachar, Ayelet. "Citizenship and Membership in the Israeli Polity." In *From Migrants to Citizens: Membership in a Changing World*, edited by T. Alexander Aleinikoff and Douglas Klusmeyer, 386–433. Washington, DC: Carnegie Endowment for International Peace, 2000.

Shalev, Eran. *American Zion: The Old Testament as a Political Text from the Revolution to the Civil War.* New Haven, CT: Yale University Press, 2013.

Shatzmiller, Joseph. "Jews, Pilgrimage, and the Christian Cult of Saints: Benjamin of Tudela and His Contemporaries." In *After Rome's Fall: Narrators and Sources of Early Medieval History; Essays Presented to Walter Goffart,* edited by Alexander Callander Murray, 337–47. Toronto: University of Toronto Press, 1998.

Shectman, Sarah, and Joel S. Baden, eds. *The Strata of the Priestly Writings: Contemporary Debate and Future Directions.* Abhandlungen zur Theologie des Alten und Neuen Testaments 95. Zurich: Theologischer Verlag Zurich, 2009.

Shelemay, Kay Kaufman. *Music, Ritual, and Falasha History.* 2nd ed. East Lansing, MI: Michigan State University Press, 1989.

Shepherd, Gary, and Gordon Shepherd. *Binding Earth and Heaven: Patriarchal Blessings in the Prophetic Development of Early Mormonism.* University Park, PA: The Pennsylvania State University Press, 2012.

Shields, Tanya L. "Rehearsing Indigeneity." In *Bodies and Bones: Feminist Rehearsal and Imagining Caribbean Belonging,* 145–66. Charlottesville, VA: University of Virginia Press, 2014.

Shipps, Jan. "An Interpretive Framework for Studying the History of Mormonism." In *The Oxford Handbook of Mormonism,* edited by Terryl L. Givens and Philip L. Barlow, 7–23. Oxford: Oxford University Press, 2015.

Signer, Michael. *The Itinerary of Benjamin of Tudela.* Malibu, CA: Joseph Simon, 1983.

Singh, Maina Chawla. *Being Indian, Being Israeli: Migration, Ethnicity, and Gender in the Jewish Homeland.* New Delhi: Manohar Publishers & Distributors, 2009.

Skog, Lindsay. "Thinking with Indigeneity: Imperatives and Provocations." *Verge: Studies in Global Asias* 4, no. 2 (2018): 2–13.

Skousen, Royal. "Towards a Critical Edition of the Book of Mormon." *Brigham Young University Studies* 30, no. 1 (1990): 41–69.

Skousen, Royal, and Robin Scott Jensen. *The Joseph Smith Papers: Revelations and Translations, Volume 3, Parts 1 and 2; Printer's Manuscript of the Book of Mormon.* Salt Lake City: Church Historian's Press, 2015.

Slessarev, Vsevolod. *Prester John: The Letter and the Legend.* Minneapolis: University of Minnesota Press, 1959.

Smith, Anthony D. *Myths and Memories of the Nation.* New York: Oxford University Press, 1999.

Smith, E. Gary. "The Office of Presiding Patriarch: The Primacy Problem." *Journal of Mormon History* 14 (1988): 35–47.

Smith, Ethan. *View of the Hebrews or The Tribes of Israel.* 2nd ed. Poultney, VT: Simon & Schute, 1825.

Smith, Hyrum G. "The Day of Ephraim." *Utah Genealogical and Historical Magazine* 20 (1929): 123.

Smith, Jonathan Z. *Map Is Not Territory: Studies in the History of Religion.* Chicago: University of Chicago Press, 1993.

Relating Religion: Essays in the Study of Religion. Chicago: University of Chicago Press, 2004.

"What a Difference a Difference Makes." In *To See Ourselves as Others See Us: Christians, Jews, "Others" in Late Antiquity,* edited by Jacob Neusner and Ernest S. Frerichs, 3–48. Chico, CA: Scholars Press, 1985.

Smith, Joseph. *History of Joseph Smith: The Prophet, by Himself.* History of the Church of Jesus Christ of Latter-Day Saints 1. Salt Lake City: Deseret News, 1902.

Smith, Mark S. *Poetic Heroes.* Grand Rapids, MI: Eerdmans, 2014.

"Why Was 'Old Poetry' Used in Hebrew Narrative? Historical and Cultural Considerations about Judges 5." In *Puzzling Out the Past: Studies in Northwest Semitic Languages and Literatures in Honor of Bruce Zuckerman,* edited by Steven Fine, Wayne T. Pitard, and Marilyn J. Lundberg, 197–212. Leiden: Brill, 2012.

Snow, Erastus. "To My Friend, 'The News.'" *Deseret News,* December 25, 1852.

Sohn, Sigrid. "The Falashas in the German Jewish Press in Germany During the First Half of the Twentieth Century." In *Jews of Ethiopia: The Birth of an Elite,* edited by Tudor Parfitt and Emanuela Trevisan Semi, 65–73. London: Routledge, 2005.

Sollors, Werner. *The Invention of Ethnicity.* Oxford: Oxford University Press, 1989.

Sorenson, John L. *Mormon's Codex: An Ancient American Book.* Salt Lake City: Neal A. Maxwell Institute for Religious Scholarship, 2013.

Soroff, Linda Begley. *The Maintenance and Transmission of Ethnic Identity: A Study of Four Ethnic Groups of Religious Jews in Israel.* Lanham, MD: University Press of America, 1995.

Sparks, Kenton L. *Ethnicity and Identity in Ancient Israel: Prolegomena to the Study of Ethnic Sentiments and Their Expression in the Hebrew Bible.* Winona Lake, IN: Eisenbrauns, 1998.

"Genesis 49 and the Tribal List Tradition in Ancient Israel." *Zeitschrift für die alttestamentliche Wissenschaft* 115, no. 3 (2003): 327–47.

Special, James Feron to The New York Times. "Israeli Court Rules a Jew Can Be One by Nationality (Published 1970)." *The New York Times,* January 24, 1970, sec. Archives. www.nytimes.com/1970/01/24/archives/israeli-court-rules-a-jew-can-be-one-by-nationality-vital-issue.html.

Spector, Johanna. "Samaritan Chant." *Journal of the International Folk Music Council* 16 (1964): 66–69.

Spector, Stephen. *Operation Solomon: The Daring Rescue of the Ethiopian Jews.* Oxford: Oxford University Press, 2005.

Stenhouse, Paul. *The Kitab Al-Tarikh of Abu'l Fath, Translated with Notes.* Sydney: Mandelbaum Trust, 1985.

Stern, Ephraim, and Yitzhak Magen. "Archaeological Evidence for the First Stage of the Samaritan Temple on Mount Gerizim." *Israel Exploration Journal* 52, no. 1 (2002): 49–57.

Stone, Michael Edward. *Fourth Ezra: A Commentary on the Book of Fourth Ezra.* Edited by Frank Moore Cross. Minneapolis: Fortress Press, 1990.

Stoneman, Richard. "Primary Sources from the Classical and Early Medieval Periods." In *A Companion to Alexander Literature in the Middle Ages*, edited by Z. David Zuwiyya, 1–20. Leiden: Brill, 2011.

The Greek Alexander Romance. London: Penguin, 1991.

Strack, H. L., and G. Stemberger. *Introduction to the Talmud and Midrash*. Translated by Markus Bockmuehl. Edinburgh: T&T Clark, 1991.

Strawn, Brent A. "What Is Cush Doing in Amos 9:7? The Poetics of Exodus in the Plural." *Vetus Testamentum* 63, no. 1 (2013): 99–123.

Strine, Casey. "Your Name Shall No Longer Be Jacob, but Refugee: Involuntary Migration and the Development of the Jacob Narrative." In *Scripture as Social Discourse*, edited by J. M. Keady, T. E. Klutz, and C. A. Strine, 51–69. London: T&T Clark, 2018.

Summerfield, Daniel P. *From Falashas to Ethiopian Jews: The External Influences for Change c. 1860–1960*. London: Routledge, 2003.

Sutherland, Heather. "The Problematic Authority of (World) History." *Journal of World History* 18, no. 4 (2007): 491–522.

Tabili, Laura. "Race Is a Relationship, and Not a Thing." *Journal of Social History* 37, no. 1 (2003): 125–30.

Taddia, Irma. "Giovanni Ellero's Manuscript Notes on the Falasha of Walqayt." In *Jews of Ethiopia: The Birth of an Elite*, edited by Tudor Parfitt and Emanuela Trevisan Semi, 43–52. London: Routledge, 2005.

Taliaferro, John. *Great White Fathers: The Story of the Obsessive Quest to Create Mount Rushmore*. New York: Public Affairs, 2007.

Talmage, James E. *James E. Talmage Collection, MS 1232*, Church History Library, The Church of Latter-Day Saints, Salt Lake City, UT.

Tamrat, Taddesse. *Church and State in Ethiopia 1270–1527*. Oxford: Clarendon Press, 1972.

Tanyeri-Erdemir, Tuğba. "Archaeology as a Source of National Pride in the Early Years of the Turkish Republic." *Journal of Field Archaeology* 31, no. 4 (2006): 381–93.

Tappy, Ron E. "The Final Years of Israelite Samaria: Toward a Dialogue between Texts and Archaeology." In *"Up to the Gate of Ekron": Essays on the Archaeology and History of the Eastern Mediterranean in Honor of Seymore Gitin*, edited by S. W. Crawford, 258–79. Jerusalem: Israel Exploration Society, 2007.

Teferi, Amaleletch. "About the Jewish Identity of the Beta Israel." In *Jews of Ethiopia: The Birth of an Elite*, edited by Tudor Parfitt and Emanuela Trevisan Semi, 173–92. London: Routledge, 2005.

Tekiner, Roselle. "Race and the Issue of National Identity in Israel." *International Journal of Middle East Studies* 23, no. 1 (1991): 39–55.

"Ten Lost Tribes of Israel." *Christian Watchman (1819–1848)*, November 28, 1828, 9, 48 edition.

The Book of Mormon. Salt Lake City: The Church of Jesus Christ of Latter-Day Saints, 1999.

The Church of Jesus Christ of Latter-Day Saints. "Are Mormons Christians?" November 1, 2013. www.lds.org/topics/christians?lang=eng.

"President Nelson Invites Record Crowd in Arizona to Help Gather Israel," February 11, 2019. www.lds.org/church/news/president-nelson-invites-recor d-crowd-in-arizona-to-help-gather-israel?lang=eng.

The Israelite Samaritan Institute. "Israelite Samaritans in Brazil," *May* 1, 2015. www.israelite-samaritans.com/brazil/

"The Ten Lost Jewish Tribes." *Western Luminary (1824–1834)*, Lexington, December 24, 1828.

"The Ten Lost Tribes." *The Christian Intelligencer and Eastern Chronicle (1827–1836)*, August 17, 1832, 12, 33 edition.

The Times of Israel Liveblog. "Interior Ministry Says It Doesn't Recognize Uganda's Abayudaya Community as Jews." News Site, January 25, 2021. www.timesofisrael.com/liveblog_entry/interior-ministry-says-it-doesnt-recog nize-ugandas-abayudaya-community-as-jews/.

Theodossopoulos, Dimitrios. "Laying Claim to Authenticity: Five Anthropological Dilemmas." *Anthropological Quarterly* 86, no. 2 (2013): 337–60.

Thomas, Matthew A. *These Are the Generations: Identity, Covenant and the Toledot Formula.* New York: T&T Clark, 2011.

Thompson, Thomas L. *The Historicity of the Patriarchal Narratives: The Quest for the Historical Abraham.* Berlin: De Gruyter, 1974.

Thorowgood, Thomas. *Iewes in America or Probabilities That the Americans Are of That Race.* London, 1650.

Tigay, Jeffrey H. *Empirical Models for Biblical Criticism.* Philadelphia: University of Pennsylvania Press, 1985.

Tobolowsky, Andrew. "History, Myth, and the Shrinking of Genre Borders." *Eidolon* (blog), May 16, 2016. https://eidolon.pub/history-myth-and-the-shrinking-of-genre-borders-e7ad46ca745.

"Othniel, David, Solomon: Additional Evidence of the Late Development of Normative Tribal Concepts in the South." *Zeitschrift für die alttestamentliche Wissenschaft* 13, no. 1 (2019): 207–19.

"Reading Genesis Through Chronicles: The Creation of the Sons of Jacob." *Journal of Ancient Judaism* 7, no. 2 (2016): 138–68.

"The Hebrew Bible as Mythic 'Vocabulary': Towards a New Comparative Mythology." *Religions* 11, no. 9 (2020): 459.

"The Primary History as Museum Exhibit: Rethinking the Recovery of the Hebrew Bible's Artifacts." *Method and Theory in the Study of Religion* 32, no. 3 (2020): 233–58.

"The Problem of Reubenite Primacy." *Journal of Biblical Literature* 139, no. 1 (2020): 27–45.

The Sons of Jacob and the Sons of Herakles: The History of the Tribal System and the Organization of Biblical Identity. Forschungen Zum Alten Testament 2. Tübingen: Mohr Siebeck, 2017.

Toon, Peter. *Puritans, the Millennium and the Future of Israel: Puritan Eschatology 1600 to 1660.* Cambridge: James Clarke & Co, 2002.

Tsedaka, Benyamim. "Families." *Israelite Samaritan Information Institute* (blog), May 1, 2020. www.israelite-samaritans.com/about-israelite-samaritans/fam ilies/.

Tuell, Steven Shawn. *The Law of the Temple in Ezekiel 40–48.* Harvard Semitic Monographs 49. Atlanta: Scholars Press, 1992.

Turner, Orsamus. *History of the Pioneer Settlement of Phelps & Gorham's Purchase, and Morris' Reserve.* Rochester, NY: W. Alling, 1852.

Tvedtnes, John A., John Gee, and Matthew Roper. "Book of Mormon Names Attested in Ancient Hebrew Inscriptions." *Journal of Book of Mormon Studies* 9, no. 1 (2000): 40–51, 78–79.

Uebel, Michael. *Ecstatic Transformation: On the Uses of Alterity in the Middle Ages.* The New Middle Ages. New York: Palgrave Macmillan, 2005.

Ulf, Christoph. "The Development of Greek Ethnê." In *Politics of Ethnicity and the Crisis of the Peloponnesian League,* edited by Nino Luraghi and Peter Funke. Hellenic Studies 32. Cambridge, MA: Center for Hellenic Studies, 2009.

Ullendorf, Edward. *Ethiopia and the Bible.* London: Oxford University Press, 1968.

"Hebraic-Jewish Elements in Abyssinian (Monophysite) Christianity." *Journal of Semitic Studies* 1 (1956): 216–56.

Ullendorf, Edward, and Charles F. Beckingham. *The Hebrew Letters of Prester John.* Oxford: Oxford University Press, 1982.

Urien-Lefranc, Fanny. "From Religious to Cultural and Back Again: Tourism Development, Heritage Revitalization, and Religious Transnationalizations among the Samaritans." *Religions* 11, no. 86 (2020): 1–15.

Valtrová, Jana. "Beyond the Horizons of Legend: Traditional Imagery and Direct Experience in Medieval Accounts of Asia." *Numen* 57, no. 2 (2010): 154–85.

Van Seters, John. *Abraham in History and Tradition.* New Haven, CT: Yale University Press, 1975.

Prologue to History: The Yahwist as Historian in Genesis. Louisville, KY: Westminster John Knox Press, 1992.

Vayntrub, Jacqueline. *Beyond Orality: Biblical Poetry on Its Own Terms.* The Ancient Word. London: Routledge, 2019.

Vermes, Geza. "The Targumic Versions of Genesis 4:3–16." *The Annual of the Leeds University Oriental Society* 3 (1963): 81–114.

Wagaw, Teshome G. *For Our Soul: Ethiopian Jews in Israel.* Detroit: Wayne State University Press, 1993.

Wasserstein, D. "Eldad Ha-Dani and Prester John." In *Prester John, the Mongols and the Ten Lost Tribes,* edited by Bernard Hamilton and Charles F. Beckingham, 213–36. Aldershot: Variorum, 1996.

Wecker, Helene. *The Golem and the Jinni: A Novel.* New York: HarperCollins, 2013.

Weil, Shalva. "Religion, Blood and the Equality of Rights The Case of Ethiopian Jews in Israel." *International Journal on Minority and Group Rights* 4, no. 3–4 (1996): 397–412.

Weingart, Kristin. "All These Are the Twelve Tribes of Israel: The Origins of Israel's Kinship Identity." *Near Eastern Archaeology* 82, no. 1 (2019): 24–31.

"What Makes an Israelite an Israelite? Judean Perspectives on the Samarians in the Persian Period." *Journal for the Study of the Old Testament* 42, no. 2 (2017): 155–75.

"שני בתי ישראל (Isa 8:14) Concepts of Israel in the Monarchic Period." In *A King Like All the Nations: Kingdoms of Israel and Judah in the Bible and History*, edited by Manfred Oeming and Petr Sláma, 21–32. Beiträge Zum Verstehen der Bibel. Hamburg: Lit Verlag, 2015.

Weiss, Shoshana. "Alcohol Use and Abuse among Ethiopian Immigrants in Israel: A Review." *African Journal of Drug and Alcohol Studies* 7, no. 1 (2008).

Weitzman, Steven. *The Origin of the Jews: The Quest for Roots in a Rootless Age.* Princeton, NJ: Princeton University Press, 2017.

Welch, John W. "View of the Hebrews: 'An Unparallel.'" In *Reexploring the Book of Mormon: The FARMS Updates*, edited by John W. Welch. Salt Lake City: Deseret Book and FARMS, 1992.

Wellhausen, Julius. *Prolegomena to the History of Ancient Israel with a Reprint of the Article "Israel" from the Encyclopedia Britannica.* Gloucester, MA: Peter Smith, 1973.

Wertsch, James V. "Collective Memory." In *Memory in Mind and Culture*, edited by Pascal Boyer and James V. Wertsch, 117–37. Cambridge: Cambridge University Press, 2009.

West, Martin L. *The Hesiodic Catalogue of Women: Its Nature, Structure and Origin.* Oxford: Oxford University Press, 1985.

Westermann, Claus. *Genesis 1–11: A Commentary.* Minneapolis: Augsburg, 1984. *Genesis 12–36.* Translated by John J. Scullion. Minneapolis: Augsburg, 1985. *Genesis 37–50.* Translated by John J. Scullion. Minneapolis: Augsburg, 1986.

Westheimer, Ruth K., and Steven B. Kaplan. *Surviving Salvation: The Ethiopian Jewish Family in Transition.* New York: New York University Press, 1992.

White, L. Michael. "The Delos Synagogue Revisited: Recent Fieldwork in the Graeco-Roman Diaspora." *Harvard Theological Review* 80, no. 2 (1987): 133–60.

Whiteway, R. S. *The Portuguese Expedition to Abyssinia in 1541–1543 As Narrated by Castanhoso with Some Contemporary Letters, the Short Account of Bermudez, and Certain Extracts from Correa.* London: Hakluyt Society, 1902.

"Why These Four Presidents? Mount Rushmore National Memorial (U.S. National Park Service)." Accessed June 5, 2020. www.nps.gov/moru/learn/historyculture/why-these-four-presidents.htm.

Widtsoe, John A. *John A. Widtsoe Papers, CR 712/2. Church History Library*, Church of Latter-Day Saints, Salt Lake City, UT.

Williams, Peter J. "Israel Outside the Land: The Transjordanian Tribes in 1 Chronicles 5." In *Windows Into Old Testament History: Evidence, Argument, and the Crisis of "Biblical Israel,"* edited by V. Philips Long, Gordon J. Wenham, and David Weston Baker, 147–60. Grand Rapids, MI: Eerdmans, 2002.

Wilson, Catherine. "Instruments and Ideologies: The Social Construction of Knowledge and Its Critics." *American Philosophical Quarterly* 33, no. 2 (1996): 167–81.

Wilson, Ian Douglas. *Kingship and Memory in Ancient Judah.* New York: Oxford University Press, 2016.

Wilson, John F. *Our Israelitish Origin: Lectures on Ancient Israel and the Israelitish Origin of the Modern Nations of Europe.* London: Nisbet, 1840.

Wilson, Robert R. "Between 'Azel' and 'Azel': Interpreting the Biblical Genealogies." *The Biblical Archaeologist* 42, no. 1 (1979): 11–22.

———. *Genealogy and History in the Biblical World.* New Haven, CT: Yale University Press, 1977.

———. "The Old Testament Genealogies in Recent Research." *Journal of Biblical Literature* 94, no. 2 (1975): 169–89.

Wisbey, Herbert A. *Pioneer Prophetess: Jemima Wilkinson, the Publick Universal Friend.* Ithaca, NY: Cornell University Press, 2018.

Wollenberg, Rebecca Scharbach. "The Book That Changed: Narratives of Ezran Authorship as Late Antique Biblical Criticism." *Journal of Biblical Literature* 138, no. 1 (2019): 143–60.

Wood, Timothy L. "The Prophet and the Presidency: Mormonism and Politics in Joseph Smith's 1844 Presidential Campaign." *Journal of the Illinois State Historical Society (1998–)* 93, no. 2 (2000): 167–93.

Woodger, Elin, and Brandon Toropov. *Encyclopedia of the Lewis and Clark Expedition.* New York: Infobase Publishing, 2014.

Worthpoint. "1931 Babe Ruth Yankees vs House of David Game Used Ticket Stub Vintage Baseball | #403210339." Accessed April 22, 2020. www.worthpoint .com/worthopedia/1931-babe-ruth-yankees-vs-house-david-403210339.

Wright, William Aldis. "Note on the Arzareth of 4 Esdr Xiii 45." *The Journal of Philology* 3 (1871): 113–27.

Xu, Xin. "Jews in Kaifeng, China." In *Encyclopedia of Diasporas*, edited by M. Ember and C. R. Skoggard. Boston: Springer, 2005.

———. *The Jews of Kaifeng, China.* Jersey City, NJ: Ktav Publishing House, 2003.

Yamauchi, Edwin. "The Eastern Jewish Diaspora Under the Babylonians." In *Mesopotamia and the Bible*, edited by Mark Chavalas and K. Lawson Younger, 356–77. Sheffield: Sheffield Academic Press, 2002.

Yasur-Beit Or, Meital. "Ethiopians Outraged Over Blood Disposal." *Ynet News*, November 1, 2006.

Yerushalmi, Yosef Hayim. *Zakhor: Jewish History and Jewish Memory.* Seattle: University of Washington Press, 1996.

Young, Brigham. "Preaching and Testimony – Gathering Israel – the Blood of Israel and the Gentiles – the Science of Life." In *Journal of Discourses*, 2:266–71. London: Latter-Day Saints Book Depot 1854–1856, 1855. http://jod.mrm.org/2.

———. "To His Majesty, L. Kamehameha the Fifth, King of the Hawaiian Islands," 24 March 1865, CHL.

Zarncke, Friedrich. "Der Priester Johannes." *Abhandlungen der philologisch-historischen Classe der königlich sächsischen Gesellschaft der Wissenschaften* 7 (1879): 827–1031.

Zegeye, Abebe. "The Beta Israel and the Impossible Return." *African Identities* 6, no. 4 (2008): 373–91.

———. *The Impossible Return: Struggles of the Ethiopian Jews, the Beta Israel.* Trenton, NJ: The Red Sea Press, 2018.

Zertal, Adam. "The Heart of the Monarchy: Pattern of Settlement and New Historical Considerations of the Israelite Kingdom of Samaria." In *Studies in the Archaeology of the Iron Age in Israel and Jordan*, edited by Amihai Mazar. *Journal for the Study of the Old Testament Supplement* 331. Sheffield: Sheffield Academic Press, 2001.

The Manasseh Hill Country Survey: The Eastern Valleys and the Fringes of the Desert. Vol. 2. Culture and History of the Ancient Near East 21. Leiden: Brill, 2008.

The Manasseh Hill Country Survey: The Shechem Syncline. Vol. 1. Culture and History of the Ancient Near East 21. Leiden: Brill, 2004.

Zerubavel, Eviatar. *Time Maps.* Chicago: University of Chicago Press, 2003.

Zevit, Ziony. *The Religions of Ancient Israel: A Synthesis of Parallactic Approaches.* London: Continuum, 2001.

Zimmerli, Walter. *Ezekiel: A Commentary on the Book of the Prophet Ezekiel.* 2 vols. Hermeneia. Philadelphia: Fortress Press, 1979.

Zitser, Joshua. "A Unique African Community Who Have Practiced Judaism for a Century Despite Persecution Say They Deserve the Right to Be Recognized as Jews by Israel." *Business Insider*, February 7, 2021. www.businessinsider .com/israel-ugandan-jews-fight-recognition-and-the-right-to-immigrate-2021-2.

Index